AMERICA'S RELIGIOUS WARS

AMERICA'S RELIGIOUS WARS

The Embattled Heart of Our Public Life

KATHLEEN M. SANDS

Yale

UNIVERSITY PRESS

New Haven and London

Yale University Press books may be purchased in quantity for educational, business, or promotional use. For information, please e-mail sales.press@yale.edu (U.S. office) or sales@yaleup.co.uk (U.K. office).

Set in Janson type by IDS Infotech Ltd., Chandigarh, India.
Printed in the United States of America.

Library of Congress Control Number: 2018962997
ISBN 978-0-300-21386-7 (hardcover : alk. paper)

A catalogue record for this book is available from the British Library.

This paper meets the requirements of ANSI/NISO Z39.48-1992 (Permanence of Paper).

10 9 8 7 6 5 4 3 2 1

For Linda

Contents

Acknowledgments

IT IS IMPOSSIBLE TO adequately thank or even to name all who have assisted, rescued, or simply put up with me during the writing of this book. That said, I humbly offer the following.

For encouraging me to pursue the study of religion and law, I am profoundly grateful to Winnifred Fallers Sullivan. For assisting my study of American constitutional law, I thank Charles Lawrence III, Aviam Soiffer, and Elizabeth Spahn. I also owe debts of gratitude to many other scholars from the fields that crisscross in this book. They include Paula Cooey, Elizabeth Shakman Hurd, and Sylvia Law. For generously reading and commenting on particular segments of this book, I thank Shirley Buchanan, Linda Guinee, Jonathan Goldberg Hiller, Linda Hamilton Krieger, Elizabeth Pritchard, Nate Walker, and Mo Wells. For allowing their own lives to be part of this book, I warmly thank Emilie Townes and Steven Greenberg.

At the University of Hawaii's Department of American Studies, I have been blessed with an unusually affable group of colleagues. In particular, I extend heartfelt thanks to Elizabeth Colwill, Jonna Eagle, David Stannard, and Mari Yoshihara, who, in addition to being wonderful colleagues, have become beloved friends. My dear sister Peg traveled far to accompany me through a health crisis that nearly derailed this book. For this and so much else she has my eternal gratitude. In the last phase of this project, Deborah Schmall gave me the kind of solitary retreat that every writer longs for but very few get. To her, and to the deer, rabbits, and redwoods of northern

California, I give thanks for refreshment beyond measure. Thanks to my agent, Susan Rabiner, for guiding me through the initial conception and formulation of this project and to my editor, Bill Frucht, for the judicious use of his red font.

For the opportunity to explore the ideas that became this book in the company of extraordinary scholars, I thank Linell Cady and Arizona State University's Center for the Study of Religion and Conflict. I also thank Sheila Greeve Davaney and the Ford Foundation. Finally, thanks to Harvard's Radcliffe Institute, where the seeds of this book were planted. There, too, I met and married Linda Hamilton Krieger, the greatest love of my fortunate life, to whom this work is dedicated.

AMERICA'S RELIGIOUS WARS

Introduction

Check Your Baggage Here

THERE ARE FEW THINGS Americans argue about more than "religion" yet few words whose meanings are less transparent. Some speak of religion with warmth and reverence, as if it went without saying that religion is essential to our national health. Others speak of religion with caution or distaste, as if it were self-evident that the public presence of religion is dangerous. In America, the word "religion" is a delivery system for sweeping judgments, whether positive or negative, not only about religion itself but about a host of other public issues. Religion-talk packs these judgments, but in baggage not meant to be opened.

Suppose you and I are on a plane headed from Indianapolis to San Francisco. We're seated in Row 17, so we can't help overhearing the people in Row 18 making conversation over their news feeds. The passenger in 18A has spotted a piece about people who want to be exempt from laws that offend their religious beliefs: Some object to providing contraception coverage in their employees' health care plans; others cannot in conscience provide wedding services for same-sex couples. To 18A, these are clear-cut issues of religious freedom: government has no right to force people to act against their convictions. The passenger in 18B is not so sure. Exemptions, if we give them, must be given to all religious groups on an equal basis. But is that really possible? What about, say, Christian Scientists, who object to almost all medical interventions, including care for their sick children? Also, does it make sense to attribute religious beliefs to moneymaking enterprises?[1] And what about government officials, whose job is to administer the law? Can they refuse to implement any laws they disagree with?

The person in 18A seems annoyed. Look, says 18A, you can't please everybody, but shouldn't government at least respect the views of the majority, rather than kowtowing to every vocal minority? The nation was founded on Judeo-Christian principles, and to this day most Americans share some version of that faith. Why in heaven's name would we tear that down? Well, 18B volleys back, aren't church and state supposed to be separate? Government shouldn't dictate our beliefs or morality. It should just protect our rights on an equal basis. Besides, isn't religion supposed to be about tolerance and compassion? Sure, allows 18A, but religion has to stand for something; it can't condone everything.

At this point 18C, who's been pretending to sleep, lets out an audible sigh, drawing inquisitive looks from 18A and 18B. Clearly, 18C doesn't want to be hearing this conversation, much less participating in it. "Sorry, I don't mean to be rude," 18C says, "but religions—all of them—ugh. I kinda wish people would keep these things to themselves." Row 18 then lapses into awkward silence, leaving you and me wondering what just happened.

Based on what we've heard, we might tell ourselves some stories about 18A, B, and C. Maybe we imagine that 18A is an evangelical Christian and a Republican who's conservative on a whole bunch of issues. We might imagine 18B as a Democrat with somewhat flexible religious views, but whose political views are firmly opposite to those of 18A. We might figure that 18C wouldn't be caught dead in a church, but it's harder to draw a convincing mental picture of this passenger's politics. If we were betting, I'd put my money on 18C's being to the left of 18A on social issues. But we'd be foolish to bet on much more.

We'd have some real-world basis for making up stories like those, because studies do show strong correlations between the religious attitudes and political views of Americans.[2] According to the Pew Research Center, evangelical Protestants are about a quarter of the population, so 18A could well be one of them. A majority of evangelicals describe themselves as conservative and vote Republican. Those factors, in turn, correlate with a set of political views that include opposition to homosexuality and legal abortion, rejection of the theory of evolution, suspicion of Islam, and espousal of the idea that America is a Christian nation.[3]

Our inferences about 18B also have empirical support. In sociological language, the difference between 18B and 18A is not necessarily that A is religious and B is not. The difference is that B is less "intense" about religion—less likely, for example, to attend religious services every week, to describe religion as personally very important, or to be intolerant of religious difference. On a number of public issues, people with lower religious intensity often hold views directly opposite to those of 18A. In 2015, for example, 68 percent of Americans who attended church infrequently supported same-sex marriage, in contrast to 34 percent of those who attended weekly or more.[4]

On the other hand, we may be making some serious misjudgments about Row 18. For instance, while there are statistical grounds for guessing that 18A goes to church regularly and votes Republican, the numbers change if race is factored in. A majority of African Americans attend church regularly yet vote for Democrats. African Americans also trend liberal on some issues but conservative on others.[5] In fact, if one looks closely at the American population—maybe even at Row 18—the whole liberal-versus-conservative paradigm becomes doubtful. Consider 18B's support for a "wall of separation" between church and state. That codes as "liberal" in American public discourse, but a good number of self-described liberals believe that the Constitution founded a Christian nation.[6] A person's age, gender, and socioeconomic status also have a statistical impact on his or her religious and political views, so it would help to have that information about the people in Row 18 before we drew any conclusions.[7] But these demographic factors have interacting effects on political views, so we'd go wrong by placing too much weight on any one of them. We'd also be curious about whether 18A, B, and C affiliate with any particular religion. But there too it's easy to go wrong, because political crevices run within religious denominations, not just between them. More than half of American Catholics, for instance, believe that abortion should be legal in all or most cases, and about 70 percent think that homosexuality should be accepted.[8] Both views, of course, are contrary to the Church's official teachings.

In other words, even if we know people's religious views, we still can't predict their politics with much confidence. And though it sounds strange, we might even misjudge the religious beliefs of the travelers in Row 18 based on what they've said about religion. That brings us back to the reluctant conversationalist in the aisle seat. Today, the fastest-growing "religious" group in America—now approaching a quarter of the population—consists of those who, when asked their religious affiliation, check "None." We might reasonably guess that 18C is a None, and we're especially likely to be right if 18C is under thirty. But we should not assume that 18C, being a None, must be an atheist or an agnostic, for more than half of Nones profess belief in God and more than a third report that they pray regularly.[9] More than a third of Nones consider themselves "spiritual but not religious." These "SBNRs," as they've been tagged, lean Democratic and, like 18C, are weary of religious contention in American politics. But, as theologian Linda Mercadante has shown, SBNRs are keenly interested in questions about God, the afterlife, human nature, and community.[10]

The Who and What of Religious Conflict

The goal of this book is not to resolve American disagreements about religion but to help us travel better in our shared political system. Disagreement is the fuel of democracy, but meaningful disagreement is a real achievement and we can fight forever without getting there. That, I'd suggest, is the condition of most religion-talk in America. We repeat lines we've uttered countless times before, as do our adversaries, and all the while everyone fumes over everyone else's intransigence. To achieve disagreement about all those issues now packed into "religion," we have to ask the questions differently. First of all: with whom are we fighting, and what are we fighting about?

Who is fighting? Abundant research now proves that our views of religion are related to who we are—our race and ethnicity, gender, age, education, sexuality, class, region, education, and so on.

The judgments we issue about religion in everyday conversation are therefore judgments about each other. Say a new acquaintance lauds America's Christian heritage, complains that God has been driven out of public schools, and laments the loss of the traditional family. If you're an atheist, a Jew, or a Muslim, or if you belong to a nontraditional family, you may feel insulted even if your interlocutor meant no offense. You may feel that he or she is labeling you as morally suspect, religiously subversive, or unpatriotic. Or suppose the new acquaintance talks scornfully about religion or a particular religion. If you're a religious person (or, worse, belong to a religion that your new acquaintance has specifically disparaged), you may feel that he or she is implying that people who hold your beliefs or come from your part of the world or belong to your racial-ethnic group don't make good citizens. Depending on our social locations, we enter such encounters with different amounts of power. For example, someone who belongs to a religious, ethnic, or sexual minority might feel (and be) disadvantaged in a conflict over religion. When we struggle, we often do so from unequal positions of power, and that goes a long way toward explaining why these conflicts are so fraught.

What are we fighting about? Debates about religion involve concrete, personal interests. One religion must contend with suspicion from the majority culture and surveillance by the government; another must watch its beliefs fall out of the mainstream. Some parents are angry that a public school is teaching their child a theory abhorrent to the parents' beliefs; others are angry that their child is being proselytized in the playground. One woman is distraught that her fifteen-year-old daughter cannot terminate an unwanted pregnancy because state laws have shut down all the clinics. Another is distraught to learn that her fifteen-year-old daughter had an abortion without the mother's consent. A gay man risks losing his job if his sexual orientation is known; a conservative evangelical risks being labeled a bigot if he voices objections to same-sex marriage.

Often, when we argue about religion, we are arguing obliquely about these other issues. This, too, helps account for the intensity of the conflicts. But it also accounts for their confused quality, because there is no fixed link between any particular religion and any particular view on a public issue. In the 1960s, if you had seen a band of clergy marching arm in arm, you'd probably have been witnessing a civil rights demonstration. If you supported that movement, you might have been glad to see those clergy in the street, but not if you opposed that movement.[11] Today, if you see demonstrators whose tee shirts have Christian symbols, odds are they're protesting against abortion or gay rights. If you agree with them on those issues, the tee shirts might trigger a positive association—even if you yourself are not a Christian. But if you're on the other side, you could develop an aversion to the display of Christian symbols—even if you yourself are a Christian. In fact, if you are a devout Christian but disagree with the demonstrators, you might feel an even stronger aversion to their tee shirts than somebody with no personal investment in Christianity.

Why Fight? The Ethical Stakes of Religious Conflict

If we listen carefully, even to the unhappy companions in Row 18, we might notice that American religion-talk is threaded through with principles of social ethics. In this book, I will refer to six: freedom, equality, community, limited government, dignity, and distributive justice.

I am not suggesting that when we fight about religion, Americans are always thinking about these and only these principles. I am suggesting that we should think about these principles, and maybe others too. Nor am I suggesting that these ethical abstractions provide concrete solutions to the conflicts related in these chapters. For one thing, the principles are tensive: each is precious, but they pull in different directions. Reconciling them is an endless balancing act. This book does not venture to say how that might be done. Rather than answering those questions, my goal is to ask them more perspicaciously by unpacking "religion," the single word into which they are usually stuffed.

In Row 18, for example, we might notice that 18A is zealous about freedom, while 18B is more worried about inequality. Even the Framers experienced that tension, trumpeting equality in the Declaration of Independence but issuing the Constitution and Bill of Rights without once using that word. It took a civil war to get the principle of equality written into the Constitution through the

Fourteenth Amendment, and it was only in the 1940s that the religion clauses of the First Amendment were applied on an equal basis in all states.[12] From the beginning, every American conflict about religious liberty has been a conflict about equality—about what counts as a "religion," who counts as a citizen, and how freedom can be safeguarded for all.

Listening to Row 18, we also might notice that nobody wants over-intrusive government, but most of us have some concern for other citizens. The principle of limited government speaks to the first concern, while the principle of community speaks to the second. People toward the left are more inclined to speak of community, while those on the right prefer to speak of limited government. But not many people want unlimited government (that is, totalitarianism), and wise people have always recognized that the less government a nation has, the more civic virtue it will need. The passengers in Row 18 probably take the principles of limited government and community as more or less axiomatic, but they interpret these principles differently and give them different weights. The person in 18A feels that when government moves onto religion's turf, tyranny soon follows, while 18B sees tyranny when religion enters the turf of government. And 18C thinks we take the first step toward tyranny when we bring religion into politics one way or the other. All three care about community, but they define it differently and therefore would protect it by different means—18A by restoring traditional values; 18B by embracing diversity, including religious diversity; 18C by silencing religion in the public square.

Freedom, equality, community, and limited government are familiar issues in American religious conflicts. But some stakes of religious conflict are more tangible than these four, and some are less tangible. The more tangible stakes have included land, money, taxes, legal protections, political power, and public education. Distributive justice is the ethical principle that should guide decisions about who gets what tangible goods, how they get them, and how they do or don't share them. But there are also stakes that, while less tangible, are just as vital. As the women's labor anthem expressed it, people need roses as well as bread. If distribution is bread, dignity is roses. When voices rise and faces flush during disputes about religion, it's often a symptom that along with everything else they are fighting about, the parties are fighting for their dignity. Dignity is like wealth: it is something everyone needs, but it has never been distributed evenly. If we bear that in mind, we'll be more equipped to discern what's going on in battles over religion.

It is perhaps not surprising that the dignitary and distributive aspects of religious conflict are most apparent to those who are least advantaged. But it is a remarkable feature of American religious conflicts that typically one side thinks that the conflict has little or nothing to do with religion, while the other side insists that it has everything to do with religion. That is why it is so illuminating to notice who uses the word "religion" and why. When we ask those questions, I will argue, we can better understand why religious conflicts are so passionate, and why they wouldn't go away even if we somehow persuaded each other to stop talking about "religion." Because religions are groups within society, religious conflicts are struggles over power. But for the same reason, we can bring principles of social ethics to the analysis of religious conflict. American religion-talk is frustrating and confused, opportunistic and self-interested. But it is not pointless; it involves principles that are worth fighting for.

Walls and Foundations

Every question of social ethics entails the meta-question of what we do or don't need to agree about. The structural flaw in religion-talk is that we use that one word to answer both questions. Sometimes Americans think of religion as private and walled off from public life. Religion then seems to be an area of benign diversity, connoting spiritual behaviors (such as attending Mass, observing Shabbat, or meditating), metaphysical beliefs (concerning, say, God or the afterlife), and voluntary acts of belonging (such as making a bat mitzvah or wearing the hijab). Understood this way, religion is separate from society and even more separate from government, the arm of society that wields the force of coercive law. Religion ends where government begins, and vice versa.

Other times, however, we may think of religion as the bedrock that upholds the basic rules of social life: control yourself, accept your responsibilities, share with others, respect the law, protect the vulnerable, do the right thing even when nobody's watching. We remember times when religion has been a solace in the face of collective loss, or when it has helped us bend the arc of history in a better direction. In those moments, religion becomes something we would like to agree about, at least on a few essentials. Imagined this way, religion is not just private but public, not just individual but shared, the sacred foundation of common life.

Alexis de Tocqueville noticed this contradiction early on, when he memorably commented that Americans, while separating church and state, nonetheless had made religion into "the first of their political institutions."[13] The contradiction remains with us today, and it pops up not only between Americans but also within our own minds. Evangelical Christians object when the government forces them to pay for the morning-after pill, yet they also call for a Christian America. The former is wall rhetoric: government has no authority to encroach on religious beliefs. The latter is foundation rhetoric: government should be based on religion. Liberal secularists may object vehemently to Christian prayers on the football field at a public school. That's the logic of wall religion: prayers should be kept to oneself. Yet a liberal secularist's eyes may mist up at the same school's winter concert, when the chorus performs Kwanzaa or winter solstice songs along with the usual fare. That's the feeling of foundation religion: warm, shared sentiments that melt individuals into a single community and cause them, at least for a while, to treat each other well.

The "wall of separation" does not appear in the Constitution; it is only a metaphor for the concept of religion implied there. But it is a venerable metaphor, first popularized in 1644 by Roger Williams.[14] And it is apt, because each time the Constitution refers to religion, the effect is to put religion and government in separate spheres. The first reference appears in article 6. "No religious Test shall ever be required as a Qualification to any office or public trust under the United States"—meaning that a citizen's religious beliefs or lack thereof have no bearing on his or her qualifications for office. The other reference is in the First Amendment: "Congress shall make no law respecting an establishment of religion or prohibiting the free exercise thereof." Again, the point was to put a barrier between religion and government. How high that barrier was meant to be, and whether it was meant to protect religion, government, or both, are matters of dispute. But that the Framers meant to erect such a barrier is clear.

As I will spell out in chapter 2, the principles of non-establishment and religious freedom were imbricated with the Framers' idea of a strictly limited, minimally coercive government. Freedom of religion, which the Framers also called freedom of conscience, was to them unique even among other inalienable rights, because those other rights (say, freedom of speech) imposed obligations only on government. Religious freedom, in contrast, also placed an obligation—an absolute obligation—upon the citizen as a person. If conscience was to be respected as absolute, government had to be strictly limited.

Notwithstanding the Framers' strict separation of religion and government, their speeches and letters are replete with paeans to religion and its importance for public life. They knew that a nation with limited government would have an especially great need for a shared ethos, and when they attempted to describe this common ethos, they usually employed the word "religion." The Framers were not contradicting themselves when they afforded religion different roles in the different contexts of government and civic life. But they did contradict themselves, just as we do today, when they thought of religion itself sometimes as wall and other times as foundation, sometimes as entirely private and other times as a common ethos.

In the Constitution, where the wall concept prevails, religion is handled as if it were simply irrelevant to public life. Jefferson expressed this rather rudely when he wrote, "It does me no injury for my neighbor to say there are twenty gods, or no God. It neither picks my pocket nor breaks my leg." Yet even Jefferson, on a more solemn occasion, could declare with satisfaction that Americans are "enlightened by a benign religion," which although "professed, indeed, and practiced in various forms," promotes the same virtues and instills faith in the same providential God.[15] For him, "religion" could refer not just to a private sphere but to the whole panoply of behaviors, attitudes, values, and practices that held the nation together. The same was true of other Framers. Sometimes they spoke of religion as private property, other times as public trust; as salubrious for the body politic or potentially poisonous; as unifying or divisive; as strictly voluntary or the basis of good citizenship.

How did the Framers overlook this contradiction? How do we? One answer can be found in the Protestant faith that most of them shared and that has shaped American culture ever since. Protestantism dispatched each soul on its own lonely pilgrimage, but it expected—even demanded—that all pilgrims would arrive at the same destination. So the Framers could tell themselves that freedom of religion would lead to consensus in religion, and that the disestablishment of religion in government would foster the unofficial establishment of a national religious ethos. Actually, they were kidding themselves. Even in their own time there was tremendous religious dissensus, not just on theological arcana but on matters of grave public import, including slavery, relations with Native Americans, and the rights of women. But there's an even larger reason for the contradictions, and it embraces not just Protestantism but an idea so familiar that it seems eternal but is really a product of the modern West: that "religion" is a quasi-natural genus with many legitimate species, distinct from but somehow underlying "secular" life.

The Circularity of Religion-Talk

In the Middle Ages, European Christians were taught that their church, and theirs alone, was "one," "true," "holy," and "catholic." Religion was what sociologist Peter Berger called a "sacred canopy," covering every area of life.[16] In the modern era, religion would be constrained from interfering with government, science, education, the market, and other spheres, which were now conceived as secular. Moreover, religion would be reimagined in the plural, a genus with a variety of species among which one could choose. Yet religion in the generic sense would still be considered an essential unity ("one"), the bastion of moral order ("holy"), and the universal marker of humanity ("catholic"). Even as religious differences were absented from the secular world, a host of Euro-Christian assumptions about morality, citizenship, and civilization were buried in the foundations of the social order. Compliance with these assumptions would seem voluntary and personal, yet this voluntary, personal faith was precisely what was publicly expected. In effect, it was required.

This double concept of religion obviously owes much to Protestantism itself, which holds that a person can be saved only through individual faith. In Protestant theology, coerced faith is not faith at all. Only free religion can be true religion. Yet because God remains one and the same, every sincere seeker of truth should arrive at more or less the same conclusions. Differences could be expected on the finer points of doctrine, the style of worship, and the authority structure of churches. But these differences are not supposed to disturb society, threaten the government, or undermine the increasingly autonomous secular spheres. On a practical basis, however, this never worked terribly well, even among Protestants. When people deeply and sincerely disagree about what is true and good, appeals to "religion" will run in circles, assuming the answers to the very questions at issue.

This circularity comes from the fact that religion-talk, while it seems to declare eternal verities, also tells people what to believe and how to act. Take for example the long-standing Christian claim that it alone is the one true church. Theologically, that claim may or may not be valid, but the historical reality is that Christianity always has been textured by local differences and riven with controversy. The words "one" and "true" were statements of conviction, but they also functioned as judgments against those deemed unorthodox. In the same way, when early modern Europeans spoke of "religion" as the hallmark of civilization, they were deciding how to classify the non-Europeans now under their colonial control—specifically, deciding to classify non-Europeans as people without religion, who therefore needed to be ruled by Christians.

This slippage from description to prescription is the sleight of hand through which religion-talk normally operates. When George Washington, in his Farewell Address, proclaimed approvingly that Americans share "the same religion," albeit "with slight differences," he was sidestepping the question of what exactly that religion was, what the differences were, and whether they were really "slight."[17] When nineteenth-century Protestants described the King James Bible as "nonsectarian," they were not really naming the sacred text recognized by all Americans. They were demanding that Protestant devotions be established in public schools and that "sectarian" (meaning Catholic) devotions be excluded. In the late twentieth century, when some Americans began to describe creationism as a "secular" and "scientific" theory while others called it "religious" and "sectarian," these words were not neutral descriptors; they were decrees about how children should be educated in public schools. And in the early twenty-first century, when many Americans insisted that marriage, by religious tradition and social definition, could exist only between a man and a woman, their point was that marriage should not be permitted between people of the same sex.

In order to understand American religion-talk, we must look at, rather than through, the judgments we normally pack into the word "religion." Here, rather bluntly, I will debunk three of them, each rooted in the history of the word in the modern West: that religion is essentially good, that religions are essentially the same, and that there is a fixed and natural division between the religious and the secular.

Fallacy 1: Religion Is Good

"Religion is good" is perhaps the most common and heartfelt judgment associated with religion. It has variants: "all religions are good"; "only certain religions are good"; or "only my religion is good." In each case, the assumption produces a circular logic: anything bad cannot really be religion. In the grip of this assumption, people might say that the Crusades were a "distortion" of the Christian gospel or that suicide bombing is a "perversion" of Islam. They admit that all manner of ignorance and cruelty are done "in the name of" religion, but by that very phrasing simultaneously dissociate religion from evil—the bad stuff is not "real" religion.

When a religious person makes such a disclaimer, he or she is saying something like the following: This is not who my God is; this is not what I mean when I say I am a Muslim (or a Christian, Buddhist, Jew, and so forth); this does not reflect my community or my aspirations. Frederick Douglass made the same type of assertion when he distinguished "slaveholding religion" (or the "Christianity of America") from the "Christianity of Christ."[18] When Douglass said that slaveholders were not real Christians, he meant that they were bad Christians. But he did not confuse these moral and theological judgments with reality on the ground. He knew all too well that the "Christianity of America" sanctioned slavery. In fact, as he chillingly recounted, some slaveholders became even more cruel after they "got religion."

Since the late nineteenth century, a permutation of this old assumption has gradually gained force: "religion is bad." It is the same circular logic moving in the opposite direction: anything good, reasonable, or progressive cannot truly be religion. There is no denying that the various religions have condoned and even mandated war, torture, slavery, the oppression of women, the violent suppression of dissent, and countless other horrors. But like the assumption "religion is good," the assumption "religion is bad" operates by sleight of hand—it substitutes a normative judgment (in this case, a condemnation) for an accurate description of reality. Faced with contrary evidence—religions that foster compassion, equality, justice, and peace—one must say that these are not really religion at all, just humanism in a state of arrested development. Moreover, everything that's not religion—say, science—is freed of the scrutiny to which religion is subjected. But that is perilous. Science has given the world much that is good, but it's also given us eugenics, weapons of mass destruction, theories of female hysteria and sexual inversion, lobotomies for the mentally ill, and many other evils. Those who place their faith in science will quickly counter that the examples just mentioned were not "real" science. But that is just like saying that the Crusades were not "real" Christianity. Both are factual-sounding but historically misleading claims that sound plausible because they appeal to our sense of how things should be.

For simplicity, I've been using the words "good" and "bad" as if we all agreed on what they mean. But often we do not, and that's one more reason it's so misleading to characterize religion, across the board, as either good or bad. It's not just that people are moved by religion to perform actions that most of us consider good (like, say, feeding the poor) as well as actions most consider bad (like, say, burning people at the stake). The larger reason is that religions disagree about so much. Whether we believe that war is never justified, sometimes justified, or sometimes morally obligatory; whether we think that men and women have different capabilities or are perfectly equal; whether we think that capitalism, socialism, or a mixed economy is best—whatever our convictions, we can find religious groups that either denounce or heartily endorse our views.

Fallacy 2: Religions Are the Same

When we speak of religions, it seems natural to assume that they share common features, just as it's natural to assume that hummingbirds, mockingbirds, and blackbirds share the essential features of birds. But religions are better understood as artifacts of history and politics than as branches of an evolutionary tree. They differ, not as hummingbirds and mockingbirds differ but as soufflés and symphonies do. Religions are not variations of the same thing; they are different things altogether.

As a category, then, "religion" does not make sense. To be clear: I am not suggesting that it makes no sense to believe in a God, or to seek salvation or enlightenment. It's an obvious point, though often elided: religion is not the same as God or the sacred. God could exist even if there were no religions, and if God does not exist there's nothing religions can do to change it. Even without religion, people can ponder the ultimate nature of reality and what it means to live a good life. One can find answers to these questions within the things we call religion, and for that reason we often conflate religion with such existential concerns. Historically speaking, however, the category of religion evolved for other purposes. As historian of religion Jonathan Z. Smith once observed, the original function of "religion" was to distinguish "us" (the Westerners, the civilized people, the moderns) from "them" (the "Orientals" and "Primitives").[19] On first encounter, it seemed that "we" had religion and "they" did not; later, "we" had the highest religions while "they" had the lower ones; still later, all civilized humans, to the extent that they truly were civilized and human, were said to have "religion."

As a category, then, "religion" developed for a variety of worldly reasons: to justify conquest, to rank races and civilizations, to explain who must be free and who could be enslaved, to determine who was or wasn't a suitable citizen. "Religion" has been invoked when people wanted to assert rights, make peace, claim equality, or stand for the inviolability of conscience. My point is not that "religion" is always uttered for nefarious purposes but that, whatever its purposes, religion-talk is legitimation: it invokes God or the sacred to authorize particular claims about how the world should be arranged. When we try to make sense of religion as a category, then, we are actually rationalizing, post facto, whatever power arrangements the category of "religion" now supports.

Fallacy 3: The Religious and the Secular Are Inherently Separate

Some Americans, like the hypothetical traveler in seat 18C, propose what sounds like a fail-safe solution to the problem of American religion-talk: could we all please just shut up? To put it more politely, it may seem reasonable to request that in public discussion, people stick to secular terms.[20]

The trouble is that there's no fixed division between the religious and the secular. "Secular," after all, only means "not religious," and if religion is a shifting concept, the secular is too. Hair length, contraception, diet, hallucinogenic drugs, medical treatment, the number or gender of one's spouses, and the origin of species may be secular subjects for most Americans, but for others they are religious. Nothing is inherently "religious" or "secular." These are just words we use to organize our world. And when the world changes, so do the meanings of the words.[21]

In medieval Europe, "secular" referred to historical time, as opposed to eternity, both regarded as dimensions of a single Christian cosmos. In America's founding period, "secular" retained this temporal connotation. The motto *Novus ordo seclorum* (a new order of the ages) meant that the birth of America inaugurated a new phase of history. That history, however, was still guided by divine providence; "secular" definitely did not imply a polity absent of God. "Secularism" only became a philosophy in the 1850s, and even then it was primarily a proposal about the moral foundations of society. As defined by British writer George Jacob Holyoake, secularism was neither theological nor anti-theological. Instead, it proposed to find common ground across religious and other differences by formulating a "natural morality" that would promote human development by "material means."[22]

In the United States, secularism was initially embraced both by freethinking atheists and by many who considered "nonsectarian" Protestantism (but not "sectarian" religion) compatible with secularist principles.[23] The emergence of a more anti-religious secularism began in the wake of the Civil War, when Euro-Protestantism began to split over modernism. By the First World War, the anti-modernist side had calcified into fundamentalism, which claimed to be the true face of American religion. On the other side was modernist Protestantism, which gradually became indistinguishable from secularism.

American secularism, then, is really a permutation of American foundational religion. For its most devoted followers, secularism does much of what religion does: it provides a worldview, a standpoint from which one looks at everything. But having repudiated its secret twin, secularism eventually became unable to discern the resemblance. This denial is enabled by the fact that secularism, like all universalistic viewpoints, does not see itself as a viewpoint but simply as "the truth." Like the ground beneath our feet, secularism is invisible until others force us to excavate it, defend it, or share it. In this book, I subject secularism-talk to the same analysis, and measure it by the same criteria, as religion-talk. Being "secular" will not count in favor of a claim any more than being "religious" will count against it. Instead, all claims will face the same questions. What freedoms were at stake, and how equitably were those freedoms distributed? What were the demands of the common good, of human dignity, and of distributive justice? What were the appropriate roles of government and civil society in protecting these goods? And how were those principles played out in these particular historical circumstances, with these particular parties?

Despite our well-practiced scripts on the subject, Americans hardly know what we're fighting about when we fight about "religion." To make sense of these conflicts, this book asks who was involved in them, what interests were at stake, and why people thought they were right. Who were these people? What did they stand to gain or lose in terms of land, wealth, political influence, legal rights, or social status? Did they have different visions of how people should relate to each other along lines of race, class, or gender? Did they disagree about how resources ought to be distributed, or how government ought to function? What kinds of people did they recognize as equals, and to whom did they deny that recognition? What were their experiences of dignity or indignity, and how did those experiences inflect this conflict? What were their views about the proper scope of freedom, and how did they balance freedom with the common good?

American religion-talk, structured around the metaphors of wall and foundation, obfuscates these underlying issues. Under the metaphor of wall, "religion" refers to matters on which we don't expect to agree; under the metaphor of foundations, it refers to matters on which we do expect to agree. Because contradictory implications are baked into the word, "religion" becomes a perfect vehicle for the expression of opposition. One can be for religion or against it, for foundations or for walls, for making one's own religion foundational while walling off the religions of others. Each metaphor also imposes its own kind of blinders on religion-talk—the wall metaphor narrowing our focus to law and politics, the foundation metaphor blurring majoritarian norms into an inchoate mass.

The "wall of separation" concerns the limits of government within our constitutional order. But what lies beyond law and government is not necessarily beyond the interest of society. Law, even at its best, is only a small part of what holds people together or remediates their tensions. It is beyond the scope of our constitutional government to pronounce upon the meaning of life, but that hardly makes the meaning of life a trivial question, or makes it easy to live among people who understand life very differently, or makes it pointless to exchange ideas about large existential questions. Nor is our government supposed to dictate most aspects of personal conduct—for example, how we raise children, relate to the natural world, spend our time and resources, or interact with the people around us. Yet these areas of personal conduct can have tremendous impact on others, so it is right that we should debate them through conversation, sermons, electronic media, art, or activism, or just by comporting ourselves publicly in the ways we think best. These are ordinary means of social influence that operate without the force of law and, in fact, are crushed when placed under compulsion.

If the wall metaphor reduces social questions to matters of law, the foundation metaphor silences social questions under a blanket of majoritarian assumptions. Until the Civil War, Euro-Americans commonly assumed that religion was the foundation of civilization; the question was which religion or religions belonged in those foundations. Euro-Protestants, who possessed the power to decide that question, thought that the proper foundation of American society was a generalized Protestant sensibility, sometimes called nonsectarianism. This sensibility put its stamp on everything—for example, on public schools, where the King James Bible was devotionally read over the protests of Catholics; on private property, which was forced on Native Americans despite their collectivist traditions; on marriage law, which forbade polygamy at a time when Mormon teaching encouraged the practice. Yet most Euro-Protestants did not worry that they might be violating the wall of separation, which they defended vigilantly against minorities and newcomers. Although they enforced their own norms as the law of the land, those norms did not seem particularly religious, because they weren't bound to any one (Protestant) denomination and were thought to be general features of civilization and citizenship.

Religious foundationalism is still a major force in American public life. But since the Civil War, it has been challenged by the secularist notion that religion is a remnant of barbarism rather than the foundation of civilization. Like nonsectarianism, secularism was introduced primarily (although not exclusively) by educated white Protestant men. Also like nonsectarianism, secularism in the eyes of its proponents is tolerant, humane, progressive, and naturally congruent with Americanism. And because secularism seems beyond reasonable controversy, its critics are said to be backward, divisive, intolerant, and un-American—the same things that were said about the Catholics and Mormons who resisted nonsectarianism in the nineteenth century.

These are the continuities, but there are also sharp differences between religious foundationalism and secularist foundationalism. Before the rise of secularism, it was commonplace for people to speak of religion both in terms of walls and in terms of foundations, with little sense of contradiction between the two. They assumed that walls were built to contain religious differences, while foundations

solidified the common features of religion. Since the rise of secularism, however, the rhetoric of wall and the rhetoric of foundation have
become increasingly bifurcated, so that people stress either the wall
of separation or the role of religion in American foundations. And
while nonsectarianism distanced itself from religious particularity,
secularism distances itself from religion generally.

Secularism disavows religion with special passion, not because
there is no connection between the two, but because its relationship
with religion is one of counter-dependence. In the creation-evolution controversy, for example, secularism has come to be equated
with science, erasing the many realms of inquiry that are neither religion nor science, and posing religion and science as singular, antag-
onistic worldviews. In controversies over sexuality, the conservative
position has come to be authorized by religion and the progressive
position by science—as if religions had the same views on sexuality,
which they do not, and as if science could answer all normative
questions, which it cannot. Disagreements on these issues remain
deep and furious, unquelled by legislation or judicial rulings. Significantly, those disagreements track fissures of class, race, ethnicity, culture, education, and region. This alone should tell Americans that
neither the ways we talk about religion nor the ways we talk against
religion get to the bottom of our problems.

In the United States, "religion" and "the secular" are symbolic
shields behind which we fight over many other things, such as access to resources, social status, authority, freedom, and dignity. Yet
Americans remain profoundly attached to our ways of speaking
about religion, as if without these tired tropes we would not know
how to talk at all. So we continue to clash, shield against shield,
with neither victory nor reconciliation in sight. We ask *which religion* should be our foundation, or *whether religion* has any place in
our foundation, when the real question is not about "religion" but
simply about foundations. What are, or should be, the norms, commitments, and sensibilities that hold the polity together? We ask
about the scope of *religious* liberty, when the real question is about
the scope of liberty itself. Under what circumstances should people
be forced to do or not do something? What is the boundary between one person's freedom and that of another? How can freedom be equally protected for all?

Using "religion" as a symbol for all that is good and true is a centuries-long habit that is very hard to break. Using religion to symbolize what is oppressive and ignorant is not quite as old a habit, but it too is deeply entrenched. In either case, it's difficult to remember that, whatever may be the nature of good and evil, "religion" is simply a word, and it changes meanings depending on when, where, by whom, and for what purposes it is used. Whether one uses "religion" as a carrier for judgments that are positive or negative, it is daunting to pick up the burdens that remain when that word no longer does our work for us.

In a benchmark 1943 decision, Supreme Court justice Robert Jackson observed that "the freedom to differ is not limited to things that do not matter much" but extends "to things that touch the heart of the existing order."[24] American conflicts about religion pertain not only to the architecture of our polity but also to the lives of the people who inhabit it. These conflicts can't be settled merely by adjusting the height and placement of walls, whether those walls are meant to protect religion or to exclude it. Nor can these conflicts be settled by repairing our foundations, if by this we hope to end up with something solid and fixed, like stone or concrete. The questions locked in our religion-talk cannot be resolved, but they can be revealed as the troubled, living heart of our democracy.

PART I

Genealogies of Religion

CHAPTER ONE

Religion as We Know It
The Career of a Contradiction

A word is not a crystal, transparent and unchanged, it is the
skin of a living thought and may vary greatly in color and
content according to the circumstances and the time in
which it is used.

—JUSTICE OLIVER WENDELL HOLMES

CHRISTOPHER COLUMBUS HAD HIS first encounter with the indigenous people of America on October 12, 1492. Among his first im-
pressions of the Taino, along with their gentleness and physical
beauty, was that they possessed "no religion at all"—a felicitous
sign, Columbus thought, for it meant they "would easily be made
Christians."[1]

But "religion" is simply a word, and as Justice Holmes would
observe centuries later, a word "may vary greatly in color and content" depending on when and why it is used. The when, in the case
of Columbus, was just as Europeans were launching their colonial
projects overseas, before the Protestant Reformation shattered the
putative unity of Christendom. The why was a rationale known as

25

the Discovery Doctrine: in lands where Christianity did not exist, Christian monarchs had both the right and the obligation to conquer and rule in Christ's name.[2] Given that his own fortunes hung upon the absence of "religion" in the New World, Columbus was hardly motivated to find it.

Over the next century and a half, a series of bloody wars would force Europeans to recognize that there existed several Christian "religions." It would take another century and a half, and a series of colonial struggles, for them to recognize what are now called the "religions of the world." In October 1492, all of that lay in the future. So when Columbus wrote the word "religion," he had in mind the meanings the word had carried throughout the Christian Middle Ages.

First of all, he took it as axiomatic that Christianity was the only true religion—*vera religio*.[3] The idea of *vera religio* was not that other religions were less true than Christianity, but that they were not religion at all. Rather than simply referring to one system of belief among others, "Christian" referred to both a people (Europeans) and their civilization (Christendom). To say that Christianity was the one true religion was also to say that only European Christians were truly civilized, that only they were fully human. The world contained four kinds of people: Christians, Jews, Mohammedans, and heathens. Jews and Mohammedans were seen not as members of legitimate religions but as people who had rejected the true religion. Heathens, also called idolaters or pagans, were people who either did not engage in any sort of worship or worshipped idols or demons. Religion, the mark of humanity, was not a mark that European Christians were prepared to discern on anyone but themselves.

In Columbus's journal, this fourfold typology showed up on the first page. He opened by addressing his sponsors, the "most Christian, very high and very excellent" monarchs of Spain, Ferdinand and Isabella. Next he praised them for their recent defeat of the last "Moors who reigned in Europe" and for having "turned out all the Jews from your kingdoms." Having vanquished the Mohammedans, expelled the Jews, and crushed heretics through the Inquisition, Columbus observed, the monarchs could now turn their attention to "the Indies," where they believed there lived a "Grand Can"

(Khan) eager for Christian conversion. With this précis, Columbus had set up his own mission: a sea voyage to these lands "with a view that they might be converted to our holy faith."[4]

As it turned out, the people Columbus would happen upon in 1492 were neither Mohammedans nor Jews, and definitely were not Christians. That consigned them to the fourth category, heathens, people who could justly be conquered for the sake of conversion. In reality, Columbus was interested only in conquest, as Dominican missionary Bartolomé de Las Casas would later recount.[5] Soon the Taino would be dispossessed of their lands, enslaved, starved, tortured, and infected with foreign diseases until they were nearly extinct.[6] Being classified as heathens had not transformed the Taino into souls worthy of salvation; it had stripped them of their humanity.

Columbus's concept of religion was far less elaborated than ours. Not having to make sense of religions in the plural, European Christians felt little need to conceive it in the singular, as a category. In common usage, "religion" mostly referred to rituals of worship or to monks and nuns, who were said to be "in religion."[7] This meaning may have predated Christianity; the Latin word *religio* seems to have referred to the customary practices, particularly devotional practices, that distinguished one people (or "race") from another. But in antiquity, race was somewhat mutable: one could change one's race by adopting new rituals. Early Christians therefore could consider themselves a new race that all people could, and should, join.[8] By the late fourth century, after Christianity became the religion of the Roman Empire, Christians did more than just assert that theirs alone was *vera religio*. Christian rulers began to enforce this assertion by suppressing other forms of worship.

If Columbus had been prepared to see religion in the New World, he would have found plenty of it, for the lives of the Taino and other indigenous Americans were rich in sacred ceremony. But even had he seriously sought to inquire about their religion, Native Americans would not have known how to reply, for nothing in their lexicon corresponded precisely to this word. The same was true of the non-Christians that Europeans encountered elsewhere. Beyond Christian Europe, as historian Jonathan Z. Smith put it, religion was "not a first-person term of self-characterization" but "a category imposed from the outside."[9] It is true that people around the world had ceremonies, deities, priests, sacred texts, and the other elements that Europeans associated with religion. The Arabic word *dīn* has often been mistranslated as "religion," but referred broadly to the beliefs and laws of the *ummah;* only in the twentieth century did Islam begin to fit itself into the Western category of religion.[10] Before that, only European Christians singled "religion" out from the rest of life and gave it unique significance, questioned whether non-Christians had "religion," or went about classifying and ranking the "religions" of the world in relation to their own.[11]

It's a long distance from the concept of religion displayed by Columbus to the one we know today. In this chapter we will travel quickly between Columbus's landing and an event that commemorated its quadricentennial: the 1893 World's Parliament of Religions. Between those two points, the "color and content" of the word *religion* would change in ways Columbus could not have imagined. Religion would become a genus with many legitimate species, such that recognizing the humanity of a people required also identifying their "religion." Religion was still expected to produce political unity and social conformity, but it was to be chosen voluntarily and cultivated internally. It would still suffuse the cultural ethos, yet it was also a distinct sphere. And in the United States, religion would be conceived both as beneath government and beyond it, both a foundation and a wall.

"Religion" in the Modern West

Three massive historical shifts forged the category of religion into its present shape: the Protestant Reformation, colonialism, and the loss of ecclesiastical control over government. The Reformation fractured Christendom into many sovereign territories, each with its own version of the Christian religion. Colonialism forced non-Europeans to reckon with the alien category of religion while bringing Europeans, very gradually, to recognize the presence of religions among non-Christian people. Alongside all this, there was the process that came to be called secularization—the separation of religion from government and also from science, trade, and other public endeavors.

The Protestant Reformation is usually traced to October 31, 1517, when a monk named Martin Luther is said to have nailed a list of Ninety-Five Theses to the door of the campus church in Wittenberg. (Actually, he may just have dispatched the Theses to the archbishop of Mainz, but nailing, not mailing, is the stuff of legend.) In any case, the Ninety-Five Theses comprised a mordant critique of the whole Catholic system. When they were printed and circulated, a public clamor arose, leading within a few years to Luther's excommunication.

Like many reformers before and after him, Luther might have ended up burned at the stake. But luckily he had won the support of some German princes by urging the nobility to "set itself against the pope as against a common enemy." He argued that because these princes were Christians, the Church in their realms was under their authority, not under that of Rome, "where the devil himself is in charge."[12] After Luther's excommunication, a powerful prince, Frederick the Elector, rescued him with a feigned kidnapping, and soon a number of other German princes were won over to the Lutheran cause. After similar challenges were issued throughout Europe, with differing models of reform, the Protestant Reformation was underway.

As Luther's alliance with the nobility illustrates, the Protestant Reformation was not only about theological issues. Questions about God, salvation, free will, the afterlife, and the proper forms of worship were certainly in play. But if the Reformation had been concerned only with theological matters, it wouldn't have precipitated a century of war. These theological disputes had major implications for the structure of government, the distribution of wealth, the regulation of marriage and divorce, and other public issues. Just as Christendom had been a way of organizing society, so were the various Protestant reformations. If for a long time it seemed that Lutherans, Catholics, Calvinists, Anglicans, and Anabaptists could not live together, it was because each version of Christianity created, in a sense, a different world.

The resolution of these conflicts, begun with the Peace of Augsburg in 1555 and extended in 1648 by the Peace of Westphalia, was based on the principle *cuius regio, eius religio*—whoever rules a region shall decide its religion. Government was regionalized into what eventually became nation-states.[13] And because religion remained linked to government, the regionalization of government demanded the pluralization of religion. At first, this pluralization was pretty meager. Only three religions were recognized on the continent and all of them were Christian: Lutheranism, Roman Catholicism, and Calvinism. Religion continued to be established, but on a more local level, and rulers promised to extend tolerance (within bounds) to religious dissenters.

In early modern Europe, then, we see two ideas of religion emerging—one rooted in the old idea of Christendom and one in the newer, Protestant idea of individual faith. In the old idea, religion had covered every aspect of culture, and church officials claimed authority (although often ineffectually) over emperors and kings. After the Wars of Religion, rulers would still need religious legitimation, but they could arrogate religious authority directly to themselves. Christian mores continued to regulate public life and were blended into moral convention and the national ethos. Yet within this public and political religious realm, there also sprouted the newer, Protestant sense of religion as private and voluntary, something that had to do with God, rather than with worldly affairs.

If the tension between the two was not obvious, it was because of the old idea of "true religion," which implied that all those who sincerely sought religious truth should arrive at essentially the same conclusions. Ideally, then, modern religion would retain tremendous power over society, but it would exert this power from the inside out, less by domination than by what philosopher Michel Foucault called "governmentality."[14] Rather than being enforced by law or inquisition, religious truth would be voluntarily embraced and cultivated by each person, who in the process would become an ideal citizen.

But what if public religion and private religion were to diverge? A few years before the Peace of Westphalia, a scholar named Alexander Ross tackled this problem in a tome modestly titled *Pansebeia: Or a View of all Religions in the World: With the Several Church Governments from the Creation till these times.* "May a state," Ross asked, "tolerate different religions in private?" His answer was a circumspect yes, bound by the following conditions: "1. If they be such religions that doe not overthrow the fundamentals of truth. 2. Nor such as impugn or disturb the government established in that State or Kingdom. 3. If the professors thereof be such as are not factious, ambitious or pertinacious; but honest, simple, tractable, obedient to Superiors, having no other end in holding their opinions of Religion, but God's glory, and satisfaction of their own conscience."[15]

Ross clearly felt the tensions between the two meanings of religion. As his subtitle indicates, he conceived different religions as different forms of government. But he also had to contend with something newer: "religion in private." How was this new thing to be understood, especially since it had the same name ("religion") as the old thing? The solution, Ross proposed, was to make "private religion" a matter of "opinion"—in particular, opinions about God. These need not be kept to oneself; Ross, by using the word "professors," assumes that they will be professed, or said out loud. Even so, they must not "overthrow the fundamentals of truth" or issue in any act of disobedience, even any expression of dissent, from the established government.

But what were "the fundamentals of truth," and which opinions would "overthrow" them? Would the Jewish faith represent such a threat? Atheism? Catholicism? In various parts of Europe and America, any and all of those positions would be deemed intolerable during the subsequent centuries. And what was entailed in "obedience to superiors"? Slavery, for example? The subordination of women to men, of the property-less to the propertied, of black and brown people to whites? All of these, too, would be embedded in the various "church-governments" of Europe and America; they also would be challenged, resisted, and defied in the name of religion. However much Ross struggled to reconcile the public and private meanings of religion, they collided at every subsequent moment.

In the following centuries, scholars would try to solve the problem by coming up with simple creeds that, supposedly, everyone would be able to accept. Natural religion (or Deism), first introduced by Edward Herbert, is perhaps the best-known example. It boiled religion down to five tenets: God exists; people should worship God; worship entails both piety and a life of virtue; people ought to repent of their sins; God will reward or punish people in the afterlife according to their individual merits.[16] Deism was attractive to many intellectuals, including some of the American Framers. But the underlying problem was still there, encoded in words like "piety" and "virtue." What, exactly, did these mean? And what if rational individuals did not define them in the same way?

In the eighteenth century, another philosopher much admired by the American Framers addressed this problem more frankly. Jean-Jacques Rousseau formulated a set of propositions he called "civil religion," which entailed the usual tenets of Deism but also required all citizens to accept *in toto* "the sanctity of the social contract and the laws." Of course, he acknowledged, nobody could be forced to sincerely believe in civil religion (or for that matter, any religion). And he cared about sincerity—so much so that he proposed execution for anyone who pretended to believe in civil religion but actually didn't. As for those who openly admitted disbelief, Rousseau advised that they be banished from the realm.[17]

Tolerable Religion

The American method of managing the tension between public and private religion owes much to John Locke, whose *Letter Concerning Toleration* (1689) and other writings greatly influenced some of the Framers.[18] Locke's answer, we often hear, was to firmly separate church and state and to sequester religion-talk from public life. But that is a partial and distorted reading of Locke, and thus of American history.

A key but often overlooked point is that Locke spoke of religion in one sense as beyond government, but in another sense as beneath government. In the former sense, a religion for Locke was a group of people "who have one and the same rule of faith and worship."[19] Government had no jurisdiction over what people believed and how they worshipped, and religious institutions had no claim on coercive power. Moreover, as Elizabeth Pritchard argued in her book on his political theology, Locke was not asking people to keep quiet about religion: he wanted religious beliefs and practices openly displayed, much as fashionable clothing is displayed, so that they could be judged in the court of public opinion.[20] I would add that while Locke made doctrine and worship easy to discuss, he also made them politically unimportant. And while he made the essence of religion hard to identify and debate, he also installed it as the foundation of the polity.

For Locke, religion also meant something both more obscure and more important than doctrines and rituals: what he (like other

Christians before and since) called "true religion." While he accepted that doctrines and worship could differ greatly from one religion to another, he thought that "true religion" was the same everywhere. Locke did not offer much by way of a definition of true religion. But as Pritchard and others have observed, it centered on belief in a God who endowed each person with inalienable rights.[21] Because Locke assumed that this belief was the moral foundation of society, he thought that people who did not share it should be shunned. Although he rejected coercive measures to enforce religious doctrines and worship, he did feel that government had a strong and legitimate interest in supporting "true religion."[22]

"True religion," because it was deeply interior, could not be worn on the sleeve. Therefore, when Locke wrote about religion as something that could be displayed and discussed, he was referring to things that are more obvious: specifically, the beliefs people professed and the ways they worshipped. Most of Locke's *Letter Concerning Toleration* speaks of religion only in this more superficial sense. That was why he could claim that "all the bustles and wars" about religion were entirely unnecessary. The cause of all that violence, he wrote, was "not the diversity of opinions (which cannot be avoided), but the refusal of toleration to those that are of different opinions (which might have been granted)." Such conflicts could be easily resolved if people would only "distinguish exactly the business of civil government from that of religion." Civil government was properly concerned only with worldly issues (life, health, liberty, and property) while religion was concerned with the "salvation of souls." The boundaries between the two were "fixed and immovable," Locke contended, and whoever confuses them "jumbles heaven and earth together." What does it matter, he asked, if a person has been "dipped" (baptized) in a certain manner? Why should we care whether, in our neighbor's church, the minister "is, or is not, clothed in white, or crowned with a mitre"?[23]

As Locke knew, these rhetorical questions had real answers. Underlying the controversies over how and when people should be "dipped," for instance, was the question of whether you had to be a Christian in order to be a good citizen. If the two were inseparable, it made sense to baptize infants. But if a person was Christian simply by virtue of being born in a Christian society, how could you tell whether that person really believed in the faith and was committed to good citizenship? Alternatively, infant baptism might be replaced by adult or "believers' baptism," but this entailed the possibility that many adults would choose not to be baptized. That was the position of the Anabaptists and later the Baptists, but it raised a different question. If a shared Christian faith was not the basis of the social order, what was? And if professing Christian faith was not how you signaled willingness to comply with the laws of society, how did you signal it? In Locke's time and for a long time thereafter, the second scenario—a society not founded on Christianity—was more widely dreaded. For that reason, the opponents of infant dipping were persecuted as political radicals in both Europe and America.

Robes and miters also were fraught with worldly implications. Fancy vestments represented not only the Anglican Church but also the king who was its head. In sixteenth-century England, there had been a major controversy over clerical vestments, foreshadowing the Civil Wars of Locke's time, when plain-dressed Puritans executed the king and installed, for a time, an alternative Christian commonwealth. Among laypeople, clothing had not only religious but social and economic meanings. Until the late Middle Ages, how people dressed was a precise indicator of their place in the world, which in turn indicated their duties and privileges. But the rise of a middle class disrupted this system of signals, because now people could "dress up"—present themselves as if born into a higher class. From the late fourteenth century until shortly before Locke's birth, English monarchs had instituted sumptuary laws in an attempt to stabilize these markers of station and duty.[24]

So it was not for nothing that Locke, the child of Puritan parents, compared religious expression to fashion. If religion is like clothing, he suggested, it can be changed without harming the body politic. And, of course, you can hate how certain people dress without needing to murder them. Yet Locke knew perfectly well that religious expressions—robes, miters, creeds, dippings, and the like—could provoke violent political conflict. When he claimed that religious differences *did not* bear on government, he meant that they *should not* bear on government. He was proposing, in effect, that the doctrines people espouse and the worship they practice no longer be read as signs of their positions on hotly contested public issues.

That people should tolerate diversity of religious expression was a sound suggestion in a time when the common way to deal with this diversity was, as Locke put it, to "persecute, torment, destroy, and kill" one's opponents.[25] Still, disconnecting religious expression from its former political meanings did not in itself resolve the underlying conflicts. Moreover, neither in religion nor in clothing did the lifting of coercive regulations mean that anything went. People were still expected to "wear" something, and what they wore would be scrutinized and judged. But now people were to choose without external regulation, to present themselves as free individuals, but individuals with finely honed social sensibilities—as people of "good taste." Atheism, for instance, was out of the question for Locke—the religious equivalent of nudism. Equally unseemly were religions that implied allegiance to a foreign power, religions that were themselves intolerant, and religions that encouraged acts or opinions that were illegal or "contrary to society."

As Locke's treatment of atheism shows, "true religion" for him was something more than, and in a sense different from, what one said. The problem with atheism, he argued, was that the atheist could not in conscience swear before God. Therefore, "promises, covenants, and oaths, which are the bonds of human society, can have no hold upon an atheist." This claim was unsubstantiated; Locke offered no examples of atheists breaking their word. Moreover, he made numerous references to hypocrisy and deceit among professed believers. Yet while recognizing that many believers did not speak truly, Locke seemed to feel that the atheist could not speak truly. In fact he contended that atheism was anti-social even if it went unexpressed. "Even in thought," he declared, "atheism dissolves all."[26]

"True religion," then, could not be reliably discerned from the beliefs people espoused or the rituals they performed; it was not measured by "purity of doctrine" or the "pomp of outward worship." Indeed, Locke opened the *Letter* with a bold new distinction between "true religion" and religious expression. "The chief characteristic mark of the true Church," he wrote, "is toleration"—an arresting declaration given that historically the true Church had been defined by doctrinal orthodoxy. Locke was proposing that instead of defining the "true church" as a community of people who say the same things, we should redefine true Christianity (and true religion generally) as a community of those who refuse to tell others what to say.[27]

Only in one short sentence did Locke assay a further definition of true religion. "The business of true religion," he wrote, is "the regulating of men's lives, according to the rules of virtue and piety."[28] He did not specify what those rules might be, but we can discern them obliquely through what he found intolerable.[29] "To come to particulars, I say, first, no opinions contrary to human society, or to those moral rules which are necessary to the preservation of civil society are to be tolerated by the magistrate. But of these, indeed, examples in any Church are rare. For no sect can easily arrive to such a degree of madness as that it should think fit to teach, for doctrines of religion, such things as manifestly undermine the foundations of society."[30]

Clearly, Locke expected that "true religion" would support "the foundations of society," but he did not state what those foundations were. It was as if people should know without being told, just as they should know what Locke meant when he said that "promiscuous uncleanness" and "heinous enormities" ought never be tolerated.[31] For Locke, what breached the bounds of "true religion" was virtually unmentionable. Conversely, what was contained within those boundaries was meant to go without saying.

In this sense, Locke's separation of religion and government was a rule about what should and should not be said: people should not speak about religion as if it were connected to government. Any religion that explicitly linked itself with government, such as Catholicism or Islam, was therefore deeply suspect. Locke denied toleration to any religious association "constituted upon such a bottom that all those who enter into it do thereby ipso facto deliver themselves up to the protection and service of another prince." And, like atheism, this political infidelity was dangerous even if unexpressed. For example, "it is ridiculous for anyone to profess himself to be a Mahometan only in his religion, but in everything else a faithful subject to a Christian magistrate," because the Muslim owed "blind obedience" to the mufti of Constantinople, and indirectly to the Ottoman emperor.[32]

By Locke's own definition, Islam was undoubtedly a religion (a system of belief and worship). Therefore, it would seem to have deserved toleration. Yet Ottoman Islam, to him, was more than a religion because it extended beyond matters of doctrine and worship and into the foundations of government and society. Christianity did the same, but for Locke the Christian underpinnings of government were to remain unspoken. Muslims living in a Christian land therefore faced an irresolvable dilemma: they somehow had to assure the civil magistrate of their allegiance, yet could not be believed if they claimed to be Muslim "only in religion." The best solution for the Muslim, Locke advised, would be "if he acknowledged the same person to be head of his Church who is the supreme magistrate in the state."[33] Christians should speak as if church and state were separate, but Muslims would do well to recognize their connection.

In the years following the *Letter Concerning Toleration*, a critic named Jonas Proast kept pressing Locke about whether he really renounced force, even "at a distance," in regard to religion. As Pritchard notes, Locke's ideal of tolerant, nonviolent religion "takes a beating" under this sort of scrutiny.[34] For although Locke continued to maintain that force in religion could never be right, he did acknowledge that it might be effective. He also offered detailed advice on how parents might forcefully (if not forcibly) instill religion into children. According to his pedagogical program, this was to be done with exquisite gentleness, but with implacable pressure. For one thing, he urged parents to introduce religion before the child was capable of reason—before the child could either consent or dissent. Parents should train children in self-control, instill feelings of pride and shame, and thus "graft the true principles of morality and religion."[35] Although he elsewhere denied that true religion could come from birth or habit, Locke's educational program was designed to make religion feel like second nature.[36] Literally before the child knew it, "there ought to be imprinted in his mind a true notion of God."[37] As Pritchard puts it, religion was to be "embedded into the body before consent is even at issue."[38]

Such children, Locke supposed, would grow up to be citizens who thought themselves religiously free, who discussed religion with reason and civility, and who spoke of religion and civil government as quite separate. But these children would long since have been molded into people whose "natural stiffness" had been softened and

who were ready to "bend to a compliance and accommodate themselves to those they have to do with."[39] They would be well prepared
to disagree on what to believe and how to worship, but the deeper
part of religion—"true religion"—would be so ingrained into their
character and cemented into society's foundations as to become hard
to notice and nearly impossible to speak.

A Dictionary of All Religions

While Locke was working out the new meanings of religion in Europe, other scholars were trying to catalog non-Christian religions.
In America, one such early compendium was *A Dictionary of All Religions and Religious Denominations: Jewish, Heathen, Mahometan and
Christian, Ancient and Modern*, first published in 1814.[40] Its author
was a self-taught American scholar named Hannah Adams, a distant
cousin of John Adams, to whom she dedicated several editions of the
book. The *Dictionary* was a massive undertaking whose interlocking
purposes are spelled out in an appendix. Among Christian nations,
Adams's goal was religious toleration; among non-Christians, she
hoped to see successful Christian missions.

To achieve these purposes, Adams proposed a simple creed composed of just five doctrines. Three were familiar Deist tenets (God,
worship, and piety and virtue); the other two were specifically Christian (the resurrection of the dead and the confession of Jesus Christ
as the messiah).[41] These five points would be the basis for inter-
Christian toleration and a gospel to share with the rest of the world.
She concluded on a missionary note, envisioning "a period when the
gospel shall be universally extended, and received with unanimity;
when all superstitions shall be abolished, the Jews and Gentiles unit-
edly become the subjects of Christ's universal empire."[42] True to the
intractable contradictions of "religion," Adams could conceive Christianity as both an empire and a matter of personal faith, both conquering the world and entirely voluntary.

As her title shows, Adams held on to the fourfold typology of
the late Middle Ages. But rather than indicating types of people,
"religion" for her pointed to a muddled collection of referents. Depending on whom or what she had in mind, it could mean a belief

system, region, race, polity, or some combination of those.[43] When she was thinking about Protestant Christianity, she took belief to be religion's most salient feature, and the bulk of the *Dictionary* is devoted to describing doctrinal differences among Christians. But for other religions, race was more important. For example, Adams placed African religions under the heading of "Negroes," indigenous American religions under the heading "Indians," and Hinduism under "Hindoos." In other cases, the key feature seemed to be regional. She placed Shintō in an entry called "Japan" and put the figures of Confucius and Lao-se (Lao-Tze) under the heading "Chinese," which for her named both a people and a region. Yet she did not describe Christianity as "the religion of whites" or "the religion of Europe"; non-Christian religions evidently were bound to their cultural particularities in a way that Christianity was not. Similarly, the religions of Jews, "Mahometans," and Catholics raised concerns about religious tyranny, while Protestant Christianity did not.

"Judaism" does not appear as a heading in the *Dictionary*; instead, the pertinent heading is "Jews." In Adams's account, the Jews were a "nation" that had lost its territory and (she incorrectly assumed) would never regain it. As a political threat, then, Jews appeared to be neutralized. Thus there was no justification for persecuting them or withholding from them the full rights of citizenship, and she strongly condemned these forms of anti-Semitism. Nonetheless, she praised missionary efforts to convert "the lost sheep of the house of Israel"[44] and in her appendix referred to the Jews' "degeneracy."[45] In any case, Jews as portrayed in her *Dictionary* did not have much of a future. As a dissolved nation, an errant religion, and a degenerate people, they seemed destined to disappear.

"Mahometans" represented different challenges. There was no doubt that Islam was centered on beliefs, and that these were as complex and in some cases as controverted as those of Christians. But because "the Christian reader would be little interested in [the] particulars" of Islamic belief, Adams declined to dwell on them.[46] Another problem was that "Mahometans," unlike Jews, could not be considered a single people, because the Muslim world embraced many regions, nations, and language groups. In fact, Islam's aspiration was the same as Christianity's—to be "a universal empire."

However, Adams argued, that aspiration was not legitimate in the case of Islam, which had spread only by promising polygamy to men and forcing conversion "by the sword."[47]

As for Roman Catholicism, Adams found that the role of beliefs was far overbalanced by its inherent authoritarianism. Catholics, she observed with apparent perplexity, were not truly committed to any doctrine. For them, "the great cardinal point" was simply "to believe whatever is taught by the church or the highest ecclesiastical authorities."[48] The entries being arranged in alphabetical order, the *Dictionary*'s first reference to Catholicism was the word "Popery," a common Protestant pejorative throughout the nineteenth century. Two letters farther on, when Adams reached "Roman Catholicism," she pointed to the papacy as the religion's most important feature. Protestants, she wrote, were troubled by the fact that popes still claimed "paramount authority beyond all temporal powers." "Intelligent Catholics" rejected those papal pretensions, but her wording suggested that intelligence might not be the norm among Catholics, given that their religion seemed to require the subjection of reason.

For Adams, and for later scholars of religion, the contrast between Catholicism and Protestantism would become a way of understanding the fourth type of religion—"heathenism" or "paganism." Where Protestantism was rational, Catholicism was superstitious; where Protestantism prized freedom, Catholicism leaned toward despotism; where Protestantism demanded personal faith and morality, Catholicism settled for collective ritual. For instance, she described "Thibetianism" (Tibetan Buddhism) as the Eastern counterpart of Roman Catholicism, with its High Lama, its theocratic government, and its many superstitious rituals.[49] Later scholars, applying the same principle, would conceive Buddhism as a reformation of Hinduism and Sufism as a reformation of Islam.[50]

A second principle for understanding contemporary heathenism was to compare it to the ancient religions such as those of Greece and Rome. Adams believed that all forms of heathenism, living or dead, could be consigned to the "childhood of humanity."[51] She divided them into four types, the first two described as ancient ("dead"), and the third comprising "the Chinese, Hindoos, Japanese and etc." The fourth type of heathenism, even more roughly described, was that of "the Barbarians," including "the Indians of North and South America and the Negroes of Africa." By the end of the nineteenth century, these last two classifications, respectively called the "Oriental" and the "Primitive," would compose a map of world religions.

"Orientals" and "Primitives"

Even today, the typical textbook on world religions displays the same confusion as Hannah Adams's *Dictionary*. Some religions are characterized by region (for example, the religions of China), others by period (religions of antiquity), others as systems of beliefs that cross time and space (for example, Christianity and Buddhism). The table of contents is also likely to show that Adams's third and fourth types of "heathenism" met different fates when processed through the conceptual mill of "religion." "Oriental religion" is now elaborated into distinct "religions," each marked as an "ism"—"Buddhism," "Hinduism," "Confucianism," "Jainism," "Taoism," "Sikhism," "Shintoism," and "Zoroastrianism." But Adams's fourth type of heathenism, now likely to be called "indigenous" rather than primitive, often lumps into one chapter traditions with no historical connection, from places as far-flung as New Zealand, Africa, Greenland, and the Americas.

If you venture beyond the introduction of a world religions textbook, you often find the author straining to depict these "religions" as varieties of the same thing. But some of the religions have one God, some have many, and others have none. Some have sacred scriptures, others rely on oral traditions; some believe in an afterlife, others do not; some have founders, many do not. In some, the human dilemma is seen in terms of suffering; in others as sin, or imbalance, or ignorance. Perhaps most bewildering of all, there is no agreement about what sorts of issues are and are not of religious concern. Everything from hair length to the origin of species is a religiously charged issue for some group. There is literally nothing that could not be a religious matter, and there is no principled way to limit the possibilities.

The truth is that the category of religion, not having been created for intellectual reasons, does not make intellectual sense. Instead it must be explained by the vicissitudes and contradictions of history. In Europe, the category grew out of the Protestant Reformation, the ensuing wars, and the emergence of more (or less) tolerant regional establishments. But the chief effect of these events was to complicate only one kind of religion—Christianity. The emergence of a whole panoply of world religions required encounter with non-Christian religions, which often happened through the distorting mirrors of conquest and colonization. Even when the relationship was not colonial—say, between Euro-Christians and Jews or with the people of Japan—the conception of religion was dominated by the Christian West. It was the Christian West that made "religion" important. Everyone else had to respond to this category, whether by resistance, negotiation, or adaptation.

Hinduism is a good example of the interests at work in the nineteenth-century discovery/invention of new religions. The *Oxford English Dictionary* records the first use of the word "Hinduism" in 1829. Before that, however, Europeans and Euro-Americans had used "Hindoo" as a name for the people of the Indian subcontinent, initially attached to inhabitants of the Indus River Valley. From ancient times, these people had an astonishing variety of spiritual practices, which formed no unified system. But as the British gained colonial control of India, they felt the need to understand the Indian "religion," and, being Protestant, they tended to identify religion with scriptures. So when they learned about the Vedas (ancient sacred texts), they thought they had found Indian religion in its pure and original form. In reality, the Vedas played little role in the lives of Indian people outside the Brahmin caste, few of whom were literate.[52] But Protestants had a familiar way of explaining this discrepancy. Just as Christianity had degenerated from its biblical roots into Catholic superstition, so Hinduism had deteriorated from its original "Brahminic" form to the extravagant displays of spirituality the British now beheld in India.

But Europeans and Americans were not the only parties involved in naming and formulating Hinduism and other Asian traditions as "religions." Local elites, particularly literate men, also played an important role. In India, for example, a Bengali Brahmin and sometime employee of the British East India Company named Ram Mohan Roy (1772–1833) was one of the first to translate sections of the Vedas into English. Based on his study of the Vedas, and influenced by Christianity, Roy contended that monotheism was India's most ancient faith. He also denounced what he saw as the idolatry and superstition practiced by most people of the subcontinent.[53]

His concept of "Hinduism" certainly was not the common view, but it appealed to certain other Brahmins who, like Roy, stood to gain by having the British regard them as the arbiters of Indian "religion." Yet there was more than self-interest at work. Roy, who objected forcefully to British imperial actions, was part of a reform movement that advocated education and opposed sati (widow burning) and the caste system. It could be argued that by formulating an Indian "religion," Roy helped forge a national identity that ultimately advanced Indian independence.

In other words, by formulating their cultural traditions as "religion," Roy and other Asian elites were not just accepting this Western concept but reshaping it. His translations of the Vedas, for example, influenced American religious consciousness. Unitarians particularly appreciated his version of monotheism, and they joined him in supporting modernization efforts in India. Ralph Waldo Emerson, Henry David Thoreau, Bronson Alcott (father of Louisa May Alcott), Walt Whitman, and Helena Blavatsky were among nineteenth-century America's Veda enthusiasts, part of a widespread enchantment among Western Orientalists with the "Sacred Books of the East."[54] Many felt that the modern West, for all its progress, had lost its sense of the eternal, and they turned to the "Mystic East" to rediscover those spiritual depths.[55] Roy and other Asian spiritual teachers did not simply succumb to Western Christian ideas; they exerted missionary influence in the other direction.

A similar push-and-pull determined the classification (and sometimes declassification) of each newly recognized non-Christian "religion." The dynamic can be easily seen in modern transformations of Shintō. In the late nineteenth century, when the Meiji government began requiring all Japanese citizens to participate in Shintō rituals, it insisted that Shintō was not a religion but simply an expression of patriotism.[56] In the government's reasoning, the fact that the required rituals were not "religious" explained how Japan, a modern nation, could expect all citizens to perform them. After its defeat in World War II, an American directive declared that

Shintō was indeed a religion and therefore could not be established.[57] Both the Japanese government and the Americans operated with the modern assumption that "religion" must be voluntary, but because they had opposing interests (respectively, to inflate or deflate Japanese imperial power), this shared assumption led them to apply the term in opposite ways.

A similar reversal occurred with Confucianism. When Jesuit missionaries arrived in China in the sixteenth century, they concluded that Confucianism was not a religion. Therefore the Chinese people did not have to choose between Christianity and Confucianism, which made Christian conversion more palatable. Over the following centuries, however, other Catholic missionaries decided that Confucianism actually was a religion and demanded that Chinese converts renounce it. In the twentieth century the Catholic hierarchy would return to the Jesuit position that Confucianism is not a religion—again, a wise move that helped preserve the Chinese Catholic church.[58] Today, the Chinese government, which sponsors Confucian Institutes all over the world, appears to agree with the Vatican. In line with communist ideology, it presents Confucianism not as a religion but as a Chinese cultural tradition.

In none of these cases is it particularly illuminating to ask, "Is X really religion?" We learn more by asking by whom, in what sense, and for what purposes X was classified as a religion. Those are also the questions to ask about the generic idea of "religion" within which these newly recognized religions were positioned. For the mostly Protestant scholars who formulated the generic concept, an overriding purpose was to legitimize the superiority of Christianity. Religions were cataloged on an evolutionary scale, with Protestant-flavored Christianity at the top.

This evolutionary scheme was elaborately laid out in 1889 by C. P. Tiele, one of the founders of *Religionswissenschaft* (the science of religion).[59] For Tiele, the highest forms of religion were universalistic; they directed their message to the whole world and were not bound to any particular region, people, or culture. Judaism, for example, could not be a universal religion because, despite its monotheism, it prescribed a detailed code of religious behavior. That, in Tiele's mind, set Judaism below the highest religions, which were based on abstract ethical principles. Another problem was that because Jews were primarily a community of descent, Judaism did not conform to the Lockean idea that religions should be voluntary societies. In Tiele's terminology, Judaism was a "race" or "national" religion, which could spread only by imposing its "nationality" or "civilization" upon others.[60] (Needless to say, he did not pause to consider that the same might have been said of Christianity, which most people followed by accident of birth, and which had spread in concert with European culture.)

For Tiele, even "Mohammedanism" flunked the universality test, although it had adherents of many cultures. Islam, he wrote, retains "its holy language, its unvarying rites, its central sanctuary around which the pilgrims from every part of the Mohammedan world assemble every year." Notwithstanding its universalist aspirations, Islam "in its external features is little better than an extended Judaism."[61] For Tiele, as for Hannah Adams, features that were oppressive and ethnocentric in Islam or Judaism—say, a community of descent, a system of government, or a shared civilization—seemed universal when they appeared in Western Christianity. Only Christianity was suited to be the universal religion—a conclusion, Tiele hastened to add, that he'd reached "from a scientific, not from a religious point of view."[62]

Most instructive of all was Tiele's treatment of "primitive" people, whose religions he termed "nature religions." These were hopelessly bound to particular people and places—stuck where they'd emerged, so to speak. Because they had no shot at universality, Tiele reasoned, nature religions could hardly be called religions at all. As he put it, religion in its earliest form "is not itself a religion, but a sort of primitive philosophy, which not only controls religion, but rules the whole life of man in the childhood of the world."[63] As a good Protestant modernist, he took it as axiomatic that religion in its most mature form had to be cabined in a discrete sphere; it could not be the whole of life but only a part of it. That was the limitation of "primitive religion": it saturated the "whole of life."

Yet for precisely the same reason, primitive people could be seen as the most religious of people. Tiele did not develop this contrary implication, but other scholars of religion did. By the mid-twentieth century, the leading American scholar of religion, Mircea Eliade, took the modernist axiom in the other direction. Modern people, he acknowledged, had reduced religion to a carefully limited segment of life. But that meant, for Eliade, that "archaic man"

Frontispiece, The World's Parliament of Religions, *ed. John Henry Barrows (Chicago: World's Parliament Publishing, 1893). From Wikimedia Commons/Public Domain.*

was the exemplar of *homo religioso*, whose essential humanity the moderns were in danger of losing.[64]

The paradox was already there in Tiele: religion was supposed to be only a part of life, yet it also was expected to provide the universal ethical principles by which everybody everywhere should live. It's similar to the paradox of religion in John Locke: religion was private and voluntary in one sense but public and effectively mandatory in another. To be only a part of life yet the foundation of everything, a separate sphere and yet "the whole of life"—this was the intractable enigma of "religion." If "primitive religion" was a mirror into which modernist religion did not wish to gaze, that was because Westerners were starting to suspect that in the modern world all religion, even perhaps their own, might soon look "primitive."[65]

The World's Parliament of Religions

September 11, 1893, was a high point in the life of the Reverend John Henry Barrows and, he hoped, in the life of humanity. That morning, as the Liberty Bell sounded ten times, leaders from ten world religions processed into the Hall of Columbus. It was the world's first parliament of religions, the finale of the Chicago Exposition, and Barrows was honored to give the opening address.

Welcome, most welcome, wise men of the East and West! May the star which led you hither be like the luminary which guided the sages of old, and may this meeting by the inland sea of a new continent be blessed of Heaven to the redemption of men from error and from sin and despair . . .

There is a true and noble sense in which America is a Christian nation, since Christianity is recognized by the Supreme Court, by the courts of the several states, by executive officers, and by general national acceptance and observance, as the prevailing religion of our people. This does not mean that church and state are united. In America they are separated, and in this land the widest possible intellectual and spiritual freedom is realized. . . . Only in this western republic would such a congress as this have been undertaken and achieved.

I do not forget . . . that devout Jews, lovers of humanity, have cooperated with us in this parliament, that these men and women . . . have come with good cause to appreciate the spiritual freedom of the United States of America. . . . But the world calls us, and we call ourselves, a Christian people. We believe in the Gospels and in Him who they sent forth as "The Light of the World," and in Christian America, which owes so much to Columbus and Luther, to the Pilgrim Fathers and to John Wesley, which owes so much to the Christian church and college, and the Christian school.[66]

The *Daily Inter-Ocean* described this opening ceremony as "a spectacle that has never been equaled in the history of the world."[67] Against a backdrop of somberly dressed Americans, the "wise men of the East" stood out splendidly. Among them, as the newspaper described it, were "the swarthy sons of India" in their "gaudy gowns of red, orange, and green," the Chinese "in their mandarin's robes and pigtails," and "from the flowery kingdom of Japan," Shintō priests

and Buddhist monks "in picturesque garb of chaste colors and varie-
gated head-dresses." All of these were seated on the great dais, in
the middle of which sat a Catholic cardinal, with scarlet cassock and
biretta. The euphoric audience cheered, applauded, shed tears, and
waved handkerchiefs. For the next seventeen days, thousands would
throng the hall, sometimes with rain pouring in through the leaky
roof, to consider how (or whether) the dream of the Parliament
might come true: "to unite all religions against irreligion."[68]

   To Barrows, the colorful holy men surrounding him on the dais
evoked the Wise Men of the Christian nativity story. By coming to
America, he imagined, they were coming to Christ. Like many in
the mostly American audience, Barrows was a Protestant modernist, which made him both open to other religions and confident
that Christianity fulfilled them all. (A few years later, he would publish a book called *Christianity, the World Religion*.)[69] And just as
Christianity was, for Barrows, more than one religion among others, so America was more than one nation among others. Only in
America, he suggested, could such a gathering take place, because
"in this land the widest possible intellectual and spiritual freedom is
realized."[70] America the nation and Christianity the religion were
uniquely universalistic and thus uniquely equipped to tame cultural
differences and harmonize dissonant beliefs. So Barrows observed
no tension between welcoming the world's religions on presumably
equal terms and insisting on the superiority of Christianity. He saw
no contradiction between lauding the religious liberty protected by
America's separation of church and state, and insisting that America
was and must remain "a Christian nation."

   For this last assertion, Barrows could claim the authority of the
nation's highest Court. The opinion to which he referred was *Holy
Trinity v. United States*, issued just the year before. The case had
grown out of a series of laws prohibiting U.S. employers from hir-
ing foreign "labor or service of any kind." The laws were originally
intended to exclude Chinese laborers, but by 1885 they were targeted more broadly.[71] Religion came into the mix when federal
prosecutors charged that Holy Trinity, an Anglican church in New
York City, had unlawfully contracted with an English clergyman
named Walpole Warren to move to the United States and become
its new rector. The charge made sense; the statute provided few

exceptions, and none that were relevant to Warren. Evidently, though, the Supreme Court was shocked that Christian ministry could be considered "labor" or that an Englishman might be the type of "foreigner" the immigration law was meant to exclude. It ruled unanimously that the immigration laws were meant only to exclude "an ignorant and servile class of foreign laborers," not those "whose toil is of the brain," and definitely not "ministers of the gospel," for "we are a Christian nation." The Court went so far as to proclaim that Congress could not have intended to constrain religion—which may have been true of Congress's intentions but would have been immediately recognized as impracticable if "religion" had conjured in their minds anything less conventional than the Reverend Walpole Warren.[72] Certainly, Justice David Brewer, who wrote the majority opinion in *Holy Trinity*, did not much appreciate religious diversity in America. A few years later, he would publish a book called *The United States: A Christian Nation.*[73]

The "wise men of the East," knowing that the religions of Asia were not entirely welcome in America because Asian people were increasingly unwelcome, might have raised an eyebrow at Barrows's opening address. One Japanese delegate to the Parliament, faced upon arrival with signs reading, "No Japanese is allowed to enter here," commented, "If such be Christian ethics—well, we are perfectly satisfied to remain heathen."[74] And surely an irony must have been noticed by the "devout Jews" who had helped Barrows organize the Parliament but who now, in its opening minutes, were reminded that in Christian America they were second-class citizens. Barrows's praise for America's "Christian schools" might have raised hackles among the Catholics in the audience, who understood that "Christian schools" meant effectively Protestant schools that were supported by public funds. In Barrows's mouth, certain words slipped easily together—"religion" and "Christianity," "Christian" and "American," "American" and "Pilgrim Fathers." Many people in the hall fell between those words, and over the coming days would say so.

Yet for all its limitations, the Parliament was a significant religious opening, made possible by extending the old Christian idea of "true religion" to the emerging idea of religion-as-such. Everyone knew that religions did harm as well as good, but most people at the Parliament would have affirmed Virchand Gandhi's claim that "abuses are not from religion but in spite of religion."[75] It was this shared belief in the goodness of religion-as-such that raised the hopes, summarized by the *Chicago Tribune* on September 24, that people might recognize "the morality that underlies every faith"; that they might arrive at "a broad and general tolerance"; and that Christians might come to see that "there are no longer pagans and heathens, at least among the Oriental religionists," but that all stood "upon the same plane of morality and humanity."[76] It was a vision not unlike John Locke's—religions, while differing in doctrine and modes of worship, shared the moral essentials that could hold society together and could perhaps bring peace to the whole world. This was the joist of orthodoxy upon which the whole gathering sat, and the stress point from which all its fault lines emanated.

The most obvious fault line concerned the Parliament's most basic premise: that the world contained more than one "religion" worthy of the name. The archbishop of Canterbury, refusing an invitation to the Parliament, wrote that "the Christian religion is the one religion" and added, "I do not understand how that religion can be regarded as a member of a Parliament of Religions without assuming the equality of the other intended members and the parity of their position and claims." The Catholic hierarchy of America decided to participate only because, in the words of John Keane, rector of Catholic University, "it is not in our power to keep the Parliament from taking place."[77] Even the General Assembly of Barrows's own denomination, the Presbyterian Church U.S.A., had condemned the Parliament. The sultan of Turkey, Abdul Hammid II, is also reported to have opposed it.[78]

At the Parliament itself, several voices spoke for religious exclusivism. Mohammad (H. A. R.) Gibb, the only Muslim to address the gathering (and himself a convert), offered a cordial address but was unequivocal about which religion was true. "There is not a Musselman on earth," he said, "who does not believe that ultimately Islam will be the universal faith."[79] The several leaders grudgingly sent by the Catholic Church were mostly (but not entirely) unwavering in their assertion that the Roman Catholic Church was the only true church.[80] But no one was more unwavering or less civil than evangelical William C. Wilkinson, who described Christianity's stance toward "religions other than itself" as "an attitude of universal, absolute, eternal, unappeasable hostility."[81] The audience, evidently, was not sure how to feel. The *Chicago Herald* described the scene following Wilkinson's speech as "bedlam," so wild was the cheering and clapping. Yet minutes later, after Julia Ward Howe rebuked Wilkinson's intolerance from the podium, the "fickle audience" did a turnabout and gave her too "a storm of applause."[82]

To defend the Parliament against such controversies, Charles Bonney, its leading official, had opened the proceedings by asking delegates to speak with "absolute respect for the religious convictions of each other" while adding that "no attempt is here made to treat all religions of equal merit."[83] Yet the religious inclusivism that was the Parliament's aim ("to unite all religions against irreligion") was hard to reconcile with the belief that Christianity alone included all religious truth. For non-Christians, that was a bit like saying a worm is "included" in the bird that eats it. Moreover, as several Asian delegates pointed out, Christian missions around the world were closely associated with imperial domination. Narasima Charya, speaking of India under British rule, told the gathering that "the religion which a conquering nation . . . condescendingly offers to the conquered nation must ever be disgusting to the recipient."[84]

While they anticipated theological disagreements, Bonney and the other organizers had hoped that the Parliament would demonstrate "the substantial unity of many religions in the good deeds of the religious life."[85] But what exactly were the ethical demands of religion? How might religious unity help alleviate injustice and suffering? No answers to those questions were agreed upon. Jewish delegates raised the issue of anti-Semitism, African Americans raised the issue of racism, and women raised the issue of male domination. But for the most part, only the groups subject to these injustices raised them; they did not become collective causes. Frederick Douglass, disgusted by the racism of the Exposition, commented that "morally speaking" the White City was really "a whitened sepulcher."[86] As historian of religion Richard Seager concluded, if the spirit of the gathering was "generally irenic," that may have been because most speeches were "theological and spiritual rather than political."[87] When conflicts erupted, the tone could change quickly.

Still, as scholar of religion Diana Eck argued, the Parliament advanced ecumenism among Christians and interfaith dialogue among religions. Before the Parliament, she writes, most Americans had never heard of Hinduism, Shintō, or Buddhism.[88] Afterwards, Hindu missionaries like Swami Vivekananda and Buddhist missionaries like Soyen Shaku had so much success in America that when the Immigration Act of 1965 finally allowed Asian people to enter the country, they found their religions already being practiced. But the forms that Buddhism and Hinduism had taken in America were quite different from what ordinary people practiced in Asia. Separated from their cultures of origin, they had become expressions of a universal consciousness that anyone, anywhere could embrace. The unity of religions, to the extent that it budded in the twentieth century, was a Western modernist unity, whose prospects were bound to those of Western modernism itself.

And the modernism that created "religion" also subjected it to the risk implied in the Parliament's motto: "To unite all religions against irreligion." Those who organized this unprecedented assembly felt it urgent to unite religions because irreligion was an ever more serious threat. Western modernity had produced the concept of religion by separating the world into parts that were religious and parts that were not. But if religion was no longer to have jurisdiction over government, science, education, or the economy, what exactly was its authority? At what point did modernist religion, in its deference to secular knowledge, come to contain nothing specifically "religious" and thus become indistinguishable from the secular? At what point did secular powers begin to create their own order of things, their own worldviews? At what point did the modern world become irreligious?

Given these haunting questions, it was extremely telling that those Americans for whom religion was "the whole of life" were not invited to the Parliament. Four hundred years after Columbus's arrival, from the podium of the hall named in his honor, no Native Americans were allowed to speak on behalf of their own religions. Asking them to do so would have been awkward given that the 1883 Code of Indian Offenses had criminalized Indian religious ceremonies. The few Native Americans who had been invited to Chicago were outside, among the "savage" and "semi-savage" people displayed on the Midway Plaisance.

In the hall itself, only one speech concerned Native Americans. Delivered by anthropologist Alice Cunningham Fletcher, it concerned the relationship between religion and science. The Parliament heard several papers on this theme, most arguing that while backward and superstitious forms of religion might have reason to fear science, modernist religion did not.[89] Modernist religions, speaking on their own behalf, claimed that they had something to teach science as well as something to learn. While ceding the universal authority once claimed by the "one true church," modernist religionists still expected to have something to say about "the whole of life." But that was not so for the religions of Native people. They were not invited to speak on their own behalf, and when science spoke of them, Native religions became objects rather than subjects of knowledge.

That was the great and ultimately irresolvable paradox of this modern concept of "religion." It was conceived by separation: the separation of Christendom into sovereign states, of religious membership from citizenship, of indigenous people from their sacred lands, of "heathenism" into distinct and respectable "religions." Yet despite all these separations, religion was supposed to remain a unity. The species were supposed to belong to a single genus. The differences among religions were supposed to be incidental compared to their common essence. Private religiosities were supposed to converge into public order. And although religion was now only a part of life, it was still expected to somehow make the world whole.

CHAPTER TWO

Walls and Foundations

Washington, Jefferson, and Religious Double-Talk

Congress shall make no law respecting an establishment of religion or prohibiting the free exercise thereof.

—FIRST AMENDMENT TO THE UNITED STATES CONSTITUTION

AMERICANS ARGUE A LOT about the Framers and religion, but often the arguments are overdetermined by our own views. If we are religiously devout, it's hard to imagine that the Framers weren't; if we are religiously skeptical, it's easy to believe that they were too. If we think of religion as the foundation of society, it may seem obvious that the Framers never intended anything like a "wall of separation" between church and state. If we view religion as ineluctably personal, politically irrelevant, or divisive, it may seem just as obvious that the Framers meant to firmly separate religion and government, for the sake of both.

In this chapter I'll argue that the Framers actually held both views at once.[1] Like Americans today, they imagined religion in terms of both walls and foundations. The same Framer who one day referred to religion as entirely the business of the individual might another day speak as if it cemented the nation. To confuse matters more, when they spoke of America's foundations, the Framers sometimes used words like "civilization," "morality," "good order," and "patriotism" interchangeably with "religion." In short, they handled religion with an unselfconscious double-talk that placed them at cross-purposes not only with each other but with themselves.

If you want to argue that the Framers were strict separationists, you could recall that many of them were Deists, Masons, or "theistic rationalists." Most had read Thomas Paine, and several were friends with him. Even those who eventually turned against Paine for his heterodox views agreed that religious zealotry could wreak havoc on a political system. You also might point out that the Framers declined to mention God in the preamble of the Constitution; that in article 2, they prescribed the presidential oath word for word with no mention of God; that in article 6, they prohibited any religious oath as a condition of federal office. You could add that when the Framers set out the principles by which the federal government was to deal with religion, they expressed these principles purely as constraints ("Congress shall make no law"). In short, you could plausibly argue that the Constitution tells the federal government to seal itself off from religion.

But if you want to argue that the Framers were proponents of religion in public life, you can marshal plenty of evidence for that proposition too. You can correctly claim that most of the Framers were professing Christians who, soon after passing the Bill of Rights, hired a pair of Christian chaplains for Congress. You could recall that those who later rose to the presidency swore their oaths of office on Bibles, conspicuously attended church, and (with the exception of Jefferson) declared national days of fast and thanksgiving. In these and innumerable other instances, you could argue, the Framers manifested the conviction that government relied on the support of religion and had a vested interest in supporting it in turn.

The Framers could think of religion in these conflicting ways because they lived in a time of conflicting exigencies. On one hand, they were anxious to neutralize the political dangers of religious differences; on the other hand, they wanted to preserve religion as the foundation of civilization. Like leading thinkers in Europe, those in America thought that the solution was to reimagine religion as a genus comprising several species. The generic aspects of religion could then be encouraged as foundational to public life, while the species differences could be cabined in the private sphere. But they could not clarify which was which. For example, should everyone believe in Christ, or was it sufficient just to believe in God? Or was it enough to adhere to the same basic moral foundations, regardless of what one believed about God or the hereafter? There was far less consensus on these points than the Framers wanted to believe. And that dissensus grew ever greater as previously excluded groups staked their claims in America's foundations.

When they crafted the Constitution, the Framers did not tackle the question of what all religions had in common. Instead, they were thinking of religion as an area of *difference* upon which government may not intrude. Religion was what Madison called a "property of peculiar value"—the most private of all matters.[2] To be religiously free was to exercise dominion over one's very self: one's own mind and conscience, accountable directly to Truth or God. Without religious freedom, this self could not exist, and self-government would be impossible. A sovereign self did not need and would not accept any rule to which he [*sic*] had not consented. In this way, the concept of limited government rested on the principle of religious freedom. And that is why the wall, although only a metaphor, is a good metaphor for religion as it appears (and disappears) in the Constitution. More than placing religion *behind* a wall, the Framers made religion itself into a wall or boundary around government.

Yet they also expected that, left free to seek religious truth, everyone would come to essentially the same conclusions, at least insofar as they bore on public behavior. Indeed, they thought that the autonomous pursuit of religious truth was exactly the sort of thing that made a person into a good citizen. Consider again the religious gestures made by presidents-elect—swearing their oaths of office on the Bible, tacking on the words "so help me God," and kissing the Bible upon concluding the oath. From one standpoint, these are expressions of religious freedom, yet there is no doubt that the American public has expected them from every president since George

Washington. Each president has been expected to precisely reenact these rituals, yet to do so sincerely and voluntarily.

In the 1830s, Alexis de Tocqueville noted that Americans were especially religious not *despite* their separation of church and state but *because* of it. Because religion looked and felt free to Americans, he argued, they surrendered more easily to the majoritarian influence. That seemed to be true also for religious minorities. Catholic clergy, for example, rarely objected to the Protestant culture around them. Instead they went "flowing without resistance" with the tide of public opinion.[3]

Tocqueville vastly underestimated the American religious conflicts of his day. But he was right to sense that Americans expected congruence between wall religion and foundation religion. This expectation was written into the early state constitutions, which defined religion in terms of certain beliefs (for example, belief in God, Protestant Christianity, or Christianity generally). Those beliefs effectively defined foundation religion and, in the same gesture, delineated the scope of religious toleration. In the rare cases when no doctrines were established, state constitutions made social conformity the criterion of true religion. Typically, this would appear right after the provision protecting religious freedom; constitutions would acknowledge religious freedom but hasten to add that it did not cover anything that violated "peace and good order" or permitted "licentiousness" or "immorality." Whether religion was described in both doctrinal and moral terms or in moral terms only, the point was that "true religion" had to support the foundations of society and government. Anything that unsettled those foundations could not be "true religion" and need not be tolerated.

But although foundation religion was inscribed into the early state constitutions, the Framers did something entirely new in the federal Constitution. Rather than just tolerate religious difference, they made religion free. Rather than just make the religious foundations of government a bit more capacious, they disestablished religion altogether. They even omitted the familiar provisos that limited religious freedom within the bounds of peace, good order, and social duty. Why they did this and what it meant remain perhaps the most vexed questions about church and state in America.

Scholars have rightly observed that federal disestablishment was partly necessitated by the continued existence of state-level establishments.[4] Nonetheless, it was a portentous innovation, imaginable because religions could now be conceived as differing from one another only in matters that did no social harm, and as sharing features that did social good. By protecting religious liberty with a metaphorical wall, and limiting government with that same wall, they hoped to provide the nation with stronger foundations. Each citizen would seek and embrace religious truth on his or her own, but each would end up with the same virtues, the same public-spiritedness, and the same sense of social order. Together these qualities would grow into a national identity that was robust and organic precisely because it was not forced.

But the religion clauses had a fatal flaw. To protect the differences among religions, one would have to know what the commonalities were—what made these different things count as "religion." The Framers did not define those commonalities and in fact could not have done so, because any definition of religion would have been either too narrow or too broad. What makes the flaw fatal, however, is not the mere absence of a definition. Many key terms, such as "speech," are not defined in the Constitution itself, and hammering out those definitions is a normal part of constitutional jurisprudence. But in none of those other cases does the Constitution call for the thing in question to be disestablished. That is the fatal flaw—the religion clauses cannot be implemented without a working definition of religion, but any definition effects not the *disestablishment* but the *establishment* of whatever is defined.

The following pages explore the inner contradictions of American religion-talk through episodes from the lives of two Framers. One of them, George Washington, leaned instinctively toward foundation religion but was also deeply committed to religious freedom. In his dealings with the Quakers, he was called upon to reconcile the two, a task in which he did not succeed. The other, Thomas Jefferson, favored a wall of separation, which he defended against the Federalist establishment by forming an awkward alliance with the Baptists. But Jefferson's wall was also a means to protect his own position in America's foundations. In both cases, the word "religion" failed to answer the questions embedded in the religion clauses—

"We can take no part in carrying on War." Fragment of a 1789 letter/address to George Washington from the Quakers. Courtesy of Quaker and Special Collections, Haverford College.

questions about liberty, equality, the limitations of government, and the needs of the political community.

Washington, the Friends, and the Enigma of Religious Liberty

In October 1789, a little delegation of Quakers made their way to the Federal Building in New York City for an audience with their nation's first president. They did not pause to remove their broad-brimmed hats in Washington's presence, although other men would have done so as an ordinary gesture of respect. To Quakers, how-ever, removing one's hat affronted divine sovereignty and human equality, so they consistently breached this protocol. Without cere-mony, they proceeded to read aloud the missive composed by their Yearly Meeting for this solemn occasion.[5]

This now-famous letter, and Washington's famous reply, were about religion. The Quakers, formally called the Society of Friends, were religiously opposed to revolution but acknowledged that "the Almighty, who ruleth Heaven and in the Kingdom of Men" had "permitted a great Revolution to take place in the Government of this Country," and evidently had left Washington in charge.[6] They urged the new president to seek God's guidance, to foster "morality and true religion," and to suppress "vice, infidelity, and irreligion."

They sang the praises of religious "toleration," one of the "greatest blessings" enjoyed by Americans. Recalling that they'd always respected the religions of others, the Quakers suggested that it was only fair for them to receive the same in return.

Then they got to the "ask"—or, more accurately, the "tell." The Friends had come before the president not to beg a favor but to issue a statement: "We can take no part in carrying on war, on any occasion or under any power." For Washington, this was no news. During the war, most Friends had refused to join his army and had disowned any members who did enlist.[7] When the British army arrived in Philadelphia on September 29, 1777, the Friends adjourned their meeting and, with somber countenances, readied their homes, barns, and meetinghouses for British occupation. A downcast spirit would have been appropriate, for the Quakers were treated badly by the rough and raucous British army. They would suffer even more the following year at the hands of Continental forces. Suspected of Tory sympathies and even of treason, Quakers saw their homes vandalized and papers seized. Dozens were arrested, jailed, or deported, and two were hanged. Not only wouldn't the Quakers go to war, they also wouldn't support it. During the Revolutionary War, they refused to pay taxes to the Continental government or even to touch its paper money.[8] Their letter was tactfully oblique on this point, simply stating that the Friends would willingly contribute to "the necessary support of civil government." But like everyone else, Washington knew that many Quakers had gone to jail or had property seized after refusing to pay war taxes.

Washington, a polite man, did not bristle openly at the Quaker demands. Instead, he affirmed the Friends' idea of religious dissent and went them one better. He said that in America, religious dissidents would enjoy religious "liberty," not mere "toleration," and this liberty would be a "right," not a privilege given or withheld at the sufferance of the majority. As he would later express it to the Jews of Newport, "It is now no more that toleration is spoken of, as if it were the indulgence of one class of people that another enjoyed the exercise of their inherent natural rights."[9] When religion was established, government could offer nothing better than religious toleration. But just weeks before the Quaker visit, the First Congress of the United States had made the revolutionary decision not to establish religion at all. With that in mind, President Washington told the Quakers that, in America, citizens would be "responsible only to their Maker for their religion." Government would not dictate conscience but existed "to protect the persons and consciences of men from oppression."

Over the centuries, these sympathetic words have been recalled as evidence of Washington's deference to religious liberty. But if the Quakers had been hoping that he would recognize religious pacifism as a constitutional right, they must have been badly disappointed. The president began with a tepid compliment, conceding that the Quakers were exemplary citizens, but for one shortcoming: "their declining to share with others the burden of the common defense." This, however, was not just any shortcoming; it was precisely the point at issue. Washington allowed that religious pacifism, like "the conscientious scruples" of all citizens, "should be treated with great delicacy and tenderness." But this would be only a statutory accommodation, not a constitutional right. "It is my wish and desire," he continued, "that the laws may always be as extensively accommodated" to conscience (and here came the mega-caveat) "as a due regard to the protection and essential interests of the nation may justify and permit."

Washington himself had tried for a long time to accommodate Quaker pacifism, and had finally given up. As a commander of the Virginia Militia during the French and Indian War, he was stuck with Quaker draftees who not only refused to fight but, when asked to help out with noncombatant chores, wouldn't do those either.[10] Early in the Revolutionary War, General Washington had been willing to exempt Quakers from military service, but by May 1777 he was fed up. Writing to Pennsylvania governor William Livingston, he complained angrily about Quaker noncompliance with Pennsylvania's Militia Law. The officers of Pennsylvania, he urged, should force the Quakers to fight—"defeat their evil intentions and bring their men into the field."[11] In the same year, he attempted to keep the Friends from attending their Yearly Meeting in Philadelphia,[12] having concluded (not wrongly) that their gatherings were forums for organized noncooperation with the Revolution. "The plans settled at these meetings," he grumbled, "are of the most pernicious tendency."[13]

Now, twelve years later, circumstances called for conciliation. So Washington's language was courteous and restrained, but his substantive response was a firm "no." Washington was telling the Quakers that despite their sincere religious pacifism, the U.S. Constitution did not entitle them to exemptions from fighting or financing the nation's wars. Legislators could choose to carve religious exceptions out of conscription laws—if they were feeling "delicate and tender" about such things, and if they determined that exempting Quakers from military service would not endanger "essential interests of the nation." But legislators were not constitutionally required to provide such exemptions. Although religious liberty was the headline of the Bill of Rights, a religious pacifist had no constitutional right to refuse participation in war. That remains true today: conscientious objector status is a statutory accommodation instituted by Congress and thus always liable to termination.[14] It is not considered a constitutional right.

This uneasy exchange between Washington and the Quakers illustrates a dilemma lodged within the free exercise clause: what the religious believer most needs from government is exactly what the government can least afford to provide. For religious people, the worst thing government can do is to outlaw what their religion commands. But for the government, the most unreasonable demand citizens could make is automatic exemption from any law that happens to contravene their religious beliefs. The dilemma reaches its greatest intensity on the issue of war. Nothing weighs more heavily on conscience than the taking of human life. If the government can make you kill in violation of conscience, what can it not make you do? Yet no obligation weighs more heavily on government than the national defense. How can that obligation be met if all citizens have the right to exempt themselves from military service as an expression of religious freedom? Although Washington and the Quakers had significantly different views of religion, both assumed that the free exercise of religion ordinarily would support America's foundations and certainly would never threaten them. Yet their own interactions show just how shaky these assumptions were.

In many ways, Quakerism fit the constitutional model of religion as a walled-off zone of personal liberty. Quakers were mystics, each one seeking a direct personal experience of the "inner light."

Quaker faith was outwardly manifest by their plain clothes, their archaic grammar, their refusal to take oaths, and their kindly demeanor. But since the inner light could not enter anyone by force, the Friends were prepared to live and let live. Their religion, in this sense, was a separate peace. Not expecting war as such to end, the Friends just wanted to be left out of it. To Washington, it looked as if Quakers were expecting others to fight and die in their place, which he found infuriating. But for Quakers, pacifism required complete self-surrender, a readiness to die rather than kill, even in self-defense. This could come only from supernatural grace; it was not a policy that could be implemented by natural means.

When Washington thought of religious freedom, he had in mind the beliefs and rituals that distinguished one religion from another. Yet neither he personally nor the Friends placed much value on doctrines and rituals. The Friends shared many tenets of Puritan belief, but had nothing like a systematic theology.[15] And apart from their meetings, where quiet waiting was punctuated by emotional outpourings of the Spirit, they had virtually no ritual.[16] Washington was no mystic, but like the Quakers he valued religion for its effects on people's behavior toward others. As he'd written to American Catholics a few months before, the public role of religion was to instill the "manners, morals, and piety" of one's society.[17] In other words, his objective was socialization, but he believed that for most people socialization had to be buttressed by beliefs and rituals. During the Revolutionary War he had required troops to attend Sunday services because he believed that it enhanced discipline and morale. And when the Jews of Newport complained about laws that denied public office to non-Christians, Washington agreed that such laws were based on mere "bigotry."[18]

Washington belonged to the Masons, a fraternal organization whose creed centered simply on the "Architect of the Universe" and which aimed to foster "polite society."[19] This was no doubt the sort of religious spirit that he meant to encourage in his Farewell Address, when he said to his fellow Americans that "with slight shades of difference, you have the same religion, manners, habits, and political principles."[20] He also was a vestryman in the Anglican Church and appears to have attended roughly once a month. Sometimes he stayed away because the rector was out of town or the weather was nasty;

other times just to visit friends or go foxhunting. It was reported that Washington never knelt when at church, and he consistently left before the most important Anglican ritual, the communion service. For this latter infraction, he was called out not too subtly from the pulpit. Evidently Washington felt duly chastised; he did not want his religious comings and goings to demoralize others. But his solution was not to start taking communion; instead, he stopped coming to church on communion Sundays.[21]

This concern for group morale animated what is perhaps Washington's most-quoted comment, also from the Farewell Address: "Of all the dispositions and habits which lead to political prosperity, religion and morality are indispensable supports." Even there, he added a subtle caveat. "Whatever may be conceded to the influence of refined education on minds of peculiar structure," he wrote, "reason and experience both forbid us to expect that national morality can prevail in exclusion of religious principle." Certainly, Washington knew people (Thomas Jefferson was one) who held virtue to be its own reward, quite apart from the question of divine rewards and punishments. But most people lacked both "refined educations" and "minds of peculiar structure." If they behaved themselves, it was mainly out of reverence for God and fear of God's punishment. No "sincere friend" of democracy, wrote Washington, could "look with indifference upon attempts to shake the foundation of the fabric of government."

Despite their many differences, both Washington and the Quakers believed that religion, though freely and individually chosen, should induce compliance with law and social convention. Quakers were sure that the experience of inner light made them better citizens, not worse. Their founder, George Fox, had advised them to "seek the peace and good of all men" and to avoid the "bustlings" and "tumults" of the world.[22] William Penn, in his first "Frame of Government" for Pennsylvania, claimed that "the powers that be are ordained of God: whosoever therefore resisteth the power, resisteth the ordinance of God."[23] In fact, Penn argued, governments had less to fear from Quakers than from any other religious society because Quakers would not "abet any contrivance destructive of the government and laws of the land."[24] That is why the Friends could issue to President Washington such a strange series of injunctions: he should support morality and "true religion," he should suppress vice and "irreligion"—and he should exempt the Quakers from what most Americans considered a basic duty of citizenship. Neither Washington nor the Quakers anticipated many conflicts between the demands of religion and those of society. But when these conflicts arose, each side defaulted toward a different explanation. The Friends assumed that the fault lay with government; Washington assumed the opposite. As he wrote in a 1789 letter to the Presbyterian General Assembly, "No man, who is profligate in his morals, or a bad member of the civil community, can possibly be a true Christian, or a credit to his own religious society."[25]

Still, on both sides there were tremendous ironies. For people who saw themselves as the most compliant of citizens, the Quakers spent an awful lot of time in jail—for refusing military conscription, withholding war taxes, and refusing to take loyalty oaths. As one Quaker historian lamented, they'd even go to jail rather than remove their hats in deference to authority.[26] And Washington, who was profoundly deferential to authority and tradition, had recently led a revolutionary war. Such an extraordinary rebellion demanded an extraordinary justification, and for Washington that justification was theological. God had made an exception of America because America was to be a place of unprecedented liberty.[27] That was why, to bring forth this nation, Americans had to break rules and defy the parent country. That was why violence had to be done. This theological faith in the Revolution—a faith that would be truly foundational for America—was precisely what the Quakers denied. Ordered to rebel for the sake of freedom, they had refused out of obedience to God and on grounds of religious liberty. Again, there was more than a little irony here.

If the Quaker stance on war strained the boundaries of wall religion, their stance on slavery directly threatened America's foundations. When there was war, the Friends had asked only to be left out of it. But once they grasped the evil of slavery, they wanted to see it ended for everyone. Since 1758 they had been urging each other to release their slaves. By 1776, the few Friends who persisted in holding slaves had been disowned, and in the mid-1770s they felt called to abolish slavery altogether. Along with several non-Quaker abolitionists, they founded the Pennsylvania Abolition Society (PAS) in 1775. In 1780, under the influence of the PAS, Pennsylvania passed an Act for the Gradual Abolition of Slavery.[28] By the time Washington was president, the Quakers were besieging Congress with anti-slavery petitions.

Like several other Framers, Washington held slaves, 164 at the time of his death, according to historian Dorothy Twohig. Also like some of his colleagues, he expressed moral discomfort about slavery. A private letter of 1794 expressed his wish "to liberate a certain species of property—which I possess, very repugnantly to my own feelings." His will provided for the manumission of his slaves upon his death, but during his lifetime Washington did not let them go. The main reasons were economic, the 1794 letter suggested; "imperious necessity" compelled him to hold on to slaves until he could find some other way to cover "expenses not in my power to avoid."[29]

When the federal government moved to Philadelphia, abolitionist law became a personal problem for Washington. According to the Pennsylvania law of 1780, any enslaved person brought into the commonwealth had to be freed within six months.[30] It was not entirely clear whether the law (which made an exemption for some federal officials) would apply to Washington's household slaves. But in case it did, he came up with an advance plan, according to Twohig. Should such a situation arise, Washington instructed his secretary, the slaves ought to be transferred back to Mount Vernon in Virginia, but "under [a] pretext that may deceive both them [the slaves] and the Public." He was similarly duplicitous in 1795, when one of his own slaves escaped. He ordered his overseer to recapture the slave but added, "I would not have my name appear in any advertisement or other measure, leading to it."[31]

But it would be too simple to say that Washington disliked abolitionism simply because it endangered his personal wealth. He correctly understood that abolitionism would endanger the Union as a whole. After Shays' Rebellion, it seemed that the Union would disintegrate without a stronger federal government that could, among other things, crush local uprisings. For that reason, the Framers had gathered in 1787, with Washington presiding, to craft what became the U.S. Constitution. The men who signed that Constitution well understood that the Union would not hold unless the South was permitted to retain its "peculiar institution," at least for the time being. Those who opposed slavery told themselves, or rather deluded themselves, that the institution would naturally end after 1808 when, as the Constitution provided, Congress could vote to end the importation of slaves.[32] Meanwhile, they were cobbling together a fragile unity, which the Quakers, in their relentless national campaign against slavery, were threatening.

As Washington's friend David Stuart reported to him, the Quaker anti-slavery petitions were creating "particular umbrage" in their home state of Virginia. Southern slaveholders resented the "Northern phalanx" of abolitionists bearing down upon them. "Many who were warm supporters of the government," Stuart reported, "are changing their sentiments, from a conviction of the impracticability of union with States, whose interests are so dissimilar with those of Virginia." Washington replied, with obvious relief, that the Quaker petition had been squelched. "The memorial of the Quakers (& a very mal-apropos one it was) has at length been put to sleep," he wrote back. Three months later, his irritation was unabated. "The introductions of the [Quaker] Memorial respecting Slavery," he recollected to Stuart, "was to be sure, not only an ill-judged piece of business, but occasioned a great waste of time."[33]

Notwithstanding their moral scruples, Washington and the other Framers saw countervailing values on the slavery question. And those values had their own religious dimensions. First, there was the Union itself, which Washington and other Framers viewed as nothing less than the will of God. By destroying the possibility of the federal union, the prohibition of slavery would have thwarted God's providential plan for the New World. Second, the Framers believed that private property was sacred. And although Washington found the idea of human property repugnant, most slaveholders disagreed. As Charles Pinckney of South Carolina recalled, the delegates to the Constitutional Convention had accepted slavery as a form of sacred property: "The property of the Southern States was to be as sacredly preserved, and protected to them, as that of land, or any other kind of property in the Eastern States were to be to their citizens."[34] Third, supporters contended that slavery was directly authorized by God. A Virginia pro-slavery petition of 1785, for example, followed its discussion of property rights with an entire paragraph of biblical proof-texts in support of slavery.[35]

Of course, none felt the religious and moral implications of the "peculiar institution" more than enslaved people themselves. For them, unlike for James Madison, slavery was not merely spiritual but physical. Freedom, conversely, was not just physical but also spiritual. Enslaved people found inspiration in the Bible, in prophetic visions, and in spirit traditions retained from Africa, all of which could and sometimes did ignite rebellion. By 1791, rebellions in Haiti prompted Washington to assure France that the United States would "render every aid in their power" to help crush "the alarming insurrection of the Negros in Hispañola."[36] Soon it would happen in the United States too. In 1800, Gabriel Prosser had spiritual visions that emboldened him to lead an unsuccessful slave rebellion in Virginia; in 1831, Nat Turner would do the same. And it was the biblically inspired rebellion led by John Brown in 1859 that would finally spark the Civil War. So Washington was quite right, in a private letter of 1794, to worry that in the United States as in the Caribbean, slaves would soon become "a very troublesome species of property."[37] Slavery was indeed cemented into the foundations of the republic, which would become irrefutably clear in the 1860s, when the weakening of this cornerstone brought those foundations so near to crumbling.

Whether one supported slavery, opposed it, or merely permitted it, the conflict was about beliefs and values, authority and order, sacred texts and divinely sanctioned traditions. It had to do with God's will and plan for America, the created nature of human beings, the moral status of private property, and the ultimate significance of differences among human beings. The same was true of war, which involved not only the power over life and death but the agonizing question of who, if anyone, may command another person to kill. All of this was fought out in the language of "religion." But how did the Quakers, or George Washington, decide when a religious conviction was a purely personal matter and when it demanded that they change their country? How did they decide which beliefs and values were the common foundation on the basis of which Americans could then disagree about other matters? And how do we decide that? What Americans might learn from the story of Washington and the Quakers is that when such complex discernments must be made, "religious freedom" has never told us which path to choose. It has only signaled, for particular people, where they had already arrived.

Jefferson, the Baptists, and the Impossible Wall

It was an unusual White House reception, but then it was an unusual cheese. Weighing 1,235 pounds, it had journeyed to Washington, DC, all the way from Cheshire, Massachusetts, accompanied by Baptist elder John Leland. History is murky as to Leland's exact proximity to the traveling cheese, which was pulled by sleigh over the winter snow, rolled along by wagon, and possibly floated on a sloop after it reached New York. But he made his association with the cheese well known by long sermons along the way, and soon they were nicknamed together: the Mammoth Cheese and the Mammoth Preacher. They arrived at the White House on New Year's Day of 1802, just as Jefferson, in another exchange with Baptists, wrote a letter containing the most famous and contentious phrase in American religion-talk—"a wall of separation between church and state." That morning, as the Mammoth Cheese made its way down Pennsylvania Avenue, the doors of the president's house swung open and Thomas Jefferson himself stepped out, arms spread, to welcome it. Painted around its thirteen-foot red perimeter was one of his favorite mottos: "Rebellion to Tyrants Is Obedience to God."[38]

Jefferson was not one to accept gifts, but this was a political godsend. Its message targeted enemies common to himself and the Baptists—the Federalist Party and its champions among the Standing Order of New England. These Congregationalist clergy were supported by taxes that the Baptists refused to pay. In Virginia, too, a religion (the Anglican Church) had been established, a situation that Jefferson had tried unsuccessfully to change with his 1779 Bill for Establishing Religious Freedom, and that James Madison finally did change seven years later. In fact, it was the sight of earnest Baptist ministers in a Virginia jail that had first impressed upon Madison the evil of religious establishment.[39] It was in Virginia, too, that Elder Leland had first met Thomas Jefferson. Leland, who lived there at the time, had allied with Jefferson and Madison in the battle against religious establishment and in the process had developed passionate loyalties both to Democratic Republicanism and to Jefferson personally.[40]

During the bruising presidential campaign of 1800, the Federalist clergy had regularly accused Jefferson of atheism. A typical ad challenged voters to choose between "GOD AND A RELIGIOUS PRESIDENT— OR JEFFERSON, AND NO GOD!"[41] Now that Jefferson was president, these same clergy were attacking him for declining to proclaim national days of fast and thanksgiving. Jefferson had thought about the establishment clause as much as anyone in America had, and it was his considered opinion that such proclamations were unconstitutional. The Federalist clergy were perfectly aware of Jefferson's separationist views, so when they demanded national days of piety, they knew he couldn't comply. That was the point: here was a fresh opportunity to make Jefferson look like the infidel and libertine the Federalists had always accused him of being.[42]

By 1802, Jefferson could benefit greatly from the visible support of a religious association—better still, a religious association consisting mostly of yeoman farmers (his favorite constituency) and whose numbers promised soon to dwarf the old established churches. So he heartily thanked the good citizens of Cheshire and invited Elder Leland to preach in the Hall of the House of Representatives the next day. Leland performed, as one shocked Federalist legislator put it, like the "poor, ignorant, clownish preacher" he was, with "stunning voice, horrid tone, frightful grimaces and extravagant gestures," with the president in attendance, "contrary to all former practice."[43] Then Jefferson sent Leland home with a payment of $200 and a generous wedge of the Mammoth Cheese for the people of Cheshire.

That Jefferson wrote to the Baptists of Danbury on the same day he received Leland and the cheese is mostly coincidence. The Danbury Baptists had written to him nearly three months earlier, complaining of the same "tyranny" that Leland and the Massachusetts Baptists were protesting: tax assessments in support of the Standing Order.[44] Jefferson hadn't received the letter until December 30 or 31, so a response was due immediately. But as he was writing it, he flirted with the temptation to make this letter do double duty as a gracious reply to the Danbury Baptists and a riposte to his

Federalist enemies. He'd written a draft of the letter in that mood but wisely held off mailing it, pending feedback from advisors. And then came Leland and his spectacular cheese, which must have reminded Jefferson that it was at least as important to attract his religious allies as to repel his religious enemies.

In the first draft, Jefferson fiercely defended his decision not to declare national days of religious devotion. That practice, he said, could be traced to "the Executive of another nation" who was also "the legal head of its church." His point, though obliquely stated, would not have missed its target: Federalists like John Adams and his clerical supporters who, Jefferson insinuated, were behaving like the king of England and his aristocratic bishops. In that draft, too, he had written of "a wall of *eternal* separation" (emphasis mine), infusing the expression with a religious vehemence all his own.

One of Jefferson's advisors thought that the first draft was fine, but attorney general Levi Lincoln did not. He cautioned the president against insulting all Federalists at a time when he needed to find some in that party with whom he could do business. Then, too, it was awkward to harp on the issue of fast days when the Baptists themselves hadn't mentioned it. Jefferson himself had acknowledged this problem, and Lincoln underscored it further by pointing out that in their home states, many Republicans rather liked government-sponsored days of fast and thanksgiving. So the lines about fast days were expunged, as was the word "eternal."[45] The letter then took its final form, in which Jefferson issued a less abrasive but still passionate defense of church-state separation.

> Believing with you that religion is a matter which lies solely between Man & his God, that he owes account to none other for his faith or his worship, that the legitimate powers of government reach actions only, and not opinions, I contemplate with sovereign reverence that act of the whole American people which declared that their legislature should "make no law respecting an establishment of religion, or prohibiting the free exercise thereof," thus building a wall of separation between Church and State. Adhering to this expression of the supreme will of the nation in behalf of the rights of conscience, I shall see with

sincere satisfaction the progress of those sentiments which
tend to restore to man all his natural rights, convinced he
has no natural right in opposition to his social duties.[46]

Only in 1998, with the aid of the FBI, did all the details of the
first draft become discernible, reinvigorating the long-running
controversy over Jefferson and his wall. For some scholars, the
new evidence suggested that Jefferson intended simply to attack
his Federalist enemies. The "wall of separation," they argued,
expressed Jefferson's deference to the establishment clause of the
First Amendment, but it was not intended to apply to the states or
put a damper on public religion generally.[47] There is some evidence for this claim. For example, in 1774 Jefferson and other as-
semblymen had "cooked up" (Jefferson's words) a day of fast and
thanksgiving as a way to arouse revolutionary fervor among lethar-
gic fellow Virginians. In 1779, no doubt with the persecuted Baptists in mind, he authored a Virginia bill to "punish disturbers
of religious worship and sabbath breakers." Certainly, Jefferson the
Republican was ever mindful of the reserved rights of state governments. On several occasions he emphasized the obvious but often
overlooked point that the establishment clause of the federal Constitution did not then apply to states. Most notably, in his Second
Inaugural Address, Jefferson defended his refusal to declare national fast days by explaining that he had left religious exercises "as
the Constitution found them, under the direction and discipline of
state or church authorities."[48]

But as other scholars observe, Jefferson had no choice but to
confine the establishment clause to the federal government. The
clause, after all, belonged to the federal Constitution and would not
be incorporated to the states until 1947.[49] Moreover, in his final letter to the Danbury Baptists, Jefferson had expressed his desire to see
"the progress of those sentiments" that protect "natural rights"—
having just written that, in the case of religious liberty, "the wall"
was the means of that protection. There is no question that Jefferson
was utterly opposed to religious assessments on the state level—by
1802, he'd been advocating that position for over twenty years. And
in the first draft of his reply to the Danbury Baptists, he had been
prepared to treat presidential fast days and state-imposed religious

assessments by the same principle—the need for a "wall of separation." In short, the contradictions in Jefferson's church-state policies
cannot be explained away either by his respect for states' rights or by
his response to different sorts of establishmentarian actions (say, tax
assessments versus fast days).[50]

When someone speaks in contradictory ways, we may assume
that they couldn't have meant both things. But Jefferson, and the
Baptists too, did think of religion in contradictory ways, because
the concept came to them with contradictions built into it. On one
hand, they felt that "religion lies solely between Man and his God."
Established religion, because it involved coercion, could never be
"true religion," and both Jefferson and the Baptists thought that
any government that established religion was, ipso facto, tyrannical. On the other hand, Jefferson and the Baptists could not help
assuming that "true" religion should be established in some sense,
because religion contributed to the social order upon which government relied. Therefore, they often permitted government to
overrun the limits that they elsewhere placed on it.

Apart from this shared pattern of contradiction, Jefferson and
his Baptist allies approached religion in ways that were wildly incompatible. For Baptists, true religion depended entirely on personal regeneration. In America, the Baptist movement had taken
off as the result of the First Great Awakening, in which thousands
of people underwent intensely emotional conversions. First came a
crushing awareness of personal sin, then terror of hell, and finally
the ecstatic assurance of personal salvation. These inner states were
manifested by behavior that under other circumstances would have
seemed bizarre. As John Leland described it, "prayer is made by
crying, weeping, lifting up the eyes, groaning, panting, breathing,
. . . veiling the face, rending the garments, kneeling and falling to
the ground."[51] Those who had undergone this experience really did
feel as if they had died and been reborn, or been condemned to
death and then reprieved.

So it galled them that in the old established churches people sat
in the pews convinced that they were Christians simply because,
when they were babies, some clergyman had sprinkled a few drops
of water on their heads. It galled them even more that the clergy
who pastored such pseudo-Christians were fattened on government

salaries. Therefore, like their forebears in Europe, these born-again "Baptists" began to set up their own churches. In those churches, baptism would be given only to believing adults and always by the dramatic gesture of full immersion, and the clergy would rely on voluntary contributions, rather than on the coerced support of taxpayers.

Believers' baptism had the immediate (and, to other Christians, disturbing) implication that the requirements of citizenship were much lower than those of salvation. Baptists believed that unregenerate people, although ultimately headed to hell, could meanwhile be decent citizens. Ideally, of course, a person would be both a true Christian and a good citizen. The first New England Puritans had tried to ensure this by withholding the full rights of citizenship until an individual could attest to personal conversion. Baptists knew this history, so they also knew that after a single generation those Puritans had been forced to lower their standards. To the Baptists, it was obvious that to condition citizenship upon conversion had never worked and never could because, as Roger Williams had put it, force extinguishes faith the way a strong wind extinguishes a candle. Writing a century and a half before Leland's cheese and Jefferson's letter, Williams had articulated what later became a key tenet of Baptist political theology. God had placed "a hedge or wall" between the "garden" that is the church and the "wilderness" that is the world. If that wall were overgrown from either side, there would be wilderness everywhere, and no garden anywhere.[52]

Jefferson does not seem to have read Roger Williams, but Isaac Backus and other leading Baptists of his time had.[53] They saw that established religion was persecuting them just as it had persecuted Williams and other dissenters before them. In Jefferson's Virginia, for example, vigilantes from the established churches liked to torment Baptists with a parody of believers' baptism, in which Baptists were forcibly "dunked" nearly to the point of drowning.[54] Backus, Leland, and the Baptists of Danbury, Connecticut, were outraged by such attacks. But they were just as outraged by something less life-threatening but, to them, no less abhorrent: in Massachusetts and Connecticut, Baptists were still expected to pay taxes to support the clergy of the established churches.

For Baptists, the problem was not just that these religious assessments took money from their pockets and gave it to Congregationalist clergy. If inequity had been their only concern, they would have settled for the exemptions that these laws provided for religious dissenters. It's worth dwelling on this point for a moment—the Baptists did not actually have to pay the taxes to which they objected. To get out of paying, they had only to be certified as members of a Baptist church.[55] But they weren't satisfied with exemptions. They wanted the law itself expunged, because (in the words of the Danbury Baptists) religious assessments meant "hierarchy and tyranny."[56] Not only did such taxes set one religion over others (hierarchy), they also made government into God (tyranny). Baptists were not just defending the equality of citizens; they also were guarding the limits of government.

As Isaac Backus explained it in 1773, God had instituted two kinds of government, civil and ecclesiastical. God had given civil government the power of "the sword," which it wielded with the consent of the people and only to restrain them from harming each other. But the church had no sword, just the power of "light and truth." It was never authorized to use force; nor should it be subject to force. It was ruled by the will of God as revealed in the Bible. Unlike civil government, the true church could hold its members to the very highest standard of holiness. And unlike the established churches, it would not hesitate to expel any members who fell short. In fact, Backus contended, true Christians wouldn't need civil law to make them behave. They'd automatically obey civil laws while obeying Christ, just as a wife (his analogy) would automatically obey civil laws while obeying her husband. As for the unregenerate—most people, in Backus's view—their condition was one of enslavement to sin. Far from compromising their liberty, civil law enabled whatever freedom they were capable of having.[57]

These assurances of civil obedience would have sounded strange coming from Baptists, who, like Quakers, were often at odds with the law. From the Baptist viewpoint, however, the laws they refused to obey were not legitimate laws, just as the religions established in their states were not "true religion." Understandably, the Baptists found it demeaning to be told that their religion—to them, the only true religion—must be certified by unregenerate others.[58] Yet in distinguishing between "true" and "false" religion, Baptists tripped on a contradiction inherent in the concept. On one hand, to separate religion from government, one first must define what religion "truly" is. On the other hand, any definition of religion will immediately tend to establish—not disestablish—whatever fits that definition.

So Baptist thinking on church and state, like that of other Americans, was riddled with contradiction. Backus, for example, often reverted to calling religion the foundation of government, despite his commitment to Williams's "wall of separation." When it came time to ratify the federal establishment clause, Backus resisted, arguing that article 6 ("no religious test shall ever be required as a qualification to any office or public trust under the United States") was sufficient to prevent the establishment of "Popery or some other tyrannical form of religion."[59] Here Backus was prefiguring the reasoning that Protestant nativists would deploy in the mid-nineteenth century: Catholicism should be sequestered behind the wall, but Protestantism was the country's foundation. Backus also supported a Massachusetts law requiring church attendance, despite having written that civil government was empowered only to prevent harm. And notwithstanding his bitter opposition to the Standing Clergy, he agreed with them that Massachusetts was a Christian commonwealth and that its elected officials should be required to take a Christian (read: Protestant) oath.[60]

John Leland, eccentric as he was, was more consistent about separating religious convictions from government coercion. Unlike Backus, he remained steadfast against religious tests for public office, and he supported religious freedom not just for Christians but for Jews and "Turks" (Muslims).[61] Still, on the crucial question of slavery, he too could waffle about the place of religion in public life. In 1789, he'd formulated a Baptist resolution condemning slavery as "a violent deprivation of the rights of nature, and inconsistent with a republican government."[62] But he ran into resistance from Baptist associations that wanted to avoid the politics of slavery. By the 1830s, Leland himself reverted to this view, fulminating against religious abolitionists. "How preposterous it is," he then wrote, possibly with the Quakers in mind, "to burden Congress with cartloads of petitions to do that which they have neither the right nor power to do." Slavery, he claimed, "belongs to the moral and religious department, and not to the legislative"; it should be ended eventually, but by religious change of heart, not by force of law.[63] Forty years earlier, Leland had found slavery both religiously and civilly abhorrent; now he implied that government had no more authority to end slavery than to command personal conversion. Unlike Backus, Leland kept his wall of separation up, but he could mentally relocate it, and everything depended on which side of that wall a given issue landed.

For Jefferson, as for the Baptists, freedom was the sine qua non of "true religion." But he believed that religious freedom lived in the mind; it was essentially a freedom of inquiry. Therefore it had to remain open-ended; there was never a point when one arrived at faith and was done with the search. "Question with boldness even the existence of a god," he once advised his nephew Peter Carr, "because, if there be one, he must more approve of the homage of reason, than that of blindfolded fear."[64] In his Bill for Establishing Religious Freedom, Jefferson compared religious opinions to "our opinions in physics or geometry."[65] The comparison was telling, because in physics and geometry, questions have right and wrong (or at least better and worse) answers, but a person must reach them for herself or himself. If people take a shortcut (say, getting the answer from the back of the book), they won't understand it. That seems to have been Jefferson's point: to become an enlightened and virtuous person, you must understand truth *for yourself* and form *in yourself* the habits of virtue. So while Jefferson himself had definite beliefs, he would not impose restrictions on anyone else's inquiry or dictate in advance where anyone should end up. For that reason, he endorsed a religious freedom that encompassed every variety of belief and unbelief—"the Jew, the Gentile, the Christian and the Mohametan, the Hindoo and the infidel of every persuasion."[66]

Although scrupulous about his beliefs, when it came to religious practice Jefferson performed only as much as others expected, and often less than they hoped. As president, he attended Sunday services in the District; when in Virginia, he continued the Anglican tradition of his family. Some scholars take these actions as evidence that he remained a pious and fairly orthodox Christian. But Jefferson, like Washington, would have participated in religion simply for the sake of social morale. No doubt he sat through many sermons with which he thoroughly disagreed; John Leland's in

Congress on January 2, 1802—the one Jefferson invited the Mammoth Preacher to deliver—must have been a prime example.[67]

When called upon to personally affirm Christian faith, Jefferson was visibly reluctant. Asked to serve as godfather to a friend's child, he declined because during the Anglican baptism ceremony a godfather was expected to recite the church's articles of faith. The problem, he explained to his friend, was that the articles of faith did not make sense to him, and "it has always appeared to me that comprehension must precede assent."[68] It was not only the Anglican creed that he found senseless. The doctrine of the Trinity, he said, was absurd on its face (equivalent to saying that "three are one and one is three"), and the doctrine of the virgin birth was akin to "the fable of the generation of Minerva in the brain of Jupiter."[69] He also rejected the divinity of Christ, the resurrection, and miracles generally—excising them all from his copy of the New Testament with a razor (or possibly a scissor).[70]

What remained after all this expurgation was "a system of morality" that Jefferson called "the most perfect and sublime that has ever been taught by man."[71] Like Jesus, he firmly believed that the world had "a Creator and Benevolent Governor," and that universal altruism was the culmination of human good. Because he embraced these beliefs, he liked to claim he was a Christian "in the only sense that Jesus wished one to be." Yet even between himself and Jesus, Jefferson had to acknowledge theological differences—accounted for, perhaps, by the fact that Jesus had died young, "his reason not having attained a maximum of its energy."[72] Two differences in particular stood out—one concerning the afterlife, the other concerning the nature of God. And they were differences on which most Americans of the time would have sided with Jesus rather than with Jefferson.

As Jefferson observed, Jesus believed "emphatically" in the afterlife and its necessity as an incentive to moral behavior.[73] Jefferson could not agree with the founder of Christianity on this point. Especially toward the end of his life, he *hoped* for life after death, and referred to it in the fond valediction of a letter to Adams: "May we meet there again," and receive "the seal of approbation, 'Well done, good and faithful servants!' "[74] But he believed that a life of true virtue had to be its own reward. After counseling his nephew

Peter to question the existence of God, Jefferson added that Peter should be virtuous even if he concluded that God does not exist, because a morally good life generates "comforts," "pleasantness," and "the love of others."[75] He himself wished to live by that counsel, comporting himself so as to be worthy of the afterlife even though he was never convinced that it existed.

Jefferson's other theological dispute with Jesus concerned the idea of God. Jesus described God as spirit, but Jefferson considered himself a materialist. "Monist" might have been a better word. Jefferson was able to imagine Being as existing in different states, but he found the concept of spirit and matter as independent substances literally nonsensical.[76] In their later-life correspondence, Adams liked to tease his old frenemy on this point, once suggesting that Jefferson "ask a mite, in the center of your Mammoth Cheese."[77] If Jefferson could not fathom a God beyond matter, Adams was saying, consider how hard it would have been for the mite to guess that reality wasn't made entirely of Cheshire cheese.

But Jefferson was quite serious. Once, having received yet another metaphysical letter from Adams, he admitted that he could not stop thinking about it. "Your puzzling letter kept me from sleep. I read it, laid it down: read it, and laid it down, again and again." The real atheists, Jefferson mused, were those who insist that God is pure spirit. "To say that the human soul, angels, god are immaterial is to say that they are nothings, that there is no god, no angels, no soul."[78] Finally, Jefferson returned to his "habitual anodyne"—a process of inquiry that began with what he could see and feel and then proceeded as far as reasonably possible—but no farther. At the limits of understanding, he liked to say, he preferred to "repose my head on that pillow of ignorance which a benevolent Creator has made so soft for us, knowing how much we should be forced to use it."[79]

Jefferson's ideas about religion, like those of the Baptists, were imbricated with his ideas about government. Famously, his Bill for Establishing Religious Freedom opened by pronouncing, "Almighty God hath made the mind free." Therefore "the opinions of men could never be the object of civil government." Several years later, in his *Notes on the State of Virginia*, he put the point even more forcefully. People do submit some of their natural rights to civil authorities, he wrote, but "the rights of conscience we never submitted, we could not submit. We are answerable for them to our God." In Jefferson's mind, religious liberty was unique even among the natural rights because, although one might honorably relinquish some measure of other rights, to surrender any portion of religious liberty was to surrender liberty itself. His wall of separation was intended not only to protect minorities from the majority but also to limit government. Civil authority, for Jefferson, extended only to "such acts as are injurious to others." And, as he put it, "it does me no injury for my neighbor to say there are twenty gods, or no god. It neither picks my pocket nor breaks my leg."[80]

That glib and often-quoted comment has led many to conclude that Jefferson was disdainful of all religious belief, but that is not accurate. He did find many religious doctrines ridiculous, but his own religious inquiries were quite earnest, and even his "pillow of ignorance" sounded a note of melancholy reverence. The deeper problem, which his detractors were correct to sense, was that he looked down on people who needed some higher authority to tell them what was true, or who needed the fear of punishment to keep them moral. Jefferson thought that few good people were like that, and that he certainly was not. The Federalist clergy thought that most people were exactly like that, and Jefferson particularly so. As William Linn, a Federalist minister, put it in an anti-Jefferson screed of 1800, "Let my neighbor once persuade himself that there is no God, and he will soon pick my pocket and break not only my leg but my head."[81] Because Jefferson fancied himself a philosopher, Linn argued, he felt accountable to nothing but his own mind. That not only cast doubt on Jefferson's personal morality but also forecast moral disaster for the nation should Jefferson become president.

For Linn and other Federalists, Jefferson was the antithesis of George Washington, who had passed away not long before the campaign of 1800. ("Thank God our Washington was no philosopher," Linn commented wistfully.) But apart from his reluctance about proclaiming days of thanksgiving, Jefferson actually espoused a public piety remarkably similar to Washington's. In his First Inaugural Address, Washington had explained history as the work of divine providence; Jefferson's First Inaugural said the same thing. In his Farewell Address of 1796, Washington had celebrated the fact that Americans "with slight shades of difference . . . have the same religion, manners, habits, and political principles." Jefferson, in his First Inaugural Address, said nearly the same. Americans were "enlightened by a benign religion, professed, indeed, and practiced in various forms yet all of them inculcating honesty, truth, temperance, gratitude, and the love of man."[82]

The real disagreement between Jefferson and Washington, and between Jefferson and the Federalist clergy, was over the issue of authority. Washington was perceived as an authoritative person, partly because he so clearly respected authority. God, of course, was the ultimate authority, which is why Washington scolded those who would "shake the foundations" of America by questioning the existence of God.[83] So when the Federalists invoked Washington, they were invoking not just one authoritative figure but authority as a general principle. As Jefferson sought to become the highest authority in America, the Federalist clergy were asking what, if anything, Jefferson recognized as having authority over himself. It did not matter to them that Jefferson actually was convinced of the existence of God. They were not interested in his reasons for believing in God, any more than in the reasons for his many religious doubts.[84] Their question to Jefferson was simply this: Would he submit to external authority, or not?

Jefferson's response was unequivocal: "I have sworn upon the altar of God eternal hostility to every form of tyranny against the mind of man."[85] These words, now inscribed in the Jefferson Memorial, are usually read as a paean to religious liberty—and implicitly, to religion itself. But Jefferson's tone was belligerent rather than devout. He was declaring support for religious freedom, but more emphatically, war against religious establishment and political tyranny—in his mind, two sides of the same coin. These were the words of a man convinced of his personal authority and furious at those who impugned his worthiness to exercise it.

While Jefferson defended the freedom of belief, he did not defend any right to behave differently from what law or convention might dictate. Instead, each time he proclaimed his wall of separation, he would reflexively add phrases like the one tacked onto the end of his letter to the Danbury Baptists: conscience is sovereign,

yet a person "has no natural right in opposition to his social duties." Similarly, in the Bill for Establishing Religious Freedom, he
boldly endorsed religious freedom—until it "breaks out into acts
against peace and good order."

These provisos were not innovations by Jefferson; they had
been boilerplate language around religious freedom for a long time.
But because Jefferson placed no doctrinal limits around religious
liberty (people were free to believe anything or nothing at all), it is
especially clear that by using terms like "social duty," "peace," and
"good order," he was effectively defining religion. Those terms, to
Jefferson, were not "religious," which is precisely why he could establish them so unselfconsciously. His wall of separation was supposed to limit government to constraining actions that harm
others. But on closer examination it seems designed only to protect
people's right to think what they want, provided that their actions
remain sequestered within the sweeping and unspecified demands
of social order.

In his *Notes on the State of Virginia*, there is a startling passage
in which Jefferson describes digging up a Native American barrow.
Jefferson knew that this burial mound was sacred to Native Americans; he repeats an old neighborhood story about a band of Indians
who decades earlier made their way there and "staid about it some
time, with expressions which were construed to be those of sor-
row." Evidently, his heart was touched by this story, but his mind
was not broad enough to consider that Native people might have
genuine religions. In his Second Inaugural, right after lauding religious freedom, Jefferson denounced Native people who stubbornly
remained "as their Creator made them" rather than adopting
Euro-American culture.[86] And throughout his presidency, Jefferson
continued the federal "civilization policy," which included efforts
to convert Native people to Christianity. In fact, his original collection of Jesus's sayings was intended both to edify himself and to
serve as a catechism for Native people. He subtitled it *For the Use
of the Indians, Unembarrassed with Matters of Fact or Faith beyond the
Level of Their Comprehensions.*[87]

The barrow, then, excited in Jefferson the desire for mastery
rather than anything like religious reverence. So he made a perpen-
dicular cut in it, "wide enough for a man to walk through and exam-

Constantino Brumidi, The Apotheosis of Washington, *Rotunda of the United States Capitol. From Wikimedia Commons/Public Domain.*

"I Have Sworn Upon the Altar of God." Statue of Thomas Jefferson, Jefferson Memorial, Washington, DC. From Wikimedia Commons/Public Domain.

ine its sides."[88] This was a big trench; the mound was forty feet in diameter and over seven feet high. Jefferson tells the story as if he personally dug the trench but, given that he held hundreds of slaves, it is more likely that he merely supervised the labor. Through the fog of history, we may then discern this scene: a white man, America's greatest champion of religious freedom, using the bodies of black men to desecrate the graves of Native Americans. Jefferson could do this because he did not think of the land as sacred ground, nor of the bodies he "owned" as animated by minds and souls fully equal to his. Having placed religious "opinions" beyond government, he did not question what remained established—his own worldview, culture, and values, and a social hierarchy in which he occupied a favored position.

From History to Hagiography

Not long after Washington's death, Americans started imagining him as a saint, lifted up to heaven by a flock of angels. Jefferson, even in his own time, was regarded as something of a genius. These men, and the others who framed the U.S. government, had their measure of virtue and intelligence, but they were neither saints nor geniuses. They were not exempt from the moral danger of maneuvering the word "religion" to affirm what they already thought was good, condemn what they already thought was bad, and avoid what they didn't want to face. They weren't beyond the intellectual inconsistency of conceiving religion sometimes as a matter of private belief and other times as the shared ethos of the nation.

In the Constitution, the Framers' overriding concern had been to build a sturdy and clearly delineated frame of government and to prevent religious differences from disturbing that structure. In that context, they conceived of religion as something like a wall. It would stand for everything that citizens did not need to agree about, and everything that government was not supposed to do. In their public lives, however, the Framers habitually spoke of religion in foundational terms—as if all religions were at heart one Religion, imparting the same virtues, shaping behavior in the same ways, and inculcating core beliefs that would reliably encourage or frighten people into proper behavior. Although they set up a government that respected religious freedom, they also fostered a nation in which, as Tocqueville put it, everyone would "let themselves go unresistingly with the tide."[89]

When the American republic was founded, however, most human beings under its jurisdiction had neither the protection of wall religion nor the power to alter the country's foundations. None of the rights of citizenship were available to enslaved Africans or nonwhite immigrants. Native Americans, placed under the federal government's jurisdiction but with no rights of citizenship, had the worst of both worlds. Even among whites, no women could vote, and in some states, men who were landless or too poor to pay taxes had no right to vote. These structural inequities infested the gap between federal and state protections, and it would take a civil war to begin to correct them. Only with the passage of the Fourteenth Amendment was the principle of equality installed into the Constitution, and even that was just the groundwork. The Supreme Court still had to rule as to whether each constitutional right would be incorporated into the Fourteenth Amendment and, by this mechanism, applied to the states. That is how, in 1940, the free exercise clause was finally applied to the states, followed by the establishment clause in 1947.[90]

Before then, the wall concept of religion as conceived in the Constitution had very little effect in public life. To the propertied Anglo-Saxon Protestant men who dominated American life, religious freedom applied first to their kinds of religion, and dubiously if at all to others. The separation of church and state, on the other hand, was not considered applicable to members of the de facto Protestant establishment but only to others (for example, Catholics, Jews, or Mormons) who might be plotting to unsettle "American" religion. Few church-state cases made it to the Supreme Court, and those that did were quickly dispatched in majoritarian terms. Rarely was anything that violated the majoritarian ethos granted religious liberty, and what was congruent with majoritarian views could be effectively established.

With the incorporation of the religion clauses to states, Jefferson's "wall of separation" became a judicial maxim rather than just a political slogan. Because the religion clauses were now being read in terms of the principle of equality, they began to be applied more evenhandedly.[91] On one hand, free exercise could be claimed by anyone with sincere religious beliefs—not only Christians but Jews, atheists, Native Americans, Buddhists, and others.[92] On the other hand, government had to be separated not only from minority religions like Catholicism and Mormonism but also from Protestant Christianity. In establishment jurisprudence, the wall reached its apex in the 1973 case of *Lemon v. Kurtzman*. According to the "*Lemon* test," all laws have to be primarily "secular" in intention, neutral in their effects on religion, and written so as to avoid the "excessive entanglement" of church and state. In free exercise jurisprudence, the wall reached its highest point in the 1963 case of *Sherbert v. Verner.* According to the *Sherbert* standard, no government action can place a "substantial burden" on anyone's religious freedom unless the government can prove, first, that it has a "compelling interest" in the action, and second, that it has restricted religious freedom as little as possible. In practice, this has usually meant that laws and policies have to make exemptions for religious objectors.[93]

But when the Framers guaranteed free exercise, they did so based on some dicey assumptions: first, that law would conflict with religion only rarely, and second, that when such conflicts arose, it would not be tremendously hard to permit religious exemptions. Even in 1789, that assumption didn't stretch far enough to cover the troublesome Quaker pacifists. Two centuries later, as the judiciary began to take seriously the full panoply of religions in America, the difficulty could no longer be ignored. Could people, for religious reasons, terminate their children's education sooner than permitted by law, or withhold medical care from their children? Could people use what otherwise would be illegal substances— say, peyote—in religious rituals? Could they engage in what would otherwise be considered fraudulent business practices?[94] Whatever the merits of particular claims, it became clear that there was no principled way to limit their number or their disruptive effects on government.

So too with the establishment clause. The Framers assumed that the phrase "an establishment of religion" had an obvious meaning—obvious enough, at least, to tell Congress what it was not supposed to do. But again, that assumption was shaky even in its

own time. Thomas Jefferson and Isaac Backus both supported a
"wall of separation" but had very different ideas of what did and did
not constitute "establishment"—which meant, in practice, that they
had very different views of what government may or may not do.
By the late twentieth century, as the judiciary faced ever increasing
religious diversity, it became excruciatingly difficult either to separate government from all religion or to accommodate all religions
equally. If a Christmas display were put up in the city plaza, was
that a government endorsement of religion? If the display included
a Santa and a Christmas tree as well as a crèche, did the ensemble
then become "secular"? Or would the display still be problematic
because it suggested that the government was unconstitutionally
endorsing Christianity over other religions? Could the establishment problem be solved by adding, say, a Jewish menorah? But
then, what about the seven symbols of Kwanzaa, the Wiccan Yule
log, or the Hindu festival of lights? And what if the Ku Klux Klan
wanted to place a large white cross in front of the state capitol? Can
a religion be excluded because most citizens believe it is false and
pernicious?[95]

Because of these difficulties, it took only half a century for
the "wall of separation" to rise to its greatest height and fall into
disrepair. By 1990, the Court was backing away from the *Sherbert*
standard, holding that nobody is constitutionally entitled to be exempt from a law simply because it happens to contravene his or
her religious beliefs.[96] All the free exercise clause really guarantees,
the Court now said, was that a religion could not be singled out for
unfavorable treatment.[97] The decline of establishment jurisprudence
followed the same trajectory. The Court began to rule that for
the government to *disfavor* religion—for example, to contract only
with secular social service agencies and refuse contracting with religious ones—was unconstitutional because it discriminated against
religion.[98]

Of course, what the Constitution textually demands is precisely
that the government treat religion differently from everything
else, whether by affording religion the unique protection called
"free exercise" or by exercising the unique restraint called "non-
establishment." The trouble is that nobody, including Supreme
Court justices, can satisfactorily explain how religion is different

from everything else, or explain why certain items end up on the list of religions and others do not. Until the principle of equality became a force in American law and society, there was little need to answer these questions: when the word "religion" was uttered, it already was freighted with majoritarian prejudgments. Imputed definitions of religion could therefore substitute for meaningful doctrines of free exercise and non-establishment. Once the Court stopped using the word "religion" to cover the problem, the un-workability of the religion clauses became obvious.

From the beginning of the republic until today, Americans have used the word "religion" as if it could help settle every public issue from war to slavery. Underlying those concrete issues are questions about basic values. For the Framers, the basic question was how to maximize the scope of freedom and minimize the coercive force of government while also fostering the common good. Less well artic-ulated by these elite men, but recognized by many others, were questions about the equality and dignity of persons and the fair dis-tribution of resources. These are the sorts of political questions that cannot be answered once and for all, so it is the process of articulat-ing them and seeking new solutions that matters. Throughout American history, the word "religion" has obstructed more than abetted this deliberative process, for it comes out of our mouths infused with our judgments about the very issues in question. It doesn't take saints or geniuses to lift those obstructions, just people who are willing to look honestly at what they mean by the words they use.

PART II

Religion against Religion

CHAPTER THREE

Protestants, Catholics, and Mormons

Religion and the Struggle for Citizenship

The Mormons and the Catholics are the most obnoxious to the sectarian world of any people, and are the only two who have not persecuted each other and others in these the United States, and the only two who have suffered from the cruel hand of mobocracy for their religion under the name of foreigners.

—PRESIDENTIAL CAMPAIGN COMMITTEE OF JOSEPH
SMITH TO ALDERMAN HUGH CLARK OF PHILADELPHIA,
MAY 24, 1844

THE NINETEENTH CENTURY WAS a time of intense religious ferment in the United States, and of equally intense religious conflict. Conflict is normal in a democracy, so it is not surprising that religious differences could disrupt communities and make or break political careers. Nor is it surprising that religious tensions found expression in salacious bestselling novels, vitriolic pamphlets, and vicious cartoons. But nineteenth-century religious conflicts went well beyond these normal channels of civic disagreement. There were gang riots and armed battles, extermination orders, lynchings, and massacres. People were beaten, jailed, and tarred and feathered. Old and young were driven into the night; convents and churches were burned to the ground.

What went wrong? Often we describe these social pathologies with words like "bigotry," "hysteria," "fanaticism," or "prejudice"— in short, religious intolerance. The implication is that intolerance is unnecessary, even inexplicable. And if a conflict was unnecessary in the first place, not much can be learned from it in hindsight. That, of course, is the logic of wall religion: as a private matter, religion need not disrupt public life. But religion in America has never existed only behind walls; it has always been embedded in the country's foundations.

Two of the century's most significant conflicts occurred between the Euro-Protestant majority and a pair of very different religious minorities: Roman Catholics and Latter-day Saints. Euro-Protestants saw Catholics and Mormons as threats to America's government, culture, and morality, and for those reasons denied them certain basic rights of citizenship. Their fears of being overtaken by these religious minorities were not entirely imaginary. By the 1840s, Catholicism was the nation's largest religious denomination, and by the 1850s Mormons controlled a significant chunk of the western United States. Each church in its own way would demand renovations, if not revolutions, in the ethos and institutions of America.

To Euro-Protestants, who had recently dismantled the last vestiges of legal establishment for their own denominations, it seemed especially dangerous that these challenges were presented in religious terms. No sooner, they thought, had intra-Protestant divisions been legally defused than Catholics and Mormons peevishly reintroduced religion as a source of public controversy. Of course, to those minorities the situation looked entirely different. It was perfectly obvious to them that Protestantism, although legally disestablished, continued to control just about everything in America, from politics to business to family life.

And they were right. American nationalism had never been either religiously neutral or inclusive. Anti-Catholicism was intrinsic to the original Euro-Protestant conception of their republic. "In the Papal system," James Madison once wrote, "government and religion are in a manner consolidated, and that is found to be the worst of governments."[1] As soon as the Church of Jesus Christ of Latter-day Saints was founded, in 1830, it was almost immediately identified with another old enemy—Islam. If Catholicism was the reference point for tyrannical, theocratic government in Europe, "Mohametanism" was the reference point for its non-European equivalent. By demanding submission to hierarchical authorities, it was said, both the Catholic and the LDS churches made people incapable of republican citizenship. Catholics were accused of fealty to a foreign power (the pope) that was said to be plotting the reconquest of America. Mormons were accused of fealty to "Pope Joseph the First," who purportedly intended to become a "second Mohammed" and subdue America by the sword.[2]

Not only were Catholics and Mormons seen as politically seditious. Euro-Protestants also felt that they were degrading the American nation or, in the parlance of the time, the American "race." Catholics, most of whom were recent immigrants from Ireland and Germany, felt to Euro-Protestants like an invasion from the Old World, underscored by the brogues of the Irish and the entirely unintelligible speech of the Germans. The Irish, who made up the majority of Catholic immigrants, seemed not just less than American but less than human, having long been caricatured as drunken, violent, ape-like beings. Latter-day Saints, though mostly white and native-born, were also subject to negative racial stereotypes.[3] They were tagged as "Mohametans" or "Turks," and were constantly compared to Asians, Africans, and indigenous people.

Irrational prejudices notwithstanding, Catholics and Mormons did pose real challenges to the Euro-Protestant sense of American identity. The nineteenth-century papacy was in no position to overtake America, but it was decidedly illiberal in its teachings. Both the Catholic and Mormon churches expected to win the populace by conversion, and Mormons were firmly convinced that the United States would soon collapse of its own accord. Moreover, both Catholics and Mormons conceived freedom in terms that disturbed the individualism of Euro-Protestants. For both groups, the point of freedom was to choose rightly, and choosing rightly meant accepting a divinely ordained structure of authority.

Even more disturbingly, Catholics and Mormons rejected American exceptionalism as Protestants understood it. Catholic immigrants arrived with a mental map not centered on the United States, and they told a story of salvation in which America was neither the beginning nor the end. Mormons presented the inverse challenge—a theology more extravagantly Americanist than Protestants had ever dreamed. Mormons held that the indigenous people of America belonged to the lost tribes of Israel, that the risen Christ had visited America, and that Joseph Smith had found an ancient scripture revealing all of this in the hills of upstate New York. The true meaning of Christianity and America had been lost, Mormons believed, and it fell to them to restore both.

Out of all the threats, real and perceived, that Catholics and Mormons presented, one issue became the focal point of each conflict. With Mormons, it was marriage; with Catholics, education. Both issues obviously bore on the foundations of society: how sex and reproduction were to be managed, and how knowledge was to be produced, preserved, and disseminated. For centuries in Christian Europe, marriage and education had been under religious jurisdiction, but in the United States these institutions came to be placed under civil law. To Euro-Protestants, the shift from ecclesiastical to civil law was emancipatory. But Americans who were not Protestant could easily see that education and marriage, even if no longer controlled by Protestant clergy, remained thoroughly imbued with Protestant norms.

For Catholics, the crisis came to a head when their children were forced to begin each public school day with Protestant devotions. For Mormons, the breaking point came when the federal government criminalized polygamy. These conflicts demonstrated that American education and family life effectively established Protestantism and suppressed everything else. That this establishment had become more cultural than legal only made it harder to displace, and that it no longer operated through the institutional machinery of churches only made it more ubiquitous. From that advantageous position, Euro-Protestants were able to win their battles against Catholics and Mormons and mold their own fractious denominations into a common national identity.

Against the grain of common narrative, but in concert with historical scholarship, I will argue that the bitter, protracted conflicts between the Euro-Protestant majority and these two religious minorities occurred for powerful reasons.[4] I do not contend that all of these reasons were *good*. Many were of the worst kind—racism, ethnocentricity, misogyny, xenophobia, and greed, to name a few. But they were not simply illusory. These were flesh-and-blood people, fighting over matters that bore on their physical, spiritual, and moral lives. If in retrospect we cannot fathom why Americans fought so bitterly over religion, it's because those who won control over the country's foundations convinced the rest of us that religion exists only behind walls.

Protestants versus Catholics

Conflagration

You might think that what went on behind the walls of Mount Saint Benedict convent was nobody else's business, but the Protestant citizens of Boston felt otherwise. People were disconcerted that the nuns took Unitarian girls, rather than Catholics, into their boarding school. And then there were the tales of "escaped" nuns like Rebecca Reed, whose hair-raising account of life at Mount Saint Benedict circulated by word of mouth and was eventually published under the title *Six Months in a Convent.*[5] Reed's publishers thought that the book was of world-historical significance, comparing it to Martin Luther's *Appeal to the Christian Nobility of Germany.* Just as Luther had stirred lay Christian leaders to free their nation from the pope, so the Protestant gentlemen who marketed Reed's bestselling story thought that they were alerting Bostonians to Rome's designs on Massachusetts.[6] They believed that Catholicism corrupted the very foundations of society, that this corruption fermented behind the walls of monasteries and convents, and that it often was spread to children through an attached school. Luther himself had lived in such a monastery and taught in its school. He'd done his bit to destroy those institutions by taking up residence in his former monastery with his wife, a former nun. In Boston, a Protestant mob would do their bit around midnight on August 11, 1834, when they looted Mount Saint Benedict, burned the place to the ground, and finished the night by desecrating the corpses of nuns interred at the convent's mausoleum.[7]

Reed's book, published in 1835, could not have been responsible for the attack on the convent. Still, her narrative—with a long introduction by an unnamed publication committee—gave native-born Protestants every reason to applaud this turn of events. Reed herself had been raised a Protestant, so was well positioned to see how Mount Saint Benedict undermined American life. Its mother superior, Mary Anne Moffatt, was a foreigner, and both she and the bishop, Benedict Fenwick, reportedly held anti-American views. As Reed described it, the convent dismantled the family, crushed individuality, infected minds with superstition, and elevated the Virgin Mary and the saints over God himself. The Bible was nowhere to be seen. When Reed requested one, she was sternly informed that only "the successors of the apostles" were permitted to interpret the Bible. In early 1832, after only six months (four, according to Moffatt's rebuttal), the young woman could bear no more. First she tried to escape the convent by climbing a trellis, but fell and hurt her wrist. Then she thought to try the front gate, which turned out to be unlocked.[8]

Distaste for Catholic religious life was a familiar feeling for Protestants. It was easy to imagine the sexual mischief that might go on behind the walls of a convent—so easy, in fact, that popular narratives often likened convents to brothels and harems. Two years after Reed's book came out, an outlandishly lurid tale of convent life called *Awful Disclosures by Maria Monk of the Hotel Dieu Nunnery* was published by another group of concerned Protestants. Eventually the book was exposed as a fabrication, and Monk herself was arrested for prostitution.[9] But that did not prevent it, like Reed's book, from becoming a national bestseller. Reed did not recount sexual sins, but she did describe convent life as filled with faintly masochistic penances such as kissing people's feet and making the sign of the cross on the floor with her tongue. She recalled that the mother superior and bishop had constantly probed her inner state. Although the inquiries seemed kind at first, they grew ever more menacing and "improper."[10] In addition, the young woman was required to make regular confessions, pouring her secrets into the ear of a priest who sat in shadow, only a breath away.

Reed's publishers worried that convent life could lead not only to excess and perversion but to the suppression of natural attachments. The Ursuline convent, they wrote in the book's intro-duction, was "destructive of all domestic and social relations."[11] In Reed's case, her mother's death had left her vulnerable to the quasi-parental attentions of the mother superior and the bishop. Once in-side, however, Reed quickly saw that this was nothing like a family. The bishop and the mother superior were inexplicably cruel to their charges. Fenwick even seemed to take giddy delight in tor-menting a dying nun. As a matter of policy, nuns were cut off from all family and friends. Reed reported that when her own people in-quired after her, they were given misleading answers, and those who tried to visit her were turned away.

Nor was convent life anything like American life, as Protes-tants knew it. The mother superior had been born in Canada, and she and the bishop would converse in French about the pope's plan to establish "the true religion" in America. Both Moffatt and Fen-wick affected the air of Old World aristocrats. Reed recalled that Moffatt described herself as "a lady of quality, brought up in opu-lence" and that she would tap on her snuffbox as a sign for the nuns to kneel. The bishop took his wine from a golden cup, and the serving nun had to wait on her knees as he drank. Reed also at-tributed to Bishop Fenwick a number of anti-American utter-ances—for example (her paraphrase) that "America rightfully belonged to the Pope, and that His Holiness would take up resi-dence here at some future day." Once when she was asked to sing a favorite song and innocently chose a patriotic tune, the bishop whispered an objection in French to the mother superior, and Reed was quickly silenced.[12]

Moffatt would later blame the convent's destruction on Reed's gossip, but the reality was that many Protestants considered Ca-tholicism an existential threat to America. In the summer of 1834, the person influential enough to excite Bostonians to act on that threat would not have been Rebecca Reed but the Reverend Lyman Beecher. Just before the convent was attacked, Beecher had delivered an anti-Catholic sermon at several sites around Boston—including, he later admitted, a sermon on the very evening of the attack, not three miles from Mount Saint Benedict. Published in 1835 as *A Plea for the West*, it would become a *locus classicus* of Prot-estant nativism.[13]

The sermon was a fundraiser for a Presbyterian seminary in Cincinnati, but its argument was 100 percent anti-Catholic. As Beecher laid it out, the problem was that the western United States was being settled so rapidly that Protestant institutions were not keeping up. A "dark-minded vicious populace"—meaning Catholics—was filling that vacuum, along with its priests, nuns, and schools. Crucially, Beecher argued, Catholic schools were not intended for Catholic children, whose parents were content that they should be "abandoned to ignorance and vice." No, the target audience for Catholic schools was Protestant children, and the obvious goal was to make them into papists. In the absence of Protestant institutions, Catholicism could win the West simply by providing "the cheap and even gratuitous education of Protestant children." Beecher did not mention Mount Saint Benedict, but to his Boston listeners, it must have come to the mind as a local example of the strategy Catholicism was advancing on the western frontier.[14]

By the time the sermon was published, Beecher was chafing under accusations that he bore some responsibility for the destruction of Mount Saint Benedict. Still, his fury at Catholicism blazed more brightly than his moral outrage over the convent's burning. Why, he asked, had Boston's Protestants been summoned to Faneuil Hall after this event and forced to hear "Catholicism eulogized"? Why did city leaders have to thank "his reverence the bishop" (Fenwick) for preventing retaliation by Catholic mobs? No such retaliation occurred, although Moffatt had brazenly threatened it at the time. But it was little comfort to know that Catholics had been restrained only by the jeweled hand of their bishop. "Will our great cities," Beecher wrote, "consent to receive protection from the Catholic priesthood, dependent on the Catholic powers of Europe, and favored by his holiness, who is himself governed by the bayonets of Austria?"[15]

Nonsectarianism

Notwithstanding the virulent anti-Catholicism of Beecher and his supporters, many Protestant Bostonians were aghast at the destruction of Mount Saint Benedict. Among them was Horace Mann, soon to found the common school movement, the progenitor of what is now American public education. Mann served on the mayoral committee that investigated the convent burning, so he knew all the incident's ugly details. He was also a Unitarian and therefore felt a special affinity with the families whose girls had been driven from the burning convent. He understood the reason why Unitarian girls sometimes ended up in Catholic schools: until the 1830s, there simply were not enough schools in the United States, especially for girls and young women. Most education was provided by religiously run "charity schools." While these charity schools often received some public funds, it was not nearly enough to make education available to all children.[16] Besides, as the convent's destruction vividly showed, parents were wary of if not violently hostile to putting their offspring in the care of teachers whose faith they did not share.

The only way to resolve tensions like those that had destroyed Mount Saint Benedict, Mann argued, was to create a system of standardized, state-supported education to which all parents could happily send their children. Girls and boys, native-born and immigrant, of all religions and social stations, could learn the same curriculum, in the same classrooms. Only then would Americans grow up experiencing themselves as citizens of a single nation.[17] Yet religion remained a challenge. Like most Americans, Mann felt that education had to include morality and that morality could not be sustained without religion. By the 1830s, however, religion had been disestablished in state constitutions. (Massachusetts was the last state to do so, in 1833.) But now that religion was disestablished, what would the religious content of the common schools be? And how would religious devotions in the common school differ from religious establishment?

Mann's solution, which would become a nationwide model, was called nonsectarianism. Schoolchildren would read passages from the King James Bible (KJV) "without sectarian note or comment," then be encouraged to ponder their moral messages. Mann believed that most children, properly guided, would come to believe in God, but his common school devotions were not meant to save souls. Instead, they served the public purpose of fostering benevolence, fairness, and self-sacrifice—in short, good citizenship.[18] Mann did not see these devotions as abridging religious freedom. Students, after all, were being urged to think for themselves, and nothing could be less coercive than that. Moreover, Mann's nonsectarian devotions would not empower or enrich institutional religion. They would be led by professional teachers, not clergy, and common school funds would add nothing to the coffers of any church.

A major lacuna with this plan, however, was that Catholics and Protestants not only used different Bibles, but utterly rejected each other's version. Catholics were specifically forbidden to read the KJV and were told to use only the Douay-Rheims (D-R) Bible. The D-R Bible was chock-full of what Protestants considered "sectarian notes and comments"—commentary by the Catholic magisterium that instructed the faithful about how passages were to be interpreted. By dividing religion into the "nonsectarian" and the sectarian, Mann had hoped to distinguish the kind of religion that government could encourage from the kind from which government must separate itself. But to many Catholics, particularly the Catholic hierarchy, "nonsectarianism" was not the benign and generic form of religion it claimed to be. It was a specific—and heretical—religion.

The first attack on nonsectarianism was mounted in New York City by the pugnacious and voluble bishop (soon to be archbishop) John Hughes, known as "Dagger John" because of the sword-like cross that emblazoned his signature. In 1840, New York, like other cities, was simultaneously struggling to create a public school system and absorb hundreds of thousands of immigrants, mostly Irish Catholics. Because elected school boards did not yet exist, the schools of New York were managed by volunteers—a cadre of wealthy men who called themselves the Public School Society (PSS). Most were Quakers and therefore did not have much of a theological axe to grind, but they were committed to the Americanization of immigrant children, and the nonsectarian model seemed to provide the proper mix of morality, piety, and patriotism. The PSS therefore determined that in the New York public schools, selections from the King James Bible would be read, a few hymns would be sung, and the Ten Commandments would be recited. Thus would the children of New York, under the care of devout but nondogmatic teachers, be formed into proper citizens.

Catholics were not the only New Yorkers to object to this program. Jews, Unitarians, and Baptists also complained.[19] But

Catholics had the numbers to form a powerful political bloc, which Hughes was determined to mobilize and control. Probably at his instigation, in September 1840 some Catholic taxpayers petitioned New York's Board of Aldermen for a share of public school funds so that they might build their own schools. Their argument was that the public schools, as run by the PSS, were really Protestant. Not only were children made to read the King James Bible, they had to recite the Protestant version of the Ten Commandments, which forbade everyday Catholic devotions as the worship of "graven images." Even the textbooks were peppered with casual anti-Catholicism. Protestants were effectively getting city funds to run Protestant schools. It was only fair, Catholics argued, that they should get the same.[20]

The petitioners might have added, although they did not, that public support for religious schools was hardly new in America. On the contrary, this was the old way that, gradually and with much controversy, had been disestablished in states. Disestablishment opened the way for a more comprehensive educational system, but it left a religious vacuum that nonsectarianism was meant to fill. But even as Protestant denominations were being asked to cede differences in favor of this supposedly generic religiosity, Catholics were demanding public support for a religion that was unapologetically, unequivocally specific. Catholicism, in other words, threw the concept of generic "religion" into question, and with it the whole idea that Americans shared a common ethos.

For over a year, in one public appearance after another, Hughes fought boisterously against the New York public schools and for the public funding of Catholic schools. Although he drew conclusions directly opposing those of Horace Mann, Hughes began from the same premises: education was essential to citizenship; moral training was essential to education; religion was essential to morality. Religion, however, was the problem: Hughes was not a man who could comfortably use that word in the plural. He did not imagine religions as incidental variations of a common essence but as distinct and incompatible options. Therefore, he argued, all religions were "sects," even Catholicism,[21] and "nonsectarianism" was a misnomer. It was really nothing but Protestantism, and all forms of Protestantism sprang from the same error—the rejection of divinely instituted authority (such as Hughes's own). This rejection of God's authority led to infidelity and then to moral collapse, evidence of which Hughes already could discern in the misbehavior of public school children.[22]

Hughes's protracted screed against public schools demonstrated that a Catholic could wield the rhetoric of Americanism just as skillfully as a Protestant.[23] He lauded the wisdom of the Constitution and its promise that Congress would make no law establishing religion. He held that Catholicism was the champion of liberty and that religious tyranny had come to Europe only with the rise of Protestantism. Centuries before the Reformation, he contended, Catholics had understood that "all authority is derived from the people." It was Protestants who had produced the unholy union of church and state. And in America, it was Protestants who were establishing their religion as the law of the land while trampling the religious freedom of others.[24]

Hughes failed to win public funds for Catholic schools, but the New York school controversy reverberated nationwide.[25] One effect was the rise of Hughes himself, heralding the ascendance of an authoritarian Catholicism over liberal strains that were not easily suppressed. Until the 1840s, for example, many Catholic properties had been controlled by boards of lay trustees. Hughes terminated trusteeism in New York, and soon bishops were firmly in charge of all Catholic properties in America. Another effect was that public schools nationwide came to be placed under the authority of elected boards rather than philanthropic volunteers. That was a minor victory for Catholics because in wards where they were the majority, they could dispose of school devotions as they saw fit, even in disregard of state law. But majority-Protestant wards could do the same, and nowhere was the system favorable to Jews, freethinkers, or other non-Christians. Elected school boards became de facto mini-establishments, always in danger of succumbing to the pressure of religious dissent or demographic change.

A final effect of the New York school controversy was to rouse Protestants to defend what they saw as America's religious foundations. As Horace Bushnell would write, public schools had called out to Catholics, "Come, be Americans with us!"[26] Catholics not only declined the invitation but demanded public funds for parochial schools whose purpose was to ensure that their children, too, would refuse Americanization. By claiming to be good citizens yet disclaiming any common religious ground with the Protestant majority, Catholics seemed to be suggesting that the American republic could be held together with no religious agreement whatsoever—at least, until such time as Catholicism would win the nation's soul, fair and square, which was the stated goal of John Hughes and other leading Catholic prelates.[27] Either way, Protestant nativists found it imperative both to curb the public influence of Catholicism and to defend the King James Bible. In nativist cartoons, literature, and parades, the KJV now appeared next to the eagle and the flag as emblems of American patriotism. And in the summer of 1844, the Protestant perception of Catholics as anti-Bible led to the worst urban conflict America had ever seen.

That spring, there were rumors that Catholics intended to remove the Bible from the public schools of Philadelphia. The rumors were inaccurate. Bishop Francis Kenrick had asked only that Catholic children be spared mandatory Protestant devotions and that, if the Bible were to be read, they be permitted to read from the D-R Bible. The school board agreed to the first request and, in response to the second, resolved that other versions of the Bible could be used provided they were "without note or comment." The former relieved some of the burden on Catholics, but the latter did not, because notes and comments were a chief feature of their Bible. Alderman Hugh Clark, the only Catholic on the school board, evidently did suggest to a schoolteacher in the mostly Catholic Kensington district that she temporarily suspend all Bible reading. But this was in response to the turmoil that went on in the teacher's classroom when Catholic students would exit the room before the Protestant devotions. Clark's goal, like Kenrick's, was to create more religiously inclusive schools, not to exclude religion from the schools.

But the accusation of Catholics' animosity toward the Bible was excellent fuel for the (nativist) American Republican Party, and on Friday, May 3, its members provocatively chose Kensington as the site for their anti-Catholic rally. Catholics drove them off, but when the Protestants returned the following Monday, a week of riots ensued. Another week of riots began on July 4, when Protestants paraded a distinctly anti-Catholic brand of patriotism. By

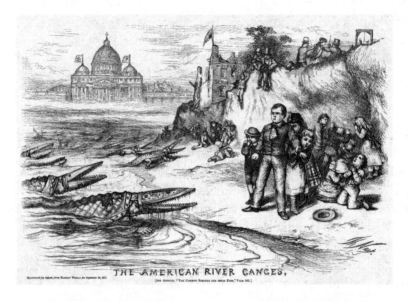

THE AMERICAN RIVER GANGES,

Thomas Nast, "The American River Ganges," depicting Catholic prelates as crocodiles attacking public schools. Harper's Weekly, *May 8, 1875. © 2001 HarpWeek. From Wikimedia Commons/Public Domain.*

the time things settled down, dozens of people had been killed, hundreds wounded, and over a million dollars of property destroyed, mainly Catholic churches, convents, and homes (including that of Hugh Clark).[28]

By the mid-1840s, nonsectarianism and sectarianism no longer connoted, respectively, a common national religiosity and its benign variations. Now they were nearly opposites—one implying Protestant, the other Catholic. Neither side was a unified group. Protestants were riven by differences of theology, class, race, ethnicity, region, and politics. American Catholicism, although numerically dominated by immigrants, also included native-born Catholics. And even immigrant Catholics were divided—German Catholics, for example, wanted to maintain their own schools to preserve their language. But just as Protestants were unified by their opposition to Catholicism, Catholics were forced into solidarity by their struggle against Protestant domination.

The Wall of Separation

In addition to consolidating Catholics into one identity and Protestants into another, the school question revivified the expression "separation of church and state." In the mouths of Protestant nativists, the wall metaphor took on strange and contrary meanings. As was evident in the 1845 platform of the American Republican Party of New York City, nativists could see themselves as champions of church-state separation. But for them, the "church" from which government must be separated was implicitly Catholic, while the "state" was Protestant.

> Our sole object is to form a barrier, as high and eternal as the Andes, which shall forever separate the Church from the State. While we regard the religion of the Bible as the only legitimate element of civilized society, and the single basis of all government, we are greatly opposed to the introduction of sectarian dogmas. ... We believe the Holy Bible, without sectarian notes or comment, to be a most proper and necessary book, as well for our children as ourselves, and we are determined that they shall not be deprived of that, either in, or out of school.[29]

While the wall was metaphorical, the division between Catholics and Protestants was a fierce reality. In 1842, a missionary priest in upstate New York publicly burned a King James Bible. In 1854, a girl named Bridget Donahoe was expelled from a public school in Ellsworth, Maine, for refusing to read from the KJV. In 1859, at Boston's Eliot School, young Thomas Wall endured a thirty-minute whipping of the palms rather than recite the Protestant Ten Commandments. To Protestants, it was of ominous significance that these events were instigated by foreign-born priests. Donahoe's family had been emboldened to civil disobedience by a Swiss Jesuit named Jean Bapst, who just a few years earlier had been tarred and feathered by the good Protestants of Ellsworth. Thomas Wall's priest, Bernardine Wiget, another Swiss Jesuit, had forbidden the children in his parish to say Protestant prayers, threatening to read from the altar the name of any child who caved.

After Wall's beating, Wiget awarded him a medal of valor, inspiring hundreds of other Catholic boys to leave the Eliot School rather than perform Protestant devotions.[30]

When these cases went to court, judges made it plain that they shared the church-state theory of Protestant nativists. In the *Donahoe* case, the Supreme Court of Maine ruled that the King James devotions appropriately reflected the will of the local community and, besides that, were not "sectarian." In Boston, a police court ruled in favor of the principal who had beaten Thomas Wall. According to the court, religious freedom did not authorize Catholics' "narrow and sectarian" behavior. Children were not required to believe in the Bible, only to read it, and to make "war on the Bible" was to undermine the common school system, "the granite foundation on which our republican form of government rests."[31]

As the Civil War approached, doubts about Catholic patriotism merged with suspicion that Catholics were enemies of the Union and supporters of slavery. There had long been Catholic slaveholders in the South, including America's first Catholic bishop. In 1863, the Irish Catholics of New York protested the draft by burning African American institutions. They also hanged several black men in the streets while (according to eyewitnesses) "shout[ing] aloud for Jeff Davis." According to police estimates, over a thousand people were killed in the New York draft riots.[32] The Catholic threat to American unity, then, was not merely ideological. It could be shockingly violent and, from the Union viewpoint, seditious.

Meanwhile, the Vatican, embroiled in its own losing battle with European liberalism, widened the chasm between Catholicism and American political principles. In 1864, Pope Pius IX issued the "Syllabus of Errors," which anathematized such liberal maxims as "that the State ought to be separated from the Church, and the Church from the State"; that "popular schools" should be "freed from all ecclesiastical authority"; that Catholics might receive education "unconnected with the Catholic faith and the power of the church"; or (in a concluding flourish) "that the Roman Pontiff can, and ought to, reconcile himself, and come to terms with progress, liberalism and modern civilization." In 1870, the First Vatican Council solemnized as dogma a word that Protestants had long used as a term of insult and accusation: "infallibility." Technically, the dogma of papal infallibility pertained only to statements made *ex cathedra* (from the throne). But it could be—and was—read as one more sign of Catholic antipathy to free inquiry and democratic deliberation.[33]

By the end of the Civil War, the rhetoric of church-state separation was further complicated by a schism within Protestantism itself. On one side were those who continued, in the tradition of the Know Nothings, to demand nonsectarian devotions in public schools while adamantly rejecting public funding of Catholic schools. After the Civil War, this faction began to demand that the Constitution be amended to state that America was a Christian nation—where "Christian" obviously meant "Protestant." Against this religious nativism, a new and more consistent position arose that called itself liberal secularism, organized in 1876 as the National Liberal League.

Some liberal secularists rejected all religion, but it would be inaccurate to cast American secularism as anti-religious. The National Liberal League included not only atheists like Robert Green Ingersoll but also some liberal Protestants, spiritualists, and Reform Jews. Their common belief was not that religion was always bad, but that religion became bad when used as a cudgel against free inquiry and individual liberty. Liberal secularists thought that the proposed Christian amendment would do just that, so they objected to it vigorously. Moreover, they cast off what had always been a point of orthodoxy in American foundation religion: that religion (as Washington had put it) "was an indispensable support" to the national character. Having seen so much blood shed in the name of God, liberals drew a new and (for most Americans of the time) scandalous conclusion: public religion was not only unnecessary for the common good but might be inimical to it.[34]

As secularism parted ways with nonsectarianism, church-state separation took on a new ambiguity. In an 1875 speech about the common schools, President Ulysses Grant warned that if another national schism were to occur, it would not set North against South but instead put "patriotism and intelligence on the one side, and superstition, ambition, and ignorance on the other." Sectarian schools were on the wrong side, Grant thought, and he called for a constitutional amendment prohibiting public aid to them. He declared that religion should "be left to the family altar, the Church and the private school, supported entirely by private contributions." And he concluded with a phrase that would become a Republican slogan in the next presidential campaign: "Keep Church and State forever separate."[35]

Grant's words held no ambiguity for Catholics; they knew that "superstition" and "ignorance" referred to their religion and "sectarian" to their schools. But Protestants could hear the speech in two very different ways. Those who supported the KJV in public schools could still think that "the separation of church and state" pertained only to (Catholic) "sectarianism," while secularists could hope that Grant was referring to religion of all kinds. The speech therefore pleased and excited most of the Euro-Protestant mainstream. It "set the nation agog," the *Chicago Tribune* reported. And the following year, it helped the Republicans hold on to the White House.[36]

For a time, "separation of church and state" had expressed the vision of both liberal secularists and Euro-Protestant nationalists. But over the remaining decades of the nineteenth century, the wishbone would break in favor of the secularist usage. Protestant religious nationalists, rather than calling for the separation of church and state, began to focus solely on their campaign for a Christian amendment. The expression "separation of church and state" became the rhetorical property of liberal secularists, who called for their own amendment inscribing that phrase into the Constitution.

Neither "Christian nation" nor "separation of church and state" ever made its way into the Constitution. But both sides would succeed in the point on which they agreed—the denial of funding to "sectarian" schools, which would be enacted in most states through so-called Blaine Amendments. In retrospect, it might be said that secularism had at least one religious doctrine, and it was one secularists shared with their Protestant opponents: anti-Catholicism.

A Separate Peace

By the 1870s, Catholics, liberal secularists, and Protestant religious nationalists were engaged in a three-way tug-of-war over public education. But the battlefront had moved west to Cincinnati, where Lyman Beecher had built his Protestant seminary as a fortress against Catholicism. Despite the seminary's success, what

Beecher dreaded had come to pass. That "dark-minded, vicious populace" had grown large enough to have its own archbishop, John Purcell, with the power to threaten the Protestant way of educating young citizens.

Purcell's initial demand was for the public support of Catholic schools. Under the Ohio Constitution that was arguably permissible, but in the political climate of the time it wasn't going to happen. As a compromise, Purcell suggested that King James devotions be prohibited in the public schools, and the school board agreed. That reignited the familiar Protestant accusation that Catholics opposed the Bible itself and set off the years of conflict now remembered as the Cincinnati Bible wars.

To the extent that the problem could be resolved in the courts, that resolution came in the 1872 case of *Board of Education of Cincinnati v. Minor*.[37] Written by John Welch, the liberal-minded chief justice of Ohio's Supreme Court, it was the first major court decision to call for the end of King James devotions in public schools. As Welch pointed out, for public schools to mandate Protestant devotions violated the Ohio constitution, which stated that "no religious or other sect or sects" could have exclusive access to public school funds.[38] Welch also took the occasion to excoriate the proposed Christian amendment to the federal Constitution as a violation of the establishment clause.

Philosophically, Welch could not have been farther from Dagger John, but he effectively ratified what the archbishop of New York City had claimed thirty years earlier: *all* religions are sectarian. Unlike Hughes, however, Welch harbored no hostility toward Protestant Christianity. In the honorable tradition of James Madison, he believed that establishment (whether de jure or de facto) was bad for Christianity. If America's Protestant majority wanted their religion to be pure, he suggested, they'd best separate it from government. And if they wanted their religion to attract others, they'd best treat others with respect.

Welch was partly motivated by the principle of equality. Recognizing that his state included, besides Protestants, numerous Catholics and Jews (enough Jews, in fact, to make Cincinnati the center of Reform Judaism), he wanted to ensure that no young citizen would suffer religious discrimination at school. But equality was not his only guiding principle. He also believed that church-state separation was entailed in the principle of limited government. In lines that the U.S. Supreme Court would quote in its school prayer decision of 1963, Welch wrote that "the great bulk of human affairs and human interests is left by any free government to individual enterprise and individual action." Religion "is eminently one of these interests, lying outside the true and legitimate province of government."[39]

Welch set up a neat conceptual division: where religion started, government left off, and vice versa. Still, on the ground in Ohio the wall of separation remained jagged and incomplete. In school districts where they could ally with Jews and liberal Protestants, lay Catholics did sometimes opt to end school-sponsored devotions. But where Protestants maintained control, school officials could dodge the *Minor* ruling by, for instance, replacing the KJV with hymns.[40] The same patchwork of practices appeared in school districts across the United States. That explains why, almost a century after the *Minor* decision, the Supreme Court would have to resolve the issue of school prayer once and for all in the 1963 case of *Abington v. Schempp.*[41]

Ultimately, the school question was settled only in the sense that Catholics pretty much gave up. Rather than challenge the public school system, they focused on building a system of their own. This was something American Catholic bishops had wanted for a long time. Since their First Plenary Council in 1852, the bishops had been cautioning Catholics about the dangers of public schools. By 1884, at their Third Plenary Council, they upgraded the warning to a decree: every Catholic parish should endeavor to build its own school. This was not possible until American Catholicism had enough religious sisters to staff these schools, but by the end of the century, that number had been achieved, and Catholics were operating four thousand schools in the United States. Over the next three decades, upwards of two thousand more were created. By the early twentieth century, the Catholic school was an American institution.[42]

The rise of the parochial school system also marked the suppression of liberal Catholic Americanism. In 1870, socialist priest Edward McGlynn had declared that public funding of Catholic schools would violate the separation of church and state, and he refused to build a school in his New York City parish. For this and other acts of defiance, McGlynn was temporarily excommunicated and then banished to a small parish upstate. Father James Nilan created a compromise system through which Catholics and Protestants could share the public schools in Poughkeepsie, New York.[43] But Nilan, for his efforts, was kicked off his diocesan school board. And when Archbishop John Ireland stepped out of line with his fellow bishops to support the Poughkeepsie Plan, it did not go well for him. In a public address, Ireland called it regrettable that a separate Catholic school system had to exist at all, and lamented that in the impasse over school prayer a "religion of secularism" was overtaking the public schools. But the address, as his editor put it, was "honored with severe criticism" from all sides.[44] The idea of Americanism was similarly honored in 1899, when Pope Leo XIII condemned it as a heresy.[45]

Ironically, even while the Catholic hierarchy was withdrawing from public education, reiterating the evil of church-state separation, and demanding the subordination of science to faith, it was shepherding its American flock toward values congruent with those of conservative Protestants. Even the pro-labor encyclical *Rerum Novarum*, though remembered fondly by Catholic progressives, was mainly a condemnation of socialism. Moreover, the encyclical's affirmation of private property was based on the supposed natural rights of fathers to head their families.[46] And although it called for negotiated agreements between workers and employers, *Rerum Novarum* contended that the Church, not the state, was most capable of mediating those agreements.

Those were the terms on which American Catholicism settled by the end of the nineteenth century into a separate peace: the defense of private property; the suppression of socialism, feminism, and other disruptive movements; an ethic of charity and obedience; and the insistence on Catholic education as a matter of religious liberty.[47] American Catholic life was conducted in orderly enclaves where the bishop ruled the diocese, the pastor ruled the parish, and the nuns ruled the schools. Rather than being roused by their priests to make trouble in public schools, Catholics were ordered by their bishops to send their children to the parish school. No longer was there any basis (if there ever had been) to fear that Catholic schools were out to convert Protestant children.

Undated Thomas Nast cartoon depicting Catholics and Mormons as "foreign reptiles." Library of Congress, Cabinet of American Illustrations.

Nor, with the temporal powers of the papacy nearly extinguished, was there reason to worry that behind the walls of Catholic institutions, plots were being hatched for the papal conquest of America. And Catholic bishops, rather than fighting with public authorities, could now broker relations between politicians and the Catholic population.

Schooled by such savvy leaders, lay Catholics learned a great deal about when and how to speak about their religion in American public life. When they emerged from those enclaves they were, not surprisingly, disposed to imagine church-state relations in terms of walls. And that was a second irony, for once lay Catholics began to win public office, they were not inclined to take political orders from their hierarchy. Asked in his 1928 presidential campaign how he would reconcile the common standards of public education with the contrary teachings of the Catholic Church, Al Smith gave an answer memorable mainly for its clumsiness: "I never heard of these bulls and encyclicals and books." In 1960, the better-prepared John F. Kennedy would respond more gracefully: "I believe in an America where the separation of church and state is absolute."[48]

Protestants versus Mormons

Theodemocracy

Hugh Clark must have been more than a little puzzled when, just weeks after his home was torched, he received a sympathetic letter from the presidential campaign of General Joseph Smith. Smith was by then notorious for proclaiming a new and seemingly fantastical revelation and, it was said, for practicing polygamy. Those sensitive points were not mentioned in the campaign pitch, nor would Smith have thought them relevant. What was relevant, the letter pointed out, was that the "city of brotherly love" was subjecting Catholics to the same treatment that Mormons had endured in three states. "And for what?" the campaign committee asked. "For our religion, though called by another name."[49] That "other name," Smith's campaign told him, was "foreigner." Clark would have known what they were talking about, because Philadelphia's Protestant nativists regularly accused Catholics of allegiance to a foreign despot (the pope), just as those in the west derided Smith as "Pope Joseph the First" and "a second Mohammed."

But for Euro-Protestants, the foreignness of Catholics and Mormons went beyond their heterodox theologies and seditious politics. These religious minorities seemed alien in a way that was conceived as racial. Catholics had floated in from abroad like an invasive species; Mormons, although native-born, had transformed into "a peculiar people."[50] They were called "white Indians," accused of "amalgamating" with blacks, and unflatteringly likened to Hindus, Turks, and the Chinese.[51] Moreover, Euro-Protestants saw a connection between the racial strangeness of these religious minorities and their odd sexual arrangements—Catholic priestly celibacy and Mormon polygamy.

Needless to say, the proposed alliance between Catholics and Latter-day Saints never got off the ground. Not five weeks later, on June 27, Smith's campaign would end with his lynching, and one week after that, Philadelphia would be embroiled in another round of Bible riots. Yet even had those bloody episodes never happened, the prospects for collaboration were dim. As much as each group disliked Protestants, they abhorred each other more. Mormons considered the Catholic Church the first and worst perversion of

Christianity, and they deplored celibacy as a blasphemous rejection of the body. Catholics reciprocated the disgust, for nothing could have affronted their ascetic spirituality more than the Mormons' rumored polygamy, and nothing could have been farther from the Douay-Rheims Bible, with its magisterial notations, than the "Golden Bible" that Smith claimed had been revealed to him personally.

The campaign letter carefully avoided these sticky questions and instead promised Alderman Clark that General Smith would restore the blessings of Jeffersonian democracy to all Americans, "no matter what their religious faith." This position was not new for Smith and his church. As early as 1835, the LDS *Doctrine and Covenants* had proclaimed, "We do not believe it just to mingle religious influence with civil government, whereby one religious society is fostered and another proscribed in its spiritual privileges."[52] In an 1839 epistle from jail, Smith had urged his followers to abjure religious "prejudices." When dealing with non-Mormons, he wrote, Mormons should remember that "our religion is between us and our God" and "their religion is between them and their God."[53] Two months before he died, Smith reiterated that "every man has a natural, and, in our country, a constitutional right to be a false prophet, as well as a true prophet."[54]

On occasions like those, Smith seemed to think of religion in terms of walls: one person's religion need not affect another's, and nobody's religion ought to unsettle public life. But in his larger vision of salvation history, religion was foundational, and in the end, only one foundation could stand. Moreover, that end was coming soon, which the religious mayhem of the time signaled. It was the proliferation of Christian sects in upstate New York that had driven the young Joseph into the woods to ask God which of them was true and to learn that none of them were.[55] So for Smith, religious freedom was not an end in itself. The point of it was to choose rightly, and there was only one right choice—the restored Christianity revealed by God to Joseph Smith.

Smith was similarly ambivalent about the U.S. Constitution. On one hand, he taught that the Constitution was a sacred text revealed by God. "We say that God is true, that the Constitution of the United States is true; that the Book of Mormon is true; that the book of covenants is true," he wrote in 1839.[56] But although he was sure that Mormons were committed to the Constitution and to Christianity, he questioned whether other so-called Christians and so-called Americans were similarly committed. The experience of his church suggested that they were not. In one settlement after another, the Latter-day Saints had been threatened, assaulted, and driven from their homes with no legal process beforehand and no legal redress afterward. In Missouri, the governor had issued an expulsion order against them, and a vigilante group had massacred a group of them at Haun's Mill. Yet when the Mormons beseeched Washington for help, they were told that the Constitution prohibited the federal government from intervening against the states.[57]

By 1842, Smith had concluded that "man is not able to govern himself—to legislate for himself—to protect himself—to promote his own good nor the good of the world."[58] A series of revelations during the last years of his life commanded Smith to replace republican government with a "theodemocracy" that wedded church and state.[59] In the spring of 1844, he quietly performed this union in Nauvoo, Illinois, by having himself (already Nauvoo's mayor, the general of its militia, and the prophet and president of the Mormon Church) crowned as the city's king. At the same time, he appointed a Council of Fifty with authority over both the church and the civil government. Theodemocracy was not even to be limited by a written constitution, for Smith and his council had concluded that no written document could anticipate future exigencies. Deadlocks would be resolved by revelations to Smith, whom God had reassured with these words: "Ye are my constitution."[60]

By the time he ran for president, Smith was implementing an idea of government that departed from the U.S. Constitution and from what he himself had publicly espoused. In fact, the men who contacted Hugh Clark were not just Smith's presidential committee but also belonged to his Council of Fifty—a fact that they neglected to mention in their letter. Justified or not, the dissimulation was at least partly a consequence of Mormon millennialism. Convinced that they were living in the latter days, Mormons had learned to think and speak in two registers, one suited to this world and the other to the imminent kingdom of God. To Clark, they spoke the language of the present world, appealing to laws, rights, and common reason. But among themselves, Mormons spoke the language of the coming kingdom, whose truth was revealed to those chosen by God.

To his followers, Smith explained that the U.S. Constitution had but one flaw: it did not "cover the whole ground."[61] It promised, but did not actually protect, religious freedom. Considering the brutal treatment of his church, Smith could well complain of religious persecution. On the other hand, the "ground" covered by his new religion extended in every direction, including government. The theological rationale for this came from the Old Testament, in which God's covenant with Israel prescribed an entire way of life. The Saints believed that this was happening again: God was choosing a new people and instituting a new covenant. Guided by fresh revelations, Mormons emigrated by the thousands, purchased land collectively, gained public office, organized local militias, and even founded a bank.[62] To outsiders, it seemed that wherever Mormons settled, the world became a different place. And that, in fact, was the Mormons' dearest hope: that through them, God would make the world anew.

Polygamy soon became the emblem of that strange new world. Smith seems to have first noticed polygamy in the Old Testament, and an 1843 revelation convinced him that God was reinstituting the practice.[63] By 1835, he had entered into a spiritual marriage with his housemaid Fanny Alger, and by 1841 was advocating plural marriage to his closest associates. At the end of his life, he had about thirty spiritual wives (several of them also were married to other men). To polygamy's many detractors, the practice stood for lawlessness and license. But Smith thought that he was obeying a higher law, newly reissued from the mouth of God.

If Smith feared that others would think him insincere or deluded about polygamy, he was correct. Whatever the reason, it cannot be denied that Smith's practice of spiritual marriage included a good deal of what his biographer Richard Bushman called "subterfuge and deception."[64] For example, much of Smith's activity around plural marriage occurred well before the revelation of 1843. In 1838, he had Apostle Oliver Cowdery excommunicated for accusing him of adultery with Fanny Alger—even though, as Bushman points out, Smith never denied the sexual involvement itself, only the charge of adultery. As Bushman writes, Smith "publicly and repeatedly denied he was advocating polygamy," perhaps because in his own mind, he was advocating "celestial marriage," which had a distinct theological meaning. He was still dissembling in 1843 when he commanded that the men of Nauvoo "set our women to work, and stop their spinning street yarns and talking about spiritual wives."[65] As in his response to Cowdery's accusation, Smith's language was equivocal. Without saying that "talk of spiritual wives" was nothing but a "street yarn," he positioned the phrases close enough to enable, if not encourage, that interpretation.

Dissent arose at every point of the Latter-day Saints' history, and because Smith expected consensus, dissent often led to schism and sometimes violence. In 1832, for example, he'd been tarred and feathered by apostate Mormons in Kirtland, Ohio.[66] But polygamy raised the level of dissent perilously high. Many women, including Emma Smith, vehemently rejected polygamy, which is perhaps why the 1843 revelation included a condemnation of noncompliant first wives.[67] On June 7, 1844, a group of Nauvoo dissenters led by William Law published a newspaper condemning Smith for, among other things, trampling on the Constitution and instituting "whoredom." Smith and the city council had Law's press destroyed, whereupon Law's faction took both judicial and extrajudicial measures. In Carthage, the county seat, they secured a warrant for Smith's arrest, and in nearby Warsaw, Illinois, they took their complaint to the anti-Mormon activist Thomas Sharp, who would fire up the mob that murdered Smith.[68]

Like William Law, Thomas Sharp couched his critique of Smith in constitutional terms. He insisted that he did not object to Mormon religion as such, finding it merely ridiculous, and that as long as Mormonism was "confined to its proper bounds," it was entitled to the same constitutional protection as other religions. "We do not believe in persecution for opinion's sake." Even the prophet's "inordinate power" over his own people seemed to Sharp pathetic but not criminal. A crisis would arise only when Mormons "step beyond the proper sphere of a religious denomination and become a political body." This, Sharp claimed, was what had happened in Nauvoo, Illinois.[69]

Other opponents of the Mormons, although not as violent as Sharp, felt the same way. Their objection was not so much to Mormonism as a "religion," but to its having overrun the "legitimate boundaries" of religion by involving itself with politics, business, landownership, and familial relations. Yet, of course, non-Mormons did the same things. They emigrated, built towns, founded banks, raised local militias, and elected their co-religionists to public office. And they regulated sex and marriage by their own religious and moral lights. The difference was that when Joseph Smith was establishing his religion, Euro-Protestants had just finished disestablishing theirs. Having recently consigned their religious differences to the private sphere, they were less inclined to think of their commonalities as religious. In this way, the struggle against Mormonism paralleled that against Catholicism. Just as Euro-Protestants thought that nonsectarian prayers in common schools were simply American and therefore perfectly constitutional, while Catholic prayers would violate the boundaries of church and state, so they saw Mormons—but not themselves—as unconstitutionally establishing religion through their public activities.

If anti-Mormons had reason to deny that the conflict was religious, Mormon theology required the opposite conclusion. Unless God had ordained the sexual, political, and economic practices that anti-Mormons found so disruptive, then all the suffering Mormons had endured and all the resistance they put up were for naught. Reassurance could be found in an 1830 revelation: "All things unto me are spiritual and not at any time have I given unto you a law which was temporal"—in other words, any command from God was, ipso facto, "religious."[70] Besides, Mormons could read the very fact of their persecution as a sign of the coming millennium, for it was to be expected that the Devil's fury would spend itself as his time grew short. As an 1842 editorial in *Times and Seasons* said, when "we see mobocracy and lawlessness prevailing," "our laws and constitutions trampled under foot," and "our once happy country bleeding at every pore," and when, in particular, the Prophet Joseph is persecuted, the church should remember that "in the last days perilous times should come."[71]

The Politics of Purity

The murder of Joseph Smith, together with the approaching Civil War, eliminated any doubt among the Latter-day Saints that those times of peril had arrived. Under the leadership of Brigham Young, they migrated to the Great Basin to escape the United States and await its imminent collapse. But with the end of the Mexican War, Mormons again found themselves under the jurisdiction of the federal government. And again, living in the end times called for a dual strategy. To the federal government, Mormon leaders proposed for Deseret a constitution mirroring that of the United States. They not only reiterated the religion clauses of the First Amendment but promised that all religions would be "equally protected under the law" and that there would be "no subordination or preference" among religions.[72] Among themselves, however, Mormons accepted the Constitution in a more qualified way—as Apostle Orson Pratt put it, "because it has good principles in it, not because we think it will last forever." The Constitution would endure only until people "were prepared to receive a more perfect government."[73]

In Utah, as it came to be called, Mormons strove to establish that more perfect government, a theodemocracy. They made Brigham Young both president of the LDS Church and governor of the territory, and packed its legislature with high-ranking church officials. The Utah Territory at the time comprised all of the present-day state, plus Nevada, about half of Colorado, and a corner of Wyoming. By controlling the territorial government, Mormon leaders ruled a significant chunk of the United States, and within that territory their church possessed greater legal powers than religion anywhere else in the country. Many other states had begun to limit the amount of property a religious association could hold; in Utah, the territorial legislature removed all such limits. Elsewhere in the United States, religious associations had no power over civil marriage. In Utah, the legislature gave the LDS Church complete legal power over its members' marriages and divorces. That set the stage for the 1852 announcement of polygamy, which the church immediately defended as a constitutionally protected religious liberty.[74]

That polygamy had the familiar earmarks of religion cannot be denied. It was found in the Bible, affirmed by new revelations, accepted in faith, and often enacted at personal sacrifice. It also was thoroughly imbricated in Mormon theology—their cosmology, beliefs about the preexistence and eternal progression of souls, and expectations for the afterlife. On the other hand, Mormon polygamy was not a religious difference that could be cabined within the private sphere. It was meant to create, and did create, an alternative social order. Plural marriage was never the sole or most common form of marriage among Mormons; that would have been arithmetically impossible. But polygamy was necessary to reach the highest spiritual exaltation, and among Mormons this correlated with worldly power. As legal historian Sarah Barringer Gordon observed, polygamous church leaders were "industrial, financial and agricultural leaders, as well as political figures." They "controlled valuable watercourses, forested canyons, and grazing pastures" and presided over "a growing structure of manufactures and directorates." Polygamy created an alternative social order—extensive, overlapping networks of kinship, wealth, and political power under the leadership of a select group of patriarchs. It made Mormons much more than a voluntary association of individuals with shared religious beliefs. It made them "a peculiar people," distinct from— and, many felt, alien to—the Euro-American nation.[75]

By choosing polygamy and everything else their church required, Mormons exposed another enigma within religious freedom: people might freely submit to an authoritarian order. Freedom, after all, is the capacity and desire to govern oneself. Mormons governed themselves more thoroughly, obediently, and hierarchically than almost anyone else in America. As Apostle John Taylor explained in 1861, Mormons "act with the most perfect freedom," but they know that "there is a correct order" and that "wisdom and knowledge proceed from God through the medium of the Holy Priesthood."[76] Given its timing—just days before the outbreak of the Civil War—Taylor's statement was especially trenchant. If the *vox populi* is the *vox dei*, he asked, "Then is it the Northern or the Southern States that are governed by the Almighty?"[77]

Hand in glove with the question of freedom, polygamy raised the question of equality. Were all people equally capable of freedom? To put a finer point on it: were women as capable as men? The Mormon patriarchs thought not. Brigham Young insisted that decisions about polygamy were entirely up to men, and the duty of women was to cheerfully submit.[78] George Q. Cannon, husband of five wives, explained that under Mormon polygamy "a woman is 'the equal of man, as far as she can be his equal.' " To Cannon, the crucial point was that men were divinely created to procreate abundantly, which required multiple female partners. Given these facts of nature, the only question was how men would treat their additional female partners. Under polygamy, he said, they were honored and protected; under monogamy, they were abandoned and disgraced.[79]

Mormon women were more ambivalent. Emma Smith broke with the main church after Joseph's death, and Brigham Young would be the subject of a salacious book by his "Wife #19," Ann-Eliza Young.[80] Yet if many women fled polygamy, it appears that even more flocked to Utah on the promise of marriage. Some were drawn by the belief that women in plural marriages would enjoy a higher station in the afterlife.[81] For others, plural marriage offered more immediate benefits. Martha Hughes Cannon, a physician, suffragist, and fourth wife of Angus Cannon (against whom she successfully ran for a seat in the state senate), commented wryly that "if her husband has four wives, [a Mormon woman] has three weeks of freedom each month."[82] Furthermore, polygamy increased the average woman's chance of marrying into a prosperous household, even as it reduced the average man's sexual and economic opportunities. Whatever their reasons, Utah women did not vote polygamy away when the Utah territorial legislature granted them suffrage in 1870. In fact, polygamous Utah was one of the very few places in America where women could vote—that is, until 1887, when Congress decided that to stamp out polygamy once and for all, it had to take the vote away from the women of Utah.[83]

But condemnation of polygamy did not necessarily correlate with support for gender equality, as shown by the failure of the women's suffrage movement elsewhere in America. In Mormon Utah, religious establishment created a patriarchy both in the home and in the public sphere. But in the rest of America, religious disestablishment had mixed effects. On one hand, it transferred religion to the domestic sphere. Women became "the angel in the home," schooling children in republican virtue and gently governing their husbands' passions. For some, this became an argument for political equality: if women could uplift the home, they could do the same for society, but to do so they would need equal political rights. For others, women's spiritual powers had the opposite implication: entry into the public world would sully women's spiritual purity, undermining their claim to public authority.

The politics of purity thus had varied implications for nineteenth-century American women. For at least some of them, the ideal of spiritual femininity empowered work for social reform.[84] But it also subjected women to an oppressive ideal of sexual purity. Women social reformers did challenge the double standard by demanding sexual purity from men as well as from women, which is why Mormon polygamists became their special nemesis.[85] But social purity movements also drew government much more extensively into the business of sexual regulation. Moreover, they precluded sexual autonomy—"pure" women were not supposed to feel sexual desire or make independent sexual decisions.

Most importantly, the ideal of sexual purity divided women along lines of race, class, and sexuality. The women leading purity movements were usually white, native-born, and economically comfortable. Presumably, it was not they whose sexuality needed taming, whose procreativity needed to be diminished, whose public demeanor needed cleaning up, or whose public activities were morally suspect. "Purity," in this sense, was a set of norms imposed by white middle-class Protestant women on women of color, immigrant women, working women, poor women—and, of course, Mormon women.

But purity is never an adequate substitute for equality, either in matters of gender or in matters of race. White abolitionists were horrified by the brutality of slavery, but few were fully committed to racial equality and many believed in white racial purity. Polygamy, in fact, was often described as "white slavery"—an expression that blended abhorrence of sexual excess with outrage that white women should be treated as if they were black. Similarly fraught was the Republican Party's 1856 denunciation of slavery and polygamy as the "twin relics of barbarism." In terms of polygamy, the meaning was fairly clear: to oppose polygamy was not to suppress a religion but to preserve civilization. But the implications for slavery were more equivocal, given the centuries-long association of barbarism with dark-skinned, non-Christian people. The racially fraught language of "barbarism" therefore could be turned either to the defense of slavery or to the cause of abolition.

Even Charles Sumner, who was beaten almost to death on the Senate floor for an abolitionist speech, denounced slavery in language that betrayed his presumption of white superiority and his aversion to racial mixing. Returning to the Senate in 1860, Sumner reminded slaveholders that, in the words of a Virginia senator, "the best blood of Virginia flows in the veins of slaves." Sumner too compared slavery with polygamy—male lust being the "disgusting element" that linked the two. Slavery was evil not only because it brutalized black people but also because it degraded whites by sexual and racial mixing. Slavery, he said, came from "barbarous Africa, . . . the ancient nurse of monsters." For Congress to tolerate it would be "to Africanize the Constitution . . . to Africanize the Territories, and to Africanize the National Government."[86] And just as he denounced slavery in sexualized terms, Sumner denounced polygamy in racialized terms. "The Slave-master hugs his disgusting practice," he charged, "as the Carib of the Gulf hugged Cannibalism, and as Brigham Young now hugs Polygamy."

Some pro-slavery legislators lent support to polygamy, but others redirected the language of barbarism away from slavery and against polygamy alone.[87] That was the tack taken by Thomas Nelson of Tennessee, chair of the Senate Judiciary Committee when it first recommended a federal law against polygamy in 1860. Surely, Nelson said, when the Framers wrote the religion clauses, "they never intended that the wild vagaries of the Hindu or the ridiculous mummeries of the Hottentot should be ennobled by so honored and sacred a name." By practicing polygamy, Mormons more resembled the people of Asia and Africa than civilized Americans. "Among barbarians," said Nelson, "[woman] is treated as an inferior," but "the precepts of Christianity have elevated her in the scale of being." Polygamy was "an insult to our wives and daughters" and should be stamped out "in the name of the respectable and virtuous women of the United States." Clearly Nelson was speaking only to men ("our wives and daughters") and only about white ("Christian") women. His actual motive was to preserve slavery by training federal attention entirely upon polygamous Utah. If the Mormons could not be brought to heel by peaceful means, he proposed, "the whole military and naval force of the United States" should be trained against them.[88]

THE MORMON OCTOPUS ENSLAVING THE WOMEN OF UTAH

"The Mormon Octopus Enslaving the Women of Utah." Republished in J. H. Beadle, Polygamy: Or, the Mysteries and Crimes of Mormonism, *2nd edition (1882; Philadelphia: National Publishing Company, 1904), xxxi.*

Vermont senator Justin Morrill, who sponsored the anti-polygamy bill, was both an abolitionist and a supporter of women's suffrage, but he too condemned polygamy not only as unconstitutional but also as racially and sexually impure. Like other opponents of polygamy, Morrill complained that Mormons had unconstitutionally established their religion in Utah. "If Congress is prohibited from making an established religion, a Territory must be equally prohibited." Mormons had imposed upon Utah "a hierarchy repugnant to the Constitution of the United States." In their penchant for hierarchy, he added, Mormons were like Catholics. But polygamy made Mormonism into something even worse than Catholicism: "a Mohammedan barbarism revolting to the civilized world." Surely, Morrill exclaimed, the religion clauses of the First Amendment cannot require us to "tamely submit to any burlesque, outrage, or indecency which artful men may seek to hide under the name of religion!" Polygamy was just such an indecency, "including in its slimy folds sister, mothers, and daughters."[89] The metaphor did not clarify who was sliming whom, but it did suggest that everything wrong with Mormonism—its seditious politics, religious heterodoxy, social corrosiveness, and racial strangeness—could be expressed in terms of sexual impurity.

Sexual Regulation and Religious Freedom

The Morrill Anti-Bigamy Act of 1862 made bigamy a federal crime punishable by up to five years imprisonment and a fine of $500. The law had little effect during the Civil War, when President Lincoln decided not to enforce it lest angry Mormons side with the Confederacy. Even after the war, when Congress stepped up measures against polygamy, they remained ineffective because Mormons kept no written records of plural marriages and, when questioned, tended to "forget" whether they'd witnessed or entered into such a marriage.[90] For the most part, they could be convicted of polygamy only with their own cooperation, which they had little reason to give.

That changed in 1874, when federal prosecutor William Carey offered a deal. If at least one Mormon polygamist would confess, polygamy charges would be dropped against high-level church officials.[91] Besides avoiding prison, Mormon leaders liked the idea that polygamy would finally have its day in court. Once they proved that plural marriage really was a core tenet of their religion, they believed, their free exercise right to practice it would surely be vindicated. So when George Reynolds, Brigham Young's personal secretary, was asked to stand trial, he gamely agreed. Reynolds was new to plural marriage, having taken his second wife only months before. The case against him therefore would be relatively simple, based on a list (provided by Reynolds himself) of fellow Mormons who could attest to his second marriage.

But when it seemed that the federal prosecutor might renege on the deal, Reynolds and his witnesses withdrew their cooperation. Even the church official who'd officiated at Reynolds's second wedding found himself unable to recall whether the ceremony had happened.[92] The case would then have fallen apart if the prosecutor had not thought to fetch the second wife, Amelia Jane Schofield. George had neglected to tell her about the change of strategy, so she arrived at court, visibly pregnant, and truthfully admitted to the marriage. The defense then returned to the argument it had wanted to make from the beginning—if he'd committed polygamy out of religious duty, George Reynolds was not guilty of a crime. Reynolds's lawyers demanded that the judge instruct the jury accordingly, which the judge declined to do. This became the point of contention that brought the case before the Supreme Court.

Given that *Reynolds v. United States* (1879) was the Supreme Court's first ruling on free exercise, it could not help running into Jefferson's "wall of separation." But upon arriving at the wall, the Court leapt it to alight on safer ground: Jefferson's statement that although religious liberty protects beliefs, it does not necessarily extend to actions, and never to actions "in violation of social duties or subversive of good order." Polygamy was exactly that sort of violation and subversion, so there could be no religious right to practice it, wrote Chief Justice Morrison Waite for a unanimous Court. To interpret the First Amendment as the Mormons proposed would "make the professed doctrines of religious belief superior to the law of the land." Each person would become "a law unto himself," and "government could exist only in name."[93]

The *Reynolds* decision did not explicitly deny that polygamy was Christian, nor did it define religion, although later anti-polygamy decisions would do both.[94] Instead, Justice Waite observed that "the word religion is not defined in the Constitution"—and then, in place of that missing definition, invoked "social duties" and "good order." These were phrases that, along with words like "morality" and "peace," had set the parameters of religion since colonial times. They had the advantage of being both vague and sweeping, capable of implying a whole worldview yet without seeming to either establish or suppress religion. Mormons, by their nonconformity, had called this bluff, forcing the Court to spell out the practical orthodoxies of American foundation religion. As it turned out, those orthodoxies had less to do with religious beliefs than with sex and race.

"Marriage, while from its very nature a sacred obligation, is nevertheless in most civilized nations a civil contract, and usually regulated by law," wrote Justice Waite. In other words, marriage is the foundation of civilization: "upon it society may be said to be built." He did not deny that Mormons considered polygamy a religious practice, but pointed out that in some parts of the world infanticide and cannibalism were considered religious too. Moreover, he added, those parts of the world were very far from Europe. "Polygamy has always been odious among the northern and western nations of Europe and, until the establishment of the Mormon Church, was almost exclusively a feature of the life of Asiatic and of African people."[95] Polygamy might be religious, Waite conceded, but different religions attached to different types of civilizations, and civilizations were definitely not equal. Just as "civilization" in its lowest forms was barely worthy of the name, so polygamy was unworthy to be considered "religion" of the sort protected by the Constitution.

Although the *Reynolds* decision also condemned polygamy for advancing "the patriarchal principle," it would be wrong to consider it a win for women's equality. In its discussion of patriarchy, the Court drew on the then-influential thought of the legal scholar Francis Lieber, who contended that polygamy led to "stationary despotism" while monogamy led to republican government and social progress. But neither Lieber nor the Court supported women's suffrage. "Some of my friends pretend to be for women's suffrage," Lieber once boasted, "but all their wives are for me." And the Supreme Court, just a few years before its *Reynolds* decision, had denied women a constitutional right to vote.[96] So when the Court denounced patriarchy, it was not denouncing male domination of women. Instead, it was worried that the majority of men would come to be dominated by a polygamous male elite—a situation that reportedly existed in Utah already and might spread from there to the rest of the nation. No doubt the *Reynolds* Court was troubled about the indignities that polygamy imposed on women; Waite twice quoted the lower court's paternalistic laments about "pure-minded women" demeaned by polygamy.[97] But it is striking that the *Reynolds* Court thought about equality only in relation to men. When it thought about women, its focus shifted from equality to purity.

As in the Supreme Court, the sentiment against polygamy throughout America was a tangle of sexual and racial anxiety. Mormons were relentlessly represented in popular media as spawning obscenely large, racially mixed families. Because of their desert habitat and polygamous families, they were called "Turks" or "Mohametans" and lumped into the vast category of "the Oriental." Political cartoons caricatured the bearded Mormon polygamist—along with the pigtailed Chinese worker, the Indian with his head feather, and the drunken Irishman—as one of "Uncle Sam's troublesome bedfellows."[98] It was not pure coincidence, then, that the campaigns to stamp out polygamy and to whiten the body politic progressed in tandem. As historian Paul Reeve notes, Congress passed the Chinese Exclusion Act and the Edmunds Anti-Polygamy Act within three months of each other during 1882. The campaign against polygamy also coincided with federally approved Jim Crow segregation, federal suppression of Native American religions, and a concerted federal effort to dissolve tribal lands.[99]

These racialized depictions of Mormons were not meant to be charitable, but they did reflect bits of truth. In the antebellum period, for example, most Mormons had objected to slavery and (to the consternation of slaveholders) sometimes preached to enslaved people. There was a black convert to Mormonism as early as 1830 and a small but steady stream thereafter. In Joseph Smith's lifetime, at least two black men were ordained to the priesthood. Moreover, Mormons believed that Native Americans were the remnants of ancient Israel and therefore directed special missionary efforts toward them. Brigham Young even urged Mormon missionaries to take Native women as wives.[100]

On the whole, however, the Mormon record on race was not better than that of other whites. The Book of Mormon is ambiguous on the subject, stating in one passage that "all are alike unto God" (2 Nephi 26:33), but elsewhere that "a skin of blackness" is a curse from God (2 Nephi 5:21). What tipped the balance, according to Reeve, was that the racialized insults hurled against them made many Mormons want to defend their "whiteness." Apostle Parley Pratt, for example, fumed that in Missouri the Latter-day Saints had been treated "as if we had been some savage tribe, or some colored race of foreigners" rather than white citizens.[101] As Pratt's mention of "savage tribes" recalls, Mormon relations with Indians ranged from alliance to (as Reeve puts it) "warfare, atrocities, and death." Black people, with no special place in Mormon theology, fared even worse. In 1852, not long before polygamy was announced (and perhaps anticipating the racial panic it would induce), Brigham Young imposed a ban on black priests. In 1863 he proposed that mixed-race couples should be executed. By the 1890s, in keeping with the nativist sentiments of the time, Mormon publications were displaying racist stereotypes of Asians.[102]

None of these gestures, however, reduced the anti-Mormon animus of Euro-Protestants. Between 1882 and 1887, Congress intensified criminal penalties for polygamy, disincorporated the LDS Church, and slashed away at Mormons' civil rights. These actions did not abridge religious freedom, explained the federally appointed Utah commission, because they were "not enacted against the religion" of Mormonism "but against a crime."[103] Yet polygamy was not wrong because it was criminal; it was criminalized because non-Mormons thought it wrong. Punishing what the majority saw as sexual sins was now explicitly within the remit, not just of state governments but of government at the federal level.

For example, according to Utah territorial law, only a spouse had been able to bring charges of adultery. In 1887, Congress annulled that law, turning adultery from a tort against injured parties into a crime against the government. It also criminalized any marriage-like solemnities that were not duly recorded and filed in probate court. If people wanted to make marriage-like commitments—asking neither the recognition nor the support of the law—they no longer were at liberty to do so. Congress even annulled inheritance provisions for children born out of wedlock. Utah and its Mormon citizens no longer had the option of providing for the children of polygamous marriages. These statutes may or may not have protected legitimate government interests, but it is telling that no such rationale was demanded. The opprobrium of the majority was sufficient to justify the criminalization of sexual dissent.[104]

Jefferson had said, and the *Reynolds* Court had reiterated, that religious freedom did not necessarily extend to religiously motivated actions. But the conflict over polygamy took the radical step of delineating religious action in sexual terms: monogamy was legitimate religion, non-monogamy was not. As the Supreme Court put it in 1890, polygamy was repudiated "by the laws of all civilized and Christian countries," so to call its advocacy "a tenet of religion" would "offend the common sense of mankind."[105] Monogamy, the Court was saying, was the teaching of a specific religion

(Christianity), but it was also what civilized people did. And if polygamy was not civilized, neither was it religious. Following this reasoning, monogamy was not just a way to frame the religious meaning of sex; it was the *only* way to frame the religious meaning of sex. And if there were no legitimate religious alternatives, monogamy itself would not need religious legitimation. It would simply be civilized, normal, and American. The effect of suppressing religiously motivated polygamy was that monogamy was both cemented into American foundation religion and stripped of its religious markers.

The American Religion

The *Reynolds* Court, quoting Thomas Jefferson, had defended its judgment against polygamy by explaining that although religious beliefs deserved unqualified constitutional protection, religious actions did not. Yet by the 1880s, even Mormon beliefs were under attack. In 1884, the Territory of Idaho denied citizenship rights to any avowed member of the Mormon Church, regardless of whether that person practiced or encouraged polygamy. And in the Edmunds-Tucker Act of 1887, Congress seized the assets of the LDS Church and used the funds to set up federally run "nonsectarian" schools.[106]

In the pair of 1890 cases (*Davis v. Beason* and *Late Corporation of the Church of Jesus Christ of Latter-day Saints v. United States*) that upheld these laws, the Supreme Court was finally moved to venture a definition of religion. Religion, it said in *Davis*, refers to "one's views of his relations to his Creator, and to the obligations they impose of reverence for his being and character, and of obedience to his will."[107] Mormons, of course, believed that "obedience to God's will" included polygamy, but as long as polygamy was a crime, neither they nor anyone else had the right to engage in it. What's striking, however, is that beyond denying Mormons a right to enact their controversial religious belief, the Court denied them a right to express that belief or even to associate with others who held it.

And once again, the Court resorted to racism and ethnocentrism in drawing the boundaries of religion and citizenship. "No doubt the Thugs of India imagined that their belief in the right of assassination was a religious belief," commented the Court in *Late Corporation*, "but their thinking so did not make it so." Similarly, "the practice of suttee by the Hindu widows" or "the offering of human sacrifices by our own ancestors in Britain" were based on "a supposed religious conviction."[108] Whether the professed belief in polygamy came from chicanery or credulity, it was at best "the pretense of religion."[109] The religion of the Latter-day Saints, in other words, could not be *seriously* believed and therefore was not entitled to any constitutional protection.

Soon after these decisions, the LDS Church issued what became known as the First Manifesto, promising that Mormons would submit to anti-polygamy laws. The next year it dissolved its political party, and by the turn of the century Mormons had become as reliable a constituency within the Republican Party as Catholics were among the Democrats. Yet neither complying with the law nor joining partisan politics was sufficient to prove that Mormons conformed unreservedly to the foundation religion of Euro-Protestant America. In 1903, when Reed Smoot became the first Mormon elected to the Senate, his colleagues refused to seat him. Smoot was a Mormon apostle but also a monogamist and an ally of Theodore Roosevelt. Nonetheless, based simply on his membership in the LDS Church, his seating was delayed until 1907.[110]

In an effort to quell these lingering suspicions, in 1904 the Mormon leadership issued a Second Manifesto, which made polygamy grounds for excommunication.[111] They also promulgated a statement called "The Kingdom of God," which not only promised that henceforth the church would conform to majoritarian norms but, remarkably, denied that it had ever refused to conform in the past. The statement accurately reiterated Smith's claim that the U.S. Constitution was divinely inspired, but omitted his eventual conclusion that "man cannot govern himself" and similar declarations by later Mormon leaders. It denied that Mormons had ever united church and state, apparently forgetting the church's experiments with theodemocracy. Perhaps most significantly, the statement played down the millennialism of early Mormon theology. The LDS Church, it said, always had understood its role as akin to that of John the Baptist—preparatory to the kingdom of God but not identical to it. Any teaching that the "dominion to come is to be exercised now," it declared, "is incorrect, no matter by whom set forth."[112]

Mormon historian Kathleen Flake describes the church's 1904 change as an acceptance of "denominational citizenship." Mormons agreed that, like any other denomination, they would obey the law, remain loyal to the nation, and tolerate other religions. By emphasizing what they called Joseph Smith's First Vision (revelations on the nature of God and similar theological points), the Latter-day Saints began to think of their differences from other Americans as purely "religious." Nonetheless, with its 1904 statement the LDS Church was doing more than shifting its emphasis. As Flake observes, it was issuing "a public renunciation of nearly sixty years of church teaching."[113]

In other words, Mormons did not simply relinquish their *non-religious* disagreements with American culture. They also shrank their notion of religion itself in order to cabin their distinctiveness nonthreateningly within the walls defined by the majority culture. It was only because of this self-shrinkage that the LDS Church was finally granted "religious freedom." Mormons' beliefs remained as heterodox as ever—they still had their Golden Bible, their esoteric rituals, their unique cosmology, and their strange stories about the lost tribes of Israel. But once those beliefs were shorn of publicly disruptive implications, non-Mormons did not much care. What mattered was whether Mormons looked and acted "American." And at least for the time being, the Latter-day Saints agreed. Rather than being a "peculiar people," they would become Americans with somewhat peculiar beliefs.

With their sexual relations in order and their whiteness no longer in doubt, Mormons began to look and feel patriotic rather than seditious. In a country worried about the feminization of its religion, the LDS Church proved that religion could still be unabashedly patriarchal. To Euro-Americans worried about "race suicide," Mormons offered portraits of large, healthy white families. To a republic lacking a spiritual connection to its land and indigenous people, Latter-day Saints shared a story of salvation centered on the American continent and encompassing its Native peoples. In contrast to the urban masses and robber barons of the East, Mormons were industrious pioneers who planted and grew their own food and managed their own communities. Born on American soil, sanctifying the U.S. Constitution, and anticipating that from this nation the reign of Christ would spread to every corner of the earth, the LDS Church had not just become a legitimate American religion; it had become, arguably, the most American religion of all.[114]

Forgetting Religious Conflict

Americans commonly look back with bewilderment on nineteenth-century conflicts among Protestants, Mormons, and Catholics. But if, in hindsight, it seems incomprehensible that these three groups found it necessary to fight so furiously and publicly about religion, that's because Catholics and Mormons, who lost at the time, made their defeats palatable by ceasing to think of them as religious. Catholics were no longer religiously required to change the public school system; Mormons were no longer religiously permitted to practice polygamy. Both groups could then enter the public square looking more like everyone else, which Protestants made easier by forgetting that institutions like public education and monogamy, foundation stones of the republic, had been hammered into place by religious conflict.

As these stories illustrate, the sequelae of American religious conflicts include misremembrance of the varied and contradictory meanings that religion held for the people involved. Euro-Protestants could think of nonsectarianism as Christian, but they could also think of it as generically religious or as simply American. Similarly, they could defend monogamy on religious grounds, but also as a feature of higher civilizations or races. Catholics and Mormons thought of these conflicts as religious when they were in the thick of them, but afterwards could adjust their own religious sensibilities to reassure themselves that, in the process of gaining full citizenship, they had not relinquished their religions.

Given that religion-talk on all sides was riddled with contradiction, it was not the strength of an argument but the relative power of the adversaries that determined who prevailed. Most Catholics were immigrants or the children of immigrants; most Mormons were economically marginal people who moved to Utah Territory in search of a better life. Their Euro-Protestant adversaries, at least in the aggregate, had more political power, cultural influence, social status, and wealth. Indeed, it was these structural arrangements that Catholics and Mormons challenged on (what to them at the time were) religious grounds, which is why Euro-Protestants objected so strenuously to these religions. When Catholics and Mormons demanded religious liberty, therefore, they were demanding much more than simply to be left alone. They wanted to affect how families were structured in America, how property was distributed, what texts were revered as sacred, how children were raised, whose versions of truth were included in the common fund of knowledge. The arguments may have been framed in terms of the wall of separation, but they were really about America's norms and sensibilities, its spirit and character—in short, its foundations.

In comparison to religious differences, foundations are hard to see, and in comparison to religious creeds, social ethics are hard to articulate. But to benefit now from these conflicts, we need to cultivate that ability to look at our foundations and articulate our social ethics. Looking back, we might notice that everyone desired freedom for themselves, but few were committed to equal freedom for others. Everyone felt the indignities suffered by their own community, yet most were insensitive to indignities inflicted on the community next door. People treasured their own vision of the common good but strained to comprehend alternative visions. They welcomed the beneficent powers of government into their lives but wanted government coercion to remain far away. Locked in religion-talk, these were the deepest stakes of the conflicts, and the questions they bequeath to us.

CHAPTER FOUR

Nicholas Black Elk and Theodore Roosevelt

Religion and the Fight for Land

We believe that a nation's memorial should, like
Washington, Jefferson, Lincoln, and Roosevelt, have a
serenity, a nobility, and a power of the gods who inspired
them and suggests the gods that they have become.

—GUTZON BORGLUM, 1930

The Great Spirit made the two-leggeds to live like relatives
with the four-leggeds and the wings of the air and all the
things that live and are green. But the white man has put us
in a little island and in the other little islands he has put the
four-legged beings; and steadily the islands grow smaller,
for around them surges the hungry flood of the white men,
and it is dirty with lies and greed.

—NICHOLAS BLACK ELK, 1931

IT IS WELL RECOGNIZED that the conflict between Native Americans and Euro-Americans has always been about land. Euro-Americans have rarely understood, however, what land might have to do with religion. This chapter will draw that connection by focusing on one region and two men whose lives intersected there. The region is the Dakotas, claimed as U.S. territory in 1803 by Jefferson's Louisiana Purchase and incorporated into the Union when North and South Dakota became states in 1889. The men are President Theodore Roosevelt (1858–1919) and Nicholas ("Nick") Black Elk (1863–1950), a Lakota warrior, healer, and visionary. Their stories show that struggles over land are not just about property and power; they also implicate questions of meaning and truth. Conversely, struggles about religion are not just about what happens after we die. They also concern how we inhabit the earth, distribute its resources, and relate to the other creatures who live alongside us.

Like religion, land has been conceived in terms of both walls and foundations—or, one could say, property and ground. Euro-Americans fought a revolution to preserve their private property, which they believed to be a sacred right. Even religion could be imagined as privately owned, which is why Madison could call it "a property of peculiar value."[1] Yet in addition to being private property, land also has been the nation's ground—its economic basis, its national home, and the territory over which the government rules. As ground, too, land has always been infused with religious meaning. To European settlers, America was a new Promised Land, given to a new chosen people. Like the ancient Israelites, they were to vanquish the land's original inhabitants on the authority of God.

For First Nations, land has had little to do with walls and everything to do with foundations. Indigenous American cultures vary widely, but they share a sense that people belong to their lands rather than the other way around. Rather than the set on which life is staged, land is the sacred wellspring of life. It cannot be transformed into something other than itself but of equal value, nor can one place be substituted for another.[2] And just as a people's land is coextensive with their life, so is religion coextensive with culture. As Native scholars point out, the very word "religion" tends to misrepresent traditional indigenous cultures, where the sacred is not consigned to a separate sphere but infuses every part of life.[3]

The lives of Nicholas Black Elk and Theodore Roosevelt reveal an almost inverse relationship between land and the Christian religion. For each, the closer he was to land, the more distant he was from Christianity. In Roosevelt's youth, religion was an indoor affair, associated with tedious sermons, softhearted clergy, and the enervating safety of the domestic sphere. As he grew up and adventured out of doors, Roosevelt began to speak of Christianity with doubt, then condescension, and finally with veiled contempt. He was one of the few presidents who chose not to follow the tradition, inaugurated by George Washington, of swearing his oath of office on a Bible. On matters of church and state he became a strict separationist, arguing that no politician should be asked about his religious beliefs, objecting to "In God We Trust" on currency, and to the dismay of Protestant nativists, confining even Protestantism within the proverbial wall.[4]

Black Elk's religious journey took him in the opposite direction. His people, from the dawn of their collective memory, had experienced their land as filled with spiritual power and beauty—in other words, as sacred. But because they did not possess land, neither did the Lakota possess "religion" in any sense that Euro-Christians could recognize. It was only the disruption of Black Elk's relationship with sacred land that made "religion" into a question and problem for him. As Euro-Americans gained control over his ancestral lands, Black Elk concluded that Christianity might be more powerful than the old ways. But even when he became a Christian, he never forgot that it was the religion of another people, from another place. And in reflecting on this, he realized that his people had their own religion, grounded eternally in their own sacred place.

Roosevelt's de facto religion became Americanism, which he conceived as the spirit of the Europeans who had forged themselves into a new nation (or "race") by mastering the American land. He took it for granted that the triumph of Americanism entailed the dissolution of First Nations. And like most Euro-American leaders, he viewed this dissolution more as an inevitability than as a policy decision. But, more than others, Roosevelt felt it essential that Euro-Americans become at home in the land—fitted to it, as Indians had been. As president, in addition to dissolving tribal lands, he initiated the nation's first conservation program, enabling Euro-Americans to encounter the land as if for the first time and become as if native to it. Native lands thus became pilgrimage sites for Euro-American patriotism. And Native religious practices, though legally prohibited for Native people, were symbolically ingested and transformed into the Americanism of non-Natives.

Between Roosevelt and Black Elk, this struggle over land took place in the Dakotas, and for each, it was a childhood illness that sealed his relationship with the region. Black Elk's illness came when he was nine, when for several days he lay in a coma while his spirit flew into the Black Hills (Paha Sapa), sacred to the Lakota people. There he encountered the Six Grandfathers, spirits associated with the directions and also with a mountain in the Black Hills called Tunkasila Sakpe. From the Grandfathers he received what he would thereafter call his Great Vision.[5] He would spend most of his remaining years as close as he could get to the site of that experience, on the Pine Ridge Reservation of South Dakota, where he would be known in his youth as a medicine man and later as a Catholic catechist.

For Roosevelt, neither the illness nor the recovery was quite as dramatic. He was plagued from early childhood with asthma and cholera, and by adolescence (according to some) had succumbed to the upper-class malady of over-civilization. He would exaggerate his time in the Dakota Badlands, which amounted to no more than three years, but the exaggeration only underscores how important the region was to him.[6] He sought no visions there, but he did seek new vitality and a new public identity, which he certainly found. Within weeks of setting foot in the region, he bought a herd of cattle. Within a year he had purchased two ranches, enabling him to truthfully (if suddenly) reintroduce himself to the world as a "ranchman" and in that persona relaunch his political career.

It cannot be said that the Dakotas completely healed either man. Roosevelt always struggled with a variety of maladies, and Black Elk suffered from tuberculosis throughout his life.[7] But each man's experiences in the Dakotas would become a part of America's public mythology—Black Elk's through the poetic offices of John Neihardt, who transformed his stories into the bestseller *Black Elk Speaks*; Roosevelt's through his three books on the Dakotas and his

The Six Grandfathers before it was carved and renamed Mount Rushmore. National Park Service Digital Image Archives.

Mount Rushmore, carved by Gutzon Borglum. National Park Service Digital Image Archives.

multivolume tome *The Winning of the West*.[8] Each man, while in the Dakotas, saw a vision of his people's future—one a vision of defeat, the other of triumph. Because nothing is forever, we should not expect or hope that these defeats and triumphs will be final. For the time being, however, those visions are inscribed on the Dakotas themselves, where Roosevelt's visage (along with those of Washington, Lincoln, and Jefferson) is chiseled into the Tunkasila Sakpe, now known as Mount Rushmore.[9]

At Pine Ridge

If Nick Black Elk and Theodore Roosevelt ever laid eyes on each other, it would have been on the Pine Ridge Reservation in the fall of 1892. They might have seen each other at one of the Indian-run stores that Roosevelt recalled visiting and where Black Elk worked for a time. Or, during the six days that he traveled around Pine Ridge (logging about 250 miles, according to his report), Roosevelt may have seen Black Elk working his allotted land in the Wounded Knee region.[10] In any event, the encounter wouldn't have been particularly memorable. Black Elk would have seen Roosevelt as just another white administrator sent to manage "the Indian problem." Roosevelt would have seen Black Elk as one of the many Pine Ridge Indians who had "only recently come out of the wild state."[11]

Roosevelt was visiting Pine Ridge in his capacity as civil service commissioner. One of his goals as commissioner was to end the spoils system, which he thought had severely compromised the caliber of federal employees. After December 29, 1890, when the army terminated the Ghost Dance at Wounded Knee by killing as many as three hundred unarmed Lakota, his concerns began to focus on civil servants working on Indian reservations.[12] Many in Washington, DC, blamed the Wounded Knee massacre on Pine Ridge agent Daniel Royer, known among the Lakota as "Young Man Afraid of Indians." Evidently the moniker was accurate: the Ghost Dance had so alarmed Royer that he'd called for military intervention.[13]

The consensus was that Royer had overreacted, but Roosevelt was not so sure. In a private letter written two months after the massacre, he commented that unlike most of his friends, he was "no sentimentalist" and had "no particular horror of bloodshed *per se.*" Reflecting on the events at Wounded Knee, he wrote, "I would put down an Indian outbreak as I would put down any mob uprising with the strongest possible hand," even if that involved "killing a few score villains and fools." On the other hand, if the investigation showed that peaceable Indians had been killed at Wounded Knee, "the hanging of a few white scoundrels" would do "incredible good."[14]

Notwithstanding those concerns, Commissioner Roosevelt had not come to Pine Ridge to search for white scoundrels. His purpose was to assess the progress of "civilization" among the Indians and check for warning signs of another Ghost Dance outbreak. He did not see much of the latter, other than a "very crafty looking Indian" named Short Bull, a member of the Ghost Dance movement who had just been released from a military prison.[15] He did not notice Black Elk, who had participated in the Ghost Dance, witnessed the carnage at Wounded Knee, and joined in the brief uprising that followed.[16] Nor could he have anticipated that Black Elk's account of those events, whose publication lay forty years in the future, would finally bring the massacre the moral condemnation it did not get from Roosevelt or from many non-Native Americans of the time.

The Ghost Dance was one in a long series of Native American prophetic movements, all of which tried to stem what Black Elk would later call the "hungry flood" of whites across the land.[17] It started in Nevada, led by a Northern Paiute messianic figure called Wovoka or Jack Wilson. The ceremony, which the Northern Paiute called the Round Dance, took place over several nights and was repeated about every six weeks. There had been a wave of the movement twenty years earlier; its revival in 1890 had been inspired by a vision that came to Wovoka during a solar eclipse, in which he was taken up to heaven and there beheld a regenerated world. Indians who had perished were alive, the earth was verdant and unscarred, and animals upon whom the people depended, such as ponies and buffalo, were plentiful again.[18] Wovoka sent word of this marvelous vision to the Lakota and other tribes in the area, prophesying that if they would perform the dance in the manner prescribed, they too would see the ghosts of the dead and help usher in the world to come.

The Lakota were renowned warriors, but notwithstanding Royer's and Roosevelt's fears, their Ghost Dance was not an armed uprising. It is true that the Lakota camped at Wounded Knee had at least a few dozen guns. We know this because Euro-American and Native American witnesses, while disagreeing on other important details, agreed that the massacre was sparked in connection with the army's attempted confiscation of guns.[19] But the weapons in the camp were only defensive. Given that the Ghost Dance camp was surrounded by five hundred well-armed federal troops, an attack would have been suicidal. Guns would not have been present in the ceremonial space because, among the Lakota, Ghost Dancers were forbidden to wear or carry metal.[20] Moreover, the tone of the Ghost Dance was lament, hardly the affect of war, and unlike a war dance, it included the whole community. That is why so many women, children, and old men were killed.[21]

Still, Euro-Americans were unnerved that Wovoka was prophesying their disappearance from Indian land. These predictions, which sometimes involved armed resistance, had long characterized Indian prophetic movements. In the Ghost Dance movement, however, whites were expected to disappear as a result of ritual rather than military action. As Smithsonian ethnographer James Mooney reported in 1896, Wovoka's followers imagined the destruction of whites by "an overruling spiritual power that needs no assistance from human creatures."[22] Black Elk pictured it as a great trembling of the earth, followed by a landslide that would drown whites while lifting Indians up to meet their returning dead.[23]

By 1890, Native people in the West had good reason to feel that restoring the world would take all the spiritual power they could muster. The Homestead Act of 1862 had brought waves of settlers to Indian territories, and the Transcontinental Railroad made it easy for them to travel from coast to coast. In the year of the Ghost Dance at Pine Ridge, the frontier was declared closed— according to the U.S. Census Department, not a single habitable square mile was unclaimed. Indians were confined to reservation lands, where they lived in near starvation, dependent on government rations that were easily and often withdrawn. As Black Elk would say, "The white man had taken our world from us, and we were like prisoners of war."[24]

The coup de grâce was the Dawes Act of 1887, also known as the Allotment and Assimilation Act, which was intended to solve "the Indian problem" once and for all by dissolving tribal lands. Its method was to break reservation lands into plots and allot them to Indian heads of households; "surplus" lands then would be sold off.[25] In 1892, Roosevelt believed that the Dawes Act was working very well at Pine Ridge. Not all Indians, he acknowledged, were quite ready to receive their lands in severalty, so the government should exercise a certain amount of caution. Sooner or later, however, Indian people would have to be thrown out on their own "to sink or swim."[26] Black Elk did not sink, but he would remain impoverished throughout his life. In 1947, the scholar Joseph Epes Brown found him, at age eighty-four, dressed in "poor cast-off clothes" and living with his family in a drafty cabin eight miles from the nearest water pump.[27] By then, nearly a third of the Pine Ridge Reservation—and, across the country, about two-thirds of reservation lands—had fallen into non-Native hands.[28]

Looking at his world in 1890, Black Elk may well have felt there was nowhere to go but up, and the Ghost Dance was a way to seek this transcendence. He'd been wary of joining the dance but had gone out to watch it and been astonished to see in the middle of the ceremonial space "an exact duplicate" of two key images from his Great Vision—the sacred hoop and the flowering tree representing the life of his people. He then joined the dance, and by his own account, painted his visionary symbols on the Ghost Shirts that became a distinctive feature of the Lakota ceremony.[29] Like other Lakota dancers, he believed these shirts to be bulletproof, especially after he rode into the Wounded Knee massacre with his arms raised and was not harmed. During the armed uprising that followed, the Ghost Shirt seemed to continue protecting Black Elk; later, he would recall that he was wounded only when he momentarily lost confidence in its power. But even if Ghost Shirts protected warriors from the soldiers' bullets, they could not protect the tribe from freezing or starving in the brutal January of 1891. On January 16, with Black Elk's reluctant agreement, the fighters surrendered.

Black Elk's bitter defeat was for Roosevelt a part of America's great triumph, the winning of the West. From the moment he set foot in the Dakotas, he had objected to the "sentimental nonsense" about "our taking the Indian's land." He believed (incorrectly) that no western Indians cultivated land, which to him meant that they "never had any real ownership" of their territories. Had whites not settled the West, Roosevelt wrote, it would have remained "a game preserve for squalid savages."[30] He contended that the government had been "abundantly generous," paying Indians "many times more than we would have paid any civilized people" in recompense for "vague and shadowy" land claims. But in the end, Roosevelt concluded, it really didn't matter "whether the whites [had] won the land by treaty, armed conquest, or, as was actually the case, a mixture of both." What mattered was that the land was won "for the benefit of civilization and in the interest of mankind."[31]

Roosevelt's 1892 report had gentler moments, like when he denounced the removal of settled Indian farmers from the eastern United States. But the Indians of the West, he reiterated, must drop their (to Roosevelt) silly accusation that whites had stolen their land.[32] And even with respect to eastern Indians, Roosevelt thought there should be a statute of limitations on sympathy. As president, he found it "amusing" but also "pathetic" when Iroquois leaders came to the White House with the "dim hope" of gaining back lost land. The meeting was conducted with "all the solemnities of calumet and wampum," Roosevelt recalled in his autobiography, but the Iroquois looked to him like people who had "walked out of a remote past."[33]

To survive—and in 1892 Roosevelt was predicting that at least half the Indian population would not—Native Americans would have to accept individual land allotments and become self-sufficient. Unfortunately, as Roosevelt saw it, missionaries on reservations didn't always agree. Like other "friends of the Indian," they tended to be "sentimentalists" who "petted and cared for" their charges rather than prepare them "for the inevitable plunge" into the "troublous sea of life." Some missionaries objected to the Dawes policy or balked at ending the federal support that, in Roosevelt's opinion, was "pauperizing" the Indians. For Roosevelt, the missionaries' job was not so much to Christianize as to Americanize the Indians. And Catholics could do that just as well as Protestants, he insisted (thrusting a finger into the eye of Protestant nativists). Moreover, federal monies should never be spent "for any sectarian purpose," such as making Indians into Christian missionaries. Sizing up the missionaries on reservations, Roosevelt concluded that when it came to violating the wall of separation, the worst culprits were to be found among Protestants.[34]

If it can be said that Roosevelt supported religious freedom for Native Americans, it was only insofar as "religion" included both Catholic and Protestant varieties of Christianity.[35] For the rest of his life, and most of Black Elk's, Native religious ceremonies would remain crimes under the 1883 Code of Indian Offenses, punishable by imprisonment or deprivation of rations.[36] At Pine Ridge in 1892, Commissioner Roosevelt thought that even the Code of Indian Offenses was not strict enough, since it had been insufficient to discourage the Ghost Dance. Roosevelt had a point, although perhaps not for the reason he imagined: even before they began to dance, the Lakota at Pine Ridge in 1890 were starving and effectively imprisoned. In the event of another "outbreak," Commissioner Roosevelt concluded, the police at Pine Ridge would need more than pistols; they should be armed with carbines.[37]

Land

In the fall of 1875, a federally appointed commission was sent to bargain the Black Hills away from the Lakota. By some accounts, an older chief named Spotted Tail offered to sell them for $70 million. Black Elk's father, who was present at the council, recalled it somewhat differently. He said that Spotted Tail, recognizing that Indians were losing their means of subsistence, had demanded that the government feed and clothe them forever and that, if the day should come when all that remained of the Indians was one of their dogs, the government should care for the dog too.[38] Not only the latter demand but also the former would have seemed facetious to the commission, because Spotted Tail's ask would have amounted to about a quarter of all the money spent by the federal government that year.[39] Either way, the message was the same: to the Lakota, the Black Hills were priceless. That, indeed, was the conclusion reached by the federal commission: "The Indians place a value upon the Hills far beyond any sum that could possibly be considered by the government."[40]

But long before the taking of Indian lands was rationalized economically, it was rationalized theologically. Chief Justice John Marshall said as much in *Johnson v. M'Intosh* (1823), the Supreme Court's first opinion on the lands of First Nations. The case concerned the sale of land belonging to the Piankashaw people, which raised the prior question of whether they (or any) First Nation legally owned their lands. To solve this dispute, Marshall noted that when European Christians arrived in the New World, they had believed it their duty to conquer "uninhabited" lands for Christ. He seemed uneasy reiterating the Discovery Doctrine, because he acknowledged that his fellow Christians had taken land mostly by brute force. But since his own court—the "court of the conqueror," as he called it—was the product of this history, he was in no position to renounce it. Moreover, Marshall shared the common Euro-Christian view that it was wrong to leave land in its natural state, as Indians appeared to do. "To leave [the Indians] in possession of their country was to leave the country a wilderness," he noted; therefore the government must claim ownership of the entire country.[41] As a sort of "apology," Marshall hoped that Indians would appreciate that Euro-Americans were "bestowing upon them civilization and Christianity."[42]

Whether or not Christian civilization was a good enough apology, it was a central objective of federal Indian policy, and missionaries were among its chief agents. Federal support for these missions was never considered a violation of the establishment clause—at least, not until Catholic missionaries got into the act. At that point, the (Protestant-run) Indian Rights Association started worrying about the wall of separation on Indian reservations, just as Protestants had worried about Catholic influence in the public schools back east.[43] Nor was the attempted conversion of Indians considered a violation of the constitutional right of free exercise, both because Native people were not yet citizens and because Euro-Americans saw Native traditions as mere superstition.[44] Native people were expected not only to adopt a Christian creed but to relinquish their names, clothing, language, healing practices, sexual arrangements, hairstyles, livelihoods, and housing for the practices preferred by Euro-Christians.

More than anything, civilization altered the relationship between Native people and their lands. Rather than the collective home of the people, land was to be divided into farmsteads, with the "additional" lands ceded to the government. If they did this, Native people were permitted to stay where they lived, create their own constitutions, and govern themselves. But that promise was made to be broken, because the ultimate goal of the civilization policy was Indian disappearance. It was expected that tribal territories would shrink by sale or cession, tribal cultures would be renounced and forgotten, and Native people would die or melt silently into the Euro-Christian mass.

The Cherokee people of Georgia were a test case. They'd done everything required by the civilization policy—converted to Christianity, turned to farming, ceded much of their land, and created a constitutional government—but the discovery of gold transformed their lands, in Euro-Americans' minds, into sheer wealth. And so the world of the Cherokee became, suddenly, a different place, much coveted by Georgia's non-Native citizens. In 1830, Congress took the state's side by passing the Removal Act, which provided that the president would "forever secure and guarantee" new lands west of the Mississippi River for any eastern tribes that agreed to move.[45] When the Cherokee declined to depart, Georgia passed a law purporting to dissolve Cherokee territory and the Cherokee government.[46]

John Marshall, perhaps regretting the effects of his 1823 decision, argued that Georgia's actions broke existing treaties between the federal government and the Cherokee Nation. In a clever but at the time ineffectual approach to Indian law, Marshall claimed that the boundaries set by treaties should be interpreted (as Indians preferred) as if intended to keep whites out, not (as whites preferred) as if intended to keep Indians in.[47] President Andrew Jackson, an aggressive proponent of the latter view, defied Marshall's ruling and signed orders expelling the Cherokee from their land, sending them on the journey that became known as the Trail of Tears. Other eastern tribes would be similarly uprooted, and in 1871, Congress stopped making treaties with Indian tribes, in effect ceasing to recognize them as sovereign nations.[48]

For the Lakota too, the catastrophic loss of land was precipitated by gold, which was discovered in the Black Hills in 1874. The Lakota did not share the Euro-Christian premise that land could be made into money—hence, the failure of the negotiations witnessed by Black Elk's father in 1875. They had every right to refuse to sell, because the Fort Laramie Treaty of 1868, which established the Great Sioux Reservation, had vouchsafed the Black Hills to the Lakota people forever.[49] When white miners tried to force their way in, the federal government was plainly obligated to prevent them. The sympathies of federal forces, however, lay in the other direction. Even while instructing subordinates to keep intruders out of the Black Hills, General Philip Sheridan wrote that he would "give a cordial support to the settlement of the Black Hills" if Congress would kindly "open up the country for settlement, by extinguishing the treaty rights of the Indians." General George Armstrong Custer went even further, broadcasting the Black Hills' mineral wealth in eastern newspapers and urging whites to come and get it.[50]

In coalition with the Northern Cheyenne, the Lakota fought hard for their lands, routing Custer at Little Big Horn in June 1876. Black Elk, only twelve years old at the time, was considered too young to fight, but he rode in anyway and, on the order of a warrior, took his first scalp. The white soldier, still alive, ground his teeth as he was being scalped, whereupon young Black Elk shot him in the forehead. He would later recall that he felt no remorse for killing whites who seemed bent on killing Indians and taking their lands. "I was a very happy boy," he said. "I wasn't a bit sorry."[51]

Despite that victory, war against the United States could only end in defeat. The following year, the federal government unilaterally terminated the Fort Laramie Treaty and informed the Lakota that they must cede the Black Hills and cease hunting outside the reservation. If they refused these demands, they would be deprived of rations; if they submitted, they would receive subsistence rations as long as necessary. A second commission was sent to the Lakota with these terms in a prewritten "agreement" (by 1980, even the Supreme Court would refer to it with scare quotes). Adding insult to injury, the 1877 agreement also demanded assent to the proposition that the government was doing all this for the Lakota's own good: "The said Indians do further agree in all things to submit themselves to such beneficent plans as the Government may provide for them in the selection of a country suitable for a permanent home, where they may live like white men."[52]

The Religious Development of Theodore Roosevelt

In 1858, the year Theodore Roosevelt Jr. was born, Thomas Wentworth Higginson published a caustic article entitled "Saints and Their Bodies."[53] For centuries, the Christian ideal of holiness had been "a strong soul in a weak body," but in contemporary America, Higginson contended, the Christian body had degenerated to a new low. If a son was "ruddy, brave and strong," parents expected him to succeed in the world, but if he was "pallid, puny, sedentary, lifeless, and joyless," they would say he was born to be a minister. The pathetic scene Higginson conjured, of anemic little boys "preaching sermons in their garret to their deluded little sisters and their dolls," reflected the feminization of American religion and consequent suspicions that male clergy were incapable of a "vigorous, manly life." Still, Higginson was heartened by burly preachers like Lyman Beecher and by stories like that of the pugilist minister who reportedly took down an assailant on Broadway. "Our American saintship," he predicted, "is beginning to have a body to it." But if that re-embodiment were to materialize, children must have plenty of outdoor exercise, and adults must "learn to regard mental precocity as a disaster to be shunned, instead of a glory to be coveted."

Theologically, Higginson was considerably more liberal than Theodore Roosevelt senior, but otherwise his "muscular Christianity" aptly described Roosevelt's father. "Thee" Roosevelt was a tall, good-looking, broad-shouldered, and athletic man, known for galloping his horse through Central Park and for taking his children on long outdoor adventures that exhausted them but not, apparently, him. Every night he read the Bible, brought to him by his namesake, "Teedie." On weekday mornings, Thee led his family through prayers, and every Sunday he shepherded them to church, after which the children were expected to recount the main points of the sermon. He was a morally exacting but loving father, a benevolent philanthropist, a rugged outdoorsman, and (until the cancer that cut short his life) the picture of health.[54]

In his autobiography, Theodore Roosevelt junior would remember his father as "the best man I ever knew."[55] But muscular Christianity was hard on a boy not blessed with a strong constitution. Young Teedie was almost constantly sick and, almost as bad, displayed just the kind of mental precocity Higginson had warned against. The medical term for this condition was neurasthenia, more commonly known as over-civilization. First identified by New York neurologist George Beard, neurasthenia was a kind of anxiety, depression, and lassitude to which women, city dwellers, and the wealthy were especially susceptible.

Suspecting that Teedie might have this condition, Thee brought his son to Beard's colleague Dr. A. D. Rockwell. Rockwell's impression, as his log recorded, was that twelve-year-old Teedie was "a bright and precocious boy." Later he told Beard, "the little fellow ought to make his mark in the world; but the difficulty is, he has a rich father."[56] Evidently Rockwell prescribed fresh air and exercise, and Thee agreed. "Theodore," he said sternly, "you have the mind but not the body, and without the help of the body the mind cannot go as far as it should. You must make your body."[57] As his sister Corinne recalled, Teedie assented with a grim nod and soon embarked on a lifelong program of strenuous outdoor activity.

Ultimately, Thee's religiosity seems to have had more impact on Teedie's muscularity than on his faith. Theodore junior would always attend the Dutch Reformed Church, his father's denomination, but he was perfectly content for his wife to take their children to the Episcopalians.[58] And although he advised his fellow Americans to attend church regularly, it was for the sake of morality rather than piety. The man who goes to church "may not hear a good sermon," Roosevelt once wrote, but he will probably hear "a sermon by a good man, with a good wife." In any case, going to church was far better than "dawdling around the house half-dressed" reading the Sunday newspaper.[59]

Even in his ethics, however, it is hard to argue that Roosevelt accepted Christianity, for he explicitly rejected the tenet of universal love. That was the target of his 1894 article "True Americanism," in which he contended that patriotism, not altruism, was the highest good. Prudently, he did not identify his opponents as Christian. Instead he called them "philosophers" and treated them to a thorough masculinist pummeling. The proponents of universal love were "silly" and "flaccid" "weaklings," "over-civilized," "over-sensitive," "over-refined," and lacking in "hardihood and manly courage."[60] Similarly, Roosevelt's 1899 speech "The Strenuous Life," which made the case for American territorial expansion, refrained from targeting William Jennings Bryan, then the nation's leading anti-imperialist. Bryan was an evangelical Presbyterian and an opponent of the theory of evolution, which Roosevelt held as gospel truth. But rather than criticize Bryan or Christianity, Roosevelt derided anti-imperialists as "cowards" and "weaklings" who were hampered by "over-civilization" and a "silly, mock humanitarianism," and who "shrank" from their "duties to the nation and the race."[61]

While casting his critique of Christianity in gendered terms, Roosevelt cast his support of Christianity in racial terms. In a 1909 speech to Christian missionaries, he extolled the importance of bringing Christianity into "the darker corners of the earth."[62] Missionaries, he assured his audience, would continue to play an important role in America's imperial age, but for reasons rather different from those they might have expected. Christianity enhanced "material well being" and "orderly individual liberty," contributed to the "growth of intelligence," and supported "equal justice in the administration of law." The missionaries might have noticed that none of those accomplishments had much to do with Christian faith. Even the title of the speech erased religion: it was "The Expansion of the White Races," not "The Expansion of Christianity."

Ultimately, however, Roosevelt's most persistent concern about Christianity coincided with the most persistent concern of his personal life: masculinity. Although as a young man he'd managed to accumulate some muscle mass, he was still considered effeminate when he graduated from college. In January 1882, when he took his first elected office, he was publicly ridiculed as a "weakling," "Jane-Dandy," "Oscar Wilde," "Punkin' Lilly," and "the exquisite Mr. Roosevelt."[63] By the summer of 1883 he found himself, once again, in what he described as a "nightmare" of asthma and cholera.[64] By September, the specter of weakness and effeminacy drove him to Dakota Territory, looking "to shoot a buffalo while there were still buffalo left to shoot."[65]

In his autobiography, Roosevelt would recall that when his father died, in 1878, he found comfort only in "the Lord Jesus Christ."[66] But in February 1884, when his wife and mother died on the same day, his solace was not indoor piety but outdoor activity. Leaving his infant daughter in the care of his sister, Roosevelt returned to his newly acquired ranches in the Dakotas and threw himself into hunting, riding, and herding cattle. The cure appeared to take, as the newspapers reported and as Roosevelt publicized with a carefully staged photo of himself decked out as a cowboy. Before long, the young man who'd left New York pale, sickly, and bereaved could reintroduce himself to eastern society as a muscled, suntanned cowboy.[67] He had restored, if not actual health, at least its appearance, and had created a personal identity, ethos, and life story that had little to do with Christianity but would become the mythology of American nationalism at the turn of the twentieth century.

The Religious Development of Black Elk

In 2013, Charlotte Black Elk wrote that "all the songs of the universe are located in the Black Hills."[68] One hundred forty years earlier, during his Great Vision, her great-grandfather had heard those songs. Everything sang—horses, birds, creeks, even the leaves on trees—and when they heard those songs, no being on earth could keep from dancing.

But what the Grandfathers revealed to young Black Elk was not entirely joyful. They showed the boy the troubles that awaited his people and conferred on him gifts of healing, prophecy, and warfare that would help in those difficult times. It was Black Elk's responsibility to use those gifts and also, one day, to return to the Black Hills and perform rituals that would benefit the whole earth. If he would do these things, they promised, the sacred tree would blossom again and the sacred hoop would be restored.[69]

His parents were astonished when Black Elk awoke from his twelve-day coma. Nonetheless, his boyhood went on more or less as normal for the next several years because, among the Lakota, it was not strange for a person to have visions. What was strange was the protracted assault upon the Black Hills after the discovery of gold. In those years, Black Elk continued to have inklings of spiritual power, but they did not really catch up with him until 1880, when his family was returning from Canada, where they'd fled after the disaster of 1877. On the journey home, he began to hear the insistent, terrifying voices of Thunder Beings (spirits of the sky) demanding that he fulfill his vision. At seventeen, at his father's urging, Black Elk finally confided these experiences to a medicine man, who told him what he was to do.

The medicine man explained that this Great Vision demanded to be enacted, piece by piece, in a series of spectacular ceremonies.[70] Most of the ceremonies centered on animals—horse, elk, and buffalo—who had appeared prominently in the vision and whose well-being was bound up with that of the Lakota people. The whole community took part, with everyone dressing, painting, singing, and dancing as Black Elk instructed. Even the natural world took part. Horses, led into dance-like movements, actually began to dance, and the Thunder Beings, called upon by Black Elk, roared and hailed in reply. The ceremonies activated Black Elk's powers as a medicine man, and soon he was a well-known and well-respected figure at Pine Ridge.

Looking back on the early 1880s, Black Elk would say that "up to this time, we had been living in accordance with the old religion and we had plenty and things were good for us."[71] But even while the gifts promised by the vision were being awakened, the trouble it forewarned was coming to pass. One calamity was the near extinction of buffalo, who occupied a central place in Lakota culture. Because they were central to his vision, Black Elk performed a ceremony for them, hoping that the herds would be restored. But this was not to happen in his lifetime. Instead, within two years, Roosevelt would arrive at the end of a long stream of white hunters, hoping "to shoot a buffalo while there were still buffalo left to shoot."

Along with their land and buffalo, the spiritual practices of the Lakota were under assault. After 1868, when President Ulysses Grant put missionaries in charge of Indian reservations, most Native people had joined a Christian church.[72] Although Native people did not necessarily see their traditional practices as incompatible with Christianity, missionaries usually did, so they objected strenuously to Black Elk's medicine practice. On one occasion, a Catholic priest interrupted one of Black Elk's healing ceremonies and took away his sacred objects. The old ways were not easily defeated; the patient was healed despite the priest's interference, and not long thereafter the priest fell off his horse and died.[73] But pressure against traditional practices intensified greatly in 1883 after secretary of the interior Henry Teller empowered the Bureau of Indian

Affairs to take action against "conjurers" and "imposters"—in other words, people like Black Elk. Not just traditional healing practices but the Sun Dance, Ghost Dance, peyote ceremony, and all other "heathenish rites and customs" were proscribed on pain of imprisonment or deprivation of rations.[74]

Although Black Elk was apparently not subjected to those punishments, the sight of his people starved, demoralized, and confined to reservations brought him to a spiritual crisis. In his effort to explain these sufferings, he wavered between blaming the people for not adhering to the old ways and finding fault with the old ways themselves. In the past, he said, the Lakota "had a way of living, but it was not the way that we were living [anymore]." He became "disgusted with the wrong road my people were going" yet couldn't persuade them to change. Eventually he began to wonder whether "the white man's ways were better." If so, "I would like to see my people live that way."[75]

To investigate this alternative path, Black Elk felt he had to experience the white man's world. The opportunity arose in 1886, when he was invited to travel to Europe with Buffalo Bill's Wild West Show. As a condition of employment, Buffalo Bill required that all Indians convert to Christianity, so by the time Black Elk arrived in Europe, he was an Episcopalian. While this conversion was clearly transactional, Black Elk's interest in the Christian God was sincere. As he'd later comment, white people's ideas about God were the *only* thing he found interesting about them.[76] Apart from their God, he found many ways of the white man "hard to endure." Especially startling to him was the fact that in Europe, kinship and place meant so little. One's fate depended only on citizenship: "Whoever has no country will die in the wilderness." Traveling around Europe, he took solace in the natural world—"that which makes me happy is always land."[77] Even so, Europe was not where he belonged. "I was in a strange land," he later explained; it was "not the place nor the habits or religion that the spirits had assigned me." He was not only out of place in Europe but also, in a sense, out of time. "At that time, the wilds were vanishing and it seemed the spirits altogether forgot me." As he traveled around Europe, Black Elk "felt almost like a dead man," and this was not just a subjective state. As he later described it, "I actually was dead at this time, that's all."[78]

One morning in 1889, this liminal state manifested itself to those around him, bringing Black Elk's time in Europe to a dramatic end. He was in Paris, dressed in "a white man's clothes" and breakfasting with his white girlfriend and her family, when suddenly he pitched over backwards. He then entered a state much like that he'd experienced during his Great Vision, when his spirit had left his body to seek the Black Hills. This time, though, the journey took him much farther, crossing an entire ocean and continent. After a day in this state, Black Elk awoke under the eyes of his worried hosts, who were relieved to learn that he would not need the coffin they had kindly procured for him.[79]

With his body and spirit together again, Black Elk headed home for real. On arriving there, he found his powers restored but his people and their lands shockingly depleted. Famine had made the people "poor and pitiful," and what remained of the Great Sioux Reservation had been hacked into five much smaller parcels. One of them was the Pine Ridge Reservation, now surrounded by the newly established states of North and South Dakota. No reservation included the Black Hills, which seemed irretrievably lost. Those living on reservations needed special permission to leave, and the reservations themselves were being broken up under the Dawes Act, which had taken effect during Black Elk's absence. Any Indian who accepted an allotment could become a U.S. citizen—provided he or she adopted "the habits of civilized life" and lived "separate and apart" from the tribe.[80] It was now beyond denial that the U.S. government intended to terminate the cultures, economies, and polities of First Nations.

Black Elk never did agree to "live separate and apart" from his tribe, nor did he detach his spirit from the Black Hills. Eventually, however, he accepted an allotment near Wounded Knee. And it was there, just a few months after his return from Europe and with a palpable sense of his world ending, that he joined the Ghost Dance movement.

The Religion of Americanism

Three months after young Black Elk took a scalp at Little Big Horn, Theodore Roosevelt headed to Harvard. There he absorbed, among other things, the ideology that came to be called social

Darwinism. From boyhood, Teedie had considered himself a naturalist; since age fourteen, when he read *The Origin of Species*, he'd been thoroughly convinced that the theory of evolution was true—as he would say later, an "established doctrine."[81] But he wondered how the tooth-and-claw story of evolution could be reconciled with Christian morality. Certain species succeeded; others did not. Within the human species, it seemed clear that whites had achieved supremacy over most nonwhites. In America they had killed or expelled Indians, and even after Emancipation, they continued to thoroughly dominate blacks. All of this was true, but was it right? From his studies at Harvard and his Dakota experiences soon thereafter, Roosevelt came up with an answer to that question, and around that answer constructed an Americanism in which being white was more important than being Christian.

Until the mid-nineteenth century, most Euro-Americans explained their national history in theological terms. In ancient times, God had given the Promised Land to the Israelites; in modern times, God had constituted a new chosen people and given them America. Obligations followed from being chosen, but God's choice was not based on human merit—a point hammered home with special force by Calvin's doctrine of predestination. By Roosevelt's time, however, educated white men were rebelling against this orthodoxy for a host of reasons, including its pessimism about human nature, its denial of human freedom, its static view of society, and its preference for revelation over scientific knowledge. Above all, these men wanted to think of history as a meritocracy in which whites had deservedly reached the top of the evolutionary ladder.

For geologist Nathaniel Shaler, one of Roosevelt's professors, one could reconcile evolution with Christianity by leavening the mixture with other ideas.[82] One was the Lamarckian theory that adaptive traits could be developed by one generation and passed on to the next. Darwin had discredited that theory, but for Shaler and others it remained a moral balm, allowing them to imagine evolutionary advancement as a reward for industry and intelligence rather than just the work of death and dumb luck. A second idea was that humans were divided into "races" that differed not just in phenotype but in the caliber of their morality and civilization. This was not a new idea, but thinkers like Francis Galton (half-cousin of Darwin) used it to transform evolution from a descriptive theory to a pre-scriptive one. Darwin believed that natural selection did not imply progress, only survival. But in the hands of the social Darwinists, evolution was both a story of progress and a program, later called eugenics, for improving the human species by racial engineering.

Roosevelt, like Shaler, thought it beyond question that the "Teu-tonic" or white race was the highest of the Western civilizations.[83] He too thought of races as bio-cultural collectives, each of which succeeded or failed on its merits. Also like Shaler, Roosevelt clung to the theory that acquired traits could be inherited; in 1894 he wrote that opposing views were "hardly worth serious refutation."[84] But more than Shaler, Roosevelt believed that the mixing of certain ra-cial groups—for example, Native Americans and whites—could be hygienically beneficial. Like Shaler and Galton, he became a propo-nent of eugenics, but only in what he considered its positive form. Rather than discouraging the propagation of nonwhites, he would campaign for raising the birth rate among native-born whites, whose declining numbers were courting "race suicide."[85] And unlike Shaler, for whom the highest civilization was distinguished by its ethic of universal love, for Roosevelt the highest civilization was America, and the love of that country was his highest good.

But what shaped his Americanism most decisively, and distin-guished it most sharply from Christianity, was Roosevelt's distaste for over-civilization. Evolution required certain natural conditions: rug-ged, uncultivated land, wild animals, and life-threatening enemies. Absent those conditions, he felt, a species stopped advancing and slipped into decline. That had been his own childhood condition, and to repair it he'd gone to the Dakota Territory. Over-civilization was also the prequel to American history as spun out in *The Winning of the West*. In Roosevelt's telling, Americans had descended from what he variously described as the "Teutonic," "English-speaking," or "white" races of Europe, where they had been left with no new lands to conquer and no more barbarians to subdue. Not needing to unite against external enemies, European whites had become divided by language, region, and religion. Their civilizations lay fallow and in danger of decline.[86]

The New World was therefore a great evolutionary boon for whites. It set before them a vast continent that they'd have to cultivate from scratch, filled with game to hunt and fierce savages to fight. Under these conditions, their Old World differences melted away, and the white people of Europe became a single robust nation—"the American race."[87] Just as Roosevelt had "made his body," so Euro-Americans had made themselves. They had won their land, not stolen it or been handed it. And in the process of making the land their own, they also had remade themselves—their language, physiques, and manners—to fit it. As Frederick Jackson Turner would express it in a renowned 1893 paper, first "the wilderness masters the colonist" but eventually "the colonist masters the wilderness." At the start of this process, wrote Turner, the European dresses like an Indian, lives in Indian dwellings, plants Indian corn, and even "shouts the war cry and takes the scalp in orthodox Indian fashion." But in time, the frontier would be conquered and closed, and the colonist would have become an American.[88]

For Roosevelt, the hero of this story was the quintessentially American character, the frontiersman—a character who had much in common with Indians yet was their implacable enemy. The frontiersman had the "stern, rough" virtues: he was strong, brave, tenacious, straightforward, and fair dealing.[89] Dishonesty and capricious violence were beneath him, but he would never turn the other cheek. As described by Roosevelt, he came off as something of a brute—often lawless, usually without family, and always ready to kill.[90] His ethic, said Roosevelt, "laid slight stress on pity, truth, or mercy." If he read his Bible, it was only the Old Testament, and mainly to take inspiration from accounts of the Israelites slaughtering the Canaanites. For what were the abominations of the Canaanites when compared with "the abominations of the red savages whose lands they, another chosen people, were set to inherit?"[91] The battle for America, however "miserable and inhuman," was "the most ultimately righteous of all wars"—because it was "war with savages."[92]

In Roosevelt's account, both whites and Indians committed atrocities, but this was out of character only for whites. "Many of the frontiersmen are brutal, reckless, and overbearing," he wrote in his first book on the Dakotas, "but most of the Indians are treacherous, revengeful and fiendishly cruel."[93] "I suppose I should be ashamed," he told a New York audience in 1886, "to say that I take the western view of the Indian. . . . I don't go so far as to think that the only good

Indians are dead Indians," he continued, but "I believe nine out of every ten are," and (going for a laugh) "I shouldn't like to inquire too closely into the case of the tenth."[94] Even when recounting the massacre of the pacifist Lenape, he cautioned readers not to issue "too severe a judgment" on the whites, considering the "extraordinary conditions of life on the frontier." Whites there knew the Indian not as "a creature of romance" but "for what he was"—"filthy, cruel, lecherous, and faithless," a "squalid and contemptible creature," unsurpassed throughout the world for "ferocity, cunning, and bloodthirsty cruelty."[95]

As president, Roosevelt would come to regret how Indians were being treated, and even rue some of his previous statements. In 1903, when he learned that Indian children were being starved at some mission schools, that Indian lands were being taken by whites, and that reservation conditions were horrific, he wrote that he was "heartbroken" and "indignant."[96] The same year, he asked William Round not to publish an 1885 letter in which he'd characterized the Plains Indians as thieves and murderers—a characterization, Roosevelt explained, that was no longer true, although it had been true when he wrote it.[97] Nonetheless, Roosevelt considered the demise of Native Americans to be their own fault. When he first went to Dakota Territory, he admitted that it was sad to see dozens of tribes "that have died out, almost before our eyes," but this was the sentence of evolutionary justice.[98] "The doctrine seems merciless," he wrote, "and so it is, but it is just and rational for all of that." Each Indian should be given a plot of land, as the Dawes policy provided, but if he failed to wrest a living from that land, then like the lazy white person, the Indian would deserve to "perish from the earth he cumbers."[99]

This constellation of social Darwinism, moralism, and white supremacy enabled Roosevelt to reconcile the miserable conditions of most Indians' lives with his firm commitment to judging individuals on their merits. In his Dakota days, Roosevelt was proud to report, he had treated Indian and white hands on his ranches exactly the same, and as president he assured Indian children that "the fundamental doctrine of our government" was the equitable treatment of individuals.[100] Yet he fully expected that the fair treatment of individuals would ratify the unequal standing of races, because nonwhites, encumbered by inferior racial constitutions, would not accomplish as much as whites and therefore would deserve worse outcomes.[101] This rationale was already worked out in Roosevelt's 1892 report on reservations, where he cautioned Indian schools against encouraging their students to reach beyond a life of manual labor. A rare Indian boy might have the right stuff to be a doctor or lawyer, Roosevelt allowed, but most did not, and it was "cruel" to make them think otherwise.

What really improved an Indian child's prospects, Roosevelt observed, was having a white parent. Of course, this formula equated success with the disappearance of "the Indian race." That was what Roosevelt had forecast since his Dakota days, and it was the framework for his (and virtually all) Indian policy.[102] At times, he felt sorrowful about this, and where he recognized abuses he demanded they be addressed. But like most Euro-Americans, he did not consider the decline of Indian populations unjust in itself, any more than he considered the loss of Indian lands to be theft. These were outcomes determined by natural law, which it was the solemn duty of whites to administer. By the time of Roosevelt's presidency, they also were the dictates of federal law, which in 1898 began to mandate the termination of tribal governments and the dissolution of reservation lands.[103]

At bottom, then, Roosevelt's Americanism was a racial affiliation. The true American was a certain kind of person, adapted to a certain environment and organically bound to a certain body politic. To be an American was a high evolutionary achievement, accessible only to people already possessed of advanced civilization and thus (oddly) beyond the ken of people who had survived in the American landscape for millennia. There is no doubt that this Americanism was Roosevelt's foundation—his mythos and ethos, the highest good of his own life and, in his mind, the culmination of history. Yet, crucially, he did not think of Americanism as religion. When "religion" came to mind, he thought in terms of walls and limits, but when Americanism came to mind, he imagined a people of infinite capacity and a territory with no fixed boundaries.

Roosevelt's separationism, therefore, had different motivations from those of the Framers. He did not have Jefferson's reverence for individual conscience or Madison's solicitude for personal faith. He wasn't worried about limiting the power of government, his view of which was notoriously expansive. Because he held that duties were far more important than rights, he wasn't even particularly concerned for religious liberty.[104] Instead, the overriding objective of his separationism was to establish Americanism as the nation's foundation. Religion was optional, but Americanism was not.

Describing the American ethos in *The Winning of the West*, Roosevelt wrote, "We regard as peculiarly American the complete severance of church and state."[105] In his article "True Americanism," he proclaimed that it was "urgently necessary" to regulate immigration so as to "keep out races that do not assimilate readily to our own." But in the same article he contended that Catholics and Jews could be Americanized, provided they ceased "cling[ing] to the speech, the customs, the ways of life, and the habits of thought of the Old World." Immigrants must understand that "we exact full religious toleration and the complete separation of Church and State."[106] Otherwise, they'd best return to their home country.

For white immigrants, the combination of Americanism and separationism had mixed implications. They had to relinquish Old

Nicholas Black Elk teaches with a rosary, 1940s. Marquette University Archives, Bureau of Catholic Indian Missions Records, ID MUA_HRM RCIS_00040. Photo courtesy of Marquette University Archives and Red Cloud Indian School.

Nicholas Black Elk in chief's regalia, 1937. Marquette University Archives, Bureau of Catholic Indian Missions Records, ID 02187. Photo courtesy of Marquette University Archives and Red Cloud Indian School.

World religious loyalties and antipathies, but by doing so they secured membership in the American nation. For Native people, however, neither Americanism nor separationism had an upside. Despite their having adapted to the American landscape longer than any other people, Roosevelt thought indigenous people largely incapable of Americanizing. His separationism, so strict on other issues, did not preclude government support for missionary schools on reservations, but his Americanism precluded any reestablishment of Native spiritual practices, even on their ancestral lands. Judging from his response to the Ghost Dance religion, he was prepared to suppress that kind of religion with military force.

Black Elk and the Problem of "Religion"

In the decade after the Ghost Dance, Black Elk struggled with increasing difficulty to fulfill the Great Vision of his youth. He still practiced as a healer, but the Jesuits interrupted his ceremonies and denounced him as "Satan." He contemplated taking up his powers as a warrior but was deterred by the prospect of women and children being killed. Nor could he, with the Black Hills lost and the Lakota people virtually incarcerated on reservations, return to the site of his vision to complete his ceremonial duties. So, on December 6, 1904, Black Elk converted to Roman Catholicism, was given the name Nicholas, and soon became a Catholic catechist.[107] Whatever else this conversion may have meant, it was at least a way he could spiritually serve his people, most of whom by then had become either Protestant or Catholic Christians. But Nicholas Black Elk's conversion transformed religion into a major question that others would have about him, and that question would remain unsettled even after his death.

Historically, as we have seen, "religion" began as a concern of Euro-Christians. It was they who insisted that each person have one and only one religion, and who insisted on knowing what that religion was. Based on those assumptions, some Catholic scholars have held that Nick Black Elk was a true and contented Catholic but was "bicultural"—the word "culture" evidently resolving the theological problem that might be raised had Black Elk possessed two "religions."[108] Others—for example, Black Elk's son Ben—suggested that in old age his father regretted converting to Catholicism and thought that his people might have done better to keep the Lakota religion.[109] Like many Native people, Black Elk may have attempted to synthesize Lakota religion and Catholicism, creating what Clyde Holler called a "theological innovation."[110] Being a lifelong seeker, he probably saw things differently at different moments in his life.

Moreover, as we have seen, it is misleading to ask what somebody's "religion" is, because the definition of religion changes depending on who is asking and who is authorized to answer. When it came to defining Catholicism, Black Elk had a high status among Lakota people but not among the Jesuits, who saw themselves as the keepers of orthodoxy. When it came to defining Lakota religion, he was given tremendous authority by Euro-Americans but less by Lakota people, who respected him as one spiritual leader among many. Still less was he an authority on the entire panoply of Native American religions, although many Euro-Americans and some Native Americans later raised him to that status.[111]

The publication, in 1932, of *Black Elk Speaks* by poet John Neihardt further complicated the question of Nick Black Elk's religion. Neihardt had arrived at Pine Ridge two years earlier, seeking both personal insight and material for his *Cycle of the West*. But after he got to know Black Elk, Neihardt decided that this one man's story was of such great interest as to deserve its own volume. Black Elk agreed to tell Neihardt the story of his life through the Wounded Knee massacre. The stenographic transcripts of those interviews, published by anthropologist Raymond DeMallie, are the main published source of Black Elk's words, but there remains much distance between the man and the printed sources. Because Black Elk spoke in Lakota, his words were first translated into the idiomatic "Indian English," spoken by his son Ben.[112] This was then transcribed in shorthand and typed in regular English by Neihardt's daughters.

As for *Black Elk Speaks* itself, it was Neihardt's own poetic creation, based on but not limited by the words of Black Elk. Neihardt himself stated this in his preface to the book, which nonetheless has been read for generations as faithfully representing not only Black Elk but the Lakota people and even all Native Americans. Most influentially, *Black Elk Speaks* has been read as if it revealed the essence of "religion"—perennial truths supposedly embedded in nature and absorbed into humanity's collective unconscious. While the book's literary value is widely recognized, whether Neihardt did full justice to Black Elk's story has been the subject of exhaustive and perhaps irresolvable debate.[113] On a couple of critical points, however, there is something of a consensus: first, that Neihardt assimilated Black Elk's story to the form of tragedy; and second, that Neihardt deliberately elided Black Elk's Christianity.

The sense of tragedy that suffuses the book was set in stone by its postscript, where Neihardt has Black Elk lamenting to the Grandfathers that "I am a pitiful old man who has done nothing" and "the sacred tree has never bloomed."[114] This closing soliloquy—

really an elegy, DeMallie says—was Neihardt's creation.[115] Black Elk did offer prayers on Harney Peak in Neihardt's presence, and he may well have wept, because weeping is a common feature of Lakota prayer. He also may have felt that he failed to fulfill the demands of his vision, and perhaps he wondered whether this explained, at least in part, the suffering of his people. None of that obviates the fact that despite everything, Black Elk and his people had survived. As DeMallie pointed out, Neihardt's "sense of irreversible tragedy" is incongruent with Lakota culture, in which "what once was, is likely to be again."[116] Neihardt may have genuinely believed that Black Elk's last and dearest wish was that his "message" be a gift for non-Indians.[117] But by framing the story as a tragedy that left behind only a "message," Neihardt (wittingly or not) relieved non-Native people of any obligation to Native people in the present. Instead, his book offered exculpation in return for nothing but a sorrowful backward glance.

The second point of critical consensus is that by failing to acknowledge Black Elk's Christian conversion, Neihardt misrepresented not only one man's spiritual life but the adaptability of Native cultures generally. It is true that the narrative ends just after the Wounded Knee massacre, well before Black Elk became a Catholic. But he had become Episcopalian in 1886 and had told Neihardt so. Not even that first conversion appears in *Black Elk Speaks*, no doubt because it would have complicated the simple, nostalgic Indian spirituality that Neihardt conjured up for non-Native consumption. Nor did Neihardt have to end the story at Wounded Knee. This was a choice, and it revealed that Neihardt, or his anticipated audience, preferred to think of Lakota history as ending in 1890.

As for Nick Black Elk himself, even before he met Neihardt he had engaged in much soul-searching on the question of religion, no doubt with the encouragement of his Jesuit mentors. In a 1911 letter to the *Catholic Herald*, he criticized Lakota people who professed Catholicism yet continued to live "the old ways." A life that is "split in two," he warned, "does not please God."[118] When Neihardt came on the scene two decades later, the Jesuits had not changed their view. Nor had the federal government, which still outlawed Native ceremonies. Strangely, however, Native practices could be permitted and even compensated when they were construed as art, education, entertainment, research material, or museum artifacts. When he met Neihardt, Black Elk had a part-time job performing bits of Lakota ceremonies for tourists. (Even Roosevelt had attended a public quasi-performance of the Hopi Snake Dance in 1913, when the dance was still prohibited on Hopi reservations.)[119] One might say that until 1934, when the Dawes-era restrictions were lifted, Indian practices were prohibited *only* when they had the seriousness of religion.

But Neihardt's view was different. Even if he separated Native spirituality from Native lives, he at least took it seriously, presenting Black Elk as a true mystic and healer. Unfortunately, that only raised more hackles among the Jesuits at Pine Ridge. They pressured Nicholas to renounce the book, and when he had a near-fatal accident, may have threatened to deny him last rites. After he recovered, Nicholas agreed to dictate a letter distancing himself from *Black Elk Speaks*. "For thirty years, I have lived very differently than the white man [Neihardt] told about me," he wrote. He went on to say that "the Indian religion of long ago did not benefit mankind," that the Sun Dance and Ghost Dance were performed "only for glory," and that medicine men (presumably including himself) had operated mainly for honor and gifts. Still, he did not call the old ways false or Satanic, as his Jesuit mentors might have preferred. Catholicism was "*better* than the Sun Dance or the Ghost Dance," and he himself "had become *better*" (emphasis mine) by converting. Insightfully, he compared his becoming Catholic to the New Testament story about Paul converting to Christianity from Judaism. Just as Christianity had fulfilled Judaism without negating it, so Lakota religion might be thought of as fulfilled but not negated by Catholicism.[120]

Black Elk once told Neihardt that long before the whites came, the Great Spirit "had given us a religion." This was in the 1930s, when Black Elk had learned the significance the word "religion" held for whites. Drawing on the authority of that word, he described the old religion as requiring, above all, love for every living being. Looking back, Black Elk could only conclude that whites did not reciprocate that love. Indians had tried "to love [whites] as we did our selves," but it had been a mistake. "On account of this we are now in misery."[121] Neihardt, according to his daughter, then asked the obvious question: Why, given all this, did Black Elk belong to a white man's church? "Because my children have to live in this world," Black Elk replied.[122]

Playing Indian

It took days of pursuit through rain and cold and mud before Roosevelt got his buffalo. When he completed the kill, in September 1883, his pleasure was so intense as to astonish even his guide, Joe Ferris. As Ferris recalled, Roosevelt jumped ecstatically from foot to foot, performing what looked like an "Indian war dance."[123]

As far as Roosevelt could tell, there were hardly any buffalo left in the region, and hardly any Indians either. In his Dakota period, Roosevelt considered the disappearance of the buffalo a "veritable tragedy for the animal world" as well as a misfortune for hunters. But it was crucial to the "advancement of white civilization in the West" because only when the buffalo were gone could Indians be confined to reservations and compelled to "abandon their savage way of life."[124]

Yet Roosevelt strove not only to terminate Native cultures but also to make them his own. This symbolic ingestion of Native culture, or what Native American historian Philip Deloria called "playing Indian," is a deeply Euro-American tradition. Famously, the Sons of Liberty pretended to be Mohawks while dumping British tea into Boston Harbor. After the Revolution, Euro-American patriotism was often expressed by membership in a Tammany Society, named after a Delaware chief called Tamanend (or "St. Tammany"). Tammany Societies admitted only white men, but their members took Indian names, performed supposed Indian ceremonies, and selected their own "sachems." In the nineteenth century, Tammany Societies were succeeded by the Improved Order of Red Men (IORM), which also confined its membership to white men. In the late nineteenth century came children's organizations, such as the Camp Fire Girls, Boy Scouts, and Girl Scouts, which provided wilderness adventures imbued with Native American ambience— imitation Indian headdresses, totem poles, and the like.[125] Some forms of "playing Indian" have gone out of style; the IORM, for example, is nearly defunct. But on the whole, Euro-Americans have felt Indian play to be more natural than odd, which bespeaks the

depth to which their nationalism has symbolically ingested indigenous America.

Roosevelt's polarized attitudes toward Indians tracked those of
other Euro-Americans. Up close, when fighting Native people for
land and resources, they have often expressed violently racist attitudes; at a distance, when Native people represent no real threat,
regret and nostalgia take over.[126] Despite his ridicule of what he
called "Indian enthusiasm," Theodore Roosevelt was listed as a no-
table member by the Improved Order of Red Men.[127] "Sagamore,"
an Algonquian word for chief and a vice presidential office in the
IORM, was adopted by Roosevelt as the name for his family home,
Sagamore Hill. He deliberately chose several part-Indians for his
Rough Riders troop, suggesting that this tableau of America would
have felt incomplete to him without an Indian presence. Most
strikingly, he included a half dozen Indians on horseback in his
1905 Inaugural Parade, followed by 350 students from the Carlisle
Indian Industrial School. At his moment of political triumph,
Roosevelt wanted to show that Indians belonged to the American
history he had so grandly narrated.[128] Riding down Pennsylvania
Avenue with stately dignity, they seemed to assure the non-Native
crowd that this land had been given to them with the blessing of its
oldest inhabitants.

More than anything else he did or said, it was Roosevelt's conservation program that enabled the symbolic ingestion of Native
cultures. Conservation is, of course, a noble cause, and when Roosevelt saw that all the land in the United States was being gobbled
up by private interests, he wisely wanted to put a curb on it.[129] His
method was to set aside more public lands than had any previous
president. But there was no room in this plan for the First Nations,
and no regard for the fact that all the lands designated as "public"
were their ancestral homes. Also forgotten was that certain national
parks, such as the Black Hills, had been vouchsafed to tribes by
treaties that were later broken. Nor did Roosevelt worry about the
reservation lands being lost by the Dawes policy of making "excess"
land available for private sale. Far from avoiding these outcomes,
Roosevelt incorporated them into his program to divide all U.S.
lands into two types—either private and settled or public and unsettled. Reservations, which were neither, literally had no place.

On public lands, Roosevelt hoped, citizens would rediscover the beauty and reenact the challenges of wilderness life. In other words, they would become as if native to America, although in practice this required the displacement of actual Native people. In an earlier period, Euro-Americans had pictured their land as a restored Eden where animals and peaceful Natives mingled in a single bucolic scene. But with the closing of the frontier, Euro-Americans began to long for "pristine"—meaning uninhabited—wilderness.[130] In 1896 the Supreme Court endorsed this desire by rescinding the right of Native people to hunt and fish in areas "destined to be settled by the white man."[131] As Black Elk would lament in 1931, Native people and animals were each consigned to their own "little islands," separately caged prisoners in what once had been their home.

Roosevelt's conservation program displayed the same logic— wild lands and wild animals were to be lovingly preserved, but "wild Indians" had to be eradicated. In 1883, when he arrived to "shoot a buffalo while there were still buffalo left to shoot," he was ready to accept the buffalo's extinction as the only way to terminate Plains Indian culture. But only four years later, with "the Indian problem" apparently resolved, he and other gentleman hunters grew concerned about preserving the game they wished to hunt. In 1887, Roosevelt co-founded the Boone and Crocket Club to encourage hunters to accept voluntary self-restraints ("fair chase rules") and to urge federal action on behalf of conservation. As president, he created the Sully Hills National Preserve for buffalo in North Dakota. Although the preserve directly abutted the Spirit Lake Reservation, Indians had no access to these buffalo. Indeed, hunting by Indians was one of the dangers against which the buffalo were to be protected.

President Roosevelt's land policies were felt in Black Elk's region, too. At Pine Ridge, Roosevelt cut a forty-nine-square-mile corner off the reservation to attract homesteaders, but the area proved more enticing to liquor merchants.[132] To make the natural beauty of the Hills available to Euro-Americans, he created the Wind Cave National Park and Devil's Tower National Monument—each a sacred site for particular tribes. Roosevelt's impression on the region kept expanding even after his death, in 1919. In

North Dakota a national park would be created in his name, and in South Dakota, his would be the fourth and final visage chiseled into Mount Rushmore.

Worlds

Nick Black Elk outlived Theodore Roosevelt by thirty-one years and, at Mount Rushmore, had another occasion to encounter him, although Roosevelt was now in stone and Black Elk was stone blind. But Black Elk was fully aware of what was going on in the twelve years it took to carve four presidents into the mountain. He probably participated in the initial dedication of the site and may have been the unnamed "Sioux chief" mentioned in a newspaper account of the event. According to Ben Black Elk, his father also partook in the solemnities surrounding the 1934 unveiling of Jefferson. Dressed in full ceremonial garb, Black Elk and a few guests were carried up in a little tram to Jefferson's gigantic countenance. As Ben recalled, his father was at first afraid even to sing. But once at the summit, he prayed at length to the Grandfathers that the workers would remain safe and, somewhat cryptically, that the greatness of the men on the mountain would be preserved "through changes of nations and races."[133]

Beginning in 1935, Black Elk also became a star attraction in the "Indian Camp" that appeared each spring and summer on the road from Rapid City to Mount Rushmore. Having picked up a bit of showmanship from his stint with Buffalo Bill, he was suited for the role of "Chief Black Elk." He may have hoped that, for some whites, his presentations of Lakota ceremonies were educational rather than just entertaining; the Indian Camp's literature actually encouraged tourists to read *Black Elk Speaks* before they arrived.[134] Whatever other motivations may have been at play, certainly Black Elk and his family badly needed the income. As Gutzon Borglum, the sculptor who designed Mount Rushmore, wrote to President Hoover in 1931, 75 percent of the Pine Ridge Lakota were starving.[135]

For the Euro-Americans who conceived it, the Mount Rushmore monument was sacred in several senses. It was a "shrine to democracy" and a pilgrimage site for the renewal of patriotism. The monument also attracted money—arguably, another sacred value to Euro-Americans. In the 1870s, the Black Hills had literally been a gold mine, but by the twentieth century most of its mineral resources had been extracted. The question then became how to draw capital to the region, and the Mount Rushmore tourist attraction was the answer.[136] Besides all this, the site was sacred to the Lakota and several other tribes. The men who headed the project were fully aware of this, but that only made the site more attractive. Looking at Rushmore, they could imagine their nation rising from the ground of its ancient past as if borne aloft by proud Native Grandparents.[137]

Many Americans would be disturbed to think of Mount Rushmore as a religious monument, because once that thought crosses the mind it's hard to ignore the monument's defiance of biblical injunctions against idolatry. For non-Native Americans, then, disavowing Rushmore's religious character can facilitate its religious work—stirring up feelings of awe, bonding a community, linking the present to the past and the future, and (above all) assuring the people that the place they occupy is where God meant them to be. But Gutzon Borglum needed no such disavowal. Raised as a Mormon, he boldly used religious language to describe the monument; the presidents, he said, had become gods. He believed that those gods were already in the mountain; his job was simply to reveal them. Washington was there because he'd created the republic, Lincoln because he had saved it, and Jefferson because of the Louisiana Purchase.[138]

It was not immediately clear that Roosevelt was in there too, but as the carving progressed, room seemed to appear for a fourth head. Some thought that Roosevelt had died too recently for such a public apotheosis, but Borglum, who'd been a friend of Roosevelt's, argued that by building the Panama Canal, Roosevelt had finished what Columbus had begun.[139] Borglum lived to see Roosevelt's face nearly completed, but not to see the project's final touch—the Hall of Records, a rectangular cave dug discreetly in the back of the mountain, which would contain copies of the Constitution and Declaration of Independence. When the hall was dedicated in 1998, Borglum's vision of Mount Rushmore was fully materialized. On its face, Rushmore would display the white men who had made America's history; inside, it would hold America's

sacred texts, revealing the land's most ancient meaning and protecting that revelation for millennia.

By the end of his life, Nicholas Black Elk had a different forecast. It can be discerned in his foreword to *The Sacred Pipe*, a book
supposedly relating Lakota rituals to Catholic sacraments.[140] Edited
by anthropologist Joseph Epes Brown, *The Sacred Pipe* was based on
interviews with Black Elk. As with *Black Elk Speaks*, however, the in-
terviewer's and interviewee's purposes were not the same. Brown
was mining Lakota rituals for Jungian archetypal images; Black Elk
(according to his foreword) had "no other desire than to help my
people in understanding the greatness and truth of our own tradition." To suggest a parallel with Catholic sacraments, the book was
structured into seven rituals, but no correspondence was established between particular Lakota rituals and particular sacraments.
Unlike the Catholic sacraments, Lakota rituals were described by
Black Elk as tied to the earth, and (even more out of kilter with
Christian practice) he addressed the earth as mother and grandmother. The rituals even resonated with Black Elk's particular
home on earth—there were buffalo, eagles, sweet grasses, and herbs
specific to the region.

In his foreword, Black Elk pointedly identified Christian doctrines as the beliefs of whites. "We have been told by the white
man," he wrote, "that God sent to men His Son, who would restore
peace and order," and that Jesus was crucified, rose, and will come
again at "the end of this world or cycle." Black Elk professed to
truly believe these doctrines ("this I believe and I know it is true"),
but he insisted on reciprocal recognition of Lakota religion. "The
white man should know that for the red people it was the will of
Wakan-Tanka, the Great Spirit, that an animal turn itself into a
two-legged person in order to bring the most holy pipe to his people; and we too were taught that this White Buffalo Cow Woman
brought our sacred pipe and will appear again at the end of this
'world,' a coming which we Indians know is now not very far off."[141]

However interested Brown may have been in the parallels between Christianity and Lakota religion, Black Elk wanted to high-
light the contrasts. Like Jesus, White Buffalo Cow was a revelation
of the one God, but she was a revelation meant for a different people and she assigned them a unique ritual, the sacred pipe. And

although, like Jesus, she was expected to come again "at the end," it is not clear that her beginning and ending were the same as his.

Perhaps, for Black Elk, these two messianic figures represented different worlds that occupied the same place but appeared and disappeared at different times. Perhaps that accounts for how he ultimately came to think of "religion" and for his portentous claim that Indians are quicker than whites to feel the end drawing near. From where he stood, this blind old seer sensed that something was on the way. To Euro-Americans, he knew, it would feel like the end of the world. But through Native eyes, it might look like a new world coming, or an old world coming back.

Law, Land, and Lifeways

When people struggle over land, we realize that we're fighting about the real world. But when we struggle about religion, we may think we're only fighting about world*views*. But as the stories of Theodore Roosevelt and Nicholas Black Elk show, conflict over the American landmass has been thoroughly intertwined with religion. This battle over land, the originary conflict of the American republic, is not considered religious by most non-Natives, but that's only because they won. Having come to possess this land, they can think of it as property and forget that it is also the ground of our existence. And having thoroughly effectuated their beliefs about land, they can forget that they are beliefs at all.

The lifetime of Theodore Roosevelt reflects a transitional moment in American religion-talk. Previously, the debate had been about which religions were true. But in the late nineteenth and early twentieth centuries, religion and public truth were becoming separate issues. The wealthy, educated white men who dominated public life put their faith in science, progress, industry, and American expansionism. Roosevelt belonged to this elite; Nicholas Black Elk did not. To Black Elk, questions of religious truth mattered very much. But for Roosevelt and his class, "religion" was a realm of private and subjective feeling concerning which it was neither necessary nor helpful to make public judgments. Conversely, beliefs such as racialism and Americanism, which Roosevelt found publicly relevant and patriotically inspiring, were to him much more than religion. They could therefore be established with all the force of government, even as religion was made entirely free.

Roosevelt's beliefs about the American land and nation were expressed with his signature bellicosity, but they commanded a large constituency in his time and still do in ours. In retrospect, his dismissal of the land claims of First Nations may look heartless, and his characterizations of the "Indian race" ignorant. But laying special blame on Roosevelt too easily exculpates everyone else. He simply exemplified, in his inimitable personal style and in the idioms of his period, the crushing incompatibility between the world founded by Euro-Americans and the worlds earlier founded by First Nations on the North American continent.

That incompatibility had been evident to many Native Americans for a long time, but it became evident to the judiciary only when Native Americans went to court and tried to make their claims on the American polity cognizable as "religion." Three such cases reached the Supreme Court between 1986 and 1990, yielding consistent losses for Native Americans and exposing intractable contradictions in the constitutional idea of religion. The first of these cases, *Bowen v. Roy* (1986), involved Social Security numbers. The second, *Lyng v. Northwest Cemetery Protective Association* (1988), centered on the issue of sacred lands. And the third, *Oregon v. Smith* (1990), showed the impracticability of religious exemptions not just for Native people but also for all Americans.

Social Security numbers might seem like bureaucratic minutiae, but to Steven Roy, an Abenaki Indian, his daughter's spirit would be harmed if the government assigned her one. Unfortunately, Social Security numbers were the vehicles through which the government provided AFDC (Aid to Families with Dependent Children), which Roy's daughter badly needed. What particularly flummoxed the Court was that Roy not only objected to writing the Social Security number on the AFDC application form, but also asked the government not to use the number in its own records. As Chief Justice Burger wrote, it was as if Roy were making "a sincere religious objection to the size or color of the government's filing cabinets," in effect demanding that the government "conduct its internal affairs in ways that comport with the religious beliefs of particular citizens."[142] Roy, in other words, wanted his beliefs treated as if they were true. But the only free exercise the Supreme Court would promise Roy was the right to *believe* that a Social Security number would harm his daughter, not (from Roy's vantage point) the right to make that harm cease.

Lyng v. Northwest involved something that both the Court and Native people could recognize as real—the Chimney Rock section of the Six Rivers National Park. This area is sacred to the Talawa, Karak, and Yoruk tribes, who call it "the high country." When the Forest Service proposed to build a road through the area, the tribes objected not only because the traffic would disturb their religious practices but because the road would desecrate the land itself. The Court could understand the former claim but was nonplussed by the latter. Justice Sandra Day O'Connor, writing for the majority, encouraged the Forest Service to do all it could to preserve the quiet and serenity of the area. But, she added, although the Court meant "no disrespect" for Native religious beliefs, these particular beliefs "could easily require the de facto beneficial ownership of some rather spacious tracts of public property."[143] Besides, O'Connor wrote, the land belonged to the government, not to the Native people.

John Marshall had come to that conclusion when he ruled that the U.S. government had original legal ownership of all the land within its borders.[144] But Marshall, writing in 1823, had felt compelled to acknowledge the Christian theological roots of these ownership claims. O'Connor, writing in 1988, no longer felt that need. By then, what Marshall had justified as Christian belief had become simply a legal reality.

Like Chief Justice Burger two years earlier, O'Connor felt that Native people were asking for much more than an accommodation; they were trying to dictate how the government itself should act. If Native American demands about the management of the high country could be justified by claiming that any or all places are sacred, where were the limits? Even worse, non-Native citizens could do the same thing, because they had the same constitutional right to free exercise as the Talawa, Karak, and Yoruk people. Native people, as the *Lyng* majority saw it, were asking for more than the Constitution promises. As Justice O'Connor explained, the promise is simply that the government will not *prohibit* religious practice; it is not, and cannot be, that government will never *inhibit* anyone's religious practice.[145]

But when faced with sacramental peyote use in *Oregon v. Smith*, the Court decided that, actually, the government *could* criminally prohibit a religious practice. The only caveat was that the government could not single out any religion, or religion generally, for legal disfavor; the law had to be religiously neutral and generally applicable. Remarkably, the *Smith* Court forgot that anti-peyote laws had originated for the express purpose of suppressing Native American religion. Sacramental peyote was one of the "heathenish practices" prohibited by the Indian Code of 1883, and the first state law against peyote, passed in Oklahoma in 1899, was targeted solely against its sale or distribution to Native Americans. Until the 1920s, non-Natives could purchase peyote at pharmacies for medicinal reasons; *The Dispensatory of the United States* even prescribed recommended dosages.[146]

Since these judicial losses, Native Americans have been able to win some victories. Congress has passed laws protecting Native peyote use and repatriating the human remains and cultural artifacts of Native people. In 2000, Congress passed a law protecting all religious land use—a measure that may prove impracticable in the ways anticipated by Justice O'Connor, particularly because it embraces all religious land use, not just that of Native Americans.[147] As for the Lakota, in 1980 the Supreme Court recognized that in taking the Black Hills, the federal government had violated the Fort Laramie Treaty. In recompense, the Court awarded the Sioux Nation $17.1 million plus $88 million in interest.[148] As of this writing, the interest is still accruing, because the Lakota have decided that no amount of money can compensate for the Paha Sapa. Instead, the tribe tries to raise funds to purchase what portions of the Black Hills it can and to create more self-sustaining economies on remaining reservation lands.

There is no predicting how the Lakota or other First Nations will find their way through their difficulties, which include poverty, unemployment, toxic dumping, substance abuse, and mortality rates far higher than those of non-Natives. What can be said is that "religion" in the constitutional sense does not adequately convey what Native people have lost, nor does "religious freedom" name what it would take to restore meaningful sovereignty to First Nations on tribal lands. At the same time, the issues are foundational, and thus religious in the deeper and older sense of the word. They bear on the origin and destiny of the earth and its creatures, the meaning of history and existence, and the obligations that living on this planet places on us. Every step we take, and every misstep, is guided by our beliefs on such matters, although we may not notice it until we cross paths with those who believe and walk differently. The lifeways and the land-ways of First Nations remind the rest of us that the world as we know it is not the world as it's always been. Different worlds have been here, and new worlds may yet come.

PART III

The Religious against the Secular

CHAPTER FIVE

Creationists and Evolutionists

Religion and the Question of Human Origins

Here is a stand on the origins of man

Some can trace a name to the family tree

But for me, I'm content with the blessed Bible plan

And you can't make a monkey out of me.

—BILLY ROSE AND CLARENCE GASKILL, "YOU CAN'T
MAKE A MONKEY OUT OF ME," 1925

IT IS A DISTINCTIVE mark of religion-talk in the United States that one in three people reject the scientific consensus that humans evolved from other forms of life and hold that God created us in our present form. As for science and religion generally, a majority of Americans think that they are incompatible, and about 30 percent consider science incompatible with their personal religious beliefs.[1]

But even Americans who don't see religion and science as mutually exclusive worldviews can understand why the question of human origins is sensitive. For *Homo sapiens*, the "being who knows," claims about origins are fraught with implications for the humanity of the

knowers themselves. What is the nature of our species, its capabilities
and limitations? Who knows best about such things, and how do they
know? Before the Civil War, Euro-Protestants thought that the chief
authority on the nature of humanity was the King James Bible, "America's book." In the controversy over evolution, however, these biblical
foundations splintered in ways that came to divide Euro-Protestants
themselves—along lines that included North versus South, urban versus rural, affluent versus poor, more educated versus less educated.

Although the disagreement about human origins went to
American foundations, it would repeatedly end up in the judiciary,
where it could be addressed only as a question about the wall of
separation between church and state. Creationism first came to the
Supreme Court in the 1960s, during what Noah Feldman calls the
era of legal secularism.[2] That era began with *Everson v. Board of Education* (1947), which revived the wall metaphor and incorporated
the establishment clause to the states.[3] Since then, the wall of separation has been the main barricade against the intrusion of creationism into the science classroom. But if ever there were a perfect
illustration of the maxim that law cannot, on its own, solve social
conflicts, this is it. Despite a half century of unfavorable rulings,
creationism endures, a crack that weakens at its base any common
fund of knowledge Americans might hope to share.

Like other conflicts about religion, this one must be understood in terms of who has been fighting and why. Because most of
the contestants have been Euro-American, the conflict cannot be
unrelated to their dominant position in America's racial hierarchy,
which produces the assumption that they know best. To be clear, I
do not contend that either creationism or evolutionism is inherently racist. Each viewpoint has been deployed both to support racial domination and to advance racial equality, and people of color
are found on both sides of the debate.[4] Nor will I suggest that the
leading participants have been motivated by racism, although as we
will see, there are some on both sides who were.

The significance of race within this conflict has less to do with
the personal attitudes of Euro-Americans than with their structural
position in a racial hierarchy that favors whites. This hierarchy is impressed on their cultural imagination as an order in which humans
are ranked from highest to lowest, with the supposedly lower races

placed closest to animals. As a legacy of slavery, the stigma of animal-
ization falls especially on African Americans. As a legacy of colonialism, it falls on indigenous Americans and other people of color.[5]

But racialization/animalization is not just something whites do
to black and brown people; it's also something whites do to each
other. This, I will argue, is the nerve that the theory of evolution
hits among Euro-Americans. The theory claims that all humans, all
animals, and indeed all forms of life are biologically related through
a long series of small changes. In the cultural imaginary, then, evolution opens new possibilities for promotion, and new risks of demotion, within the order of being. This helps account for the
weakly comical but always insulting monkey imagery that appears
whenever the conflict resurges. People rely on humor when they
don't quite know, or can't quite say, what pleases or worries them.
In the creationism conflict, people have been fighting for the dignity and equality that ought to come with being human but that in
America (although we might not wish to acknowledge it) have historically been attached to being white.

For many centuries, Euro-Christians conflated the categories
we now call race and religion, deeming themselves the best of people and their religion the peak of civilization. But with the rise of
the modern research university in the nineteenth century, that story
was turned upside down. The so-called conflict thesis, laid out in
popular works like Andrew Dickson White's 1896 book *A History of
the Warfare of Science with Theology*, cast Christianity as the enemy,
and science the savior, of true and useful knowledge.[6] Following the
influential theory of Auguste Comte, scholars had begun to consider whether religion, far from the basis of higher civilization,
might actually be a vestige of the primitive. Comte maintained that
society develops through three stages—the religious, the metaphysical, and the scientific. In its infancy, humanity spontaneously attributes earthly events to supernatural agents. With the European
Enlightenment, humanity advanced to the metaphysical stage by
replacing supernatural beings with an abstract God. The third and
ultimate stage, Comte thought, was arriving in his own period, the
mid-nineteenth century. Soon, all meaningful questions would be
asked and answered in terms of science (or "positive knowledge"),
and the subject of religion would be humanity, not God.[7] In this

schema, whites knew best, and whites who had abandoned religion for science knew best of all.

In modern universities, religion itself became an object of study, through the new "science of religion." Particularly troubling to Protestants, even the Bible was subjected to the rule of experts. For one's claims about the Bible to be considered publicly legitimate, it was no longer sufficient to have undergone a personal conversion, be an inspired preacher, or even be called and ordained by a denomination. Now one needed advanced training in ancient languages, cultures, and history. America's book no longer seemed to belong to ordinary Americans, and the beliefs that animated Christian lives seemed vulnerable at every moment to new academic discoveries.

The movement that came to be called fundamentalism, which began between 1910 and 1915 and has driven creationism ever since, was an effort to build a doctrinal barrier against these modern threats. *The Fundamentals* was a series of short books laying out what were said to be the central doctrines of Christian faith. These included the virgin birth, the bodily resurrection of Christ, the necessity of Christ's atoning death, the miracles of Jesus, and the literal inerrancy of the Bible. Only about a fifth of the essays in *The Fundamentals* addressed the theory of evolution, and even these were not always entirely opposed to it.[8] But when public figures like William Jennings Bryan took up the torch of creationism, the question of human origins was transformed from a theological disagreement to a hundred-year political war.

Before the 1920s, the debate over creationism mostly concerned what should be preached in pulpits and taught in seminaries. Bryan, in the denouement of his political career, made it into a public fight about the use of tax funds, the control of schools, and the ethos of the nation. By setting up fundamentalism as the true American religion, and himself as its champion, he hoped to recover something of the national stature he'd had at the turn of the century. That was not to be, nor were Bryan and other fundamentalists able to convert the whole nation to their beliefs. But they had a different, highly consequential impact on religion in America. They managed to convince a large segment of the population that liberal religion (such as that propounded by biblical scholars and theological modernists) was not religion at all. The debate over human origins was thus reduced, on the creationist side, to a battle between religion and irreligion, and on the evolutionist side, to a battle between religious backwardness and scientific progress.

This confluence of interests between religious fundamentalists and anti-religious evolutionists had two persistent effects. First, by marginalizing modernist religion, it reduced Americans' capacity to think critically about religion, as distinct from merely believing or disbelieving. Second, it radically transformed the terms of American religion-talk. Because of the creationist controversy, it became widely possible to ask not just which religion was best, but whether religion itself was good or bad.

This chapter traces the creationist controversy in the United States through its four major phases. The first was the *Scopes* era, in which the conflict was expressed in foundationalist terms, as a battle for civilization. In the second phase, which began with the 1968 case *Epperson v. Arkansas*, the courts raised the wall of separation

Faustin Betbeder, illustration of Charles Darwin, London Sketchbook, *1874. From Wikimedia Commons/Public Domain.*

between creationism and the science classroom. In the third phase, culminating in the 1987 case *Edwards v. Aguillard*, creationism battered that wall with the argument that creation could be understood as a scientific theory and evolution as a religious doctrine. In its fourth and current phase, creationism morphed yet again, into a theory called "intelligent design" (ID), which a Pennsylvania federal court tried and found wanting in 2005.[9]

At each phase, the dispute about human origins was fueled by conflicts among Euro-Americans that were associated with disturbances in the prevailing racial hierarchy. These group conflicts, together with the profound influence of the Bible in American history, account for why the dispute about human origins has become a lightning rod for some of the deepest inequities that exist among Americans, as well as their deepest indignities, resentments, and fears.

"Monkey Biz Ness Down in Tennessee"

The 1925 case of *Tennessee v. Scopes* came to be called the "monkey trial" thanks to the nasty wit of Baltimore journalist H. L. Mencken, who gave the first of his many pieces on the trial the title "Homo Neanderthalensis." As Mencken told it, the real "primates" were the fundamentalist "morons" who had passed a law forbidding public schools "to teach any theory that denies the story of the Divine Creation as taught in the Bible, and to teach instead that man has descended from a lower order of animals."[10] This law, called the Butler Act, was a stubborn denial of scientific knowledge, and for Mencken only confirmed Darwin's claim that humans are linked to lower forms of life. The spectacle of John Scopes being tried for teaching Hunter's *Civic Biology* was, in Mencken's words, a "religious orgy." In his acerbic commentaries, religion connoted histrionics, vulgarity, and excess—in a word, barbarism. "No man of any education or other human dignity," he wrote, still rejected Darwin's theory. Such "ignoramuses" were found only among "the lower orders," but unfortunately the lower orders comprised most of humanity. "Even in this inspired Republic, the great masses of men ... are precisely where the mob was at the dawn of history."[11]

Despite his contempt for fundamentalists, Mencken implicitly agreed with them that the controversy over evolution (pronounced "*ee*volution" in Tennessee, as Clarence Darrow would note) was a zero-sum game.[12] Like the creationists, he believed that religion founded one type of civilization and science another. And despite his contempt for the Ku Klux Klan, he agreed with the "mountain yokels" about white supremacy. But while they turned to the Bible to legitimate their racial ideology, Mencken preferred more modern means. In 1910, he'd written that although it might be possible, by "careful breeding" and other measures, to improve the "stock" of the American Negro, it would be a "ridiculous waste of energy" because there was "a high caste stock of whites ready at hand."[13] So when he ridiculed Bryan, fundamentalism, and the KKK, Mencken was not suggesting that they were wrong to believe in the general superiority of whites. Instead, he was suggesting that, in their antipathy toward civilization, these whites demonstrated that they were perhaps not as "white" as they thought they were.

In the summer of 1925, Mencken's monkey theme captured the American imagination. During the trial, a nattily dressed chimp named Joe Mendi entertained visitors in the streets of Dayton. Radios rang with songs like "Monkey Biz Ness Down in Tennessee" and newspapers around the country published cartoons portraying one side or the other as monkeys. One cartoon depicted the jury box of the Rhea County Courthouse crammed with monkeys, who presumably would have rendered a more rational decision than the jurymen of Tennessee. Bryan himself was caricatured as a monkey, over captions like "He Denies His Lineage." But cartoonists had been picturing Darwin as a monkey for decades. And Bryan's favorite barb was that although evolutionists might think of themselves as descended from monkeys, they "can't make a monkey out of me."[14]

In the mainstream press, coverage of the monkey trial often had a jocular tone, but for African Americans it was not a laughing matter. A cartoon in the *Chicago Defender*, for example, showed monkeys trembling in a tree above Dayton while, in the distance, an American flag flew from the Capitol and, just below, whites lynched a black man.[15] African Americans were well aware that monkey-talk was racially coded, for whites had been comparing darker-skinned people to primates for a long time. Before Darwin, many whites in Europe and America had contended that the various shades of humanity had originated in different regions (polygenesis) and belonged to different species.[16] Around the turn of the twentieth century, when Euro-Americans split over the theory of evolution, the association of black people with primates intensified on both sides.[17] Although Anglo-Protestants saw the theory of evolution as a conflict mostly among themselves, African Americans were keenly aware that the conflict began in the age of lynching. Ever since then, African Americans have been especially conscious of the resonance between the dispute over human origins and the ongoing realities of race-based discrimination and violence.

Evolutionists, although they considered humanity a single species, often ranked human subgroups based on skin color. This "scientific racism" was exactly the view put forth in *Civic Biology*, the textbook at issue in the *Scopes* trial. Its author, biologist George Hunter, wrote that although "there is an immense mental gap between monkey and man," the gap was smaller for the darker races, some of which were still uncivilized. Hunter laid out five races of men—"the Ethiopian or negro type, originating in Africa; the Malay or brown race, from the islands of the Pacific; the American Indian; the Mongolian or yellow race, including the natives of China, Japan, and the Eskimos; and finally, highest type, Caucasians, represented by the civilized white inhabitants of Europe and America."[18]

Notably, Hunter referred not to the "civilized *Christian* inhabitants" of Europe and America but to the "civilized *white* inhabitants." This marked a sea change in the self-concept of Europeans and Euro-Americans, who for centuries had equated civilization with Christianity. By the time Hunter wrote his textbook, whiteness was competing with Christianity as the foundation of higher civilization. On the question of race, Hunter could assume a consensus among the overwhelmingly white scientists, teachers, and students who would use his book. But on Christianity he was silent, because his readers were divided about whether Christianity was the basis of higher civilization or a remnant of something old, dark, and primitive.

Yet many of the people behind the *Scopes* trial were hoping for a rapprochement between religion and science, not a tectonic collision. The ACLU, which instigated the case, wanted to argue that Darwin's account of human origins did not necessarily conflict with the Bible. To that end, the organization lined up a cast of heavy-hitting expert witnesses—both religion scholars who could explain how the Bible might be read less literally, and scientists who were prepared to profess belief in both religion and evolution. According to historian Edward Larson, the ACLU hesitated to have Clarence Darrow argue Scopes's case because of his well-known animosity toward religion. Even the Dayton town leaders who collaborated with the ACLU were not uniformly opposed to Darwinism. George Rappleyea, who proposed the collaboration to the other town leaders, was a Methodist whose minister had persuaded him that Darwinism could be synthesized with Christian faith. When Rappleyea and the other leaders got together to plan the arrest of John Scopes, the site of their meeting was Mayor Robinson's drugstore—where, along with Coca-Cola, sandwiches, and incidentals, one could purchase a copy of *Civic Biology*.[19]

But the sweaty match between Bryan and Darrow melted away any modernist position that might have mediated between them. Actually, neither man had an interest in mediating positions. Bryan wanted to be the champion of American religion, and to claim that title he had to discredit religious modernism. He liked to say that the Christian evolutionist was "more dangerous for the Christian faith than the atheist" and that theological modernism was "an anesthetic which deadens the pain while the patient's faith is being gradually removed." Darrow was perversely eager to accept Bryan's premise that fundamentalism was true religion. As passionately as Bryan believed that Christianity was the ground of civilization, Darrow believed that "the origin of what we call civilization is not religion but skepticism."[20] And if biblical literalism really were the essence of religion, as Bryan so ardently held, refuting religion would be as easy as shooting fish in a barrel.

As the result of the *Scopes* trial, the public face of religion would become anti-modern and the public face of science would become anti-religious. But both faces would remain white and both views of evolution would often attach to racialist ideologies. On the creationist side, where the KKK was regularly found, this wasn't hard to notice. The pro-evolution side evoked racism more subtly, in the eugenicist impulse to identify "inferior" types of people and reduce their numbers. The children of Dayton, Tennessee, learned their eugenics from Hunter's *Civic Biology*, which devoted a whole section to the subject. Hunter wrote that if "parasitic people"—meaning the poor, the immoral, and the disabled—"were lower animals, we would probably kill them off." Such a solution would be inhumane, Hunter hastened to add, so it was better to halt the growth of a "low and degenerate race" by separating the sexes and preventing inter-marriage in undesirable populations.[21]

For Bryan, the eugenicist potential of Darwinism was as disturb-ing as its defiance of the Bible. Survival of the fittest, he said, was a "law of hate" and incompatible with the "Christian law of love." Bryan failed to acknowledge that for Darwin, natural selection was descriptive, not prescriptive. But he was right that ever since Francis Galton, social Darwinists had espoused what Bryan called the "sci-entific breeding" of humans, directed by "a few supposedly superior intellects."[22] Nor was Bryan wrong to fear that eugenics was the wave of the future. Within ten years after the *Scopes* trial, thirty-five states would pass laws of the kind Hunter endorsed. In that same pe-riod, inspired by sterilization programs begun in California, Nazi Germany inaugurated the most systematic and catastrophic eugenics program of all time, advised by some of the American scientists who had been witnesses for John Scopes's defense.[23]

But Bryan's horror at eugenics was partly a fear that what had long been inflicted on African Americans might also be inflicted on vulnerable whites. The eugenic policies of which he so disapproved were built on anti-miscegenation laws of which he thoroughly ap-proved. His treatment of African Americans was paternalistic rather than violent, but he was an open, unrepentant white supremacist. In 1901, he'd published an essay defending racial segregation and re-strictions on black suffrage, especially in localities where the Afri-can American population was large enough to endanger white control. Twenty years later, he repeated the same views on the edi-torial page of the *New York Times*.[24]

Bryan did not belong to the Ku Klux Klan, and according to Larson, he "despised" the organization.[25] "Despised" may be too harsh a word, however, because Bryan counted on the Klan to sup-port his anti-evolution campaign and it, in turn, relied on him. In 1924, the same year he came to Tennessee to crusade for the Butler Act, he quashed an anti-Klan resolution at the Democratic Na-tional Convention. It is said that when Bryan died, Klansmen in Ohio burned a cross to honor him as "the greatest Klansman" of his time. According to historian Wyn Craig Wade, the Grand Dragon of Ohio pledged to "take up the torch passed by William Jennings Bryan" by demanding that if evolution were taught in public schools, the book of Genesis be taught as well. On August 8, just two weeks after Bryan's death, some fifty thousand white-robed Klansmen and Klanswomen marched down Pennsylvania Avenue in Washington, DC. Had he lived to see it, Bryan might have been abashed at the display, but many of the marchers thought they were honoring his memory.[26]

Clarence Darrow, a perceptive critic of racism, recognized eugenics as a racial project advanced by "Nordic" types who falsely thought themselves superior to others, and he denounced it as an abridgement of basic liberties. Curiously, however, he thought that its main victims would be white Christians, such as Italian immigrants to the United States. Evidently he did not think of people with disabilities, upon whom eugenics was already being practiced, or of Jews, soon to be targets of the most monstrous eugenics program of all time. Still more curiously, he contended that socially engineered human breeding had never been attempted, as if forgetting that enslaved Africans had been bred (often through rape) for most of American history.[27]

Whatever his personal qualms, Darrow's six most prominent scientific witnesses for the defense were all eugenicists. One of them, Charles Davenport of Harvard, was the main source for *Civic Biology*'s section on eugenics; in the 1930s, Davenport would instruct Nazis on the subject. Another, David Starr Jordan of Stanford, was a leading supporter of California's sterilization policies and held that no intelligent person could deny that some races were superior to others. Zoologist Maynard Metcalf, the only scientist permitted to testify at the trial, was a Bible teacher in his Congregational church. Darrow made sure that the court heard all about that. But whether from ignorance or guile, he avoided mentioning that Metcalf had espoused eugenics in a 1914 article for *Popular Science*.[28]

As historian Jeffrey Moran has shown, African Americans held views on religion that paralleled those of Euro-Americans—fundamentalism, religious modernism, and secular intellectualism.[29] But just as white domination inflected Euro-American views on evolution, so defiance of white domination shaped those of African

Americans. For black fundamentalists, according to Moran the largest constituency within the Black Church, the primary imperative was to defend the Bible—that is, the Bible as read by the Black Church, not necessarily as read by whites. For the educated elite, who spoke through the African American press, the *Scopes* trial exposed the ignorance of white racists like Bryan. And for African American religious modernists, most of whom occupied pulpits in the North, the challenge was to avert a rift between the other two groups.

As a disagreement within the African American community, the evolution issue bore some similarities to the Euro-American culture war. But as a public issue—specifically, a conflict about public schools—race and racism made the issue quite different. For one thing, schools were segregated—de jure in the South, de facto in the North. African American children in the South rarely made it to high school, when biological science would normally be introduced, and the schools they attended were notoriously underresourced. Rather than fret about whether their children might read Hunter's *Civic Biology*, African American parents worried about whether their children could get to school in the first place and, if so, whether they got any decent books at all.

African Americans tended to have a greater stake in the Bible than in *The Origins of Species* or *The Descent of Man*. And the proposition that humans had descended from animals could be especially repugnant to people whose close relatives had been bred, worked, and killed like animals. As the Reverend Charles Satchell Morris would preach during the summer and fall of 1925, humanity came "down from God," not "up from the monkey." The Bible taught that all humans, whatever their skin colors, were made in the image of God. AME minister John Norris explained that God "did not make a white man, nor a yellow man, nor a black man, nor a brown man, or red man. He made a man, regardless of colors." God commanded this man to master himself and animals, but not other humans, proving that "man was never made to be a slave."[30]

If some of African Americans' biblical claims seemed to contradict what educated whites believed, that was nothing new. At the time of the *Scopes* trial, there was a famous example of how the Black Church held to biblical truth in apparent defiance of scientific knowledge: the sermon entitled "The Sun Do Move and the

Earth Am Flat," by the Reverend John Jasper. Jasper, a former slave, first delivered it in 1878 and was invited to deliver it so many more times that it became one of America's best-known sermons. His text was the biblical story of Joshua's battle with the Amorites, where God commands the sun to stop so that the day might be prolonged and Joshua might win his battle (Joshua 10:12–13). Jasper reasonably concluded that if the sun could be stopped on this special occasion, on ordinary days it must move around the earth. Hence, the sermon's strikingly counterfactual title.

Today, we might call this science denial, but in context it could more accurately be called an act of intellectual resistance. Jasper, a former slave, was not an educated man. He'd learned to read through the Bible; it was both his schoolbook and prayer book. He recognized that learned folk might scoff at his sermon, and he said so. But he spoke for a Black Church whose life was sustained precisely by defying white versions of truth, and that was the main point of his sermon. Despite what "philosophers" might say, his congregants should stick with the Bible and there find proof that, despite all contrary evidence, God was on their side and, at the end of a very long day, would give them victory.[31]

But African American intellectuals, who were not accountable to the Black Church, saw the *Scopes* trial as a display of white stupidity. In an editorial titled "If Monkeys Could Speak," the *Chicago Defender* explained that southern whites hated Darwinism because, by showing the common origins of all people, it refuted their claims to superiority. The *Topeka Plaindealer* editorialized that both evolution and human mixing belonged to the law of nature, which was God's own law. "The Tennessee legislature is not able to stop evolution by its anti-evolution law, any more than it stops intermarriage by its miscegenation laws." The *Pittsburgh American* noted that the all-white jury faced by Scopes was "typical of the bar before which black men and women must stand." W. E. B. Du Bois wrote acerbically that "Dayton, Tennessee is America—a great, ignorant, simple minded land," and those who kept white Tennesseans mired "in blank and ridiculous ignorance" were the same as those who "would leave black Tennessee and black America with just as little education as is consistent with fairly efficient labor and reasonable contentment."[32]

Just days after the passage of the Butler Act, tensions between African American fundamentalism and modernism came into public view when AME pastor James Hatcher decided to revive John Jasper's sermon. Hatcher's version, called "The Sun Do Move and the Earth Hath Four Corners," was first delivered to his own congregation but, like Jasper's, was repeated by invitation to thousands more hearers. But times had changed. When Jasper was preaching, few African Americans could read, and they experienced the Bible more as story, song, and sermon than as text. But by the 1920s most African Americans were literate, making the debate between fundamentalism and theological modernism more salient. Most chose to align with fundamentalism, but African American intellectuals were keenly aware that this exposed the Black Church to the same ridicule that Bryan and other white fundamentalists were drawing from the northern press. One newspaper said that nobody outside Richmond liked Hatcher's rendition; others insinuated that he was appropriating Jasper's sermon for personal gain.[33]

Theological modernists in the Black Church had the sensitive task of both preserving and revising sermonic traditions like Jasper's. A small delegation of them, including university professors, preachers, students, and doctors, attended the *Scopes* trial. They were led by the Reverend W. H. Moses of the National Baptist Convention, who reported on the trial for the *Pittsburgh Courier*. His well-founded concern was that the perceived gap between religion and science was driving a wedge into the African American community. On one side were fundamentalist preachers, whom Moses described as "proverbially hostile" to science; on the other side, "college Negroes" who'd become dangerously alienated from the religion of their forebears.[34] Moses thought that the trial might heal this breach and enable the progressive marriage of religion and science, to African Americans' benefit. But his hope of finding respect for his faith among the defense lawyers must have faded when Arthur Garfield Hayes opened his case by stating that Tennessee, in passing the Butler Act, might as well have declared that the sun goes around the earth.[35] Later that day, Darrow would make the same disparaging point.

Darrow began by lauding religious freedom and nonpreferentialism. But he was soon conjuring the fading specters of

Turks and polygamists, thus associating religion with people whom Euro-Protestants found alien. If Tennessee could establish the Bible, he asked, why could it not establish the Qur'an or Book of Mormon?[36] Condemnation of "religious intolerance" and "religious bigotry" was constantly on Darrow's lips, but these expressions were tricky: they could connote both injustice and irrationality inflicted *on* religion and injustice and irrationality inflicted *by* religion. Usually, Darrow meant the latter. He took it as axiomatic that whatever the standard of religious liberty, religious minorities must not be shortchanged—an axiom definitely not shared by the prosecution, which openly endorsed a Christian nation.[37] But most of Darrow's statements about religious intolerance were like this: "There is nothing else, Your Honor, that has caused the difference of opinion, of bitterness, of hatred, of war, of cruelty, that religion has caused."[38]

A few months later, in their appeal of Scopes's conviction, Darrow and his colleagues would reject religion more explicitly, explaining that "the historical conflict between theology and science" had always proceeded in three stages. First, theology would label a threatening scientific claim as heresy and attempt to crush it. Then, as the claim gained acceptance, the Church would try to compromise by adjusting its doctrines as needed. Finally, the Church would "retreat" by asserting that the scientific claim (say, evolution) had nothing to do with religion. Certainly, this account implied a critique of theological modernism. It was less picturesque than Bryan's image of the theistic evolutionist as a man who'd fallen over a cliff and was clinging to a fragile bit of scrub for what was left of his life.[39] But the idea was the same: religious modernism, the willing consignment of religion to a separate sphere, was religion's last stop before deportation. Darrow's battle for science, like Bryan's for religion, was not just for a place in the world of knowledge. For both, it was a war for control of the whole territory.

During the trial, Darrow tried to contain his contempt for religion, but it sometimes popped out anyway. Fairly enough, he complained about the court's practice of beginning the day's proceedings with a prayer, or as he put it, "turning this courthouse into a meeting house." Curiously, however, he counterbalanced this objection with an assurance that he "did not object to the jury or anyone else praying in secret or private"—as if permitting people to pray even in private were a magnanimous concession on his part.[40] In the heat of his exchange with Bryan, he spat out that "no man of science and learning" believes "in your fool religion." Later he backpedaled, directing the insult against "your fool ideas that no intelligent Christian on earth believes." But by that point it would have taken a fool to believe that Darrow considered Christianity an intelligent point of view.[41]

The Rhea County Court met Darrow's separationism with belligerent establishmentarianism. Judge John Raulston entered his courtroom each day displaying the Bible in one hand and the Tennessee statutes in the other. "Read Your Bible" banners were draped everywhere, including over the jury box.[42] When the defense objected to the banners, outraged prosecutor Ben G. McKenzie allowed as how he'd "never seen the time in the history of this country when any man should be afraid to be reminded of the fact that he should read his Bible." And if such a time should come, McKenzie added, we might as well "tear up all of the Bibles, throw them in the fire and let the country go to hell." As a compromise, Darrow wryly suggested that the court post a sign of equal size saying "Hunter's Biology" or perhaps "Read Your Evolution."[43]

If for Darrow, skepticism was the basis of civilization, for Bryan it was faith. That was exactly what bothered Darrow when he first encountered Bryan at the 1896 Democratic National Convention. Bryan struck him as someone who "never cared to read, much less study," and who felt that he "knew, without investigation or thought."[44] Less antagonistically, we might say that for Bryan, majoritarianism was not just a political theory but an epistemology. Truth was what ordinary people—people like himself—knew to be so. He was claiming something far bolder than that the theory of evolution shouldn't be taught because it disturbed religious faith. He was claiming that it shouldn't be taught because it was *false*, and it was false because it contradicted the common sense of ordinary Christians.

Bryan was positively hostile to the kind of scholarly testimony that Darrow had hoped to put on the stand. He could not countenance the idea of experts telling him what his own Bible—and his own religion—meant. As he said in court, to great applause, "The one beauty about the word of God is it does not take an expert to understand it."[45] Nor could Bryan grant scientists the authority to define what it meant to be human. In this sense, Bryan's intellectual resistance toward modern knowledge was not unlike that of African American fundamentalists. The loyalties were different, but the guiding maxims were the same: hold fast to the truth of your tradition, and don't let powerful people with fancy titles tell you otherwise.

Judge Raulston, sharing this populist resentment, terminated expert testimony after hearing just one scientist. That gave Darrow the chance to call upon Bryan himself as an expert witness on the Bible. It was an ingenious trap, because although Bryan had no relevant academic training, he couldn't admit lacking knowledge about the book on which his public authority had come to depend. Darrow, having made himself conversant with the study of religion, proceeded to hammer Bryan with questions about ancient languages, comparative religions, and the age of the earth. Almost every question began with "Do you know?," "Don't you know?," or "Don't you think?" Time and again, Bryan had to acknowledge that he'd not previously considered the question and therefore did not know. Increasingly flustered, he finally stammered, "I do not think about . . . what I do not think about," walking smack into Darrow's devastating rejoinder: "Do you think about what you *do* think about?"[46]

Even so, Bryan was not as literalist as Darrow had hoped. As he announced on the stand, he did not think that the six days of creation were of twenty-four hours, and he was reluctant to assign definite dates to the age of the earth or the creation of humans. Unfortunately for Bryan, however, the prosecution had put into evidence a Scofield Bible whose notes assigned far-fetched dates to biblical events. Darrow began to throw those dates at Bryan and then, bringing a pencil to the stand, led his confused adversary through an absurd series of calculations. Before long, Bryan conceded that, yes, the earth must be only about six thousand years old, an insupportable position with which he'd not previously encumbered himself. He tried to bear his humiliation in Christ-like fashion, but eventually sputtered that the defense's real purpose was to "cast ridicule on everybody who believes in the Bible." Darrow, not denying the charge, shot back: "We have the purpose of preventing bigots and ignoramuses from controlling the education of the United States."[47]

Bryan was not an ignoramus, but the truths most important to him were moral and theological rather than empirical: God existed; humanity was uniquely endowed with a soul; natural history was guided by divine benevolence rather than survival of the fittest. Those were the truths for which he had hoped to testify. So when Darrow asked him about Confucianism, Bryan explained why altruism was better than reciprocity. To Darrow, that was irrelevant; he only wanted to hear whether Bryan knew how old Confucianism was (Bryan did not). Asked about Buddhism, Bryan told of meeting a Buddhist agnostic in Burma, his point being that Buddhism, lacking a God, is not a valid religion. Again, Darrow wanted only the facts. How tall was this Buddhist? "About as tall as you but not so crooked," Bryan quipped. How old was he? "Old enough to know what he was talking about." Exasperated, Darrow complained that the judge was allowing Bryan "to regale the crowd with what some black man said to him." Bryan, defending his source, retorted that the man was "not black, just dark skinned."[48] And so they battled in front of the whole country, one with science as his cudgel, the other with religion as his shield. After two exhausting hours, they stood there, two aging white men, shaking their fists at each other and trembling with rage, until Judge Raulston gaveled the fiasco to a close. It took the jury only nine minutes to find John Scopes guilty.[49] Five days later, William Jennings Bryan died while taking a nap after a hearty meal.

The African American press assessed Bryan's life in negative terms but maintained a certain restraint. The *Pittsburgh Courier* called him a "militant disciple of colorphobia, racial discrimination, and religious bigotry" and stated bluntly that "Negroes have nothing to treasure out of the life of Bryan." Yet the *Courier's* obituary concluded by noting that Bryan was widely liked and would be "mourned by the whole people." The *Chicago Broad Axe* was equivocal, or perhaps sarcastic, describing Bryan as having won "a victory over Satan" in Tennessee, yet adding that all people "who have one ounce of gray matter in the top of their heads" know that evolution is a settled fact. The *Norfolk Journal and Guide* said that Bryan, by taking up the Bible's cause, had "lived just long enough to ingratiate himself" to African Americans.[50]

H. L. Mencken, having less compunction against speaking ill of the dead, chided other journalists for going easy on the Great Commoner. He described Bryan as "vulgar and common," "ignorant, big-oted, self-seeking, blatant, and dishonest," consumed with hatred, bald, lisping, and looking strangely dirty even when freshly shaved and dressed in clean clothes. As always, the contumely that Mencken poured on Bryan spilled over onto the masses. In Tennessee, he wrote, Bryan was a "peasant come home to the dung pile." The spectacle of the *Scopes* trial had embarrassed the "civilized minority" of the South, and although Darrow's humiliation of Bryan might have offended millions of religious Americans, the "delusions of *homo neanderthalensis*" needed to be broken down. Religion was pro-tected from government interference but not from public opinion. When half-witted fundamentalists spurted "such bilge as would gag a Hottentot," Mencken wrote, contempt and ridicule were the only proper responses.[51]

The Tennessee Supreme Court found the *Scopes* case embar-rassing too, but the ACLU was determined to appeal it up to the U.S. Supreme Court. To thwart that appeal, the Tennessee Court overturned Raulston's ruling on a technicality. There remained, however, the problem of the Butler Act, which by this point was universally known to represent fundamentalism. It was difficult to deny that in passing that law, Tennessee had endorsed a particular religious viewpoint and thus violated its own constitution. But overturning the act would have been politically perilous, so the jus-tices came up with a clever, if implausible, solution: they saved it by reading religion out of it. Yes, the Court admitted, the statute en-dorsed the "divine creation of man as taught in the Bible," but that was just a rhetorical flourish. The key point was simply that Ten-nessee public schools must not teach "that man has descended from a lower order of animals."[52] Now creationism in Tennessee could evade scrutiny as "religion," even as it became more deeply ce-mented into the law. It would simply be instilled into children as public truth while they attended segregated schools.

Evolution and Integration in Little Rock

Inherit the Wind, that popular parable of the *Scopes* trial, begins with a cryptic note about its setting: "Summer, not too long ago."[53] Actu-ally, thirty years had passed between the monkey trial and the debut

of *Inherit the Wind*. What was "not long ago" in 1955, however, was
the televised scene of attorney Joseph Welch angrily demanding of
Senator Joseph McCarthy, "Have you no decency, sir?"—an exchange that left McCarthy looking as pathetic as William Jennings
Bryan after his drubbing by Clarence Darrow. By the time the film
version of *Inherit the Wind* was released in 1960, two other Cold
War tableaux had been imprinted on the national screen. One appeared in newspapers around the world and seemed tailor-made for
communist propaganda, although sadly it was an all-American production: nine black teenagers entering Little Rock Central High
School in September 1957 under the protection of federal troops.
The other, which appeared the following month, was the launch of
Sputnik, which instantly transformed science education from a religious dispute into a matter of national defense. In the ideological
fight with communism, both counted as defeats. As historian Mary
Dudziak put it, the Little Rock Nine and the launch of Sputnik were
"a double blow to U.S. prestige, in Arkansas and in the heavens."[54]

By 1968, when *Epperson v. Arkansas* reached the Supreme
Court, it was not surprising that the first nationwide creationism
case had come from Little Rock Central High. Many then thought
of McCarthyism and creationism as two examples of a kind of
Americanism whose time was nearly over—more precisely, of a
kind of *American* whose time was nearly over. This imagined American, represented by the William Jennings Bryan character in *Inherit the Wind*, was anti-intellectual, anti-modern, racially bigoted,
southern, rural, jingoistic, and fundamentalist.

This was, of course, something of a caricature of the white South
of the time. For example, the groups supporting the Little Rock Nine
included (in addition to black clergy and the NAACP) the predominantly white Greater Little Rock Ministerial Association.[55] A decade
later, the Little Rock Ministerial Association also would assist biology
teacher Susan Epperson, a devoted Presbyterian. (Epperson later recalled that her pastor even offered to serve as her bodyguard during
the controversy.)[56] And in Arkansas, unlike in Tennessee, the campaign to dump the anti-evolution law did not have to be instigated
from outside. It came from the Arkansas Education Association,
which had supported desegregation in the 1950s and in 1969 would
merge with an advocacy group for African American education.

Still, like many caricatures, the picture of creationism painted by *Inherit the Wind* contained some truth. In Arkansas as in Tennessee, supporters of evolution would be compared to monkeys. Epperson's most memorable piece of hate mail commented that "there is a striking resemblance between you and the monkey," an insult that she took in stride by calling it an "astute observation on comparative anatomy."[57] Moreover, Arkansas's 1928 anti-evolution law had been a direct outgrowth of the *Scopes* trial. The campaign for its passage had been led by a Baptist minister named Ben Bogard, whose American Anti-Evolution Association was closed to "Negros [sic], and persons of African decent [sic]" as well as to atheists, drunks, and "despoilers of domestic life."[58] And in Arkansas, as in *Inherit the Wind*, creationism was a creed that also embraced anti-communism and southern chauvinism. Bogard's ad in the *Arkansas Gazette* said it all. "THE BIBLE OR ATHEISM, WHICH? Shall conscientious church members be forced to pay taxes to support teachers to teach evolution which will undermine the faith of their children?" Creationists would be ridiculed, Bogard warned, but the true source of the derision was communism, so there was nothing to do but face it down. "The Gazette said Russian Bolsheviks laughed at Tennessee. True, and that sort will laugh at Arkansas. Who cares? Vote FOR Act No. 1."[59]

There was also some truth behind the representation of creationism as a phenomenon of southern fundamentalism. In the early twentieth century, six states had passed anti-evolution laws or resolutions, and all of them were in the South.[60] Fundamentalism, though born in the North, flourished in the South in reaction to northern intrusions on the issues of evolution and integration.[61] And although segregation was practiced throughout the country, only in the South was it the law of the land until 1964 and, both before and after that, a badge of regional pride for many whites.

Leading segregationists were also creationists, and they found warrants for both positions in the Bible. Arkansas governor Orval Faubus, who'd called out his National Guard against the Little Rock Nine, defended the anti-evolution law by declaring the Genesis account "good enough for me."[62] Attorney general Bruce Bennett, who'd fought alongside Faubus against school desegregation, would later defend the anti-evolution law in court by calling upon the Bible and the memory of William Jennings Bryan. When the battle against integration was lost, Bennett infamously attempted to punish the NAACP by demanding the names of all its members.[63]

But by the time of the *Epperson* case, views about race and evolution had become entangled throughout the United States, not just in the South. After 1925, publishers had begun to remove evolution from biology textbooks, but they kept "scientific racism," which increased the apparent significance of racial differences by ignoring the evolutionary unity of life. Hunter's 1926 revision of *Civic Biology*, for example, expunged the word "evolution" and charts showing the development of species, but still described the "five races of man" and implicitly ranked them by level of civilization. Also intact were Hunter's proposals about preventing marriage among the sexually immoral, the feebleminded, and others whose progeny would perpetuate "a low and degenerate race."[64] In 1964, a cartoon in a New Jersey fundamentalist magazine blended these themes by depicting "Civil Rights 'Bill' " as a grimacing Neanderthal, wielding a cudgel labeled "federal power" and dragging by her blond hair a slender woman named "private property."[65]

What brought the theory of evolution back into public high schools was not a commitment to science, academic freedom, or human equality. Certainly many proponents of the theory shared those commitments, but what turned the tide was the launch of Sputnik, which made many think that America was losing the Cold War. In immediate response, Congress passed the National Defense Education Act (NDEA), which provided up-to-date science textbooks to public schools. The NDEA also helped birth the Biological Science Curriculum Study, a program that paired university-trained scientists and high school teachers to build world-class science curricula for American public schools.

These opportunities were hard to take advantage of in Arkansas, because teaching the theory of evolution was still against the law. Nonetheless, in 1965, Central High School decided to take the professional advice of its biology teachers and adopt a textbook that included a chapter setting forth "the theory about the origin . . . of man from a lower form of animal."[66] For Arkansas science teachers like Susan Epperson, this was a chance to show students that one could be a good scientist, a good American, and a good Christian all at once. But to do that, they had to accomplish what educators in the 1920s could not: get the courts to rule that laws prohibiting the teaching of human evolution were unconstitutional.

Legally, the crucial difference between the 1920s and 1960s was that in the 1947 case of *Everson v. Board of Education*, the Supreme Court had finally ruled that the federal establishment clause applies to the states. Only once before had the Court referenced Jefferson's "wall of separation." That was in the *Reynolds* case of 1879, where the Court had summarily concluded that the wall did not protect religious polygamy. But in 1947, when applied to the school question, the wall metaphor led to decisions more critical of the foundation religion of the previous century. In the nineteenth century, it had been axiomatic that the younger the children, the more incumbent it was on public schools to contribute to their religious formation. But in the *Everson* era, jurists started to say just the opposite: the younger the child, the greater the government's duty to protect him or her from religious indoctrination. In the 1948 case of *McCollum v. Board of Education*, the Court invoked the wall of separation to rule against a release-time program for the religious education of public school children.[67] In the 1962 case of *Engele v. Vitale*, the Court ruled against a theistic prayer recited each day by public school children. And in the renowned 1963 case of *Abington v. Schempp*, it ruled against two school districts that began the day with Bible verses or the Lord's Prayer.[68]

These decisions were victories for religious minorities, dissenters, atheists, and those whose spiritual seeking took them outside the bounds of organized religion. But many Protestants felt that the words and gestures that had held the nation together were being vetoed by a handful of misanthropes. In the Supreme Court, this anxiety was manifest in the paeans to foundation religion that appeared even in the Court's most separationist decisions. For example, in *Abington v. Schempp*, the Court consigned religion to "the inviolable citadel of the individual heart and mind" but also declared that "the history of man is inseparable from the history of religion."[69] In *Zorach v. Clausen* (1952), within a few pages of firmly supporting the wall of separation, the Court pronounced magisterially, "We are a religious people, whose institutions presuppose a Supreme Being."[70]

If the judiciary displayed uneasiness about church-state separation, the public displayed bursts of unmitigated fury. Atheist Madalyn Murray O'Hair, one of the complaining parents in the *Abington* case, received so many death threats that in 1964 she could tell *Life Magazine*, with evident pride, that she was "the most hated woman in America." O'Hair was willfully obnoxious, but even the mild humanist Vashti McCollum, who had brought the 1948 case against religious education in public schools, suffered physical threats, lost her job, and found the family cat hanging from a tree. Unitarian teenager Ellery Schempp, who resisted his school's Protestant prayers by bringing the Qur'an to school, received letters smeared with excrement from anonymous supporters of school prayer and, from his school principal, a letter of *dis*commendation for college.[71]

So when Susan Epperson's case came to the Supreme Court in 1968, the subject of religion in public schools could not have been more touchy. Adding to the awkwardness was the fact that the state of Arkansas had crafted its anti-evolution law to omit any mention of the Bible, God, or religion. Initiated Act One simply made it unlawful for any public school teacher to "teach the theory or doctrine that mankind ascended or descended from a lower order of animals."[72] To strike the law down on establishment grounds, the Supreme Court would have to rule that the anti-evolution law was religious despite Arkansas's claim that it was not, and that the theory of evolution was not irreligious, despite Arkansas's claim that it was. Several judges were loath to take that stand, including Hugo Black, who had rebuilt the wall of separation in his *Everson* decision but now seemed unwilling to enforce it. But Justice Abe Fortas would win the day, transforming America's debate over the theory of evolution into a debate about the meaning of the establishment clause.

Both men's perspectives on the *Epperson* case were shaped by the fact that they knew the South, but from very different social angles. Hugo Black was born, raised, and spent much of his adult life in Alabama. At the time of the *Scopes* trial, he belonged to the KKK and taught Sunday school at his Baptist church. By the time he joined the Supreme Court, he had long since left the Klan and had come to consider himself a liberal. He'd also made many rulings, including those separating church and state, that cost him friends in the South. Nonetheless, when the *Epperson* matter came before the Court, he staunchly defended the right of Arkansas to decide what to put in—or keep out of—its public school curriculum. He voted to strike down the Arkansas law, but only on grounds of vagueness. If Black had had his way, Arkansas could have saved its anti-evolution law simply by rewording it.[73]

Abe Fortas, only the fifth Jewish justice to sit on the Supreme Court, had grown up in Memphis, Tennessee, where he knew racism and anti-Semitism from firsthand experience. Having been a teenager when the *Scopes* circus took place in his home state, Fortas could not be persuaded that the Arkansas anti-evolution law had nothing to do with religion. In his opinion for the *Epperson* majority, he held that the Arkansas anti-evolution law of 1928 had undoubtedly resulted from the "upsurge of 'fundamentalist' religious fervor" in the 1920s and was clearly "an adaptation of the famous Tennessee 'monkey law.' " The only difference was that Tennessee had "candidly stated" its religious purpose, while Arkansas, perhaps chastened by "the sensational publicity attendant upon the *Scopes* trial," chose "to adopt less explicit language."[74]

Fortas's reasoning rested most heavily on the uncontroverted principle that government may not prefer one religion or set of religions above others. Although his opinion was short, Fortas managed to use the words "particular," "sect," "sectarian," or "fundamentalist" a dozen times. Arkansas, he wrote, had tailored its law to a specific "religious sect"; it had established "a particular religious doctrine," "a particular interpretation of the Book of Genesis by a particular religious group."[75] It was sensible to lean on this lowest and least controversial bar of church-state separation, but Fortas was also avoiding the prickly question of whether government could favor religion in a general way.

Twenty years earlier, in Hugo Black's *Everson* opinion, the Court presumably had answered this question: the establishment clause prohibited government not only from favoring "one religion or religions," but also from favoring "all religions." But the Court almost immediately betrayed its discomfort with this position. In 1952 it added that just as government could not favor religion, neither could it treat religion with "hostility."[76] No wonder, then, that Fortas did not answer the riddles that have bedeviled jurists ever since: What is neutrality toward religion, and is it even possible? If the establishment clause forbids government to favor religion, does this not amount to "hostility"? But if government does favor religion in general, does this not disfavor citizens who are not religious? And what does "religion in general" even mean?

Neither the events of the fall of 1957 nor the *Epperson* case a decade later changed much at Little Rock Central High. As Susan Epperson would recall, teachers were still afraid to discuss human origins. Epperson herself eventually moved to Colorado to teach in a less repressive environment. The few black teenagers who went through Central High School in the 1960s mostly continued on to college and successful lives. But as I write this, Little Rock schools are still residentially segregated, and predominantly black schools remain shockingly under-resourced.[77]

But *Epperson* did have one fateful impact: the Court ruled that the problem with anti-evolution laws was that they violated the establishment clause. It was not enough, in the Court's view, to show that creationism was not science (although it clearly was not), that laws prohibiting the teaching of evolution would produce educational deficiencies (although they did), or that the anti-evolution campaign was linked, perhaps inextricably, to segregationism (although it was). Instead, all the cultural, regional, and racial conflicts packed into the creation/evolution controversy were condensed into the single issue of religion. That was the seam along which the Court, beginning in 1968, tried to stitch up the wound, and along which it would continue to tear open.

Bonzo's Balance

In 1951, Ronald Reagan appeared in a movie that would gain notoriety less for his acting than for his co-star, an African chimpanzee named Bonzo. Reagan played Professor Peter Boyd, an emotionally arrested psychologist who is engaged to marry the brilliant but icy Dr. Valerie Tillinghast. Valerie's father, who happens to be the dean of the college, demands that the engagement be broken off after he discovers that Peter's father was a lifelong criminal. To prove that he is not genetically shackled to his father's criminality, Peter must show that moral character is a product of one's environment. So he brings Bonzo home and undertakes to raise him with the assistance of a pretty farm girl named Jane, who pretends to be Bonzo's "Momma" while Peter acts the part of "Papa." The results are ambiguous: on the minus side, Bonzo commits grand larceny; on the plus side, he does it out of love for Momma. "Even if Bonzo gave a lecture on Darwinism it wouldn't do me any good now," Peter sighs. But all's well in the end, because the real experiment was not to see whether Bonzo could be transformed from wild monkey to civilized human but whether Peter could be transformed from cold scientist to warm family man. Here the results are unambiguous. Dumping his over-educated fiancée, Peter elopes with Jane, whose only desire is to have "at least ten" children.[78]

Three decades after *Bedtime for Bonzo*, presidential candidate Ronald Reagan was rousing the nation to what he would call "Morning in America." On August 22, 1980, in Dallas, Texas, he told ten thousand evangelicals that their entry into partisan politics was nothing short of a third Great Awakening.[79] The speech is remembered especially for Reagan's pronouncement, "You can't endorse me, but I can endorse you." That statement was nearly the reverse of reality, because the Reverend Jerry Falwell had already endorsed Reagan.[80] It was also a historical reversal of what presidential candidate John Kennedy had said about church and state on a visit to Texas twenty years earlier. Kennedy, a Catholic, had reassured the Houston Ministerial Association that under his presidency the church (meaning, primarily, *his* church) would remain absolutely separate from the state.[81] But since Kennedy's speech, the Supreme Court had raised the wall of separation not just against Catholics but also against the Protestant majority, many of whom now felt like exiles in their own land. Reagan denounced the Court's separationism as an assault on both "old time religion" and the "old time Constitution." In America's new morning, he promised, old times would be back.

Like most politicians, Reagan defended his policy with a tendentious account of early America. Citing John Winthrop, Roger Williams, and James Madison, he argued that the sole purpose of the First Amendment was to protect religion from government. Actually, Winthrop's Massachusetts was a theocracy that banished

Roger Williams for advocating the separation of church and state. As for James Madison, he was every bit as worried about the incursions of religion into government as about the reverse.[82] But Reagan was out to make myth, not to teach history. He was proffering an origin story that would authorize the political campaign on which his audience had collectively embarked. At a news conference the same day, Reagan affirmed another origin myth sacred to the new religious right: the book of Genesis. Avowing a policy that had been adopted in his home state of California, he proposed a "dual" approach: whenever the theory of evolution is taught in public schools, the Genesis account of creation should be taught alongside it.[83] Within two years, this proposal had become law in Louisiana: public schools were required to "give balanced treatment to creation-science and to evolution-science."[84]

When Reagan was elected president, Nell Segraves felt that she and other creationists were "about to repossess our land."[85] As governor of California, Reagan had supported Segraves's and her friend Jean Sumrall's campaign to outlaw the theory of evolution. They didn't succeed, but they did get California to adopt the dual approach.[86] Like others on the new religious right, Segraves believed that the theory of evolution led to atheism and that it replaced "Absolutes and Eternal Verities" with moral relativism. The people who championed evolution were the same ones pushing for gay rights and the Equal Rights Amendment (ERA). So, she felt, it was unsurprising that belief in evolution increased the rates of abortion, divorce, venereal disease, and sexual promiscuity.[87]

Segraves was part of a significant new element in creationist leadership—white antifeminist women. In the *Scopes* era, most creationist leaders had been Euro-Protestant men whose place in the social hierarchy was threatened by the rise of white urban elites. In the 1970s, some white women felt similarly threatened by feminism and the gay rights movement. They included Beverly LaHaye (wife of creationist Tim LaHaye), who founded Concerned Women for America; Phyllis Schlafly, nemesis of the ERA, who founded the Eagle Forum; and anti-gay activist Anita Bryant.[88] Although creationist constituencies remained predominantly white, their shared focus on the father-headed family overshadowed the enduring theme of white supremacy.

Those who wished to distance creationism from racism could even turn to the founder of creation science himself, Henry Morris, who in 1973 had made the case that evolutionism, not creationism, was responsible for racism in America.[89] There was an important element of truth in Morris's accusation, given that so many evolutionary scientists had embraced eugenics. But there was an equally important element of distortion, given that white segregationists remained a core constituency of the creationist movement. Moreover, both conservative white Christian leaders and a number of liberal white Christians had denounced the civil rights movement—if not because of racial ideology, then on the grounds that the church should not get involved in politics. Martin Luther King's classic "Letter from Birmingham Jail" was written to address just this criticism from white clergy.[90]

So when conservative Christians boldly entered partisan politics in the late 1970s, it called for some explanation. Jerry Falwell would later popularize the idea that the *Roe v. Wade* decision of 1973 had mobilized Christian conservatives. Yet Falwell hadn't founded the Moral Majority until six years after *Roe*, so his explanation was missing something. According to historian Randall Balmer, the missing element was race. Among the "segregation academies" that sprang up after the *Brown v. Board of Education* decision were a number of avowedly Christian institutions, including Falwell's Lynchburg Christian Academy. These schools received tax exemptions as not-for-profit charities until African American parents in Mississippi convincingly argued that segregationist schools ought not to be classified as "charitable." In the 1971 case of *Coit v. Green*, the Supreme Court ruled in favor of the African American parents. Christian segregationists were incensed. Evangelist Bob Jones, founder of Bob Jones University, stubbornly defended racial segregation on biblical grounds, but Falwell shrewdly took a different tack. Rather than appealing to the increasingly unpopular principle of racial segregation, he appealed to something Americans find harder to disparage: "religious freedom."[91]

In his 1980 speech in Dallas, Reagan did the same. Despite Falwell's later claim that the abortion issue had mobilized the religious right, Reagan did not mention abortion. He did, however, excoriate the federal government for forcing "all tax-exempt schools—including religious schools—to abide by affirmative action orders drawn up by—who else?—IRS bureaucrats."[92] African Americans were the real targets of the religious-freedom sentiments Reagan was invoking. But rather than linger on the fraught subject of race, he deftly redirected his listeners' anger against (presumptively white) government bureaucrats. Repurposing Cold War rhetoric, he implied that such government-enforced egalitarianism was, like communism, irreligious. In this way, his audience was reassured that what they were defending was not racial segregation so much as religious freedom and family values.

The creationist idea of fixed, divinely ordered "kinds," referenced by Reagan a day later, would be a potent conductor between the new theme of family order and the older theme of racial order. But although it seemed more important than ever to defeat the theory of evolution, the *Epperson* decision had made it impossible to simply outlaw teaching it in public schools. A new legal strategy was needed, and Henry Morris provided its underpinnings in his book *The Genesis Flood: The Biblical Record and Its Scientific Implications.*[93] Morris acknowledged that creationism could not be conclusively proven, but he argued that the same was true of evolution. Moreover, he treated apparent gaps or contradictions in the evidence for evolution as confirmation of what he considered the only alternative theory—the biblical account of creation. Based on this tortured reasoning, Morris concluded that the earth was not more than several thousand years old, that humans and dinosaurs had once roamed the earth together, and most importantly, that fossils, which most scientists saw as evidence of evolution, actually had resulted from Noah's flood.[94]

Only those sharing Morris's religious beliefs could be convinced by these arguments, yet the book sold hundreds of thousands of copies, illustrating the growing gap between scientific and public opinion in the United States. Morris's reasoning also served an important legal role because, since 1971, the Supreme Court had been approaching establishment issues via the "*Lemon* test."[95] The *Lemon* test requires every government action to serve purposes that are "primarily secular" and, to most Americans, science seemed to be the most secular of purposes. If creationism could be put forth as a science, people might come to agree that excluding it from the science classroom was doctrinaire, unreasonable, and unscientific.

But the representation of creationism as a scientific idea was only one side of the Reagan-era strategy. The other side was the startling claim that evolution, rather than being a neutral and objective scientific theory, was actually a religion. This argument was inadvertently made available to the creationists by a *dictum* of the Supreme Court in the 1961 case of *Torcaso v. Watkins*. Torcaso, an atheist, had objected to being made to affirm a belief in God as a condition for taking public office in the state of Maryland. Finding in favor of Torcaso, the Supreme Court for the first time recognized the existence of nontheistic religions, including Confucianism, Buddhism, and "secular humanism."[96]

This was a sleight of hand on the Court's part, for Torcaso had not identified himself with secular humanism or a nontheistic religion; he simply did *not* believe in God and was *not* religious. But the Court's elision of the difference between nontheistic religion and simple nonreligion invited creationists to venture a similar gambit. They began to argue that the theory of evolution, although presented by scientists and educators as religiously neutral, was really a doctrine of "secular humanism." Therefore, went the rationale, by teaching the theory of evolution, the public schools were establishing religion in violation of the federal Constitution. The only solution was to also teach the "other" theory—creation science.

This odd couple of assertions—that creationism was a science and evolutionism a religion—first appeared in 1978 as an anonymous note in the *Yale Law Journal*.[97] The author was Wendell Bird, who would be Louisiana's chief counsel when it defended its balanced treatment law before the Supreme Court. Bird had a gift for capitalizing on the contradictions of religion-talk. When he wanted to claim the protections of the free exercise clause, Bird would avow the religious character of creationism. He argued, for instance, that teaching the theory of evolution to creationist children abridged their religious freedom by unsettling their beliefs. But when he wanted to evade the establishment clause, he would disavow the religious character of creationism, contending that it could be taught strictly as science. Yet again, when he wanted to turn the establishment clause against the opposition, he would argue that evolutionism was at least as religious as creationism. In fact, Bird claimed that all views on evolution are "religious" in the sense that all religions either accept or reject the theory—in effect, dividing religions into those that shared Bird's beliefs and those that did not.

But Bird's Jesuitical subtleties were lost on ordinary creationists like Senator Bill Keith, who introduced the Balanced Treatment Bill in 1980 after his son came home from school in tears, having been ridiculed for believing in God.[98] Unlike Bird, Keith did not try to present evolution as religious; to him it was irreligious, consonant with "cardinal principle[s] of religious humanism, secular humanism, theological liberalism, aetheistism [*sic*]." He defined creationism in plainly religious terms—"the belief that the origin of the elements, the galaxy, the solar system, of life, of all the species of plants and animals, the origin of man, and the origin of all things and their processes and relationships were created *ex nihilo* and fixed by God." Only in the second draft of the bill, guided by Wendell Bird, did Louisiana legislators remove the word "God" and adopt the expression "creation science." Both versions claimed that the act had the "secular purposes" of "protecting academic freedom" and "teaching all the evidence."[99] The question for the Supreme Court, then, would be whether these purported secular reasons were sincere, or whether they were simply a sham for religion.

The majority's answer to that question, and a vigorous dissent, were put forth in the 1987 case of *Edwards v. Aguillard* by the Court's two Catholic justices. William Brennan (b. 1909) and Antonin Scalia (b. 1936) both had immigrant parents, grew up in New Jersey, attended public elementary schools, and took their legal training at Harvard. But in the generation between their comings-of-age, American Catholicism had been transformed from an ostracized minority religion to a securely fixed bloc in the Euro-American establishment. Brennan, an old-fashioned Catholic Democrat, was most concerned with the protection of minorities, which he believed required a high wall of separation. But Scalia, a Reagan Republican, identified with the "moral majority" that felt displaced from its former centrality in American public life. For him, Brennan's wall was destroying America's foundations.

The question of whether "creation science" was a cover for religion would have reminded William Brennan of *Epperson v. Arkansas* for many reasons. In 1968, Brennan had voted with the majority against the Arkansas anti-evolution law, agreeing with Abe Fortas that although the law did not mention the Bible, it was clearly motivated by "fundamentalist religious fervor." And in the 1958 case of *Cooper v. Aaron*, Brennan organized the Court's *per curiam* ruling denying Arkansas's last-ditch request to delay school integration. Here, too, he found the state's professed motives disingenuous. Arkansas officials had contended that they needed time to restore law and order after the "violence and disorder" caused by the enrollment of the Little Rock Nine. The Court, led by Brennan, found that the "violence and disorder" had been largely produced by the officials' own resistance to desegregation.[100]

So when Louisiana claimed that its balanced treatment law was intended only to provide better science education, Brennan would have remembered that in Arkansas and elsewhere, people routinely rationalized unlawful discrimination by claiming to be acting from nondiscriminatory motives. Just as sham nondiscriminatory reasons were a typical feature of unlawful discrimination, so sham secular reasons might be offered to cover the unlawful establishment of religion. As Brennan noted in his opinion against Louisiana's Balanced Treatment Act, a lower court had already found that another state had enacted just such a religious sham in the form of a balanced treatment law like Louisiana's. Once again, the state was Arkansas, whose balanced treatment act had been struck down by Judge William Overton in a case widely publicized as "Scopes II." Although the phrases "balanced treatment" and "creation science" were obviously crafted to avoid religion, Judge Overton ruled that the Arkansas law was "simply and purely an effort to introduce the biblical version of creation into the public school curricula."[101]

But Antonin Scalia found the whole notion of legislative motivations suspect. To begin with, he claimed, jurists were obligated to assume that legislators meant what they wrote. The Creationism Act had stated its secular purpose, and for the majority to discount this purpose was to call the legislators of Louisiana liars. Besides, Scalia asked, what did it even mean to assess the intentions of a whole legislature? Individual lawmakers might have cast their votes for reasons that were *both* religious and educational. They might also have been motivated by (his examples) friendship, party intrigue, publicity seeking, spousal conflict, or intoxication. Moreover, the Constitution itself makes protecting religion a permissible and sometimes even a required basis for government action. To disallow religious motives was profoundly discriminatory, Scalia wrote, because it "would deprive religious men and women of their right to participate in the political process."[102]

But perhaps the most influential factor behind their *Edwards* opinions, albeit one that neither Brennan nor Scalia would have been eager to probe, was their fundamentally different sensibilities about religion itself. For Brennan, religion was positive in private life but divisive in public. Although he wrote appreciatively of "the good mothers, fathers and ministers" who inculcate religion in homes and churches, he firmly opposed school-sponsored prayer. And having learned from the history of the Bible wars to be skeptical of anything claiming to be "nonsectarian," Brennan's wall of separation applied to all religion, including that of the majority.[103] Unlike Scalia and the Moral Majority, Brennan did not assume that the moral teachings of his religion should be the basis of legislation. In opposition to Catholic teachings (and, by some accounts, under threat of excommunication), he voted for abortion rights in *Roe v. Wade*.[104] In 1986, when a divided Court upheld the criminalization of homosexual sodomy, Brennan sided with the dissent, anticipating the position the Court would adopt six years after his death.[105]

Scalia's religiosity, by contrast, was extremely, even nostalgically conservative. On Sundays he would travel to a traditional Latin Mass rather than attend the Catholic church nearest his home.[106] He expected government to acknowledge majority religion and lend it support. This would inevitably disfavor minorities and dissenters, Scalia recognized, but it was a natural consequence of the democratic process.[107] Although public religious expressions might make some minorities feel a little excluded, Scalia found that "nothing, absolutely nothing, is so inclined to foster among religious believers of various faiths a toleration—no, an affection— for one another than voluntarily joining in prayer together."[108] Provided that individuals' rights were not directly abridged, disfavoring moral or religious minorities was, in his estimation, far preferable to the effacement of a common moral and religious culture.

In his dissent in *Edwards v. Aguillard*, Scalia offered a pair of hypotheticals that preserve, as if in amber, the bewilderment of many religious Americans about the implications of science for their faith and their nation. Suppose, he suggested, that "a history teacher falsely told her students that the bones of Jesus Christ had been discovered, or a physics teacher that the Shroud of Turin had been conclusively determined to be inexplicable on the basis of natural causes." In those cases, he argued, surely state officials could demand a correction, even though the officials would no doubt be "prompted by concern for the religious beliefs of the mis-instructed students."[109]

Considering Justice Scalia's usual toughness, these questions revealed an almost touching naiveté. Of course, corrections would be warranted in the cases he mentioned, but not for the reasons he gave. In the case of the bones of Jesus, a correction would be needed simply because the purported discovery was false, not because it had shaken students' beliefs. And in the case of the Shroud of Turin, a correction would be needed not because the shroud has natural explanations (although no doubt it does), but because science never declares a phenomenon "inexplicable on the basis of natural causes," only that its causes have not been identified.

Yet Scalia was expressing the painful anxiety felt by Americans whose religious beliefs, once counted as public truth, were now being expunged from the canon. Did this not imply that those who held such beliefs were ignorant and backward? And are not ignorant, backward people considered lesser specimens of *homo sapiens*? For religious and racial minorities, such humiliation was nothing new. But for those who considered themselves America's "moral majority," it was nearly unbearable.

Intelligent Design in Dover, Pennsylvania

In August 2002, Bertha Spahr was disturbed to notice that a large mural called "The Descent of Man" had gone missing from Dover High School. It had been painted by a student several years earlier and had been on casual display ever since, resting on the ledge of a chalkboard. Theft or vandalism would have been bad enough, but for Spahr, who headed the biology department, this was also the loss of an excellent pedagogical tool. So she asked the school superintendent, but was told that the mural's whereabouts were none of her business.[110] It took almost two years and a heated series of school board meetings for her to learn, from board member Bill Buckingham, that the mural had been removed and set aflame while Buckingham, in his own words, "gleefully watched."[111]

Before 2002, Dover High School had been using a well-respected biology textbook by Kenneth Miller of Brown University. New editions, published every several years, were known by their cover photos—the dragonfly book, the lion book, the elephant book.[112] When Miller's new edition came out, expectations were that Dover would purchase it, because the school had always acquired new biology textbooks without much fuss. But that year, Alan Bonsell was elected chair of the school board and had informed the teachers that he had two priorities (both of which would have defied Supreme Court rulings): to restore school-sponsored prayer and to counter evolutionism with creationism. Bonsell had appointed Buckingham head of the curriculum committee and assigned to him to review Miller's latest edition. Buckingham found the book "laced with Darwinism" and refused to purchase it unless the school promised that an image like the one he'd seen burned that summer would never again be displayed at Dover High.[113]

By the fall of 2004, Bonsell, Buckingham, and their allies on the school board had passed what became known as the Dover ID policy. The policy was predicated on an apparently fortuitous event—the anonymous donation to the school of sixty copies of a book called *Of Pandas and People*. Ninth-grade science classes were to be read the following disclaimer, casting a cloud of suspicion over the theory of evolution and urging students to read *Pandas*, which would counter evolution with an alternative theory called intelligent design:

> The Pennsylvania Academic Standards require students . . .
> to take a standardized test of which evolution is a part. Be-
> cause Darwin's Theory is a theory, it continues to be tested
> as new evidence is discovered. The Theory is not a fact.
> Gaps in the Theory exist for which there is no evidence. . . .
> Intelligent Design is an explanation of the origin of life

that differs from Darwin's view. The reference book, *Of Pandas and People*, is available for students who might be interested in gaining an understanding of what Intelligent Design actually involves.[114]

Like every previous creationism conflict, the one in Dover was rife with monkey imagery. First there was the burned mural, which had depicted humans evolving from primates. Then there was Buckingham repeatedly challenging Spahr and other advocates of modern biology to "trace your roots to the monkey you came from."[115] Children whose parents opposed the ID policy were taunted as "monkey girl" or "ape boy."[116] And inevitably, the monkey-talk boomeranged against the creationists themselves. A cartoon in the *York Daily Record* portrayed creationism as a wolf in the sheep's clothing of intelligent design, ridden by a clownish monkey identified as "the Religious Right."[117]

But in Dover, as in other creationist hot spots, monkey imagery was also a racialized code for status conflicts among whites. A rural borough in western Pennsylvania with a population of 1,800, Dover was about the size of Dayton, Tennessee, in 1925, and the vast majority of its residents (96 percent) were white.[118] Most adults were employed and owned their homes, but half had only a high school education and just a fifth, post-secondary degrees. Those who supported the theory of evolution—teachers like Bertha Spahr and Bryan Rehm, or journalists like Laurie Lebo— belonged to a fairly elite segment of the community, although they probably would not have described themselves that way. As far as Bill Buckingham and Alan Bonsell were concerned, education and sophistication had made those people forget what it meant to be human, moral, and American. And as far as the teachers and intellectual leaders of Dover were concerned, Bonsell and Buckingham were leading the community straight back to the past.

Like its racial dynamics, the religious dynamics of creationism in Dover were obscured—some would say obfuscated. Ever since Tennessee's Butler Act, creationism had been reformulating itself to avoid establishment clause challenges. In Arkansas, the anti-evolution campaign of the 1920s had been based on the Bible, but references to the Bible were carefully expunged from the final wording of the 1928

statute. Louisiana, in its 1981 Balanced Treatment Act, had edged farther from Christianity by pointing out that the special creation was
harmonious with several religions, and by asserting that creationism
could be taught as a purely scientific theory. The theory of intelligent
design, formulated by Phillip Johnson in his 1991 book *Darwin on
Trial*, claimed to be independent of all religions, deities, and sacred
texts.[119] While proving that nature was full of intelligent designs, it
would refrain from asserting anything about the existence or character of the designer.

Opponents of the ID policy argued that this distancing from
religion was, as Judge John Jones III would later put it, "at best disingenuous and at worst a canard."[120] Considering Buckingham and
Bonsell's antics, which would come out in court, this judgment was
not entirely unfair. Yet the religious, intellectual, moral, and political implications of ID were so thoroughly blended in its proponents' minds that they could present the theory, in fairly good
conscience, as something other than religion. In Dover and around
the country, intelligent design was more than a theory about the origin of species—more, even, than a doctrine about God and nature.
It was the key doctrine of a certain kind of Americanism. According
to the Discovery Institute, ID's main think tank, the theory implied
positions on everything from market regulation and same-sex marriage to abortion and American exceptionalism. Intelligent design
was felt to authorize an entire social vision, as if by pulling a single
switch one could save or annihilate a world.

While proponents of the ID policy felt religion to be foundational for their community, opponents saw it as a personal belief that
should neither intrude on public life nor be dictated by public officials. For lead plaintiff Tammy Kitzmiller, religion belonged in the
home, under the authority of parents. Plaintiff Bryan Rehm had an
additional way of compartmentalizing religion and science: he
taught biology during the school year and Bible school in the summer. Noel Wenrich, who eventually resigned from the school board
over its ID policy, put it this way: "My religion is personal. It's between me, God, and my pastor." Casey Brown, another board member who ended up resigning, said something similar: "An individual's
religious beliefs should have no impact on his or her ability to serve
as a school board director."[121]

In this way, religion in Dover displayed a pattern that sociologists had been noticing since the late twentieth century. Previously, the most important religious differences had been along denominational lines, but after World War II, political views gradually became more determinative.[122] At the same time, conservative congregations grew in the number and intensity of their membership while liberal congregations declined. In Dover, church membership seems to have been fairly high, but the division between liberal and conservative churches was quite marked. For example, Buckingham attended Harmony Grove Baptist Church while Bryan and Christie Rehm belonged to the United Church of Christ—congregations at opposite ends of the political spectrum that also take opposite views on evolution.[123] While proponents of ID repeatedly demanded to know whether those who disagreed with them had been "born again," opponents of the policy resented having the content or intensity of their religious beliefs subject to public judgment.[124]

In tandem with the chasm between liberals and conservatives, the numbers of religiously unaffiliated Americans began to rise sharply in the late twentieth century. For many liberal-leaning people, especially youth, it was easier to leave religion behind than to find a progressive religious community. Atheism became a lively option. For most of American history, freethinkers had faced American religion in patient silence, even while being excoriated as immoral and unpatriotic. But in 1986, when English biologist Richard Dawkins published *The Blind Watchmaker*, atheism took off the gloves. Not content to leave religion in a separate sphere, Dawkins set out to disprove it. Also abandoned was the modernist truce in which science promised not to deal with questions of meaning or value. Instead, Dawkins proposed (as Auguste Comte had done in the nineteenth century) that such questions could be answered in purely rational and scientific terms.[125] *The Blind Watchmaker* was widely read in the United States and was followed over the next decades by a series of bestselling books by three American authors—Christopher Hitchens, Daniel Dennett, and Sam Harris. Together they inspired a loose movement called the New Atheism, and even an ironic religion, the "Church of the Flying Spaghetti Monster."[126]

In Dover, the New Atheism didn't have much impact other than on journalist Laurie Lebo, who, after reporting extensively on the *Kitzmiller* case, decided to have the Flying Spaghetti Monster tattooed, as she described it, "just above my butt."[127] But it had a large impact on the ID controversy, because the founding text of the intelligent design movement, Johnson's *Darwin on Trial*, had been written to refute Dawkins.[128] And just as the New Atheism needed creationism as its foil, so the ID movement needed the New Atheism. Both sides had built totalistic, opposing systems of meaning upon their particular positions on the origins of life. Moreover, they had a shared interest in erasing any mediating positions. ID proponents denied the validity not just of atheism and non-Christian religions, but of any form of Christianity that was not "born again." And the New Atheists, like Comte before them, rejected efforts to reconcile religion and science, which they saw as efforts to shirk the rigors of scientific inquiry. That left only the two positions, locked in furious battle like Darrow and Bryan, with no oxygen for anyone else.

The quintessentially modernist assessment of religions is that they are good in their commonalities, if potentially divisive in their differences. That, probably, is how Dover residents managed religious differences before the ID controversy. But with the Christian right insisting that only its religion was good, and the New Atheists insisting that all religions were bad, the modernist settlement was disrupted. Then came September 11, 2001, when a professedly religious form of political violence hurled itself at the foundations of the American government and economy. Ironically, the attacks produced additional confluences between people like Johnson, who saw themselves as the champions of American religion, and the New Atheists, who saw themselves as the sworn enemies of all religion.

Johnson saw only two ways to respond to 9/11: either by affirming the United States as a Christian nation or by "cringing in fear of these Muslim terrorists." The New Atheists were of course repelled at the thought of a Christian nation, but they were, like Johnson, particularly repelled by Islam. Sam Harris called it a "religion of war"; Christopher Hitchens, deliberately inverting "Allah Akbar," published a book entitled *God Is Not Great*. Daniel Dennett would describe Islam as a "brain virus." To both the New Atheists and the new creationists, the events of 9/11 proved that Islam was evil, that liberal relativism must yield to absolute truth, and that religious toleration, at least toward Islam, was inimical to global peace and the national defense.[129]

Because Dover sits just a hundred miles east of Shanksville, Pennsylvania, where the third plane crashed on 9/11, the day echoed especially loudly in its ID debate. "This country wasn't founded on Muslim beliefs or evolution," said Buckingham at a public meeting on the ID policy. "This country was founded on Christianity and our students should be taught as such." He and other school officials accused the evolutionists in their midst of atheism and disloyalty to the nation, implicitly connecting the two charges. Noel Wenrich, who fought the ID policy, recalled that "I was referred to as unpatriotic, and my religious beliefs were questioned." More or less reflexively, Buckingham, Bonsell, and other ID supporters equated ID, evangelical Christianity, and Americanism. "Two thousand years ago, someone died on a cross," Buckingham pleaded. "Can't someone take a stand for Him?" They also denounced the separation of church and state as a "myth."[130]

Judge Jones was well aware that the "wall" is not in the Constitution, but he nonetheless saw separation as an apt expression of what the establishment clause requires. Sticking with the modest self-description of mainstream science (and avoiding the hubristic claims of the New Atheists), he wrote that science is simply not concerned with questions of purpose or meaning. The "bedrock assumption" of the ID policy—that the theory of evolution contradicts belief in God—was therefore "utterly false."[131] Rather than accept the argument that only one of the two theories could be true, Jones asked a different set of questions. First, was intelligent design a religious concept or, as its supporters claimed, could it be considered a scientific theory? Second, were the effects of the ID policy and the intentions of those who created it primarily religious? Or did the policy have the primarily secular purpose of fostering critical thinking and science education, as the school board claimed?

By tracing its history from fundamentalism in the 1920s, through its transformation into creation science after the *Epperson* decision of 1968, and finally to its reincarnation as intelligent design after the *Edwards* decision of 1987, Jones concluded that ID was a religious theory. Moreover, it turned out that *Of Pandas and People* had originally been drafted as a creationist text. Bertha Spahr had gathered as much when, upon unpacking the box of donated books, she had found a catalog of works on creation science.[132] Spahr's impression was confirmed by testimony from philosopher Barbara Forrest, whose meticulous study revealed that after the *Edwards* decision the manuscript had been redacted to replace "creationism" with "intelligent design." The redaction changed none of the book's creationist substance and was done so hastily that it left telltale typos such as the "cdesign proponentsists."[133] *Pandas*, although held out by Dover to prove ID's scientific pedigree, became almost comical proof of its religious ancestry.

To assess whether the effects of the ID policy were religious, Jones used the "reasonable observer" standard that had been formulated by Sandra Day O'Connor in 1984.[134] O'Connor's standard, called the endorsement test, asks whether a reasonable observer would conclude that the government was favoring or disfavoring people on the basis of religion. Jones decided that any reasonable observer in the United States would know something about ID's descent from fundamentalist creationism, and that a reasonable observer living in Dover would have read some of many letters and editorials about the ID controversy that had appeared in local papers. Most importantly, he concluded, no reasonable observer could miss the fact that in most of those letters and editorials, the ID controversy was considered to be about religion.[135]

To assess whether ID might be considered a scientific theory, Jones heard days of testimony from scientists, both mainstream ones like Kenneth Miller and ID proponents like biochemist Michael Behe. Jones learned that ID had not been published in peer-reviewed scientific journals or presented at scientific conferences. Behe's examples of "irreducible complexity," which he advanced as evidence of intelligent design, were refuted by Miller and other mainstream scientists as not irreducible at all. On the stand, Behe also was forced to admit that his definition of science, formulated to include ID, would logically have to include astrology as well. Worst of all for the defense was Phillip Johnson's "Wedge Document," the mission statement of the ID movement, which stated frankly that its ultimate goal was to "replace science as currently practiced with 'theistic and Christian science.' " That, for Jones, settled the question. ID could not possibly be science because, by replacing methodological naturalism with an untethered supernaturalism, it rejected the very "ground rules" of science.[136]

Finally, Jones returned to the *Lemon* test, asking whether those who put the policy in place had acted from primarily religious intentions. Here the proceedings became almost gruesome, as Bonsell and Buckingham were publicly hoisted on their own petards. Both had sworn that they'd never advocated creationism, only intelligent design. But in fact they hadn't shifted from "creationism" to "intelligent design" until August 2004, when they were sternly ordered to do so by their solicitor.[137] Neither man, it turned out, really understood the difference between the two theories—and not for nothing, because there was little substantive difference. Witness after witness reported having heard Bonsell and Buckingham endorse creationism. Buckingham had even done so in a television interview, which he was forced to watch from the witness stand.

The last straw was that Buckingham and Bonsell had lied about how the sixty copies of *Pandas* had materialized at Dover High. Both had denied any knowledge of how this came about, insisting that the books arrived through the miraculous generosity of an anonymous donor. Actually, Buckingham had solicited contributions from his church, then sent a check for $850 to Bonsell's father, who purchased the books and had them delivered to the high school. Jones, on discovering this, was struck by the "breathtaking inanity" of the machinations leading up to the ID policy, and furious that witnesses had perjured themselves. All of this was more than enough to convince him that ID was religion and *not* science.

Jones's memorandum opinion in *Kitzmiller v. Dover* is arguably the best decision ever written on the creation/evolution controversy. But even his rock-solid reasoning contains peculiarities resulting from the awkward demands of establishment jurisprudence. For example, in showing that ID was not science, Jones's point was that the ID policy did not serve a *secular* purpose. Yet plenty of topics are secular but are not science. To put it differently, plenty of topics are neither science nor religion. Consider, for instance, math, music, or history. A school board that forced any of these subjects into the biology curriculum would be making bad education policy. Yet the establishment clause could not be used to correct that mistake, because the establishment clause pertains only to things marked "religion."

Had the history of ideas gone a bit differently, ID itself might never have become what we call religion, because (although Jones didn't mention this) it was formulated by the ancient Greeks as what we usually call philosophy. In his brief history of ID, Jones correctly pointed out that the theory had passed through many religious stations on its way to Dover—Thomas Aquinas in the thirteenth century, William Paley in the nineteenth century, the fundamentalists of the twentieth century.[138] But what if none of that had ever happened? What if the theory of intelligent design had survived only as a bit of Aristotelian philosophy? Might public schools then mandate its teaching?

From an educational standpoint, the answer should still be no. It would be as wrong to require Aristotelian ID in the science classroom as to require musical training in that context. But the reason, in each case, is not that these subjects *are religion*, but simply that they *are not science*. In other words, what made Dover's policy legally wrong (the similarity between ID and religion) was not pedagogically on point, while what made the policy pedagogically unwise (the dissimilarity between ID and science) was not legally dispositive. In Dover, like everywhere else, it was hard to discern between truth and bias, objectivity and subjectivity, partisan ideologies and the common good. These difficult judgments had to be made, but religion-talk once again proved inadequate to making them.

Inheriting the Wind

On the last day of the *Kitzmiller* trial, a production of *Inherit the Wind* opened in Theater Harrisburg, a block from Judge Jones's courthouse. Near the end of the play, the Drummond/Darrow character says to Cates/Scopes, "You don't suppose this kind of thing is ever finished, do you?" Reportedly, the line drew a weary laugh from the audience.[139]

But as tired as Americans claim to be of this story, we've been reprising it for nearly a century. For those who like the way the story is told in *Inherit the Wind*, the moral is that American progress must always be protected against the regressive urges of religion. For creationists, the moral is that America must not be led by those who, thinking themselves gods, would make us all less than human. Whatever version of the story we prefer, each retelling makes us more sure that religion and science are antagonists, more ready to typecast the actors, and more adept at performing our scripted lines.

And because the story is about "religion," it's been shaped by the contrary metaphors of wall and foundation. In the *Scopes* era, before the wall of separation was resurrected in the judiciary, foundation was the dominant metaphor on both sides. Creationists held that civilization rested on an eternal, divinely instituted order; evolutionists equated civilization with progressive change. By the *Epperson* period, the wall of separation had climbed to its all-time high, yet the Fortas majority cautiously applied it only to religion that was "particular" or "sectarian." That left open the possibility that government might support religion in a more general way, as it had often done in the past. But twenty years later, William Brennan foreclosed that possibility by reiterating what the Court said in the *Everson* decision of 1947: that government is prohibited not only from supporting particular religions but from supporting "all religions."

That was a turning point. Previously, the judiciary had managed church-state relations by distinguishing between sectarian religion (from which government had to remain separate) and nonsectarian religion (which government could support). In that framework, wall and foundation seemed to cohere. Government would avoid the hot spots of religious difference but support those aspects of religion that belonged to the common ethos. But to the extent it ever existed, that common ethos belonged mainly to Euro-Protestants, and by the time of the *Edwards* case, it was badly fractured even among them. The first fracture appeared when fundamentalists broke with modernists who declined to read the Bible literally. The second fracture appeared in the Reagan era, when the religious right captured the flag of public religion for a controversial vision of family, society, and politics. "Religion," rather than evoking unity, became the ensign of what its own proponents call a "culture war."

But like most religious controversies, this one is more about inter-group conflict than about law. Nationally, creationists are demographically similar to the people who supported Dover's intelligent design policy. They are likely to be middle-aged or older, to live in rural areas or the South, and to have never attended or not finished college. Those who accept the theory of evolution, by contrast, are more likely to reside in the Northeast or Northwest, to have a college degree, and to hold professional jobs.[140] This is a rough demographic portrait, but it is enough to suggest that the creationist picture of a divinely ordered hierarchy of life may appeal most to those whose socioeconomic status is precarious, while the picture of a progressively evolving world may appeal most to those who are either secure in their status or hopeful about their prospects. Most creationists want to protect a faith that seems threatened by an evolutionary worldview, and most evolutionists value the humane and rational aims of science. Yet more often than not, the rhetoric of the conflict is inflected with assumptions about the moral, cultural, or intellectual superiority of one's own side. And because most of the principals are white, the "culture war" often looks like a competition to control the top of the American social hierarchy.

Democracy depends on the ability to learn, deliberate, and make decisions together. But collective learning depends on social trust, because much of what we "know" depends on whom we trust. People resist trusting those who threaten their dignity, their status, or (for some) their sense of superiority. Confronted with such threats, whether real or perceived, people can put up an intellectual resistance that no argument or evidence can penetrate. For those trying to teach science, it may be tempting to blame this intellectual resistance on religion. But doing so amounts to intellectual resistance of another kind. What ails knowledge in the United States cannot be reduced to religion, nor can the remedy be reduced to science. What ails us is being human, which means that we need to know; what heals is knowledge of ourselves and our relations.

CHAPTER SIX

Religion, Race, and Science
The Battle over Sexuality

Condemnation of these practices is firmly rooted in Judeo-Christian moral and ethical standards. . . . To hold that the act of homosexual sodomy is somehow protected as a fundamental right would be to cast aside millennia of moral teaching.

—CHIEF JUSTICE WARREN BURGER, CONCURRING OPINION IN *BOWERS V. HARDWICK*, 1986

The fact that the governing majority in a State has traditionally viewed a particular practice as immoral is not a sufficient reason for upholding a law prohibiting the practice; neither history nor tradition could save a law prohibiting miscegenation from constitutional attack.

—JUSTICE JOHN PAUL STEVENS, DISSENTING OPINION IN *BOWERS V. HARDWICK*, 1986

NO AMERICAN CONFLICT IN the twenty-first century has been more intense than the one about sexual difference and same-sex marriage.[1] But more than any conflict before it, this one is typically represented as pitting people either for or against religion as such. On one side, goes the familiar narrative, are those who support religion and therefore oppose LGBT rights; on the other, those who support LGBT rights and therefore oppose religion. One side defends the heterosexual norm as a basic tenet of religion, a consistent feature of American history, and a cornerstone of civilization. The other side says that religious beliefs should have no bearing on law or public policy, and appeals instead to the scientific consensus that being homosexual, bisexual, or transgender is a fact of nature. One side considers homoeroticism a sinful choice. The other side says that sexuality is an identity, not a choice, and that opposition to LGBT rights is akin to racism—at best explained by ignorance, at worst by animus.

This picture of the conflict is useful in small ways. If you want to figure out where a new acquaintance stands on sexual nonconformity, just drop the word "religion," gauge their reaction, and you'll probably know. And yet this familiar picture is both counterfactual and counterproductive. It is counterfactual because religions in America are profoundly divided on the question of sexuality. It is counterproductive because instead of debating the real issues, we fight about whether religion should be the foundation of public life or walled off in a separate sphere. Once again, we use the word "religion" in ways that don't facilitate communication but obstruct it.

One illustration of the diversity of American religions was the flurry of amicus briefs that hit the Supreme Court in the 2015 case of *Obergefell v. Hodges.* Briefs opposing same-sex marriages came from major religious organizations including the Southern Baptist Convention, the LDS Church, the U.S. Conference of Catholic Bishops, the Missouri Lutheran Synod, the Assemblies of God, the Free Methodist Church, the National Coalition of Black Pastors, and Agudath Israel (ultra-Orthodox Judaism). Yet some of the nation's oldest denominations weighed in on the other side: the United Church of Christ, Reform Judaism, the Society of Friends, the Unitarian Universalist Association. Alongside them were scores of newer religious voices, including the Reconstructionist Rabbinical Council, the Metropolitan Community Church, the Hindu American Foundation, the Sikh American Legal Foundation, and the American Humanist Association. Even religions that were divided about or officially opposed to same-sex marriage included organized subgroups that signed amicus briefs for same-sex marriage. Among them were the More Light Presbyterians, Lutherans for Full Participation, Affirmation Methodists, the Progressive National Baptist Convention, and Muslims for Progressive Values.[2]

Like the other conflicts in this book, this one merits a place because religion-talk has played a decisive role. But unlike those other conflicts, where religion appeared front and center, in this one it has been shuttled from center stage to the wings and is now angling for a comeback. In the 1986 case of *Bowers v. Hardwick*, where this chapter's narrative begins, the Supreme Court kept the civil rights of homosexuals under the authority of majoritarian religion and morality. But beginning in 1996, the tide began to turn when a slender majority of Supreme Court justices began to compare discrimination based on sexual orientation with discrimination based on race.[3] Although they respectfully acknowledged religious and moral objections to homosexuality, they held that these objections could no longer justify the denial of gay civil rights. Since then, the Court by narrow margins has managed sexuality like race, much to the distress of religious conservatives, who find their beliefs equated with ignorance and their moral compunctions with phobia or brute hatred.

I propose to shift the terms of our national debate by switching out some of the participants. I will tell the judicial story of LGBT civil rights in conversation with individuals whose perspectives differ from those of the familiar leading voices. Usually we have one party who likes religion and wants more of it in public life and another who dislikes religion and wants less of it. I will instead write about people who are deeply religious but whose religious traditions distinguish what they expect of their members from what they expect of the world. I have not chosen individuals who are neutral about LGBT civil rights, because nobody is neutral. Nor have I chosen one person who is for and one who is against civil same-sex marriage, because I do not think it productive to re-litigate this issue. Instead I have chosen people whose lives, although very different from each other's, display the intersection of forces that many Americans keep apart: religion, sexuality, and racial/ethnic identity.

One of these individuals is Steven Greenberg; the other is Emilie Townes. Both are ordained clergy—he in the Orthodox Jewish tradition of Yeshiva University, she in the American Baptist Church, USA (ABCUSA). Both are highly accomplished, admired (and sometimes criticized) on the national and international stage. Rabbi Greenberg rose to prominence in 1999, when he came out as gay and Orthodox in an Israeli newspaper, and again in 2001, when he appeared in a film called *Trembling before G-d*, which documented the struggles of gay and lesbian Orthodox Jews. In 2004 he published *Wrestling with God and Men: Homosexuality in the Jewish Tradition*, and in 2012 he founded Eshel, an organization for gay and lesbian Orthodox Jews.[4] Reverend Townes, dean of Vanderbilt Divinity School, is the first African American woman to lead a major Protestant seminary in the United States. She is also openly and comfortably lesbian. Townes has taught in a number of venerable Protestant institutions, including Yale Divinity School and Union Theological Seminary. She has lectured widely, produced a long list of publications (including *Womanist Ethics and the Cultural Production of Evil*, published in 2006), and served as president of the American Academy of Religion, the world's largest organization for scholars of religion.

Both baby boomers, Townes and Greenberg have lived through astonishing changes around sexuality in the United States. They were in their early teens, and far from New York City's Greenwich Village, when the Stonewall Rebellion of 1969 sparked the gay liberation movement. They were in their thirties and coming out as gay when the Supreme Court ruled, in the 1986 case of *Bowers v. Hardwick*, that homosexuals have no right to sexual privacy. A decade later, when Townes and Greenberg were already well-known advocates for gay rights, the Supreme Court made its first ruling favorable to LGBT people, saying that they could not be excluded from the political process simply because of their sexuality. Greenberg and Townes were nearing fifty when the Supreme Court finally decriminalized homosexual sex (i.e., their own intimate lives) in the 2003 case of *Lawrence v. Texas*. And each was approaching sixty and had been in a committed partnership for years when the

Supreme Court legalized same-sex marriage in the 2015 case of *Obergefell v. Hodges.*[5]

Townes and Greenberg have steered their own courses and guided many others through these sea changes. In a society still deeply at odds about how people may or may not touch each other, how men and women may or may not relate, how people of different colors, religions, and heritages can coexist in peace, their insights cannot but enhance our navigational skill.

Spiritual Formations

When Emilie Townes was growing up, Durham, North Carolina, was so segregated that until she was in the fourth grade she did not know that white people even lived there. She remembers Durham as an "all-black world" where "everything that we needed to survive was in the black community."[6] Townes got a single message from her church, her parents, and her grandmother, Nora Jackson, known to her neighbors as Miss Nora: "God loves you, you are a child of God, and that's all you ever need to know. There's nothing anyone can do to take that from you." By the age of four, she knew better than to believe the fire-and-brimstone sermon of a visiting preacher. "That is not God!" the preschool future theologian mused. "He's got it wrong!"

Until her early twenties, Townes belonged to predominantly black churches. Not everything about them was wonderful; services could induce anything from ecstasy to extreme boredom. But the Black Church was Townes's first spiritual home, and it permanently shaped the way she likes to worship—that is to say, ecstatically. In her twenties she joined the American Baptist Church, the shoot of the Baptist tradition that grew from its 1845 schism over slavery, and that today prides itself on being one of the most racially diverse denominations in the United States. Religion then became not only her home and heritage, but a commitment and, eventually, a career.

What drew Townes to the Baptists was their insistence on adult baptism—in other words, their insistence on personal choice. Since colonial times, this theological position has had important political implications: it was the belief that genuine faith can only be based on personal conversion that led Roger Williams to call for a "hedge or wall of separation" between church and state. But Baptists have never been of one mind on the implications of these two principles. While all are evangelicals, called to spread the "good news" of Christ, they've disagreed mightily about what the headline should be, and what story the church should write beneath that headline. For Townes, the headline is love. With Cornel West, she holds that "justice is what love looks like in public."

Even in childhood, Townes had to learn that beyond her safe neighborhood the world was not ruled by the law of love, nor did it abide by her community's maxim: "Treat people right." The momentous 1954 *Brown v. Board of Education* decision meant that desegregation was on the way, and that white resistance to it would bring an ugliness that, to the young Emilie Townes, was quite new. In grade school, teachers constantly warned her and her classmates that "you need to learn" (meaning, you need to learn *now*) because "if you had white teachers they wouldn't care about you." And she did learn, landing in the handful of "academically talented" students who were transferred to a white school in the sixth grade. Few of the children, black or white, were ready to make close friendships across racial boundaries, but mostly they approached each other's different cultures with simple curiosity. In the black neighborhood, children were not necessarily enthusiastic about this development, taunting Townes and her little cohort for going to the "white" school, until one of them replied that it was not a "white" school they were attending but simply a "red brick" school.

When I asked Townes how her encounters with racism affected her spirituality, she replied that it was the other way around. It was not that racism had affected her spirituality, but that when she encountered racism she was already grounded in the experience of God's love. As an illustration, Townes told me how her mother, Mary, mediated her daughter's first exposure to segregationist Jesse Helms. Each night before bed, Mary would sit her daughter down in front of the evening news to braid her hair, then send her to bed with a stocking cap so the braids would stay put for school the next day. The channel was WRAL, where in those years Helms was executive vice president for news operations. A perk of this job was that Helms got to deliver editorials on the nightly news. Between 1960 and 1972 he would present about 2,700 of these "viewpoints," which elevated him to national prominence and helped him win the Senate seat that he would hold for thirty years.

So young Emilie sat, with Jesse Helms in front of her complaining about "the nigras" and "the northern sympathizers," and her mother behind, silently braiding her hair. Mary knew very well what Helms meant, but her daughter did not. "I couldn't figure out who he was talking about," Townes recalls. "And mom never said a word." Night after night, this hard lesson continued, until "finally, it clicked who the 'nigras' were." Townes looked at her mother and said, "Who is he talking about? I don't know any people like that who are my friends or your friends. This isn't right." Her mother replied, "I want you to always remember that. It's not right; it's wrong. You are valued and you are loved and you are a child of God."

Subsequent experience would prove just how large racism looms among the many social evils in America. "As poorly as we do on issues of gender and sexuality," Townes told me, "we do an even worse job when it comes to race and racism." For Townes, oppression based on sexual orientation is never separated from other injustices. Most LGBT people would agree, but the movement does not often reflect it. So it sticks out in her memory that the day before the Supreme Court struck down a key section of the Defense of Marriage Act, it also gutted the Voting Rights Act. She could not celebrate one decision while failing to protest the other.[7]

If injustices are connected to each other, Townes says, so is love connected to justice, its public face. "Treating people right" boils down to three principles: fairness, truthfulness, and honesty. Fairness requires that "we treat folks consistently" with "dignity and respect." This does not guarantee equality of outcomes, because people have "different abilities and gifts." ("We are different, different, different all over the place," she adds, a mantra of her life.) But fairness is socially doable, and therefore morally requisite. Truthfulness and honesty, her other two guiding principles, are related but not the same. Asked for an example of each, Townes replied, "Truth would be 'Black lives matter'; honesty would be 'We don't act like it.' "

Steven Greenberg was raised in Columbus, Ohio, by parents he describes as "nostalgically" Jewish.[8] In the Hebrew school he attended as a child, he was taught that "the purpose of science was to sift through religion to clean out its primitive notions."[9] In his early teens he sang with his father on High Holidays in the local Conservative synagogue choir and worked on odd Sundays at the Huddle, his family's diner near Ohio State University, where he cooked, served, and often ate sausage cheeseburgers.

Yet despite the limits of their religiosity, his parents were keenly aware that their Jewishness had been marked by persecution. His mother, Francoise, was among the 1,300 Jewish children of Paris who were hidden and saved during the Nazi occupation. His grandfather, Simon Silberstein, was dragged from his bed and transported to the Drancy internment camp, then to Auschwitz, where he was gassed. After Simon was taken, his wife, Jeanne, struggled to stay in Paris with her two daughters. When she could not care for them safely, Jeanne arranged for them to be hidden with Catholics. Greenberg carries both their names (Steven is for his grandfather Simon, and his middle name, Jay, is for his grandmother). With this family history, the question of what Jewishness means—identity, choice, privilege, obligation, trauma, survival, or all of these—was imprinted on his life from the moment it was given to him.

Jewishness, as Greenberg describes it, is "not quite a religion, and not quite a nationality." It didn't matter to the Nazis that his grandfather was not observant. To them, Jewishness was in "the blood," regardless of whether a person affirmed or rejected Jewish belief and practice. Judaism is surely grounded in faith, but it is much more than religion in the Protestant sense, because it requires action. For Orthodox Jews, to be religious is to live according to *halacha*, Jewish law. *Halacha*, literally "walking," applies the 613 biblical commandments (*mitzvot*) that guide and sanctify every part of life. Judaism, says Greenberg, is a way of responding to God as Abraham did when he left Ur at God's command—but also as Abraham did when, on the borders of Sodom, he dared to interrogate God's justice. It is both obedience and questioning, and it is both personal and communal.

At fifteen, Greenberg chose to walk the Jewish way, even though to his parents, this was like a "bodysnatching." Suddenly, this son (and no one else in the family) insisted on keeping 100 percent kosher and on observing Shabbat until the stars came out. The change was

enabled by Joseph Vilensky, whom Greenberg describes as "a gentleman rabbi from Manchester, England." Somehow, Vilensky had
landed in Columbus and, almost as surprisingly, invited Greenberg
to study Torah with him each week "over tea and oranges." The
invitation, Greenberg recalls, "swept him off his feet," as did the texts.
Soon he and Rabbi Vilensky were studying the Talmud as well as
the Torah, meeting twice a week along with several of Greenberg's
friends. It was like joining a conversation among great rabbis from
every time and place of Jewish history, all there at the table with
Vilensky, Greenberg, and the other young men. At issue were countless questions about how *halacha* should apply to new circumstances.
But to Greenberg, those technical questions were elaborations of
questions more basic and perennial: "What does it mean to be a
human? How do you manage a moral dilemma?" Captivated by those
questions, he eventually would pursue rabbinical studies in Israel and
New York.

But the study of *halacha* also heightened Greenberg's private
dilemma about the attractions he sometimes felt for the men he
was studying with. Three parts of the Torah were especially daunting: the Genesis creation stories, in which the male and female are
made by God for each other; the story of Sodom, destroyed by God
after its men threatened to rape a pair of male travelers; and the book
of Leviticus, chapters 18 and 20, which state that for men to "lie
with" each other "as with a woman" is *to'evah* (usually translated
"abomination"). In Leviticus 20:13, the punishment for this *to'evah*
is death.[10]

Like many biblical scholars, Greenberg eventually concluded
that to read the creation stories and the story of Sodom as prohibiting homoeroticism is both inadequate and inaccurate. In Genesis,
adama means earth, so originally *adam* was not a proper name,
much less a male name. The original image of God was not a male
but a human creature who was beyond gender, or perhaps composed of all genders. And the perversion of Sodom was not that
its men were what we would call gay, but that they rejected the
duty of hospitality, instead visiting violence and degradation on the
wayfarers who came to them.

As Greenberg points out, the *sameness* of gender (the "homo" in
homosexuality) is not even the issue. Although the Torah prohibits

sex between men, it says nothing about sex between women. (This lacuna would later be addressed by rabbinical rules against female "rubbing.")[11] Moreover, in the Torah a particular kind of sex act between men—anal sex—is uniquely troubling. Greenberg argues that the verses in Leviticus should be read in the light of Genesis, where anal penetration is associated with rape and humiliation. The implication of Leviticus, he believes, is that a man must not sexually treat another man, or allow himself to be treated, "like a woman," because throughout history women have been dominated and debased by men. As he put it in *Wrestling with God and Men*, "If a man may not do to his fellow man what he ordinarily does to women because it 'feminizes' the other man, then femininity itself is the worst of humiliations."[12]

Greenberg hopes that someday these passages will be read to forbid any use of sex, including that between men and women, to dominate or humiliate another person.[13] In the meantime, most Orthodox Jews find homosexuality to be absolutely forbidden. By Greenberg's estimate, about 80 percent of LGBT Orthodox Jews walk away, either from religion altogether or to a non-Orthodox form of Judaism. For *haredi* (ultra-Orthodox) Jews, there is no such thing as an actively homosexual Orthodox Jew. As one rabbi put it, "It's like eating a cheeseburger on Yom Kippur"—something a Reform Jew might do but that for a "real" (meaning Orthodox) Jew is beyond the pale.

But as Greenberg observes, nobody commits suicide or undergoes electroshock therapy for the sake of a cheeseburger. As he sees it, either God created a whole group of people who, by God's own law, can have "no reasonable life," or the *halacha* of Leviticus 18:22 and 20:13 must be subject to remediation. Tragedy and injustice happen in the world, but Greenberg believes deeply that a good and just God would never prescribe them. Jews either have "a troubled law" or "a troubled God," he says. For him, it's the law that is troubled, and it is that trouble into which he's chosen to walk.

Walls and Closets

Each of the Supreme Court cases about gay sex began with police bursting into somebody's bedroom. In the first instance, a police officer with a grudge against gays invaded Michael Hardwick's home in Atlanta, Georgia, there to discover Hardwick having sex with a man. In the second instance, Houston police were falsely informed (by a white man who turned out to be a spurned lover) that "a black man was waving a gun around" in the apartment of John Geddes Lawrence. Police entered Lawrence's bedroom with guns drawn to find Lawrence and Tyron Garner having sex. The first of these events led to the 1986 case of *Bowers v. Hardwick,* in which the Supreme Court ruled that although heterosexuals have a right to sexual privacy, homosexuals do not. The second led to the 2003 case of *Lawrence v. Texas,* in which the Court overturned its previous decision and ruled that homoerotic relations, like hetero-erotic relations, are constitutionally entitled to privacy.

In the United States, we have counted on the distinction between public and private to manage religion and many other problems. As conventional thinking goes, matters on which individuals differ should be private, but matters on which the majority agrees may be supported or even enforced by public law. But the social institution known as the closet belies any fixed distinction between public and private. Hardwick, Garner, and Lawrence were all denied privacy, but the reason they could be denied privacy was their nonconformity with public norms. In other words, there was a connection between the dangers these gay men faced on the streets and the fact that police could freely enter their bedrooms. That is the condition of the closet: on one hand, forced invisibility, on the other hand, constant vulnerability to exposure, ostracism, and punishment.

Separatist religions know the benefits of walls, but also the risks. Orthodox Jews have understood themselves as a people apart, called to a more exacting standard of life than others. Yet Jewish separation has been imposed as well as chosen. The ghetto of the Middle Ages, for example, protected Jewish lifeways but also made it easy for Christians to target Jews for attack or expulsion. Similarly, the "all-black world" of Townes's childhood was, in some ways, like the church envisioned by Roger Williams—a world of Christian love and faith where everyone was a "child of God." But it was also a place to which black people were confined by law, intimidation, and raw violence.

Baptist and Jewish separatisms are complicated by the fact that they exist for the benefit of everyone, not for the religious community alone. In the Torah, Jews are called a "nation of priests." As Greenberg puts it, this implies that "your congregation is the world." Judaism shows that "the parochial can serve the universal" without imposing itself on the universal. Rather than trying to make everyone Jewish, Jews are to be "a blessing to all the families of the earth."[14] For Baptists, the point of maintaining a pure church is not just to get individuals through the gates of heaven. Even though (as Townes points out) some Baptists have adopted this cramped view of salvation, historically they have concerned themselves with the well-being of all God's children, not just the salvation of the individual.[15]

Whether it's called repairing the world (*tikkun olam*) or spreading the good news, these missions are the tallest of orders. For both Jews and Baptists, it has been crucial to discern which of the commitments they live by should be encoded into law, and which should be commended as good choices for free people. Roger Williams managed the question by distinguishing between "the two tables" of the Ten Commandments, the first table binding only Christians, the second binding everyone. Jewish tradition has distinguished between the 613 commandments required of Jews and the seven laws that, according to tradition, were given to the children of Noah (i.e., all of humanity) after the flood.[16] But again, which is which? In this sense, the question of sexuality has two levels for Baptists and Jews. First, what theological stance should the denomination take within its own membership? Second, what laws and public policies should it endorse for everybody?

Since the early 1990s, the ABCUSA has acknowledged internal disagreement on homosexuality, but officially hewed to what it considers the biblical position. In the popular paraphrase, that position is to "love the sinner" but "hate the sin."[17] Yet this theological rejection of homosexuality did not translate into support for the kinds of laws that snagged Hardwick, Lawrence, and Garner. Townes recalls that in the late 1980s, when the ABCUSA began to debate gay civil rights, respected leaders like E. Spencer Parson argued that Baptists had no business telling people what to do with their private lives. "That is not what we *do*," he said emphatically.[18] Others in the ABCUSA must have shared Parson's cautionary attitude, because the denomination did not file briefs in either *Bowers v. Hardwick* or *Lawrence v. Texas*.

Greenberg describes the consensus Orthodox position as pretty much the same as that of the Baptists. Also like the Baptists, Orthodox Jews had not shown much love for the "sinner" until the catastrophic failure of so-called reparative therapies showed that sexual orientation cannot be changed. That softened Orthodox views on sexual orientation but did not shake the consensus that homosexual activity is forbidden. Moreover, many Orthodox Jews believe that homoeroticism violates the Noahide law and therefore is wrong for everyone, not just for Jews. Yet no Orthodox Jewish group filed an amicus brief in *Bowers v. Hardwick*. By 2003, *haredi* Jews had decided to speak out against decriminalization, and Agudath Israel filed a brief supporting Texas in *Lawrence v. Texas*. But the Orthodox Rabbinical Council of America did not, and its journal published an article stating that although the government should not affirmatively support homosexual conduct, "no one in the Orthodox Jewish community . . . is urging the state to vigorously enforce sodomy laws."[19]

But while Jews and Baptists in the 1980s were debating whether to discipline homoeroticism only within the walls of their denominations, the Supreme Court was ready to justify the criminalization of sodomy on the basis of religious foundations. In 1986, the Court ruled in a 5–4 decision that "homosexual sodomy" was not a "fundamental right." That was a deliberately selective wording, for the Georgia law prohibited sodomy (an act "involving the sexual organs of one person and the mouth or anus of another") without reference to the gender of the parties.[20] In fact a heterosexual couple known to history only as "John and Jane Doe" admitted they would like to practice "sodomy," thus defined, in the privacy of their home. They challenged the law on their own behalf, but the Court declined to consider this challenge on grounds that the Georgia law had not (yet) done them any harm, so they had no concrete grievance.

In constitutional law "fundamental rights" is a term of art. Certainly the rights enumerated in the Constitution are considered fundamental, but the Ninth Amendment states that those are not the *only* rights people have. But what are these un-enumerated yet still fundamental rights? That is a critical question, because if something is a "fundamental right," laws about it cannot be made without the most serious ("compelling") government interest. Within constitutional jurisprudence, two phrases have been used to delineate what might count as a "fundamental right." One, from a 1937 case, says that a fundamental right is "implicit in the concept of ordered liberty," such that without it "neither liberty nor justice would exist." The other, from a 1977 case, says that a fundamental right must be "deeply rooted in this nation's history and traditions."[21]

In 1986, the question facing the Supreme Court was whether, in his bedroom that night, Michael Hardwick was exercising a "fundamental right." To answer "no" required the Supreme Court to account not only for the fact that the Georgia law didn't single out same-sex partners, but also for the fact that the Court itself had previously affirmed a fundamental right to privacy for both married and unmarried people within "the sacred precincts of the bedroom."[22] Those opinions had not drawn the curtain of privacy only around *heterosexual* sex. It fell to the *Bowers* Court to decide whether homosexual sex was excluded from the protection to which other private sexual acts were constitutionally entitled.

In effect, the *Bowers* majority decided that in those prior decisions, it had gone without saying that only heterosexual sex was constitutionally protected. Writing for the majority, Justice Byron White contended that proscriptions against "homosexual sodomy" had "very ancient roots" in English common law, American colonial and state laws, and American religions. Given all that, White concluded, to say that a right to homosexual sodomy is " 'deeply rooted in this Nation's history and traditions' or 'implicit in the concept of ordered liberty' is, at best, facetious." Justice Burger, in concurrence, put it even more strongly: "Condemnation of [homosexual] practices is firmly rooted in Judeo-Christian moral and ethical standards," and under Roman law they were a capital crime. Burger approvingly quoted Blackstone's comment that "the infamous *crime against nature*" was an offense worse than rape, an act so heinous that "the very mention of [it] is a disgrace to human nature," and "a crime not fit to be named."[23]

"Not fit to be named" well describes the situation of the closeted person, whose intimate behavior is so severely prohibited that the prohibition need not even be spoken. One is forbidden to be visible, yet constantly exposed to negative judgments. The closet, in these ways, resembles the diabolically efficient prison called the "panopticon," conceived by Jeremy Bentham (ironically, an opponent of anti-sodomy laws) in the late eighteenth century.[24] In the panopticon, single-inmate cells would be arranged around a central guardhouse that emitted a constant, punishingly bright light. The side walls of each cell would be solid, so that the prisoners could never see each other; the front and rear walls would be made of glass, so that the guard could see in at any time. Always aware that they had no privacy, but never knowing whether they were being watched at that very moment, inmates of the panopticon would learn to watch themselves.

As Emilie Townes observed when the AIDS crisis hit the African American community, the panopticon was a good metaphor for what white-dominated society had done to black bodies. Those bodies had been the objects of external monitoring and reporting, yet stripped of their own subjectivity; talked about, but not expected to speak for themselves. In response, the African American community had learned to repress or ignore sexual realities that seemed less than respectable. The Black Church, as the chief monitor of sexual conformity, was therefore fatally unhelpful when the AIDS epidemic began. HIV-positive members were unlikely to disclose their condition and, if they did, were often met with "condemnation or stony silence."

Two decades into the crisis, Townes wrote that "our sexual repression will kill us and kill others if we do not begin to grapple with the reality of HIV/AIDS. . . . We must refuse to submit to the panopticon." By then, she knew this in a personal way; AIDS already had killed her uncle Pete. Pete's homosexuality was known to his immediate family, who cared for him until the end of his life. But he did not feel free to disclose his condition in the Black Church, where many believed that AIDS was a punishment for sin—just as many had once believed that black skin was a punishment from God.[25]

Steven Greenberg's experience of the closet started early and lasted long. From a very young age, perhaps seven, he felt as if he were "playacting" a role in which he was miscast. He also sensed that to fail in this performance would be dangerous. Having become observant at age fifteen, he found shelter under the *halachic* prohibition against premarital sex. But by the age of twenty, Greenberg no longer could deny that strong attractions to men were part of who he was. But to consciously admit homosexuality, even in his own mind, was unthinkable. As he recalls it, to say "I am gay," even to himself, would have "set me at the edge of a precipice." Even in his fantasies, "every decent, good future" had to be straight. "All gay futures were shameful, ignominious, and threatening, . . . even deadly."[26]

After he was ordained, in 1983, it was another ten years before Greenberg began to acknowledge being gay. At first he did this while remaining closeted, publishing an article in *Tikkun* called "Gayness and God" under the pseudonym Yaakov Levado ("Jacob Alone").[27] The article moved many similarly closeted Jews, who contacted Greenberg through the magazine. In this way, a small community of gay and lesbian Orthodox Jews began to collect in the shadows, not even knowing each other's names.

In his prescient dissent in *Bowers v. Hardwick*, Justice Harry Blackmun began by evoking the importance of walls. Quoting Louis Brandeis, the Supreme Court's first Jewish justice, he wrote that the largest and most significant right of all is the "right to be left alone." That simple right, said Blackmun, was linked with the Constitution's protection of the home as a place to engage in the "pursuit of happiness," where happiness, besides material satisfactions, also includes the individual's right to beliefs, thoughts, and feelings. Privacy has both spatial and decisional aspects, Blackmun argued, and the latter embraced sexual and reproductive choices because those choices "form so central a part of an individual's life." The right to privacy "embodies the moral fact that a person belongs to himself, and not others nor to society as a whole."[28]

In 2003, overturning *Bowers* by a 6–3 vote, the Court followed Blackmun's lead in connecting the need for privacy with the principle of limited government. Anthony Kennedy began his majority opinion by stating that "liberty protects the person from unwanted government intrusions into a dwelling or other private places." But where Blackmun had referred to the "decisional" dimensions of privacy, Kennedy put a finer point on it by substituting the word "transcendent." Quoting Justice O'Connor from an earlier decision, he defended the sexual privacy of John Geddes Lawrence in terms redolent of religion: "At the heart of liberty is the right to define one's own concept of existence, of meaning, of the universe, and of the mystery of human life." These, O'Connor had written, belong to the "attributes of personhood" and cannot be "formed under compulsion of the State."[29]

In 1986, the *Bowers* majority had represented religion in foundationalist terms, as a national commonality and an appropriate basis for law. For them, the question of homosexuality came down to religion versus irreligion, morality versus immorality. For the *Bowers* dissent and the *Lawrence* majority, however, religion was a matter of differences. For these jurists, the history of religious objections to homosexuality did not secure anti-sodomy laws as a part of American foundations. Instead, it suggested just the opposite: that religious and moral opinions, even those of the majority, should not be given the force of law over conduct that does not harm others. This marked an important shift in the relationship between religion and privacy. In 1986, religion was an *obstacle* to homosexual privacy; in 2003, it was refigured as a *protection* for homosexual privacy.

In his dissent in *Bowers*, for example, Blackmun had pointed out that some "but by no means all" religious groups disapprove of homosexuality. More importantly, he argued that religious disapproval as such "gives the State no license to impose their judgments on the entire citizenry." Noting that his colleague Warren Burger had invoked the "Judeo-Christian tradition" and that the state of Georgia had appealed to the book of Leviticus, the Epistle to the Romans, and the writings of St. Thomas Aquinas, Blackmun argued that these references spoke against rather than for the legitimacy of Georgia's anti-sodomy law. "Far from buttressing [Georgia's] case," he argued, those religious warrants "undermine the suggestion that [the anti-sodomy statute] represents a legitimate use of secular coercive power."[30]

Tellingly, Blackmun's dissent called upon two of the strongest opinions the Court had ever issued on freedom of conscience. The first was a 1943 decision in which the Court (overturning its own ruling of just three years earlier) found that, as a matter of constitutional right, Jehovah's Witness children could refuse to recite the Pledge of Allegiance. Quoting what Justice Robert Jackson had written then, Blackmun repeated that the "freedom to differ is not limited to things that do not matter much.... The test of its substance is the right to differ as to things that touch the heart of the existing order."[31] The second was a 1972 decision in which the Court exempted Amish parents from a Wisconsin law requiring parents to send their children to school until age sixteen. "A way of life that is odd or even erratic, but interferes with no rights or interests of others, is not to be condemned because it is different," wrote the Court in 1972.[32] Applying the same principle to sexual privacy, Blackmun wrote that "in a Nation as diverse as ours, ... there may be many 'right' ways of conducting [sexual] relationships."[33]

Where Blackmun had referred to religious freedom, Kennedy referred to dignity. This was the pivotal theme not only of Kennedy's *Lawrence* opinion but also of his next three opinions for gay rights. In all of them, the words "dignity" and "dignify," as well as antonyms including "stigma," "humiliate," and "demean," appear with striking frequency.[34] No doubt this owed something to the fact that dignity is a cornerstone of social ethics in the Catholic Church. Kennedy, a Catholic, would deploy this principle in a different way from the American Catholic bishops, who did not object to the decriminalization of sodomy but would strongly object to civil same-sex marriage.[35] For Kennedy, the principle of dignity added a transcendent dimension to privacy. A given sexual encounter might or might not be "one element in a personal bond that is more enduring," but either way, a person needed moral autonomy to make such a decision. By stripping homoerotic sex of these moral and relational dimensions, he argued, Texas had "demean[ed] the claim [that Lawrence] put forward, just as it would demean a married couple were it to be said marriage is simply about the right to have sexual intercourse."[36]

The *Bowers* and *Lawrence* cases also concerned the constitutionality of morals legislation generally, a question closely related to religious freedom. Traditionally, the protection of public morality was seen as falling within the legitimate powers of state governments, but since 1947 it has been unconstitutional for states to establish religion.[37] Since that time, many states have tacitly adopted a strategy that's been around since the beginning of the republic: protect religious difference but demand moral conformity. Yet most of the moral rules encoded in law are rooted in religion. Once religion is disestablished, those moral rules must be either dislodged from the foundations or stripped of their religious markers. Washington and Jefferson, recall, did the latter. They emphasized in magnanimous tones that government was to take no position on religious doctrine, but for them religious doctrines were "things that do not matter much." What did matter to them were "peace and good order," and here they were unyielding, confining religious liberty strictly within those vaguely worded but practically nonnegotiable boundaries. Just where those boundaries should be placed was the question that, if spoken, would have touched the "heart of the existing order." But that was precisely the sort of question that religion-talk holds at bay.

And this perhaps explains why the cases about homosexuality so upset the judiciary and the general public: they forced into words moral norms that had not even needed to be stated, much less defended. In his 1986 *Bowers* opinion, Justice White could state without apology or elaboration that law is "constantly based on notions of morality."[38] In 2003, when the Court reversed *Bowers*, Justice Antonin Scalia echoed that sentiment, predicting that the *Lawrence* decision would undermine all morals legislation and cause "a massive disruption of the current social order."[39] Moreover, these jurists could back their support for morals legislation with the constitutional argument that "fundamental rights" had to accord with "this nation's history and tradition." They, like many other Americans, were simply dumbfounded that people could claim a fundamental right to engage in conduct that historically had been considered indecent.

The *Bowers* dissenters and the *Lawrence* majority also understood that sexual behavior could have moral implications. But to them this signaled the possibility of conscientious *disagreement* rather than the need for conformity. As Justice Stevens put it in his *Bowers* dissent, "The fact that the governing majority in a State has traditionally viewed a particular practice as immoral is not a sufficient reason for upholding a law prohibiting the practice; neither history nor tradition could save a law prohibiting miscegenation from constitutional attack."[40]

Yet Stevens's clever sentence involved a certain sleight of hand, which was being simultaneously performed by many supporters of decriminalization, between respect for moral pluralism and the demand for moral conformity. He pointed to both the legitimacy of moral *dis*agreement on one topic (homosexuality) and the growing moral *agreement* on another topic (racial equality). In mentioning laws against miscegenation, Stevens was referring to the aptly named 1967 case of *Loving v. Virginia*, in which the Court struck down laws prohibiting marriage between people of different races.[41] Justice Blackmun made the same connection, going so far as to find an "uncanny" resemblance between *Loving v. Virginia* and *Bowers v. Hardwick*. In both cases, Blackmun added, religion was used to buttress a prohibition that could be seen, in retrospect, as unjust.[42]

Exactly ten years after *Bowers v. Hardwick* was decided, that fateful comparison between sexual difference and racial difference—and therefore between discrimination against LGBT people and racial bigotry—would permanently enter American discourse. In the process, the old habit of managing sexual difference by invoking religious authority would be permanently unsettled.

Coming Out: Exodus Stories

Michael Hardwick, Tyron Garner, and John Geddes Lawrence learned from experience that their lack of public protection went hand in glove with their lack of personal privacy. In the years between the *Bowers v. Hardwick* ruling of 1986 and the *Lawrence v. Texas* ruling of 2003, many LGBT people came to the same conclusion. Stepping deliberately out of the closet, they entered the public sphere to insist on the civil rights granted to other citizens.

Most people describe coming out of the closet as a matter of being themselves, but it's important to remember that it is quite possible not to "be oneself." It has often been demanded of LGBT people that they not be themselves, on pain of ostracism, isolation, even death. In this sense, coming out is not only an act of personal liberation, but also a public stance adopted at significant risk and cost. This intersection of freedom and obligation, what one wants to do and what one must do, characterizes decisions of conscience. It also characterizes the Bible's own coming-out story, the Exodus. There too, a people felt called to leave their place of confinement and move into a freedom that would bring its own responsibilities and troubles.

In the 1970s and 1980s, these comings out prompted some localities to pass gay civil rights ordinances, but also brought a

powerful backlash from religious conservatives. The conflict between the two camps set the terms in which the American debate
about sexuality is still cast. Gay rights advocates insisted that religious strictures should have no bearing on law or public policy. Instead, they rested their case on the growing scientific consensus
that homosexuality is a natural variation of human sexuality and
not subject to change. Religious opponents held that, as Justice
White had stated in his *Bowers* ruling, "laws are constantly based
on notions of morality" and that, as Justice Burger had written, the
Judeo-Christian tradition was a major source of moral norms. Homosexual attractions might be unchosen and unchangeable, but
homosexual conduct remained a choice. Moreover, religious conservatives pointed out, to publicly *affirm* homosexuality as natural
and good was not something one had to do; it was definitely a
choice. That was the choice gays were making by publicizing their
sexuality—or, in the parlance of the gay rights movement, by coming out. From the vantage point of religious conservatives, that
action had extremely negative social consequences, and gay civil
rights laws were forcing those consequences on everyone.

If sexuality and religion were the two most obvious terms of
this conflict, a third term toggled between them: race. The movements for and against gay rights both claimed to be the true heirs
of the civil rights movement. There was some irony in this, given
that both sides were dominated by Euro-Americans, many of whom
had come to regard the civil rights movement with reverence only
in retrospect. Moreover, the civil rights movement was often invoked as if the battle against racial injustice were over and had been
won by the right side—a perspective not shared by many people of
color in the United States. Although patterns of discrimination
based on sexuality and on race were linked, particularly for LGBT
people of color, the race-related messages from both sides could
have an opportunistic ring. From one side came the implication
that people of color must support gay rights; from the other side,
that all true believers must oppose homosexuality.

Like the predominantly white religious right, the Black
Church leaned conservative on homosexuality. But especially due
to the AIDS crisis, the Black Church felt more pressure to contend
with gays in its midst than to support or oppose gay rights in the

public sphere. For example, most Baptists, regardless of skin color, held that homosexuality was incompatible with the Bible. But when it came to the question of civil rights for gays, they varied discernibly along racial lines. From the 1980s to the present, the predominantly white Southern Baptist Convention has stridently opposed gay rights laws, but the predominantly black Baptist National Convention (BNC) has chosen not to enter the fray.

The position of Orthodox Jews resembles that of black Baptists; they have found it theologically impossible to support gay civil rights yet imprudent to oppose them. When same-sex marriage became legal, the Union of Orthodox Congregations stated that it had always opposed discrimination against individuals. Yet the Union also reiterated that "our [Jewish] law ... represents a universal morality" and that Judeo-Christian morality "has long had a place in American law and jurisprudence." To thread that needle, the Union advised that when the democratic process results in the expansion of civil rights, Orthodox Jews should defer.[43]

If the battle over gay civil rights was awkward for black Christians and Orthodox Jews, it could be agonizing for those denominations' gay members. That was especially so for Steven Greenberg, whose coming out was tightly and painfully bound up with his entry into Orthodox Judaism. At twenty, while studying in a Jerusalem yeshiva, he became ever more entranced with rabbinical studies but simultaneously aware of his attraction to young men in his dormitory—"one in particular," he recalls. Every morning at 6:00 a.m., the showers would turn on and Greenberg's heart would leap. He'd ask himself, "What is this feeling?" But as he says, "I knew; I'd always known."

Rather than retreat from the tension, Greenberg decided to face it. He requested an audience with an aged, revered rabbi in Jerusalem named Yosef Shalom Eliashiv. Describing his dilemma, as he then understood it, Greenberg said (in Hebrew), "Master, I am attracted to both men and women. What should I do?" To Greenberg's astonishment, the rabbi replied, "My dear one, my friend. You have twice the power of love. Use it wisely." Greenberg says he virtually danced away from the meeting, yet he knew that the rabbi had not given him permission to have a homosexual relationship. Although he would strive to become a great and loving rabbi,

Greenberg would endure many more years of inner torment before coming out publicly.

Emilie Townes began to come out to friends and family in her
late twenties. Almost everyone greeted her with a level of acceptance that surprises and touches her even many years later. There
was no particular moment when she announced herself as a lesbian
to the ABCUSA. As she recalls, "I just started being myself." It
made the denomination uncomfortable, to say the least, but by
then the ABCUSA was used to being made uncomfortable by Emilie Townes over the church's response to AIDS, its treatment of
women, and other social justice issues.

But although Townes left the closet many years ago, like all
LGBT people she can be re-closeted by others. After becoming
dean of Vanderbilt Divinity School, she was asked to meet with a
group of evangelical Christians, potential donors, in Orlando,
Florida. It was not long after June 12, 2016, when forty-nine people, mostly gay Latino men, had been massacred at the Pulse
nightclub. So the topic of homosexuality arose quickly, but in an
extraordinarily insensitive way. It emerged that some evangelical
ministers had offered to conduct a prayer service at the Pulse site
but had been turned down by Orlando's gay community. The people at the meeting, offended by this rejection, talked about the importance of "hating the sin" while "loving the sinner." They did not
pause to consider that the dean herself might be one of those "sin-
ners" or to ask why Orlando's gay community might feel wounded
by religion. Listening to all this, Townes decided that she would
visit the Pulse site not in the company of the other ministers but
on her own. When she arrived there, she found it enclosed in a
chain-link fence that was shrouded in black and covered with the
haunting faces of the young victims. Quite without the help of
clergy, Pulse had become a shrine.[44]

In the years that Townes and Greenberg were struggling to
come out and stay out, the state of Colorado was battling over gay
civil rights laws. Denver, Aspen, and Boulder had passed statutes
prohibiting discrimination based on sexual orientation. Conservative
evangelicals argued that these laws violated the liberty of people
who objected to homosexuality, and wasted state resources that were
needed for "real" civil rights. Once again, the rhetoric was polarized

in the very terms that crisscrossed Townes's and Greenberg's lives. Opponents of gay civil rights spoke of religion, choices, and the moral foundations of society. Proponents spoke of science, fixed sexual identities, equal rights, and the wall of separation.

As usual, race was something of a political football. The NAACP and Coretta Scott King firmly supported gay civil rights.[45] But the religious right, with the support of some African American leaders, argued that gay rights were nothing like the hard-won civil rights of African Americans. Skin color was visible and involuntary, they said, whereas homosexuals chose to flaunt their lifestyle and then demanded social approval and legal protection for doing so. LGBT people, they argued, already had all the normal protections of law. The only thing gays did not have was legal protection specifically *for being gay;* they did not have "special rights." The rhetoric of "special rights" moved enough Coloradans that in 1992 they voted to amend their state constitution not only to rescind existing gay rights laws but to prohibit "any minority status, quota preferences, protected status or claim of discrimination" that would be based on "homosexual, lesbian or bisexual orientation, conduct, practices or relationships."[46]

Four years later, when this amendment, known as Amendment Two, was challenged in the Supreme Court case of *Romer v. Evans,* the tangled web of questions around gay rights could be examined in full public light. Was discrimination based on sexual orientation like racial discrimination, or not? Was homosexuality chosen or involuntary, changeable or immutable? Was it an inner disposition, an action, a way of identifying oneself, or something that was ascribed to one by others? Were the religious objections to homosexuality a legitimate justification for Amendment Two? Or was the measure so broad as to compel the conclusion that, in this case, religion was really a cover-up for an animosity akin to racism?

The majority opinion opened in a way that suggested that the category of race was indeed going to be dispositive for gay rights. Its first sentence recalled the sole dissent in the infamous 1896 case of *Plessy v. Ferguson,* when the Supreme Court had ruled that "separate but equal" facilities for blacks and whites did not violate the equal protection clause.[47] Now, exactly a hundred years later, six justices were resolving not to repeat that mistake. "One century ago," began Justice Kennedy for the majority, "the first Justice Harlan admonished this Court that the Constitution 'neither knows nor tolerates classes among citizens.' "[48] Colorado had singled out a group of people for the specific purpose of treating them worse than everyone else. This, Kennedy argued, violated the core of the equal protection clause. Rather than merely regulating actions, Colorado had "deem[ed] a class of persons a stranger to its law."[49]

Legal scholar Carlos Ball has observed that the *Romer v. Evans* decision stopped short of making sexual orientation discrimination and racial discrimination *legally* equivalent, while implying a moral equivalence between the two.[50] Legally, race is the paradigm of what is called a "suspect classification"—meaning that any law that divides people in terms of race will be subject to "strict scrutiny" under the equal protection clause and has a good chance of being struck down. But race is not the only form of unconstitutional discrimination, so over time the judiciary came up with a more general formula. Unlawful discrimination occurs when the law intentionally targets a "discrete and insular minority" based on an "immutable characteristic" that bears no relationship to a legitimate government interest. Furthermore, the targeted group must lack the numbers or power to alleviate the discrimination by "ordinary political means."[51]

But if sexuality is being compared to race, it's important first to ask whether race itself is actually "immutable." Intuitively, the answer seems to be yes; the color of any person's skin is what it is. Yet the "races" easily can procreate, blend, and, over time, merge. Laws against racial mixing, although defended on grounds that "the races" are ineluctably different, actually functioned to produce and magnify shades of difference that can easily disappear. In Europe and the United States, whites invented the idea that differences of skin color signal differences of temperament, character, intelligence, and worth, and this racial ideology was used to justify the conquest, killing, dispossession, colonization, and enslavement of black and brown people. So: is race real? According to Emilie Townes, yes and no. "As a fixed immutable category, no, race does not exist." But, she adds, "as a relational process of shifting boundaries and social meanings, constantly engaged in political struggle—yes, race does exist."[52]

Most scholars say that sexuality, too, is a social construction. This does not mean that people do not have different sexual preferences, any more than recognizing the social construction of race eliminates the different shades that humanity comes in. People have all sorts of preferences about how, where, when, with whom, and with what frequency to have sex. Some of these preferences may be lifelong—we might say, "immutable." But there is nothing natural or necessary about making any of these sexual preferences the basis for deciding who gets honored and who gets stigmatized, who is rewarded and who is punished, who is considered decent and who is considered indecent. As historians of sexuality have shown, the particular sexual preference that today seems all-important—preference concerning the gender of sexual partners—is a relatively new focus. In other places and times, humans have thought about sexuality very differently, and usually much less.[53] As with race, the apparent naturalness and significance of sexual orientation is the effect, not the cause, of the weighty norms that have been built around it.

Sidestepping these tricky questions, the *Romer* majority chose not to treat the amorphous collection of people who stood to be harmed by Amendment Two as a "discrete and insular" minority marked by an "immutable trait."[54] Instead, Justice Kennedy made a more subtle point: he argued that the amendment was "a classification of people undertaken for its own sake." Colorado had identified people by "a single trait" (whether real or imagined) for the specific purpose of "denying them the possibility of protection across the board." That, he wrote, was "unprecedented" and "a denial of equal protection in the most literal sense."[55]

Although it deftly avoided the question of whether sexuality was an "immutable trait," the *Romer* majority had an additional problem: the *Bowers* ruling was still in place, meaning it was still constitutionally permissible for a state to criminalize homosexual sodomy. Proponents of Amendment Two argued that there was nothing wrong with declining to afford "special rights" to people who committed what some states still considered a crime. The gay rights ordinances in Denver, Aspen, and Boulder had avoided this problem by phrasing their anti-discrimination laws in terms of "sexual orientation," a category based on status rather than on conduct.[56] To counter those ordinances, Amendment Two precluded legal protection of gay, lesbian, or bisexual "conduct, practices or relationships." But it also precluded civil rights protection based on "sexual orientation." With this terminology, Amendment Two not only underscored that homoerotic conduct was criminal in some places, but also implied that a person might be discriminated against for simply being gay without necessarily "doing" gay. It might even have permitted discrimination against those who neither "were" gay, "did" gay, nor called themselves "gay," but were simply perceived as gay by others.

Justice Kennedy addressed this problem by recalling the 1890 case of *Davis v. Beason*, in which the Supreme Court upheld an Iowa law denying voting rights to members of the LDS Church. To the extent that the law targeted people who'd been convicted of polygamy, Kennedy did not question the 1890 ruling. But the Iowa law had also targeted people based merely on their *advocacy* of polygamy or their *status* as members of the LDS Church. Kennedy suggested that in this respect the *Davis* ruling was invalid, because to participate in the making, contesting, and changing of laws is a basic right of democratic citizenship.[57] His point was that citizens retain the right to political participation even when the law is unfavorable to them—which, of course, is when the right to political participation is most needed.

Besides the questions of immutability and potential criminality, the *Romer* majority had to address whether homosexuals lacked the power to alleviate discrimination by ordinary political means. Amendment Two's proponents had contended that homosexuals, far from being politically powerless, were disproportionately powerful—a claim that Justice Scalia, joined by two other justices, reiterated in a furious dissent. Scalia argued that far from being oppressed minorities, homosexuals were "elites" whose wealth and numbers in "certain neighborhoods" enabled them to hold sway over other elites—such as his own colleagues. Both in Colorado and at the Supreme Court, this claim was racially fraught, contrasting the "special rights" demanded by homosexual "elites" with the "civil rights" of racial minorities.[58]

Scalia's argument rested on the incorrect premise that memberships in the gay community and in a racialized minority are mutually exclusive. But it would have been difficult in 1992 to make a demographic case about the relative power or powerlessness of homosexuals, because accurate demographics cannot be obtained when discrimination forces people to live closeted lives. Instead, Kennedy argued that regardless of how well LGBT people were doing in Colorado before 1992, Amendment Two itself had deprived them of the "ordinary political means" of effecting change. Unlike any other citizens, those targeted by Amendment Two would have to change the state constitution before they could even hope to make or change a law. That, to the majority, was an extraordinary imposition of political powerlessness.

Despite beginning with a portentous reference to *Plessy v. Ferguson*, the *Romer* majority ultimately did not make sexual orientation a suspect classification and did not subject Amendment Two to strict scrutiny. Instead, Kennedy's opinion applied only the lowest standard of judicial review, called rational basis review. For Amendment Two to pass muster, Colorado had only to show that it advanced a legitimate government interest by rational means. Kennedy found that the amendment "fails, indeed defies, even this conventional inquiry."[59] Colorado had said that Amendment Two would protect the freedom of those who objected to homosexuality on religious grounds and would conserve state resources for combatting discrimination against groups already covered by civil rights laws. The majority did not question the legitimacy of those reasons, but it found that the means Colorado used to implement them were so excessive as to make the reasons unpersuasive. As Kennedy put it, "the breadth of the amendment is so far removed from these particular justifications that we find it impossible to credit them." Amendment Two, he concluded, is "inexplicable by anything but animus toward the class it affects."[60]

Here, in the explosive word "animus," was the *moral* equivalency between discrimination against gays and discrimination by race. The word was difficult for the majority to avoid, for a key element of any equal protection violation is that discriminatory treatment is motivated by animosity—the "bare desire to harm a politically unpopular group."[61] But for religious conservatives and the three dissenting justices, "animus" was a bewildering inversion of the intentions behind Amendment Two. Scalia found it "nothing short of insulting." The majority opinion, he wrote in his dissent, "places the prestige of this institution behind the proposition that opposition to homosexuality is as reprehensible as racial or religious bias." The "grim, disapproving" tone of the majority opinion insinuated that "Coloradans have been guilty of 'animus' toward homosexuality, *as though that has been established as un-American*" (emphasis mine).[62]

For the dissenters, the difference between racism and opposition to homosexuality had become a boundary of Americanism itself. To their thinking, racism was un-American and, apparently, had always been. They made no acknowledgment that racism had ever been established in America or that it was now only partially dislodged from the country's foundations. And just as they ignored America's history of race, the dissenters ignored the historical fact that views of sexuality change. For them, disapproval of homosexuality was "established," and to question that disapproval—or, worse, to invert it by disapproving of it—was to unsettle the whole social order.

From the perspective of the *Romer* majority, finding "animus" in Amendment Two was not an attack on religion and morality as such. Instead, it was a rebuke to Colorado for politically suppressing religious and moral disagreement. Proponents of Amendment Two, however, couldn't or wouldn't imagine any religious or morally serious person standing *for* gay rights. Unfortunately, by the 1990s many LGBT people and their allies had come to almost the same view: religion itself was the enemy. After decades of hearing the religious right condemn homosexuality and blame AIDS on the supposed immorality of its victims, they found even moral language repugnant. Understandably, many had learned to prefer the languages of science and individual rights to those of religion or social responsibility. By the time of the *Romer* decision, then, people on both sides were finding it hard to grant their opponents any presumption of moral seriousness.

Greenberg's long coming-out story is a tale about taking moral disagreement seriously. Fifteen years after seeking the guidance of Rabbi Eliashiv in East Jerusalem, he was an ordained rabbi, nationally known as a teacher and leader in the Orthodox community. In all those years he'd continued trying to reconcile himself to marrying a woman, but eventually had begun a relationship with a man.

The conflict was tearing him apart, and on Yom Kippur (the Day of Atonement) in 1996 it would reach a breaking point. Greenberg describes Yom Kippur as "a rehearsal for death." Jews dress in white, as if in a shroud, and fast (because "dead people do not eat"), while the Torah is read and each person reviews his or her life as if this day were the last. Each year, Greenberg knew that he would hear his love life condemned as *to'evah*. When the service was about to reach Leviticus chapter 18, he would retreat to a corner, pull his *tallis* overhead, and quietly weep.

After nine years, he says, he was out of tears. The next year he arranged that when the service got to Leviticus, he personally would be called up before the congregation to read from the Torah scroll. He walked up trembling, but to his astonishment, the words of the text brought him a new and profound calm. By his opening himself to the sacred text, it was as if the doors of the sacred had opened to him. From then on, he felt convinced that the meaning of Leviticus could not be understood without the testimony of those "who have carried that text on our backs."[63]

Rabbi Steven Greenberg officiates at the wedding of Gil Wiener and Leon Bernstein, 2017. Photo by Gruber Photographers.

Some might say that Greenberg was hearing what he wanted to hear rather than what the Torah actually says. But if he was hearing what he wanted, the same is true for those who want to hear only a condemnation of homosexuality. That the dominant viewpoint is not the only viewpoint is an insight more available to those who have lived in the closet than to those who have not. This added insight is not unlike what W. E. B. Du Bois, speaking of the African American experience, called double consciousness.[64] An oppressed person learns to see himself as the dominant order sees him, but also to see the dominant order in ways that are invisible to those who control it. To be a "stranger to the law" is to be an exile, but it also affords a wider angle of vision. From that angle, one might discern a path into freedom that carries its own law forward. How to travel with such a weighty freedom is no easy question, but it is good to take counsel from those who have been carrying the law on their backs.

African American women exchange wedding rings in California.
Ted Soqui/Getty Images.

Foundations and Renovations

In his dissent in *Obergefell v. Hodges*, the Supreme Court's closely divided 2015 decision affirming a right of same-sex marriage throughout the country, Chief Justice John Roberts commented with evident dismay that until recently, "the meaning of marriage went without saying." Like the other dissenters, he felt that the question should have been left up to the states. "Whether same-sex marriage is a good idea," he wrote, "should be of no concern" to the Supreme Court. But clearly he thought it was a bad idea. To his mind, heterosexual marriage was a simple biological given—not the result of "a prehistoric decision to exclude gays and lesbians," but something that had "persisted in every culture throughout human history," from the "Kalahari Bushmen and the Han Chinese, the Carthaginians and the Aztecs." It had been assumed by the Framers of the Constitution and, until very recently, by the laws of every state. To change such an institution, Roberts felt, was to take a sledgehammer to the foundations of civilization. "Just who do we think we are?"[65]

Emilie Townes and Steven Greenberg know something about marriage, civil and religious, pastorally and personally. Long before they could have had legal spouses of their own, both had counseled dozens of engaged couples, officiated at weddings, and signed civil marriage licenses. They have ritualized marriages both in accordance with their own religious traditions and somewhat differently, and they've debated with their own denominations about what a wedding is and how it should be done. It is fair to say that they have earned a place in the discussion about same-sex marriage. Here, I will bring them into dialogue with the majority opinion and dissent in *Obergefell v. Hodges*. Greenberg, being at heart a traditionalist, falls more naturally into dialogue with the Roberts defense of traditional marriage. Townes, whose life's work is to identify and correct social injustices, offers a critical extension of the majority opinion.

In the United States, for both better and worse, marriage has long been tied to religion. It was peculiar, therefore, that although Chief Justice Roberts emphasized the foundational character of heterosexual marriage, he did not identify these foundations as religious. In fact, he took pains to say that heterosexual marriage had not arisen from "a religious doctrine" or any other historical force.[66] Conservative jurists had earlier defended the suppression of homosexuality on religious grounds, but by 2015, most recognized that banning same-sex marriage based on religion would violate the establishment clause. An appeal to religion, which just a few decades earlier would have clinched any argument against same-sex marriage, would now have weakened that argument and therefore was no longer made.

However, all four dissenters argued forcefully that permitting same-sex marriage would assault religious liberty. This claim was puzzling, because if the ban on same-sex marriage had not been grounded in religion, why would lifting that ban harm religion? The answer may lie in the unselfconscious opportunism to which American religion-talk lends itself: those who want to diminish religious influence on a given issue will decry religious establishment, while those who want to increase religious influence will extol religious freedom. The opponents of same-sex marriage belonged to the latter category. They had not lost all place in American foundations but had lost the cultural dominance that could "go without saying." In reaction, they seized upon the language of religious freedom, but they repurposed that language to establish, or reestablish, majoritarian religious norms as the law of the land.

In a Canadian case concerning same-sex marriage, Steven Greenberg offered a different take on the relationship between religion and civil marriage. He had been unsettled by the testimony of a fellow Orthodox rabbi who claimed that because *halacha* does not permit same-sex marriages, neither should civil law. Greenberg countered that *halacha* forbids many marriages that are regularly permitted by civil law—for example, marriage between Jews and non-Jews, or between any Jew and the child of an adulterous union. Orthodox Judaism, he argued, doesn't object to non-*halachic* civil marriages of opposite-sex couples, so why do non-*halachic* civil marriages become a problem when they occur in same-sex couples? In fact, Greenberg contended, the distinction between religious and civil marriage is good for religions themselves, because it allows them to enforce strict marriage standards within their denominations without shutting anyone out of their legal rights. Giving legal

force to majoritarian religious beliefs does not protect religious liberty, he argued, but destroys it. Jews, whose religion is the majority
in only one nation on earth, should know this better than anyone.[67]

Chief Justice Roberts and the other dissenters also argued
against same-sex marriage on the grounds that confinement of
marriage to opposite-sex couples is very ancient. For them, that
settled the constitutional question of whether same-sex marriage
can be a fundamental right. As mentioned above, constitutional jurisprudence contains two definitions of fundamental rights. By the
1937 definition, fundamental rights are "implicit in the concept of
ordered liberty," such that "neither liberty nor justice would exist if
they were sacrificed." By the 1977 definition, a fundamental right
must be "deeply rooted in this nation's history and tradition." The
Obergefell majority appeared to read the two definitions as alternatives, but the dissenters read them as co-requisite.[68] The dissenters
could see that the *right to marry*, which the Court already had
classed as fundamental, fit both the 1937 and the 1977 criteria. But
the purported right to *same-sex* marriage was undoubtedly a new
idea and therefore could not possibly be a fundamental right.

In Canada's same-sex marriage debate, Steven Greenberg too
confronted the claim that the institution of marriage had not
changed since ancient times. He pointed out that even within Judaism, marriage traditions had evolved. "Abraham ended up with a
wife and a concubine, Jacob with two wives and two concubines,"
he said, and the Babylonian Talmud relates without criticism that
"day marriages" were contracted by wealthier Jewish men, including highly respected rabbis.[69] With these examples, Greenberg
showed that marriage is not a "natural" phenomenon but a product
of culture and thus subject to change. Why, he asked, would this
particular change—the extension of civil marriage to same-sex
couples—be thought to upend marriage in a way that previous
radical changes had not?

For Chief Justice Roberts and the other dissenters in *Obergefell*,
the ancient and enduring character of heterosexual marriage was
due to the necessity of propagating the species. He did not acknowledge that for at least a century the ideal (if not always the
reality) of marriage in America has centered on companionship
rather than procreation. Most Americans would consider a loving

but nonprocreative marriage at least adequate, while few would be content with a marriage that was procreative but loveless. In this respect, the *Obergefell* dissenters were out of step with American marriage norms and insufficiently acquainted with historical scholarship on the subject.[70] Their dissent even seemed out of step with marriage law, which does not deny marriage to nonprocreative couples.

As an Orthodox Jew, Steven Greenberg places a very high value on procreation. As he puts it, "Jesus made disciples; Abraham and Sarah made a baby."[71] But although nonprocreative Jewish couples may be seen as failing in a duty, he says, that does not invalidate their marriage under Jewish law. Judaism recognizes the need for sexual intimacy, and it traditionally has not expected anyone to remain celibate throughout his or her entire life. Greenberg argues that the benefits of marriage should be equally available to all people, but his larger point is that marriage is about obligations. As he put it in the Canadian case, marriage "is a conservative institution, expressing lifelong commitment, caring, love, and support." To deny gays and lesbians the opportunity to fulfill this duty, he argued, is "hardly an expression of family values."[72]

Greenberg also made the somewhat more delicate point that when it comes to procreation, "same-sex marriages would not preclude such endeavors any more than heterosexual marriages require them."[73] He did not elaborate, but it takes little reflection to know what he meant. Many gay or lesbian couples have raised a child that is genetically related to one of them—whether as the product of a previous heterosexual relationship, a surrogacy agreement, a sperm donation, or *in vitro* fertilization. In a lesbian couple it is possible for both partners to have a biological although not genetic relationship to the child, by implanting one partner's fertilized egg to gestate in the other's womb. And of course gay and lesbian couples can and do adopt children.

Straight people enact the same range of options, and their efforts to create and rear children are usually met with acceptance if not admiration. Yet for opponents of same-sex marriage, and no doubt for the *Obergefell* dissenters, the same endeavors by same-sex couples appear to evoke shock, disgust, and incomprehension. The point of the procreation argument against same-sex marriage, then, is not that same-sex couples cannot conceive or rear children, but that they *should* not. It is an old, visceral, and pre-reflective judgment whose deep reasons have been covered by a logical *trompe l'œil*—the need for a sperm and an egg seems to dictate that every child must be raised by a man and a woman, although one is a biological given and the other a changeable social norm.

In *Wrestling with God and Men*, Greenberg wrote that the rejection of homosexuality is so intertwined with misogyny that we cannot resolve the first without addressing the second.[74] If we apply this observation to same-sex marriage, it becomes clear that the ban on such marriage in the United States served to regulate not just sexuality but also gender. Its real social significance, in other words, was less in what it prohibited (the legal recognition of gay relationships) than in what it enforced: the legal establishment of male and female gender roles. The former applied to only a small portion of the population, but the latter applies to everyone.

The first state-level ruling for same-sex marriage, the 1993 Hawai'i case of *Baehr v. Lewin*, embraced this important insight, buttressed by the fact that Hawaii's constitution makes sex a suspect classification, meaning that any measure that treats men and women differently is subject to "strict scrutiny" by the courts.[75] Federal constitutional law has not gone that far, but it has determined that sex is an "inherently suspect" or "quasi-suspect" classification. Unlike laws based on race, those based on sex are not presumptively invalid, but they are subject to "heightened scrutiny." They must advance an important (not just "legitimate") government interest and must use means that are "substantially related" (not just "rationally related") to that interest.[76] The *Obergefell* dissenters declined to ask those questions about sex (so did the majority, a point to which I will return). Instead, Chief Justice Roberts simply asserted that "distinguishing between opposite and same sex couples is rationally related to the legitimate State interest in 'preserving the traditional institution of marriage.' "[77] The reasoning ran in an obvious circle—we should not extend marriage to same-sex couples because we should preserve the tradition that limits marriage to opposite-sex couples.

But perhaps the greatest challenge facing the opponents of same-sex marriage was the 1967 case of *Loving v. Virginia*. There, the Supreme Court had described marriage as a "fundamental right" and unanimously concluded that this right may not be abridged due to race.[78] By 2015, this was a familiar question: was or was not discrimination based on sexuality like discrimination based on race? Also familiar by now were the insulted feelings this question aroused in some members of the Court. Justice Scalia, with his usual rhetorical intemperance, complained that marriage traditionalists were being treated like "unhinged members of a wild-eyed lynch mob."[79] Justice Alito, in language reminiscent of the closet, suggested that opposition to same-sex marriage would be as stigmatized as homosexuality had once been. "I assume," he wrote, "that those that cling to old beliefs will be able to whisper their thoughts in the recesses of their homes, but if they repeat those views in public, they will risk being labeled as bigots."[80]

Chief Justice Roberts, in a calmer tone, explained that the reason mixed-race marriages are acceptable while same-sex marriages are not is that mixed-race marriages do not alter the definition of marriage as a male-female union. He argued that anti-miscegenation laws were like the coverture laws (not ruled unconstitutional until 1971) that subordinated a wife's legal existence to her husband's. Coverture, in his view, had never affected the core meaning of marriage. During the centuries when these laws were in place, "no one would ever have said, 'Marriage is the union of a man and a woman where the woman is subject to coverture.' "[81] But Roberts was off the mark: people would have been still less likely to say, "Marriage is a union of a man and woman as legal equals" (and, if they had said this, would likely have been corrected). Although aware that racial and gender hierarchy had been integral parts of marriage for most of American history, Roberts did not appear to think that these structural injustices had penetrated the institution at its base.[82]

This intersection of race and gender is a particularly good site for Emilie Townes to enter the discussion. As a womanist ethicist, she understands that rearing children, caring for the ill and aged, and the quotidian tasks of keeping a home are socially necessary forms of labor. Almost always, that labor has been performed by women and has been either unpaid or underpaid. In the antebellum South, enslaved women did this work in many white households, generating the durable stereotype that Townes describes as the

"Black Mammy," an African American woman who happily raises the children of whites while lacking the time and resources to care adequately for her own children.[83] After the Civil War, when the racial hierarchy was no longer maintained by chattel slavery, anti-miscegenation laws were enacted to reinvigorate white supremacy.[84] With the beginning of integration and the end of anti-miscegenation laws, racial hierarchy was justified by the supposed moral failures of African Americans. For black men, the problem was said to be their criminality and the solution was mass incarceration.[85] For black women, the problem was said to be their lack of sexual and reproductive restraint and the solution was marriage.

In *Womanist Ethics and the Cultural Production of Evil*, Townes traced the evolution of the Black Mammy and other stereotypes of African American women. As she pointed out, Daniel Patrick Moynihan's 1965 report titled *The Negro Family* popularized the stereotype of the "black matriarch" or, as Townes called it, "the Black Mammy gone bad."[86] In Moynihan's analysis, the supposed domination of the Negro family by women was a symptom of pathology. When not under white or male control, Moynihan suggested, black women's sexuality posed a grave social danger. For Townes, the Reagan-era stereotype of the (presumptively black) "welfare queen" was a direct descendent of the "black matriarch." Just as the black matriarch could not be trusted to responsibly bear and rear children, so the welfare queen was said to bear children for the sole purpose of collecting AFDC payments.

Given this historical context, Townes refuses to glorify marriage as a solution to social and moral problems. Yet she is hardly opposed to marriage. She has officiated at many wedding ceremonies and will proudly tell you that nearly every one of the couples she's married has stayed married. But marriage, she says, has been a "lazy" institution; couples lean so heavily on the legal and social supports it provides that they neglect to nurture the relationship itself. Worse than individual laziness, she believes, is the collective laziness that expects marriage to solve social problems. Although she certainly favors committed relationships, she does not favor any institution that is structured on gender domination, that transforms children from a social responsibility into private property, that requires childbearing women to surrender their independence, or that grants reproductive freedom to women of color only at the sufferance of whites. If these are the legal and social structures of marriage, then for Townes, marriage as such is not the solution to African American problems, much less a curative for American society.[87]

The *Obergefell* Court, however, was not about to inspect the structural soundness of marriage as a foundation of American society. Instead, Justice Kennedy's majority opinion undertook to unravel the circular claim that marriage, because traditionally defined as exclusively heterosexual, had to remain so. Those who insisted on this definition were not answering whether marriage could be extended to same-sex couples, Kennedy argued, but refusing to entertain the question. The *Loving* Court had not asked whether there was a specific right to *interracial* marriage but whether the right to marry, having been recognized as "fundamental," could be abridged on the basis of race. Similarly, in *Lawrence v. Texas*, the Supreme Court of 2003 had concluded that the Supreme Court of 1986 had been wrong to ask whether there existed a right to *homosexual* privacy; the real question had been whether the well-established right to *sexual* privacy could reasonably be denied to homosexuals.[88]

Rather than presupposing a definition that automatically precluded same-sex marriage, Kennedy proposed that the Court step back and ascertain why marriage was a fundamental right. The first reason, he argued, is personal autonomy. Marriage is "among the most intimate decisions a person can make," a "momentous act of self-definition" that people must be free to make on their own terms. The second reason is that marriage is "intimate to the degree of being sacred," a phrase the Court first used to explain the right to sexual privacy. As Kennedy had argued in 2003, the protection of sexual privacy was a necessary condition for the dignity of gay and lesbian people. But he added in *Obergefell* that privacy was not sufficient; public recognition was needed as well. "Outlaw to outcast may be a step forward, but it does not achieve the full promise of liberty." Third, he argued that marriage is fundamental because it addresses the needs of children. Like all children, those of same-sex parents need the "permanency and stability" of marriage. And like their parents, these children suffer dignitary wounds when their families are demeaned.[89]

Finally, quoting Alexis de Tocqueville, Kennedy made the most traditional of arguments for why the right to marry must be fundamental: because marriage is the foundation of society. With evident admiration, Tocqueville had written that there exists "no country in the world where the tie of marriage is so respected" as it is in America. "When the American retires from the turmoil of public life to the bosom of the family, he finds in it the image of order and peace" and then "carries that image with him into public affairs." Picking up Tocqueville's torch, Kennedy concluded that because married couples support society, society must in turn support them.[90]

Significantly, each of Kennedy's reasons had religious and ethical tones—moral autonomy, the right to be responsible, the dignity of public commitment, the sanctity of sexual love, the care of children, the common good. But unlike the dissenters, who downplayed religious warrants for their view of marriage, Kennedy acknowledged that there were religious and moral warrants on both sides. He took sober note that many Americans object to same-sex marriage on "decent and honorable religious or philosophical premises," and he stressed that "neither they nor their beliefs are disparaged here." But, he added, many Americans believe with equal sincerity "that allowing same-sex marriage is proper or indeed essential." Opponents of same-sex marriage must be free to express their views, but "when . . . sincere, personal opposition becomes enacted public law and policy, the necessary consequence is to put the imprimatur of the state itself on an exclusion that soon demeans and stigmatizes those whose own liberty is then denied."[91]

Without adverting directly to religion, the majority handled same-sex marriage with principles related to religious freedom and non-establishment. Kennedy was saying, in effect, that while the traditionalist view of marriage is perfectly legitimate, it must not be established by force of law. Where the dissenters argued that permitting same-sex marriage would shut down debate and severely threaten religious liberty, the Kennedy majority drew the opposite conclusion: that permitting same-sex marriage, far from ending the discussion, would create the conditions under which people with different views "may engage those who disagree . . . in an open and searching debate."[92]

Having explained why the right to marry is fundamental, Kennedy then had to explain why that right must be as available to homosexual as to heterosexual people. In *Obergefell*, as in his previous opinions supporting gay rights, Kennedy declined to produce a full-blown equal protection analysis. The *Obergefell* majority thus avoided the hot-button question of whether sexual orientation (like race) should be a "suspect" classification or (like sex) a "quasi-suspect" classification. Instead, Kennedy relied on what he called the "synergy" between liberty and equality: the principle that, once the judiciary recognizes a constitutional right, it immediately follows that this right cannot be denied to any citizen. Rather than subject bans against same-sex marriage to the exacting standard that the judiciary applies to racially discriminatory laws, Kennedy again made the simpler but perhaps more devastating argument that bans on same-sex marriage do not even pass rational basis review. To put it more bluntly and colloquially than he would, denying the right to marry based on a couple's genders does not even pass the "stupid test."

Although he largely avoided equal protection analysis, Kennedy did note that according to scientific consensus, "sexual orientation is both a normal expression of human sexuality and immutable."[93] Calling sexual orientation "immutable" was a first for him. In equal protection jurisprudence, this word is the bell-ringer, because it links sexual orientation to what the judiciary has said about race. It also resonates with the thinking of Steven Greenberg and many other theologians and ethicists. Greenberg compares homosexuality to left-handedness—a natural, immutable variation with no normative significance.[94] Within a theology of creation that affirms the goodness of all God has made and the humaneness of all God prescribes, this is a compelling argument. Together with the legal wallop of the word, it explains why immutability has been the hinge on which American arguments about sexuality swing.

But as Townes observed, "immutability" is a questionable descriptor. Even in describing race, it confers upon skin color a significance and intergenerational stability that it simply does not have. Although at the individual level one's sexual orientation may be as settled as one's skin color, at the collective level *how we think about* sexuality and race are social choices that carry profound consequences. In this sense, the most significant word in Kennedy's opinion was not "immutable" but "normal." Immutability, as an empirical finding, does not answer the question of whether homosexuality can be healthy and positive. Again, the crucial question—and the one about which we really have a social choice to make—is how we evaluate homosexuality, or to put it generally, how we determine social norms.

To return to the example of handedness: the reason left-handedness is morally neutral is that left-handed people do exactly the same things right-handed people do, only differently. But are same-sex married couples really doing exactly the same thing opposite-sex married couples do, only differently? Were Mildred and Richard Loving really doing exactly the same thing as racially unmixed couples in Virginia? If racial hierarchy penetrated the foundations of American society, then Mildred and Richard were *not* doing exactly the same thing as racially unmixed couples. They were shaking American social foundations in a way that affected not only themselves and other mixed-race couples, but everyone. In the same way, same-sex marriage shakes the gendered order that historically has been built into the foundations of the American society. And because it does, it affects everyone.

Indeed, Tocqueville's words celebrating marriage as the foundation of society, quoted by Kennedy, were an unselfconscious celebration of patriarchy. "When the American retires ... to ... the family, he finds in it the image of order and peace" and he "carries that image with him into public affairs." For Tocqueville, the husband and father was the true citizen who moved freely from the public to the private and back. The wife and mother remained closeted in the home, a private "bosom" ever available to nurture the public world of men. And this gendered distribution of liberty was precisely the order that Tocqueville saw male citizens replicating in the public square.

If from Tocqueville's time to ours it's been thought essential that marriage be opposite-sexed, that is because it's been thought essential that the sexes *be* "opposite." To change the gendered order of the home is to rock the social world. This is not to deny that opposite-sex couples can achieve true equality or to claim that same-sex couples are flawlessly egalitarian. But gender inequality was built into traditional marriage, and same-sex marriage lets us imagine private and public life without this systemic inequality.

The Supreme Court took a long time to conclude that, in matters of race, "separate" is inherently unequal.[95] The legalization of same-sex marriage raises similar questions about gender. As with skin color, the implication is not that we should make the differences go away—indeed, the drift of social change suggests that American society will soon have more genders, not fewer. The implication of recognizing that "separate is almost never equal" is that the empirical reality of differences must not be deployed to settle normative questions about the liberties and opportunities different sorts of people should have.

This shake-up of gender foundations goes a long way toward explaining the alarmed statements by Chief Justice Roberts and many others that the legalization of same-sex marriage will radically undermine traditional marriage in America. Justice Kennedy, in response, gently suggested that it was "counterintuitive" to think that heterosexuals will abandon traditional marriage simply because they can now legally marry someone of the same sex.[96] But if same-sex marriage provides an alternative to the gender arrangements in which we all have lived, then perhaps we must acknowledge that it really does shake things up for everyone. It is not that people who wish to live in traditional marriages may no longer do so, or that people who think same-sex marriage is wrong may no longer express that belief. But same-sex marriage makes it impossible to believe in traditional marriage in quite the same way one did before, just as exposure to religious difference makes it impossible to believe that one's religion is the only way to see the world.

Rather than thinking in terms of fixed sexual identities, we may better understand the tense division over same-sex marriage by comparing it to the challenge of living with religious pluralism and without religious establishment. To live among people whose beliefs differ from yours does not keep you from maintaining your own beliefs or practicing your religion. But it does unsettle the kind of belief that goes without saying. The beliefs of others become imaginable in a way that they previously were not. And one's own beliefs, which once abided in comfortable silence, are called into articulation. The position from which one sees the world suddenly becomes a position at which one can look, as if from the outside.

Even more disturbingly, one's own position becomes visible to the judgmental gaze of others.

People who are positioned as religious, racial, sexual, or ethnic minorities get regular practice in these difficult exercises. But we should admit that they are difficult. When asked to justify norms they used to assume, such as the norm of opposite-sex marriage or stereotypes about race that are so deeply seated as to appear factually true, people usually respond with bewilderment. People can feel demeaned and insulted when their social rank seems diminished, even if the perceived demotion results only from others rising to equality. But to return to Justice Jackson: "the freedom to differ does not pertain only to things that do not matter very much."[97] It includes the freedom to conscientiously but profoundly disagree on how our society should be ordered.

Beginnings

After same-sex marriage was legalized, both Greenberg and Townes tied the knot. Townes did so with some hesitancy, recognizing the many social injustices with which marriage can be entangled. Neither she nor her spouse, theologian Laurel Schneider, is at peace with the fact that our society distributes health care, wealth, property, social inclusion, and almost every other good thing on the basis of marriage. They did not really need the government to formalize their relationship, given that each of them is an expert ritualist and they know how to throw a good party. Yet they did need the legal protections of marriage so that they could securely live out their lives together and become "the kind of old ladies we'd so admired as children."[98] So they got married, with a ceremony that combined a congregational chant, jumping the broom, poetry, and a clarinet performance by Schneider's father. Today their Nashville home includes a large, lovely suite for an elderly relative as well as two other well-traveled guest rooms and a spacious dining table around which it's not unusual to find eight or ten people eating well, thanks to the quiet beneficence of the women of the house.

When Steven Greenberg met opera singer Steven Goldstein, they quickly knew they were right for each other, but civil same-sex marriage was not yet available in New York State. Several years

later, after New York's law changed, they were married by a
justice of the peace with some friends and family in attendance. A
Jewish wedding remained beyond the pale, because there is no *halacha*-approved marital ritual for same-sex couples. When Greenberg officiates at same-sex Jewish weddings, he does not perform
the standard ceremony called *kiddushin*, but he encourages couples
to include *halachic* elements such as a *huppah* (wedding canopy), a
shtar shutafut (partnership agreement), and *nedarim* (formal vows).
But he and Goldstein, not wishing to add fuel to the fire ignited by
Greenberg's coming out, have not had such a ceremony for themselves. As Greenberg says, "It was enough to be an out Orthodox
rabbi who wrote a book about it."[99]

Greenberg trusts that, in time, Orthodoxy will find ways to
better affirm the same-sex couples and families in its midst. But for
him, the larger question is whether gay couples and families can be
integrated into Orthodox communities. That question became
even more important when Steven and Steve decided to become
parents. Greenberg shared his husband's eagerness for a child, but
he was nearing fifty at the time. On a summer day in 2009 the couple made the decision. Hours later, they found an antique wooden
cradle on the sidewalk outside their New York apartment. This
they took for an omen, which perhaps it was. Their daughter, Amalia, was born in Mumbai, India, in 2010. The family now lives in
Boston, where they belong to a (mostly) welcoming Orthodox
community. The old cradle, salvaged from the street and lovingly
refinished, is now home to Amalia's menagerie of stuffed animals.[100]

Americans like stories to end with marriage, when all that remains is to live "happily ever after." But we all know that marriage
is the beginning, not the end, and that even in the happiest of marriages the greatest of difficulties can be expected. That's true not
only for the same-sex couples who have married since 2015, but
also for our national conversation about how sex should be managed, what family should be, and how people of different genders
should relate to each other. A decision like *Obergefell*, which shakes
the foundations of these arrangements, is not an ending, only a beginning. But although we should not expect such profound social
questions to be settled quickly, we might learn to ask them more
productively.

The logic of the *Obergefell* decision was that because marriage is good for individuals and foundational to society, and because people in same-sex couples can't change their sexual orientation, they must, as citizens entitled to equality under the law, be allowed to marry. But the decision avoided addressing the underlying normative questions about the structures of our society, just as Roberts's dissent avoided normative reflection on same-sex marriage by pointing to the biology of sperm and egg. To tackle the normative issues, we might instead ask whether there is anything *good* about specifically same-sex marriage. We might ask, as well, whether there is anything *not so good* about the foundations of our society. Conversely, we might ask whether broadening our gender arrangements does real harm to society and, if so, precisely what those harms might be.

Such questions cannot be answered in a purely linear way. Just as there was circularity in Roberts's argument that same-sex marriage cannot be a fundamental right because marriage can only be between opposite-sex people, so there is a circularity about the question of whether an openly gay man can be an Orthodox rabbi or whether an openly lesbian woman can be a Christian minister. To seriously ask whether LGBT people should be allowed to do things of which they are perfectly capable is almost automatically to answer in the affirmative—just as to seriously ask whether gays and lesbians can be civilly married is to conclude, as the *Obergefell* majority said more politely, that the answer is a no-brainer.

But the no-brainer quality of this judgment suggests not that the opposite judgment is foolish, but that in neither case is the judgment made primarily with the head. Similarly, the sense that traditional marriage "went without saying" does not indicate obtuseness on the part of its supporters, but shows how it is with "things that touch the heart of the existing order." We cannot force people to feel the same way about whom and how to love. We can only create the structural conditions under which people who see the world differently can coexist in peace, make their own homes, and perhaps invite others to come and see how the world looks from a different site.

Conclusion
Heart Conditions

LTHOUGH AMERICANS USUALLY ARGUE about religion through the architectural metaphors of wall and foundation, Justice Robert Jackson wisely spoke of these conflicts in more organic terms, as matters that "touch the heart of the existing order."[1] The heart is a good metaphor for our spirit, sensibilities, and dreams, and also for our terrors and biases, resentments and revulsions. The measure of our respect for the "right to differ," Jackson was suggesting, is taken when the differences hurt and run deep. Moreover, these differences are not solely about religion. The case at hand involved religious objections to the Pledge of Allegiance, but Jackson emphasized that people could also object to the Pledge for conscientious but nonreligious reasons. Carrying his reasoning a step forward, we might say that America's heart trouble is not caused by religion and cannot be healed by the excision of religion. It's a condition we must learn to live with. To do that, we will need a better diagnosis than the ones usually ventured.

Architecture is artifice, rarely designed to reveal the lives or tangled relations of those who inhabit it. So it has been with American religion-talk, which by its opacity hides speakers from each other, by its absolutism prevents negotiated solutions, and by its manipulability makes it all but inevitable that "religion" will be used to ratify judgments one has already reached while obscuring the reasons behind those judgments. As the stories related in this book illustrate, behind those judgments are the social locations, interests, and values of the people who are judging and being judged. But the contradictory yet interchangeable metaphors of wall and foundation not only leave the reasons for religious conflict unspoken but render those reasons virtually unspeakable.

For about the first century of the American republic, what could not be said (or, if said, could not be heard) is that religions are not necessarily good or the same. This was the age of foundation religion in America, when Euro-Americans held that religions (meaning, mostly, varieties of Protestantism) were salubrious in their commonalities and benign in their differences. The Quaker pacifists who met with President Washington in 1789 were sure that their religious devotion made them the best of citizens, even though, in the name of religion, they rejected what most other Americans considered a basic duty of citizenship. Because this contradiction could not be expressed, popular history would forget that Washington, far from deferring to the Quakers, politely rebuffed them.

Aporia followed by amnesia were also symptoms of Euro-Protestant conflicts with Mormons and Catholics in the nineteenth century. Aware that these minority traditions significantly challenged the dominant American ethos, Euro-Protestants for a long time refused to consider them genuine religions. Mormonism was "fanaticism," Catholicism was "superstition" or "papism," and both were utterly "foreign." Only after the disruptive demands of Catholics and Mormons on public life were beaten back would Anglo-Protestants acknowledge Catholicism and Mormonism as legitimate American religions. Then, quickly forgetting that foundational institutions such as public education and marriage law had been pounded into place by religious conflict, they began to wonder why it ever seemed necessary to fight over mere "religion." By virtue of this forgetting, an anti-Islamic nativism could emerge in the twenty-first century that closely recapitulated the anti-Catholic and anti-Mormon nativism of the nineteenth century, but hardly anyone would notice the resemblance.

Americans have never ceased to argue about which religions are appropriate to American citizenship, but since the late nineteenth century it has become possible to suggest that religion, at least in its public expressions, might actually be a bad thing. This view was not entirely new: there had always been two faces to the "wall of separation." From one side, it was a fortress to protect something precious, but from the other side it was a barricade against dangerous divisions. Before the Civil War, few Euro-Protestants thought much about the wall of separation, and those who did believed that its purpose was to cabin the religions of others, not their own. Criticism of public religion was rare and voiced mostly by freethinkers, Reform Jews, and Unitarians. After the Civil War, however, Euro-Protestantism itself fractured between those who wanted to restore Christianity as America's foundation and those who, like President Grant, believed that to avoid a new national schism, America must "keep Church and State forever separate."[2] For the first time, a significant part of the population came to believe that the "wall of separation" should apply to all religions and that American society should be founded on something other than religion. That something, more often than not, was "science," which over the twentieth century would be conflated with the secular and posed as the antithesis of religion.

Theodore Roosevelt was a pivotal figure at this turn. His career peaked at a time when it was too soon for a politician to openly reject religion, but not too soon to sacralize Americanism itself. Here it is instructive to compare Roosevelt's Americanism with that of Joseph Smith. Each elaborated a mythos that placed America at the center of world history, gave European settlers roots in the New World, and incorporated the sacred lands of indigenous people into Euro-American nationalism. And each explained, also in mythic terms, the subordination of women to men and of nonwhites to whites. But Smith's Americanism, emerging in the 1830s, was religiously authorized; Roosevelt's, articulated a half century later, was not. Smith's Americanism was heralded by a theophany, codified in a new sacred scripture, and amplified by direct, ongoing revelations. Roosevelt's Americanism drew its authority from the "doctrines" of evolution and strenuous living, nature's cruel but righteous law that only the fit survive, and the historical triumph of the "white race." It was, in fact, subtly authorized by *not* being "religion." "Religion," as Roosevelt understood it, had to be strictly separated from government, while Americanism was the living spirit of the nation-state. And while "religion" could be a symptom of over-civilization (to which white women were prone) or under-civilization (found, he thought, mostly among the "dark races"), Americanism cultivated the balance of moral, intellectual, and physical rigor best suited to the leading civilization on earth.

Following Roosevelt, the twentieth century became the age of wall religion, when American religion-talk came to rely on the putative distinction between "the religious" and "the secular." Americans now began to position themselves not simply for and against particular religions, but for or against religion-as-such. The most famous mid-century example of the pro-religion position was President Dwight Eisenhower's 1952 comment that "our form of government has no sense unless it is founded in a deeply felt religious faith—and I don't care what it is." Eisenhower added that in America, this faith was "Judeo-Christian," but his point was that democracy could only rest on "a religion that [*sic*] all men are created equal." Three decades later, speaking to ten thousand members of the Moral Majority, presidential candidate Ronald Reagan endorsed "old time religion." Eisenhower's version of American religion was formulated to fight communism, while Reagan's was meant to fortify Euro-Protestant conservatism against domestic challenges like affirmative action, feminism, and the gay rights movement. But both consolidated "American religion" into a single political platform. People who favored those platforms could signal their support by speaking favorably about "religion"; those opposed could signal their dissent by speaking unfavorably of "religion."[3]

The problem with identifying oneself politically as either for or against religion is not, of course, that there's anything wrong with either engaging or disengaging with religion. But when "religion" becomes a signal for a wide-ranging political platform, everything important is elided—the relative merits of the positions bundled into the platform, disagreements within and among religions, and disagreements among nonreligious people. The axiom that religions are essentially the same, which was always untenable, is only intensified when religions are concentrated into a singularity that must be condemned or vindicated in one sweeping judgment. The thought-stopping axiom that "religion is good" is now counterbalanced by the equally thought-stopping axiom that "religion is bad."

The secularist ethos still organizes the world in relation to religion, but now the relation becomes one of exclusion or containment. This implicit negativity toward religion can be sincerely disavowed—just as, in the age of foundation religion, many sincerely believed that nonsectarianism was not hostile to anyone but was simply the best formulation of a generic American religion. Similarly, in a secular world, religion has its own proper sphere, alongside (for example) the market, public education, science, and the arts. And within its proper sphere, religion is duly protected. Yet a secular world does not treat religion just like other spheres, because its relationship with religion is uniquely counter-dependent. Without religion, there can be no secular world, yet with religion present there is always the threat (or promise) that the world might be conceived and organized in very different ways.

Secularism is also the legal framework in which church-state jurisprudence blossomed in the late twentieth century, and it was the contradictions of secularism that made this jurisprudence go quickly to seed. The First Amendment assumes that the religious is categorically distinct from the secular. Otherwise it would not be possible to single out religion for unique government protection, as the free exercise clause does, or for unique government constraints, as the establishment clause does. But given the broad reach of government into our daily lives and the nation's burgeoning religious pluralism, this imagined division between the religious and the secular has proven hard to sustain. This problem bedevils every theory of church and state, from separationism to establishmentarianism. Whether one prefers the special liberties the Constitution confers on religion or the special constraints it imposes concerning religion, neither these liberties nor these constraints can be maintained if the boundary around religion gives way.

In establishment clause jurisprudence, the purported boundary between the religious and the secular is supposed to delineate the kinds of things government may not do or say. But what if something seems to be both religious and secular, such as a crèche displayed on public ground alongside a Santa Claus, reindeer, and other Christmas decorations? Or, if the goal is to include all religions on an equal basis, how is that logistically possible? If a religiously homogeneous town begins its public meetings with a sectarian prayer, must it (can it?) strive for neutrality by importing representatives of world religions to its meetings? If a school district provides vouchers for parents to send their children to private schools of the parents' choice, may that district (or must it?) deny parents the choice to use those vouchers at private religious schools? In each of these cases, religion won, and the "wall of separation" was lowered because the Supreme Court wished to avoid appearing hostile toward religion. Yet caution and constraint (if not hostility) toward religions are actually what the establishment clause requires, and when these constraints are not applied, neither is the establishment clause.[4]

One of the few places the wall of separation remains high is where it barricades creationism from the public school biology classroom. But keeping it out has proven increasingly difficult, because with each reiteration, creationism has put a greater distance between itself and religion. To date, the greatest distance has been achieved by the theory of intelligent design (ID), which omits any reference to the Bible, Christianity, or religion. ID distinguishes itself from theism by claiming only to prove the existence of the design itself, and leaving students to wonder about the existence of a Designer. It has not been hard for jurists to determine that ID, like the creationists' earlier curricular proposals, is not science. But to bar those curricula on establishment clause grounds, it is not enough to find that they do not promote *science*. Courts must also find that these theories actually promote *religion*. As creationism distances itself from religion, a certain sleight of hand seems increasingly necessary: the finding that creationist proposals are not science becomes a proxy for the finding that they are not secular—and that therefore, by implication, they must be religious.

In the Pennsylvania case of 2005, for example, Judge John Jones III showed that ID had been promulgated by the same individuals and institutions that had promoted creation science, that they had switched to ID precisely because creation science laws had been struck down, and that the theory had been espoused over the centuries by various Christian theologians.[5] All of that was true, but it was no more than historical accident. Had history gone differently, ID might be known today only as a theory created by

Aristotle, and it might be taught purely as philosophy. Of course, the integrity of the biology curriculum would suffer as much from a hostile invasion by philosophy as from a hostile invasion by religion. But the establishment clause protects public schools only from religion. And if the establishment clause is one's only hammer, religion is one's only nail.

While the establishment clause cannot be invoked without an implicitly negative judgment about religion, the free exercise clause cannot be effectuated without an implicitly positive judgment. When the Framers guaranteed that citizens had a constitutional right to freely exercise their religions, they were assuming that religions contribute to the common good and that different religions would have compatible visions of the good. On those assumptions, religious exemptions to general laws would seldom be necessary, and when necessary, would not be disruptive. Those assumptions were not true even in 1789, when the Quakers spoke up for a vision of the good that did not include war. They had stumbled on a paradox inherent to the free exercise clause that would reveal its full dimensions as America became more religiously heterogeneous: while believers understandably want to be exempt from laws that punish their own religious practice, exemptions from general laws are what government can least afford to promise.

In 1879, with its first free exercise case, the Supreme Court would have to face a religious practice that challenged majoritarian norms even more than pacifism did. In *Reynolds v. United States*, the Court acknowledged the "wall of separation" that was supposed to protect religion from government intrusion—in this case, protect Mormon polygamy from anti-polygamy laws. But the Court instantly breached that wall, partly on the ground that polygamy was found only among "Asiatic and African people." While such explicitly racist logic has long since disappeared from Supreme Court decisions, another claim of the *Reynolds* ruling would have more staying power: if the First Amendment were interpreted to require religious exemptions to general laws, every citizen "would become a law unto himself."[6]

The full disruptive potential of the free exercise clause would not reveal itself until after 1940, in the rush of cases that followed the clause's incorporation to the states. The Supreme Court soon noticed that, despite having done so at times in the past, it had no business deciding whether a religious belief was true. In 1944, it found that even a religious belief that to others seemed preposterous, demonstrably false, or harmful to its adherents could be the basis of a free exercise claim. The standard of free exercise reached its high-water mark with the *Sherbert* test of 1963, which prohibited government from placing a "substantial burden" on religion unless it had a "compelling interest" for doing so and used the "least restrictive means."[7]

For a brief period, some religious individuals won remarkable exemptions, even from criminal law. But the major victories were won by small Christian denominations, such as the Amish and the Seventh-day Adventists.[8] These groups were, if anything, more doctrinaire and strait-laced than the majority culture, so accommodating them hardly rocked America's foundations. That was not the case, however, with Native Americans, whose sovereignty claims and relationship to land fundamentally challenged the Euro-American order. When Native American sacred land claims came to the Supreme Court in 1988, the Court rebuffed them by pointing out that the First Amendment says only that government must not *prohibit* religious practice, not that government mustn't *inhibit* religious practice. Only two years later, however, the Court decided that the state of Oregon could criminally *prohibit* the use of peyote without carving out any exemption for the sacrament of the Native American Church.[9]

In finding for Oregon, the Supreme Court in effect swung back to where Washington stood two hundred years earlier, and where the *Reynolds* Court had stood in the century between. Like Washington, the Court in *Oregon v. Smith* decided that although legislators might choose to carve religious exemptions out of a law, they were not constitutionally obligated to do so. Quoting the *Reynolds* decision, the majority in *Smith* pointed out that if the First Amendment were interpreted to require religious exemptions to general laws, everyone would become "a law unto himself." A person's obligation to obey the law would be "contingent upon the law's coincidence with his religious beliefs" unless the government could show that the interest the law furthered was "compelling" and that religious exemptions would undermine that compelling interest—a standard the vast majority of laws do not meet. This would be "courting anarchy," said the *Smith* Court, and the peril would increase "in direct proportion to the society's diversity of religious beliefs, and its determination to coerce or suppress none of them." In other words, as the realities of religious pluralism stretched the bounds of the religious, all kinds of actions formerly considered secular (such as drug use) could make colorable free exercise claims. Under these conditions, the Court determined, the *Sherbert* standard could not be applied on an equal basis and therefore should rarely be applied at all.[10]

In this decision, the Supreme Court acknowledged that abandoning the *Sherbert* standard would unavoidably disadvantage minorities.[11] This prediction has been so fully borne out that it might as well have been the Court's intention. The vehicles of this renewed majoritarianism are Religious Freedom Restoration Acts (RFRAs), first passed by Congress in 1993 and later by many states.[12] Contrary to the misconception of some RFRA enthusiasts, neither this law nor any other can overrule the Supreme Court's interpretation of the Constitution. So RFRAs do not change the fact that, since 1990, there has been no constitutional entitlement to religious exemptions from laws. However, as Washington obliquely said to the Quakers, legislators may choose to protect *more* liberty than the Constitution promises. That, essentially, is what RFRAs do. They represent a promise on the part of legislatures to craft their laws so as to maximally accommodate religious freedom, thus restoring a semblance of the *Sherbert* standard—but only as a statutory accommodation, not as a constitutional right.

But if the *Sherbert* standard proved impossible to apply on an equal basis, why do RFRAs not fail in the same way? The answer is that RFRAs would fail in exactly the same way if they were applied equally, but to date they have not been. One reason is simple: laws, and the regulations that implement them, cannot possibly carve out exemptions for every imaginable religious objector. Instead, laws are written to exempt those whose views have the most public recognition and influence as "religion," and since the 1970s, those people have been the constituents of the religious right. So, for example, the Affordable Care Act of 2010 provided exemptions for employers who religiously object to contraception, but not for employers who religiously object to blood transfusions or to all medical care. Far from denoting a liberty that is equally available to all, "religious freedom" has become a code for opposition to laws that protect the equality of women and LGBT people, just as it once served as a code for white Christian opposition to school desegregation.

With the assistance of well-funded legal foundations, religious conservatives have sued to extend their RFRA exemptions beyond anything imagined by the authors of the free exercise clause. RFRAs have been deployed not only to protect religious individuals and churches but to benefit for-profit corporations. They have been called upon not only to protect acts of worship and decisions of obvious moral weight but in defense of activities as prosaic as cake decorating. "Religious freedom" has been invoked not only to protect the believer from being made to act against his or her own conscience, but to permit the believer to prevent *others* from doing things of which the believer does not approve.[13] Rather than being few and nondisruptive, as the Framers assumed, religious exemptions have become so numerous as to disrupt the implementation of laws—which, in some cases, appears to be exactly their intention. "Religious freedom" has become a way to reestablish formerly majoritarian but non-egalitarian norms.

But the religious right's ability to dominate the discourse of religious liberty also owes much to the confluent interests of antimodernist religion and anti-religious modernism that began in the *Scopes* era and persists today. Socially conservative Christians, believing that they are the true face of American religion, have little interest in acknowledging progressive forms of religion. LGBT and feminist organizations have a greater interest in recognizing religion among their members and allies, and over the years have learned to do so. But in the public sphere, they encounter religion as their self-identified opponent and shield themselves from it with the principle of church-state separation. So the conflict once again freezes into the familiar pattern of religion versus its foes. And the chief opposition to religion becomes science—medical standards of care for women's reproductive health, for instance, or the scientific consensus that sexual orientation cannot be changed.

Although the religion-versus-science framework has won victories for social equality, it has hardly improved the quality of public debate. To disagree meaningfully with one another, or to offer each other the presumption of moral seriousness, parties have to speak the same language. Progressives are right that sound public decision making must be informed by science. But religious conservatives are right to point out that while science can tell us what is, it cannot tell us what should be. That homosexual orientation is immutable does not mean that it is "normal" in anything more than a statistical sense. In an ethical sense, the "normality" of a transgender, gay, bisexual, or lesbian life depends on our norms: on how we envision good lives, characters, and societies. Yet so does the "normality" of being heterosexual or gender-conforming. In either case, it is far easier to appeal to an absolute authority than to expose our interests and aspirations to honest dialogue.

Today's religion wars, mostly waged by and against the religious right, are a new permutation of the problems that have ever bedeviled American religion-talk: "religion" is almost always the vehicle for prejudgments, and prejudgments are the enemy of good judgment. Arguably, this is what happened with church-state jurisprudence. Thinking carefully about these cases, jurists had to examine and eventually relinquish most of their assumptions about "religion"—for example, the assumption that there's a clear line between the religious and the secular, or that religious people will rarely refuse to obey a law. When those assumptions dissolved, church-state jurisprudence fell into what is now widely regarded as a state of disarray.

Both in the judiciary and in public life as a whole, it appears that "religion" can no longer make our judgments for us. That being the case, we are left with no choice but to probe beneath that word (and its twin, "secularism") to identify what is at stake and for whom. Within the Constitution, the stakes include freedom, equality, and the principle of limited government. But law is only one of the forces that hold a political community together or pull it apart. American religious conflicts have also embraced a host of extra-constitutional values, including the common good, the need for dignity, and the fair distribution of resources.

As history shows, these values are not absolute. They do not exist in a hierarchy that determines what is most important in any given situation. Nor should they be forced into a rational consistency that life does not obey. Even the richest description of social values is meaningless apart from lived experience, and inert until embodied in social practice. The value of freedom, for example, is better understood by those who have experienced subordination than by those who have never known what it is to be unfree. To expose the roots of our religious conflicts and imagine how they might be remediated, Americans must understand our *relations*—not just as individuals but as groups, not just now but in the history we've shared and the future that is unfolding.

American conflicts about religion, though often phrased in terms of walls, always come down to questions about how we should live together. Those questions are undoubtedly foundational, which is why they so unsettle us. It is rightly said that we live in a post-foundational age, but this does not mean that we stand nowhere, make no promises, and share no assumptions. It means that we no longer can plead innocence about history or pretend not to know that mandates once held out as natural or divine may turn out not to be so. In a post-foundational age, what's beneath our feet feels more like water than earth, and repairing it is more like adjusting sails on a windy sea than sealing cracks beneath a familiar home.

That America is morally unmoored is no news to the many victims of our history. They know that troubles like those recounted here do indeed go to the "heart of the existing order." Life at sea can be good for the heart, although not always by the reduction of stress, for we must live at close quarters with tense disagreements, yet cooperate greatly to get anywhere. Let us hope we rise to the effort.

Notes

Introduction

1. Burwell v. Hobby Lobby Stores, Inc., 573 U.S. ___ (2014).
2. Robert Wuthnow, *The Restructuring of American Religion* (Princeton: Princeton University Press, 1988); Pew Research Center, *Religious Landscape Survey: Religious Beliefs and Practices; Diverse and Politically Relevant* (Washington, DC: Pew Research Center, 2008), 2.
3. Pew Research Center, *Religious Landscape Survey;* Pew Research Center, "Public's Views on Human Evolution," December 30, 2013, http://www .pewforum.org/2013/12/30/publics-views-on-human-evolution/; Pew Research Center, "How Americans Feel about Religious Groups," July 16, 2014, 5, 15, http://www.pewforum.org/2014/07/16/how-americans-feel-about-religious-groups/; First Amendment Center at Vanderbilt University and the Newseum, "The State of the First Amendment," July, 2013, 9, https://www.freedomforuminstitute.org/wp-content/uploads/2014/08 /FAC_sofa_2013report.pdf.
4. Pew Research Center, "Support for Same-Sex Marriage at Record High, but Key Segments Remain Opposed," June 8, 2015, 10, http://www. people-press.org/2015/06/08/support-for-same-sex-marriage-at-record-high-but-key-segments-remain-opposed/.
5. Pew Research Center, "A Religious Portrait of African Americans," January 30, 2009, http://www.pewforum.org/2009/01/30/a-religious-portrait-of-african-americans/.
6. First Amendment Center, "The State of the First Amendment."
7. Rutgers Center for American Women and Politics, "The Gender Gap: Attitudes on Public Policy Issues" (New Brunswick, NJ: Rutgers University, 2014).

8. Michael Lipka, "Majority of U.S. Catholics' Opinions Run Counter to Church on Contraception, Homosexuality," Pew Research Center, September 19, 2013, http://www.pewresearch.org/fact-tank/2013/09/19/majority-of-u-s-catholics-opinions-run-counter-to-church-on-contraception-homosexuality/; and Pew Research Center, "In Gay Marriage Debate, Both Supporters and Opponents See Legal Recognition as Inevitable," June 6, 2013, 19, http://www.people-press.org/2013/06/06/in-gay-marriage-debate-both-supporters-and-opponents-see-legal-recognition-as-inevitable/.

9. Michael Lipka, "Religious 'Nones' Are Not Only Growing; They're Becoming More Secular" (Washington, DC: Pew Research Center Fact Tank, November 11, 2015); and Lipka, "Why America's 'Nones' Left Religion Behind" (Washington, DC: Pew Research Center Fact Tank, August 24, 2016).

10. Linda Mercadante, *Belief without Borders: Inside the Minds of the Spiritual but Not Religious* (New York: Oxford University Press, 2014), 27; Michael Hout and Claude S. Fisher, "Why More Americans Have No Religious Preference: Politics and Generations," *American Sociological Review* 67 (April, 2002): 165–66.

11. Stephen Carter, *The Culture of Disbelief: How American Law and Politics Trivialize Religious Devotion* (New York: Basic Books, 1993), 38.

12. Constitution of the United States, Amendment XIV, Section I; Cantwell v. Connecticut, 310 U.S. 296 (1940); Everson v. Board of Education, 330 U.S. 1 (1947).

13. Alexis de Tocqueville, *Democracy in America*, vol. 1 (1835), ed. Eduardo Nolla, trans. James T. Schliefer (Indianapolis: Liberty Fund, 2012), 475.

14. Roger Williams, *The Bloudy Tenet of Persecution for Cause of Conscience* (London, 1644). *See also* John Witte Jr., "Facts and Fictions about the History of Separation of Church and State," *Journal of Church and State* 48, No. 1 (Winter, 2006): 15–45.

15. Thomas Jefferson, *Notes on the State of Virginia* (1787), Query XVII, Avalon Project, http://avalon.law.yale.edu/18th_century/jeffvir.asp; Jefferson, Second Inaugural Address, March 4, 1801, Avalon Project, http://avalon.law.yale.edu/19th_century/jefinau2.asp.

16. Peter Berger, *The Sacred Canopy: Elements of a Sociological Theory of Religion* (Garden City: Doubleday, 1969).

17. George Washington, Farewell Address, September 17, 1797, George Washington Papers, Series 2, Letterbook 24, April 3, 1793–March 3, 1797, Library of Congress, https://cdn.loc.gov/service/mss/mgw/mgw2/024/024.pdf.

18. Frederick Douglass, *Narrative of the Life of Frederick Douglass, an American Slave* (Boston: Anti-Slavery Office, 1849), 118–24.

19. Jonathan Z. Smith, "Religion, Religions, Religious," in *Critical Terms for Religious Studies*, ed. Mark C. Taylor (Chicago: University of Chicago Press, 1998), 269–84, 269.

20. John Rawls, "The Idea of Public Reason Revisited," *University of Chicago Law Review* 64, No. 3 (Summer, 1997): 765–807; Winnifred Fallers Sullivan, Robert Yelle, and Mateo Taussig-Rubbo, eds., *After Secular Law* (Stanford: Stanford University Press, 2011).

21. Talal Asad, "Reading a Modern Classic: W. C. Smith's *The Meaning and End of Religion*," *History of Religions* 40, No. 3 (February, 2001): 205–22; and Asad, *Formations of the Secular: Christianity, Islam, Modernity* (Stanford: Stanford University Press, 2003).

22. George Jacob Holyoake, *Principles of Secularism*, 3rd ed. (London: Austin and Company, 1871), 11, 15.

23. Susan Jacoby, *Freethinkers: A History of American Secularism* (New York: Metropolitan Books, 2004).

24. West Virginia State Board of Education v. Barnette, 319 U.S. 624 (1943) at 642.

Chapter One. Religion as We Know It

Epigraph: Towne v. Eisner, 245 U.S. 418, 425 (1918) at 425.

1. Christopher Columbus, "Journal of the First Voyage of Christopher Columbus," in *The Northmen: Columbus and Cabot, 985–1503; The Voyages of Columbus and John Cabot*, ed. Julius E. Olson and Edward G. Bourne (New York: Scribner's, 1906), 87–258, 111.

2. Pope Nicholas V, *Romanus Pontifex* (1455); Pope Alexander V, *Inter Caetera* (1493), in *European Treaties Bearing on the History of the United States and Its Dependencies to 1648*, ed. Francis Gardiner Davenport (Washington, DC: Carnegie Institute, 1917), 9–32, https://archive.org/details/europeantreatieoopaulgoog/page/n42.

3. Tertullian, *Apology against the Heathens* (circa 198); Augustine of Hippo, *On True Religion* (circa 390).

4. Columbus, "Journal of the First Voyage," 89–90.

5. Bartolomé de las Casas, *An Account, Much Abbreviated, of the Destruction of the Indies* (1542), ed. Franklin Knight, trans. Andrew Hurley (Indianapolis: Hackett, 2003), 68–71.

6. Irving Rouse, *The Tainos* (New Haven: Yale University Press, 1992), 150–61.

7. Jonathan Z. Smith, "Religion, Religions, Religious," in *Critical Terms for Religious Studies*, ed. Mark C. Taylor (Chicago: University of Chicago Press, 1998), 269–84, 271.

8. Denise Kimber Buell, *Why This New Race? Ethnic Reasoning in Early Christianity* (New York: Columbia University Press, 2005).

9. Smith, "Religion, Religions, Religious," 269.

10. Brent Nongbri, *Before Religion: A History of a Modern Concept* (New Haven: Yale University Press, 2013), 39–45.

11. Daniel Dubuisson, *The Western Construction of Religion: Myths, Knowledge and Ideology*, trans. William Sayers (Baltimore: Johns Hopkins University Press, 2003).

12. Martin Luther, *Appeal to the Christian Nobility of the German Nation* (1520), trans. Charles Jacobs, in *Three Treatises* (Minneapolis: Fortress Press, 1970), 1–112, 45, 41.

13. Kal Raustiala, *Does the Constitution Follow the Flag? The Evolution of Territoriality in American Law* (New York: Oxford University Press, 2018), 11–13, 23; Derek Croxton, "The Peace of Westphalia of 1648 and the Origins of Sovereignty," *International History Review* 21, No. 3 (September, 1999): 569–91.

14. Michel Foucault, "First Hour, February 1, 1984," in *The Courage of Truth: The Government of Self and Others II*, ed. Frédéric Gross, trans. Graham Burchell (New York: Palgrave Macmillan, 2011), 1–15, 9.

15. Alexander Ross, *Pansebeia: Or a View of all Religions in the World: With the Several Church Governments from the Creation till these times: Also, a Discovery of all known Heresies in all Ages and Places, and choice Observations and Reflections throughout the Whole. Written in the year 1640 by Alexander Ross, Chaplain in Ordinary to King Charles the First; and now brought down to the present times by a clergyman* (London, 1755). University of Hawai'i at Manoa Library, https://www.gale.com/primary-sources/eighteenth-century-collections-online. As the long subtitle indicates, Ross served as a chaplain to King Charles I, whose commitment to absolute monarchy and the Anglican Church helped ignite the English Civil War in 1642 and, ultimately, led to the execution of Charles by the Rump Parliament in 1649.

16. Edward Lord Herbert of Cherbury, *De Veritate* (1624) (Bristol, England: J. W. Arrowsmith, 1937).

17. Jean-Jacques Rousseau, "Civil Religion" (1762), in Rousseau, *The Social Contract and the First and Second Discourses*, ed. Susan Dunn (New Haven: Yale University Press, 2002), 245–53.

18. John Locke, *A Letter Concerning Toleration* (1689), trans. William Popple (London: J. Crowder, 1800).

19. Ibid., 123.

20. Elizabeth A. Pritchard, *Religion in Public: Locke's Political Theology* (Redwood City: Stanford University Press, 2014), 14–35.

21. Pritchard, *Religion in Public*, 6.

22. Barbara McGraw, *Rediscovering America's Sacred Ground* (Albany: State University of New York Press, 2003).

23. Locke, *Letter Concerning Toleration*, 11, 12–13, 39, 48, 118.

24. Marjorie Garber, *Vested Interests: Cross-Dressing and Cultural Anxiety* (New York: Routledge, 1991), 25–31.

25. Locke, *Letter Concerning Toleration*, 3–4.

26. Locke, *Letter Concerning Toleration*, 103–4.

27. Ibid., 1.

28. Ibid., 2.

29. Pritchard, *Religion in Public*, 84–86.

30. Ibid., 98–99.

31. Ibid., 70.

32. Ibid., 102–3.

33. Ibid., 103.

34. Jonas Proast, *The Argument of the "Letter Concerning Toleration" [by John Locke] Considered and Answered* (London: George West and Henry Clements, 1690); Pritchard, *Religion in Public*, 98.

35. John Locke, *Some Thoughts on Education*, in *The Harvard Classics* 37, pt. 1, ed. Charles W. Eliot (New York: P. F. Collier and Son, 1909–14), § 200.

36. Locke, *Letter Concerning Toleration*, 20.

37. Locke, *Some Thoughts on Education*, § 136.

38. Pritchard, *Religion in Public*, 8.

39. Locke, *Some Thoughts on Education*, § 143.1.

40. Hannah Adams, *A Dictionary of All Religions and Religious Denominations: Jewish, Heathen, Mahometan and Christian, Ancient and Modern*, 4th ed. (Boston: James Eastburn, 1817).

41. Ibid., 371–72.

42. Ibid., 376.

43. Ibid., 55, 106, 107, 142, 195.

44. Ibid., 128–32.

45. Ibid., 373.

46. Ibid., 161.

47. Ibid., 157.

48. Ibid., 248.

49. Ibid., 289–90.

50. Tomoko Masuzawa, *The Invention of World Religions* (Chicago: University of Chicago Press, 2005), 121–46, 202–3.

51. Nongbri, *Before Religion*, 133–43.

52. Richard King, *Orientalism and Religion: Postcolonial Theory, India, and "The Mystic East"* (New York: Routledge, 1999), 101–8.

53. Jogendra Chunder Ghose, ed., *The English Works of Raja Rammohun Roy*, vol. 1 (Calcutta: Srikanta Roy, 1901).

54. Max Müller, ed., *Sacred Books of the East* (Oxford, UK: Oxford University Press, 1879–1910).

55. King, *Orientalism and Religion*.

56. Helen Hardacre, "Creating State Shinto: The Great Promulgation Campaign and the New Religions," *Journal of Japanese Studies* 12, No. 1 (Winter, 1986): 29–63.

57. SCAPIN 448, "The Shinto Directive" (December 15, 1941).

58. Congregation for the Doctrine of the Faith, *Plane Compertum Est* (1939).

59. C. P. Tiele, "Religions," in *The Encyclopedia Britannica*, 9th ed., vol. 20 (New York: Scribner's, 1886), 358–71.

60. Ibid., 366, 369.

61. Ibid., 369.

62. Ibid., 369, fn. 1.

63. Ibid., 367.

64. Mircea Eliade, *The Sacred and the Profane: The Nature of Religion*, trans. Willard Trask (New York: Harper Books, 1961).

65. Emile Durkheim, *The Division of Social Labor* (1893), trans. W. D. Hall (New York: Free Press, 2014); Max Weber, *The Sociology of Religion*, trans. Ephraim Fischoff (Boston: Beacon, 1963, 1991).

66. John Henry Barrows, "Address to the World's Parliament of Religions," in *The World's Parliament of Religions: An Illustrated and Popular History*, ed. John Henry Barrows (Chicago: World's Parliament Publishing, 1893), 1:73–74.

67. *Daily Inter Ocean*, September 12, 1893, cited in Richard Hughes Seager, ed., *The Dawn of Religious Pluralism: Voices from the World's Parliament of Religions, 1893* (La Salle, IL: Open Court, 1993), 30–31.

68. Charles Carroll Bonney, "Address," in Barrows, *World's Parliament of Religions*, 1:72.

69. John Henry Barrows, *Christianity, the World Religion: Lectures Delivered in India and Japan* (Chicago: A. C. McClurg, 1897).

70. Barrows, "Address," 1:74.

71. Church of the Holy Trinity v. United States, 143 U.S. 457 (1892); Chinese Exclusion Act (1882); Alien Contract Labor Law (1885).

72. Holy Trinity v. United States at 465.

73. David J. Brewer, *The United States: A Christian Nation* (Philadelphia: John C. Winston, 1905).

74. Diana Eck, foreword to Seager, *Dawn of Religious Pluralism*, xvi.

75. Virchand A. Gandhi, "The History and Tenets of the Jains of India," in Barrows, *World's Parliament of Religions*, 1:144–45.

76. "Outcome of the World Parliament of Religions," *Chicago Tribune*, September 24, 1893, reproduced in Seager, *Dawn of Religious Pluralism*, 353–54.

77. Seager, *Dawn of Religious Pluralism*, 153.

78. John Henry Barrows, "The World's Response to a Great Idea," in Barrows, *World's Parliament of Religions*, 1:18–61.

79. Mohammed A. R. Webb, "The Spirit of Islam," in Barrows, *World's Parliament of Religions*, 2:989–96, 989.

80. Merwin-Marie Snell, "The Future of Religion," in Barrows, *World's Parliament of Religions*, 2:1325–27.

81. William C. Wilkinson, "The Attitude of Christianity to Other Religions," in Barrows, *World's Parliament of Religions*, 2:1243–49, 1249.

82. Julia Ward Howe, "What Is Religion?," in Barrows, *World's Parliament of Religions*, 2:1250–51. The audience's reactions to the speeches were described by the *Chicago Herald*, September 27, 1893, cited in Seager, *Dawn of Religious Pluralism*, 79.

83. Bonney, "Address," 1:71–72.
84. Narasima Charya, "Criticism and Discussion of Missionary Methods," in Barrows, *World's Parliament of Religions*, 2:1094–95.
85. Bonney, "Address," 1:72.
86. Seager, *Dawn of Religious Pluralism*, 133.
87. Ibid., 7.
88. Eck, foreword, xv–xvi.
89. Henry Drummond, "Evolution and Christianity," in Barrows, *World's Parliament of Religions*, 1:67–72.

Chapter Two. Walls and Foundations

1. Gregg L. Frazer, *The Religious Beliefs of America's Founders: Reason, Revelation, and Revolution* (Lawrence: University Press of Kansas, 2012); David G. Hackett, *That Religion in Which All Men Agree: Freemasonry in American Culture* (Berkeley: University of California Press, 2014); Susan Jacoby, *Freethinkers: A History of American Secularism* (New York: Metropolitan Books, 2004); Isaac Kramnick and R. Laurence Moore, *The Godless Constitution: A Moral Defense of the Secular State*, updated ed. (New York: Norton, 2005); Daniel Dreisbach et al., eds., *The Founders on God and Government* (Lanham, MD: Rowman and Littlefield, 2004); Jon Meacham, *American Gospel: God, the Founding Fathers, and the Making of a Nation* (New York: Random House, 2007); Steven Waldman, *Founding Faith: How Our Founding Fathers Forged a Radical New Approach to Religious Liberty* (New York: Random House, 2008).
2. James Madison, "Property," March 29, 1792, in *The Founders' Constitution* 1, Ch. 16, Document 23, http://press-pubs.uchicago.edu/founders/documents/v1ch16s23.html.
3. Alexis de Tocqueville, *Democracy in America* (1835), trans. Gerald Bevin, ed. Isaac Kramnick (New York: Penguin Classics, 2003), 342, 518.
4. Steven Smith, *Foreordained Failure: The Quest for a Constitutional Principle of Religious Freedom* (New York: Oxford University Press, 2004); Philip Hamburger, *Separation of Church and State* (Cambridge: Harvard University Press, 2004); Van Orden v. Perry, 545 U.S. 677 (2005), Thomas, J., concurring.
5. "Address of the Religious Society Called the Friends to the President of the United States"; George Washington, "Address to the Religious Society Called the Friends," circa October 13, 1789, Founders Online, http://founders.archives.gov/documents/Washington/05-04-02-0188.
6. Rufus M. Jones, *Quakers in the American Colonies* (London: Macmillan, 1911), 562–64.
7. Ibid., 151.
8. Ibid., 564–68.

9. George Washington to the Hebrew Congregation in Newport, Rhode Island, August 18, 1790, Founders Online, http://founders.archives.gov/documents/Washington/05–06–02–0135.

10. Paul F. Boller, *Washington and Religion* (Dallas: Southern Methodist University Press, 1963), 129; Vincent Philip Muñoz, *God and the Founders: Madison, Washington, and Jefferson* (Cambridge: Cambridge University Press, 2009), 63–65.

11. George Washington to William Livingston, May 11, 1777, George Washington Papers at the Library of Congress, Series 4, General Correspondence, https://www.loc.gov/item/mgw447222/. Hereafter, Washington Papers.

12. Boller, *Washington and Religion*, 132.

13. George Washington to John Lacey Jr., March 20, 1778, Washington Papers, Series 4, https://www.loc.gov/item/mgw449815/.

14. § 7(j) of the Military Selective Service Act of 1967, as amended, 50 U.S.C.A. §3806(j).

15. J. William Jones, "The Dry Bones of Quaker Theology," *Church History* 39, No. 4 (1970): 503–23.

16. Jones, *Quakers*, 34.

17. George Washington to the Roman Catholics of America, c. March 15, 1790, Founders Online, http://founders.archives.gov/documents/Washington/05–05–02–0193.

18. Washington to the Hebrew Congregation in Newport.

19. Hackett, *That Religion*, 56–57, 60–65.

20. George Washington, Farewell Address, September 17, 1796, https://cdn.loc.gov/service/mss/mgw/mgw2/024/024.pdf.

21. Boller, *Washington and Religion*, 29, 33–34; Waldman, *Founding Faith*, 57–59.

22. George Fox, *Journal of George Fox*, 7th ed., vol. 2 (London: W. and F. G. Cash, 1852), 279.

23. William Penn, "Frame of Government of Pennsylvania," May 5, 1682, Avalon Project, http://avalon.law.yale.edu/17th_century/pa04.asp.

24. William Penn, "The Great Case of Liberty of Conscience," 1690, in *The Political Writings of William Penn*, ed. Andrew R. Murphy (Indianapolis: Liberty Fund, 2002), 86.

25. George Washington to the Presbyterian Church Assembly, May, 1789, Washington Papers, Series 2, Letterbook 38, https://www.loc.gov/resource/mgw2.038/?sp=44.

26. Jones, *Quakers*, 169.

27. George Washington, First Inaugural Address, April 30, 1789, Founders Online, https://founders.archives.gov/documents/Washington/05–02–02–0130–0003.

28. Jones, *Quakers*, 517–20; Richard S. Newman, "The Pennsylvania Abolition Society: Restoring a Group to Glory," *Pennsylvania Legacies* 5, No. 2 (No-

vember, 2005): 6–10; "Address to the United States Congress from the Yearly Meeting of the People Called the Quakers," October 4, 1783, https://www.wikitree.com/wiki/Space:1783_Quaker_Anti-Slavery_Petition.

29. Dorothy Twohig, "That Species of Property: Washington's Role in the Controversy over Slavery," in *George Washington Reconsidered*, ed. Don Higgenbotham (Charlottesville: University of Virginia Press, 2001), 128, 135, 132.

30. Pennsylvania Act for the Gradual Abolition of Slavery, March 1, 1780.

31. Twohig, "That Species of Property," 129, n. 48.

32. Constitution of the United States, Article I, § 9, clause 1.

33. David Stuart to George Washington, March 15, 1790, Founders Online, http://founders.archives.gov/documents/Washington/05-05-02-0155; George Washington to David Stuart, March 28, 1790, and June 15, 1790, in *The Writings of George Washington*, vol. 31, ed. John C. Fitzpatrick (Washington, DC: U.S. Government Printing Office, 1939), 30, 52.

34. Annals of Cong., 16th Cong., 1st Sess., 1310–29, 1316.

35. Inhabitants' Petition, Halifax County, November 10, 1785, Legislative Petitions of the General Assembly, 1776–1865, Accession Number 36121, Box 97, Folder 21.

36. George Washington to Jean Baptiste de Ternant, September 24, 1791, in *Writings of George Washington*, vol. 31, 375–76.

37. George Washington to Alexander Spotswood, November 23, 1794, in *Writings of George Washington*, vol. 34, ed. John C. Fitzpatrick (Washington, DC: U.S. Government Printing Office, 1940), 48.

38. C. A. Browne, "John Leland and the Mammoth Cheshire Cheese," *Agricultural History* 18, No. 4 (October, 1944): 145–53; Daniel Dreisbach, "Mr. Jefferson, a Mammoth Cheese, and the 'Wall of Separation between Church and State': A Bicentennial Commemoration," *Journal of Church and State* 43, No. 4 (Autumn, 2001): 725–45.

39. James Madison to William Bradford, January 24, 1774, in *The Founders' Constitution* 5, Amendment I (Religion), Document 16, http://press-pubs.uchicago.edu/founders/documents/amendI_religions16.html.

40. Mark S. Scarberry, "John Leland and James Madison: Religious Influence on the Ratification of the Constitution and on the Proposal of the Bill of Rights," 113 *Pennsylvania State Law Review* 733 (2009): 733–800.

41. *Gazette of the United States*, September 11, 1800, 2.

42. James Hutson, "Thomas Jefferson's Letter to the Danbury Baptists: A Controversy Rejoined," *William and Mary Quarterly* 56, No. 4 (October, 1999): 781.

43. William Parker Cutler et al., eds., *Life, Journals and Correspondence of Rev. Manasseh Cutler*, vol. 2 (Cincinnati: R. Clarke, 1888), 66–67.

44. Danbury, Connecticut, Baptist Association to Thomas Jefferson, October 7, 1801, Thomas Jefferson Papers at the Library of Congress, https://www.loc.gov/item/mtjbib010633/. Hereafter, Jefferson Papers.

45. Hutson, "Thomas Jefferson's Letter," 783–85.
46. Thomas Jefferson to Danbury, Connecticut, Baptist Association, January 1, 1802, with copy, Jefferson Papers, https://www.loc.gov/item/mtjbib010955/.
47. "Forum: Thomas Jefferson's Letter to the Danbury Baptists—a Controversy Rejoined," *William and Mary Quarterly* 56, No. 4 (October, 1999): 775–824.
48. Thomas Jefferson, *Autobiography, 1743–1790*, Avalon Project, http://avalon.law.yale.edu/19th_century/jeffauto.asp; Jefferson, "A Bill for Punishing Disturbers of Religious Worship and Sabbath Breakers," June 18, 1779, Thomas Jefferson Papers, Founders Online, http://founders.archives.gov/documents/Jefferson/01-02-02-0132-0004-0084; Jefferson, Second Inaugural Address, March 4, 1805, Avalon Project, http://avalon.law.yale.edu/19th_century/jefinau2.asp.
49. Everson v. Board of Education, 330 U.S. 1 (1947).
50. Ian Bartrum, "Of Historiography and Constitutional Principles: Jefferson's Reply to the Danbury Baptists," *Journal of Church and State* 51, No. 1 (Summer, 2009): 102–25.
51. John Leland, *The Writings of the Late Elder John Leland* (New York: G. W. Wood, 1845), 340; Janet Moore Lindman, *Bodies of Belief: Baptist Community in Early America* (Philadelphia: University of Pennsylvania Press, 2011).
52. Roger Williams, *The Bloudy Tenet of Persecution for Cause of Conscience* (1644), ed. Edward Bean Underhill (London: J. Hadden, 1848), 435.
53. Edwin Gaustad, *Sworn on the Altar of God: A Religious Biography of Thomas Jefferson* (Grand Rapids, MI: Eerdmans, 1996), 72.
54. James Hutson, curator, *Religion and the Founding of the American Republic*, Library of Congress, http://www.loc.gov/exhibits/religion/rel05.html#obj141.
55. Isaac Backus, *An Appeal to the Public for Religious Liberty* (Boston: John Boyle, 1773), 30–43.
56. Danbury Baptists to Thomas Jefferson, October 7, 1801.
57. Backus, *Appeal to the Public*, 13, 45, 8.
58. Danbury Baptists to Thomas Jefferson.
59. William G. McLoughlin, *Isaac Backus and the American Pietistic Tradition* (New York: Little, Brown, 1967), 198–99.
60. William G. McLoughlin, "Isaac Backus and the Separation of Church and State in America," *American Historical Review* 7, No. 3 (1968): 392–413.
61. John Leland, "The Rights of Conscience Inalienable," in *Writings*, 191.
62. Lindman, *Bodies of Belief*, 143–44.
63. John Leland, "Address Delivered at Bennington," August 16, 1839, in *Writings*, 697–98.
64. Thomas Jefferson to Peter Carr, August 10, 1787, Founders Online, http://founders.archives.gov/documents/Jefferson/01-12-02-0021.

65. Thomas Jefferson, "A Bill for Establishing Religious Freedom," June 18, 1779, Founders Online, http://founders.archives.gov/documents/Jefferson/01-02-02-0132-0004-0082.

66. Jefferson, *Autobiography*, 1743–90.

67. Hutson, "Thomas Jefferson's Letter," 785–86; Thomas Buckley, "Reflections on a Wall," *William and Mary Quarterly* 56, No. 3 (October, 1999): 795–800.

68. Thomas Jefferson to J. P. P. Derieux, July 25, 1788, Founders Online, http://founders.archives.gov/documents/Jefferson/01-13-02-0302.

69. Thomas Jefferson to John Adams, April 11, 1823, Jefferson Papers, https://www.loc.gov/item/mtjbib024623/.

70. Gaustad, *Sworn on the Altar of God*, 129.

71. Thomas Jefferson to Joseph Priestley, April 9, 1803, Jefferson Papers, https://www.loc.gov/item/mtjbib012297/.

72. Thomas Jefferson to Benjamin Rush, April 21, 1803, with Syllabus of an Estimate of the Merit of the Doctrines of Jesus, Jefferson Papers, https://www.loc.gov/item/mtjbib012336/.

73. Ibid., 3.

74. Jefferson to Adams, April 11, 1823.

75. Jefferson to Carr. *See also* Thomas Jefferson to John Adams, October 14, 1816, Jefferson Papers, https://www.loc.gov/item/mtjbib022614/.

76. Jefferson to Adams, April 11, 1823.

77. John Adams to Thomas Jefferson, March 2, 1816, Jefferson Papers, https://www.loc.gov/item/mtjbib023421/.

78. Thomas Jefferson to John Adams, August 15, 1820, Jefferson Papers, https://www.loc.gov/item/mtjbib021117.

79. Thomas Jefferson to Isaac Story, December 5, 1801, Jefferson Papers, https://www.loc.gov/item/mtjbib010798/; Thomas Jefferson to John Adams, March 14, 1820, https://www.loc.gov/item/mtjbib023756/.

80. Jefferson, "A Bill for Establishing Religious Freedom"; Thomas Jefferson, *Notes on the State of Virginia* (1787), Query XVII, Avalon Project, http://avalon.law.yale.edu/18th_century/jeffvir.asp.

81. William Linn, *Serious Considerations on the Election of a President* (New York: John Furman, 1800), 19.

82. Thomas Jefferson, First Inaugural Address, March 1, 1801, in *The Papers of Thomas Jefferson*, vol. 33, ed. James P. McClure (Princeton: Princeton University Press, 2006), 148–52; Matthew Holland, " 'To Close the Circle of Our Felicities': 'Caritas' and Jefferson's First Inaugural," *Review of Politics* 66, No. 2 (Spring, 2004): 181–205.

83. Washington, Farewell Address.

84. Linn, *Serious Considerations*, 8.

85. Thomas Jefferson to Benjamin Rush, September 23, 1800, Jefferson Papers, https://www.loc.gov/item/mtjbib009434/.

86. Jefferson, Second Inaugural Address.

87. Henry S. Randall, *The Life of Thomas Jefferson*, vol. 3 (New York: Derby and Jackson, 1858), 654.
88. Jefferson, *Notes on the State of Virginia*, Query XI.
89. Tocqueville, *Democracy in America*, 518.
90. Cantwell v. Connecticut, 310 U.S. 296 (1940); Everson v. Board of Education (1947).
91. Mark De Wolfe Howe, *The Garden and the Wilderness: Religion and Government in American Constitutional History* (Chicago: University of Chicago Press, 1967).
92. United States v. Ballard, 322 U.S. 78 (1944); Torcaso v. Watkins, 367 U.S. 488 (1961).
93. Lemon v. Kurtzman, 403 U.S. 602 (1971); Sherbert v. Verner, 374 U.S. 398 (1963).
94. Wisconsin v. Yoder, 406 U.S. 205 (1972); Lundman v. McKown, 530 N.W. 2d 807 (1995); Oregon v. Smith, 494 U.S. 872 (1990); United States v. Ballard (1944).
95. Lynch v. Donnelly, 465 U.S. 668 (1984); County of Allegheny v. ACLU, 492 U.S. 573 (1989); Capitol Square Review Board v. Pinette, 515 U.S. 753 (1995).
96. Oregon v. Smith (1990).
97. Church of Lukumi Babalu Aye v. City of Hialeah, 506 U.S. 520 (1993).
98. Bowen v. Kendrick, 487 U.S. 589 (1988); Agostini v. Felton, 521 U.S. 203 (1997).

Chapter Three. Protestants, Catholics, and Mormons

Epigraph: Central Campaign Committee to Hugh Clark, Esq., May 24, 1844, in Joseph Smith, *History of the Church of Jesus Christ of Latter-Day Saints* (Salt Lake City: Deseret Book Company, 1948–1961), 6:404.

1. James Madison to Jasper Adams, 1832, James Madison Papers at the Library of Congress, https://www.loc.gov/item/mjm.23_1175_1176/.
2. E. D. Howe, *Mormonism Unvailed* (Painsville, OH: E. D. Howe, 1834), 145; Smith, *History of the Church*, 3:167, n. 2.
3. W. Paul Reeve, *Religion of a Different Color: Race and the Mormon Struggle for Whiteness* (New York: Oxford University Press, 2015), 52–55; Hokulani Aikau, *A Chosen People, a Promised Land: Mormonism and Race in Hawai'i* (Minneapolis: University of Minnesota Press, 2012), 31–54.
4. Jenny Franchot, *Roads to Rome: The Ante-Bellum Protestant Encounter with Catholicism* (Berkeley: University of California Press, 1994); John T. Mc-Greevy, *Catholicism and American Freedom: A History* (New York: Norton, 2003); Robert Emmett Curran, *Shaping American Catholicism: Maryland and New York, 1805–1915* (Washington, DC: Catholic University Press, 2012); Steven K. Green, *The Second Disestablishment: Church and State in Nineteenth-Century America* (New York: Oxford University Press, 2010);

J. Spencer Fluhman, *"A Peculiar People": Anti-Mormonism and the Making of Religion in Nineteenth-Century America* (Chapel Hill: University of North Carolina Press, 2012); Kenneth Winn, *Exiles in a Land of Liberty: Mormons in America, 1830–1846* (Chapel Hill: University of North Carolina Press, 1990); Reeve, *Religion of a Different Color.*

5. Rebecca Reed, *Six Months in a Convent* (Boston: Russell, Odiorne, and Metcalf, 1835).

6. Franchot, *Roads to Rome,* 146.

7. George T. Curtis, Theodore Lyman, and Charles G. Loring, eds., *Documents Relating to the Ursuline Convent in Charlestown* (Boston: Samuel N. Dickinson, 1842).

8. Reed, *Six Months,* 133, 174; Mary Ann Moffatt, *An Answer to "Six Months in a Convent"* (Dublin: William Powell Jr., 1835), 3.

9. *Awful Disclosures by Maria Monk of the Hotel Dieu Nunnery* (New York: Maria Monk, 1836), University of Alberta Libraries, https://archive.org/details/cihm_38885/page/n5; Sandra Fink, "Women, the Family, and the Fate of the Nation in American Anti-Catholic Narratives, 1830–1860," *Journal of the History of Sexuality* 18, No. 2 (May, 2009): 237–64.

10. Reed, *Six Months,* 139.

11. Ibid., 6.

12. Ibid., 115–16, 129, 141, 168.

13. Lyman Beecher, *A Plea for the West,* 2nd ed. (Cincinnati: Truman and Smith; New York: Leavitt, Lord, 1835).

14. Ibid., 39, 99.

15. Charles Beecher, ed., *Autobiography, Correspondence, and etc. of Lyman Beecher, D.D.,* vol. 2 (New York: Harper and Brothers, 1865), 334–35.

16. Steven K. Green, *The Bible, the School, and the Constitution* (New York: Oxford University Press, 2012), 13–20.

17. Jonathan Messerli, *Horace Mann: A Biography* (New York: Knopf, 1972), 191–92, 204; Curran, *Shaping American Catholicism,* 207.

18. Green, *The Bible, the School, and the Constitution,* 20–30.

19. Martin L. Meenagh, "Archbishop John Hughes and the New York Schools Controversy of 1840–1843," *American Nineteenth Century History* 5, No. 1 (Spring, 2004): 45.

20. "Petition of the Catholics of New York for a Portion of the Common School Fund," September 21, 1840, in *Complete Works of the Most Reverend John Hughes,* vol. 1 (New York: Lawrence Kehoe, 1866), 102–7.

21. Ibid., 50.

22. Ibid., 103.

23. Meenagh, "Archbishop John Hughes and the New York Schools Controversy," 51.

24. John Hughes, Speech at St. James Church, September 7, 1840; Hughes, Speech in Carroll Hall, October 25, 1841; Hughes, Speech in Washington Hall, February 11, 1841, in *Complete Works,* 1:83, 273–74, 244.

25. Ian Bartrum, "The Origins of Secular Public Education: The New York Schools Controversy, 1840–1842," 3 *NYU Journal of Law and Liberty* (2008): 267.

26. Horace Bushnell, *A Discourse on the Modifications Demanded by the Roman Catholics* (Hartford: Case, Tiffany, 1853), 1.

27. John Hughes, "The Decline of Protestantism and Its Cause," in *Complete Works*, 2:87–102.

28. *Sunbury (PA) American and Shamokin Journal*, May 18, 1844, 2; John B. Perry, *A Full and Complete Account of the Late Awful Riots in Philadelphia* (Philadelphia, 1844), 55; A Protestant and Native Philadelphian, *The Truth Unveiled: A Calm and Impartial Exposition of the Origin and Immediate Cause of the Terrible Riots in Philadelphia* (Philadelphia: M. Fithian, 1844), 20–22; Katie Oxx, *The Nativist Movement in America: Religious Conflict in the Nineteenth Century* (New York: Routledge, 2013), 53–82.

29. *Address of the General Executive Committee of the American Republican Party of the City of New York to the People of the United States* (New York: J. F. Trow, 1845), 10. See also Tracy Fessenden, "The Nineteenth Century Bible Wars and the Separation of Church and State," *Church History* 74, No. 4 (December, 2004).

30. John Hughes, "Alleged Burning of Bibles," letter to the *Evening Post*, January 1, 1843, in *Complete Works*, 1:501–4; "Dastardly Outrage in Ellsworth Maine," *Liberator*, October 27, 1854, 17; McGreevy, *Catholicism and American Freedom*, 7–19; Curran, *Shaping American Catholicism*, 213.

31. Donahoe v. Richards, 38 Me. 379 (1854); Commonwealth v. Cooke, in the Police Court of Boston, Massachusetts (April 1859), *American Law Register* 7, No. 7 (November 1858—November 1859): 421.

32. Cyprian Davis, "Black Catholics in Nineteenth Century America," *U.S. Catholic Historian* 5, No. 1 (1986): 1–17; Curran, *Shaping American Catholicism*, 92–110; A. Hunter Dupree and Leslie H. Fisher, "An Eyewitness Account of the New York Draft Riots, July 1863," *Mississippi Valley Historical Review* 47, No. 3 (December, 1960): 472–79.

33. Pope Pius IX, *Syllabus Errorum* (1864), http://www.papalencyclicals.net/pius09/p9syll.htm.

34. Francis Abbott, "The Nine Demands of Liberalism," *Index*, April, 1872; Tisa Wenger, "The God-in-the-Constitution Controversy: American Secularism in Historical Perspective," in *Comparative Secularisms in a Global Age*, ed. Linell Cady and Elizabeth Shakman Hurd (New York: Palgrave Macmillan, 2010), 87–106; Jonathan D. Sarna, "Church-State Dilemmas of American Jews," in *Jews and the American Public Square: Debating Religion and Republic*, ed. Alan Mittleman, Jonathan D. Sarna, and Robert Licht (Lanham, MD: Rowman and Littlefield, 2002), 56.

35. Ulysses S. Grant, Speech at the Reunion of the Army of the Tennessee, October 6, 1875, Ulysses S. Grant Papers, Series 10, Addition III, 1819 to 1969, https://www.loc.gov/item/mss233330375/.

36. *Chicago Tribune*, October 9, 1875, 5.

37. Board of Education of Cincinnati v. Minor, 23 Ohio St. 211 (1872).

38. Constitution of the State of Ohio, Article VI, §2 (1851).

39. Cincinnati v. Minor at 253; cited in Abington v. Schempp, 374 U.S. 203 (1963) at 214–15.

40. Linda Przybyszewski, "A Forum on the Law: Cincinnati Bible Wars of 1872," Address at the Ohio Supreme Court, April 1, 2009, http://www.ohiochannel.org/video/a-forum-on-the-law-cincinnati-bible-war-case-of-1873.

41. Abington v. Schempp (1963).

42. McGreevy, *Catholicism and American Freedom*, 118–26.

43. Curran, *Shaping American Catholicism*, 162–68, 171, 174, 188–89, 200.

44. John Ireland, "State Schools and Parish Schools," in *The Church and Modern Society* (Chicago: D. H. McBride, 1896), 197–214, 198.

45. Pope Leo XIII, *Testem Benevolentiae* (1899), http://www.papalencyclicals.net/leo13/l13teste.htm.

46. Pope Pius X, *Pascendi Domenici Gregis* (1907), http://w2.vatican.va/content/pius-x/en/encyclicals/documents/hf_p-x_enc_19070908_pascendi-dominici-gregis.html; Pope Leo XIII, *Rerum Novarum* (1891), http://w2.vatican.va/content/leo-xiii/en/encyclicals/documents/hf_l-xiii_enc_15051891_rerum-novarum.html; McGreevy, *Catholicism and American Freedom*, 131.

47. Pierce v. Society of Sisters, 268 U.S. 510 (1925).

48. McGreevy, *Catholicism and American Freedom*, 149; John F. Kennedy, Speech to the Greater Houston Ministerial Association, September 12, 1960, John F. Kennedy Library, Pre-Presidential Papers, https://www.jfklibrary.org/Asset-Viewer/Archives/JFKSEN-0911-027.aspx.

49. Central Campaign Committee to Hugh Clark, Esq., May 24, 1844, in Smith, *History of the Church*, 6:404.

50. Brigham Young and Williams Richards, "Election and Reprobation," *Times and Seasons* 4, No. 1 (November 15, 1842): 3. *See also* Fluhman, "A Peculiar People."

51. Reeve, *Religion of a Different Color*, 52–55.

52. *Doctrine and Covenants* 134:9 (August 17, 1835).

53. Smith, *History of the Church*, 3:304.

54. Ibid., 6:304.

55. Ibid., 1:5–6.

56. Ibid., 3:304.

57. Ibid., 3:183–86.

58. Joseph Smith, "The Government of God," *Times and Seasons* 3, No. 18 (July 15, 1842): 856.

59. Joseph Smith, "The Globe," *Times and Seasons* 5, No. 8 (April 15, 1844): 508–10.

60. Revelation, April 25, 1844, in Council of Fifty Record, http://www.josephsmithpapers.org/paper-summary/revelation–25-april–1844/1#source-note; Winn, *Exiles in a Land of Liberty*, 182–207; Andrew F. Ehat, "It Seems Like Heaven Began on Earth: Joseph Smith and the Constitution of the Kingdom of God," *Brigham Young University Studies* 20, No. 3 (Spring, 1980): 258.
61. Smith, *History of the Church*, 6:57.
62. Sarah Barringer Gordon, *The Mormon Question: Polygamy and Constitutional Conflict in Nineteenth-Century America* (Chapel Hill: University of North Carolina Press, 2002), 25–26.
63. *Doctrine and Covenants* 132 (July 12, 1843).
64. Richard Lyman Bushman, *Joseph Smith: Rough Stone Rolling* (New York: Knopf, 2005), 323–27, 437–39, 473, 490–91.
65. Bushman, *Joseph Smith*, 491; Smith, *History of the Church*, 6:58.
66. Winn, *Exiles in a Land of Liberty*, 83.
67. *Doctrine and Covenants* 132 (July 12, 1843); Bushman, *Joseph Smith*, 493–96.
68. Seceders from the Church at Nauvoo, "Preamble," *Nauvoo Expositor* 1, No. 1 (June 4, 1844): 1–2; Smith, *History of the Church*, 6:448; Winn, *Exiles in a Land of Liberty*, 209–14.
69. Thomas C. Sharp, "The Mormons," *Warsaw Signal* 2, No. 2 (May 19, 1841).
70. *Doctrine and Covenants* 29:34 (September, 1830).
71. "To the Saints of God," *Times and Seasons* 3, No. 24 (October 15, 1842): 951.
72. Constitution of the State of Deseret (1850), Article VIII, § 3, https://archive.org/details/constitutionofsto2dese/page/no.
73. Orson Pratt, "The Kingdom of God," *Journal of Discourses* 3:71 (July 8, 1855).
74. Orson Pratt, "Celestial Marriage," *Journal of Discourses* 1:53–66 (August 29, 1852); Gordon, *The Mormon Question*, 25–26.
75. Gordon, *The Mormon Question*, 27.
76. John Taylor, "Union: Human and Divine Government," *Journal of Discourses* 9:8–15, 10 (April 6, 1861).
77. Ibid., 9, 10.
78. Brigham Young, "The Gospel: The One-Man Power," *Journal of Discourses* 13:272 (July 24, 1870); and Young, "In Obeying Counsel There Is Salvation," *Journal of Discourses* 17:159–60 (August 9, 1874).
79. George Q. Cannon, "Celestial Marriage," *Journal of Discourses* 13:197–209, 204, 206 (October 9, 1869).
80. Ann-Eliza Young, *Wife #19, or The Story of a Life in Bondage* (Hartford, CT: Dustin, Gilman, 1875). *See also* Maria Ward, *Female Life among the Mormons: A Narrative of Many Years' Personal Experience* (New York: J. C. Derby, 1855).

81. Gordon, *The Mormon Question,* 96–99.

82. Martha Hughes Cannon, interview, *San Francisco Examiner,* November 8, 1896, cited in Gordon, *The Mormon Question,* 101, n. 29.

83. Edmunds Tucker Act of 1887, 44 Stat. 635 (1887) §20; 49th Cong., 2d Sess., CH. 397, §20, "Female Votes Prohibited in Utah" (March 3, 1887).

84. Nancy Cott, "Passionlessness: An Interpretation of Victorian Sexual Morality, 1790–1850," *Signs* 4, No. 2 (Winter, 1978): 219–36.

85. Shoshanah Ehrlich, *Regulating Desire: From the Virtuous Maiden to the Purity Princess* (Albany: State University of New York Press, 2015).

86. Cong. Globe, 36th Cong., 1st Sess., 2590–603 (1860).

87. Cong. Globe, 33rd Cong., 1st Sess., 1094, 1110 (1854).

88. S. Rep. No. 36–83, at 2 (1860) (Comm. Rep.); Cong. Globe, 36th Cong., 1st Sess., app. 190–94 (1860).

89. Cong. Globe, 34th Cong., 3rd Sess., app. 284–89 (1857).

90. Morrill Anti-Polygamy Act of 1862, Pub. L. No. 37–126, 12 Stat. 501 (1862); Poland Act of 1874, 18 Stat. 253 (1874).

91. Gordon, *The Mormon Question,* 114.

92. Ibid., 115.

93. Reynolds v. United States, 98 U.S. 145 (1879) at 164, 167.

94. Ibid. at 162.

95. Ibid. at 165–66, 164.

96. Francis Lieber to Emory Washburn, July 14, 1867, Francis Lieber Papers, Huntington Library, San Marino, CA; Minor v. Happersett, 88 U.S. 162 (1875).

97. Reynolds v. United States at 152, 168.

98. "Uncle Sam's Troublesome Bedfellows," *Illustrated Wasp,* February 8, 1879.

99. Chinese Exclusion Act of 1882, 22 Stat. 58; Plessy v. Ferguson, 163 U.S. 537 (1896); Dawes Act of 1887, 24 Stat. 387.

100. Reeve, *Religion of a Different Color,* 11, 52–74, 103, 123–24.

101. Parley Pratt, *The Autobiography of Parley Parker Pratt* (New York: Russell Brothers, 1874), 191.

102. Brigham Young, "The Laws of God Relative to the African Race," *Journal of Discourses* 10:110 (March 8, 1863); Reeve, *Religion of a Different Color,* 77, 135, 244.

103. Alex Ramsey to Henry Teller, November 17, 1882, in *The Edmunds Act, Reports of the Commission* (Salt Lake City: Tribune Printing and Publishing, 1884), 13.

104. Edmunds Tucker Act of 1887, 44 Stat. 635 (1887) § 6, 9, 11, 13, 25.

105. Davis v. Beason, 133 U.S. 333 (1890) at 341–42.

106. Idaho Laws, 13 Sess., Section 16; Edmunds Tucker Act (§ 25).

107. Davis v. Beason at 342.

108. Late Corporation of the Church of Jesus Christ of Latter-Day Saints v. United States, 136 U.S. 1 (1890) at 49–50.

109. Davis v. Beason at 343.

110. Kathleen Flake, *The Politics of American Religious Identity: The Seating of Senator Reed Smoot, Mormon Apostle* (Chapel Hill: University of North Carolina Press, 2004).

111. James R. Clark, *Messages of the First Presidency*, vol. 4 (West Valley City, UT: Bookcraft, 1970), 84–85.

112. *Elders' Journal of the Southern States Mission of the Church* 1 (January–February, 1904): 57–59, 73–74.

113. Flake, *Politics of American Religious Identity*, 54, 157.

114. Harold Bloom, *The American Religion* (New York: Simon and Schuster, 1992).

Chapter Four. Nicholas Black Elk and Theodore Roosevelt

Epigraphs: Gutzon Borglum, foreword to *Mount Rushmore National Memorial: A Monument Commemorating the Conception, Preservation, and Growth of the Great American Republic* (Washington, DC: Mount Rushmore National Historical Commission, 1941), 2; Nicholas Black Elk to John Neihardt, in *The Sixth Grandfather: Black Elk's Teachings Given to John Neihardt*, ed. Raymond DeMallie (Lincoln: University of Nebraska Press, 1984), 50.

1. James Madison, "Property," March 29, 1792, in *The Founders' Constitution* 1, Ch. 16, Document 23, http://press-pubs.uchicago.edu/founders/documents/v1ch16s23.html.

2. Vine Deloria, *God Is Red: A Native View of Religion*, 30th anniversary ed. (Golden, CO: Fulcrum, 2003), 61–76; Joel Martin, *The Land Looks After Us: A History of Native American Religion* (New York: Oxford University Press, 2001), 5–31; Keith Basso, *Wisdom Sits in Places: Landscape and Language among the Western Apache* (Albuquerque: University of New Mexico Press, 1996).

3. Clara Sue Kidwell, Homer Noley, and George Tinker, *A Native American Theology* (Maryknoll, NY: Orbis, 2001), 12.

4. Theodore Roosevelt, *Americanism in Religion* (Chicago: Blakely-Oswald, 1908), 15; "Roosevelt Dropped 'In God We Trust,' " *New York Times*, November 14, 1907.

5. Raymond DeMallie, ed., *The Sixth Grandfather: Black Elk's Teachings Given to John Neihardt* (Lincoln: University of Nebraska Press, 1984), 111–18. All quotations from Nicholas Black Elk are taken from the above source, which provides the original transcripts of his interviews with Neihardt, as well as supplemental materials and biographical information.

6. "Address of Colonel Roosevelt at Laying of the Cornerstone of the Carnegie Library, Fargo College, Sept. 5, 1910," *Christian Work and the Evangelist* 89, No. 2278 (October 8, 1910): 474; Edmund Morris, *The Rise of Theodore Roosevelt* (New York: Modern Library, 2001), 261–312, 363–70; Roger DiSilvestro, *Roosevelt in the Badlands: A Young Politician's Quest for Recovery in the American West* (New York: Walker and Company, 2012), 235–41, 258;

Hermann Hagedorn, *Roosevelt in the Badlands* (Boston: Houghton Mifflin, 1921); Chester Brooks and Ray Mattison, *Theodore Roosevelt in the Badlands* (Washington, DC: National Park Service, 1958), 39–45.

7. DeMallie, *Sixth Grandfather*, 24.

8. John G. Neihardt, *Black Elk Speaks* (New York: William Morrow, 1932); Theodore Roosevelt, *Hunting Trips of a Ranchman: Sketches of Sport on the Northern Cattle Plains* (New York: Putnam's, 1886); Roosevelt, *Ranch Life and the Hunting Trail* (New York: Century, 1888); Roosevelt, *The Wilderness Hunter* (New York: Putnam's, 1893); Roosevelt, *The Winning of the West*, 4 vols. (New York: Putnam's, 1889–1896).

9. Peter Gardella, *American Civil Religion: What Americans Hold Sacred* (New York: Oxford University Press, 2014), 232–33, 240. *See also* Christina Rose, "Native History: Construction of Mount Rushmore Begins," *Indian Country Today*, October 4, 2013, https://newsmaven.io/indiancountrytoday/archive/native-history-construction-of-mount-rushmore-begins-nNaLMzte1kKPJmtJoLoFZA/; Jesse Larner, *Mount Rushmore: An Icon Reconsidered* (New York: Thunder's Mouth/Nation Books, 2002), 89; Larry Stetler and James Sanovia, "The Heart of Everything That Is," Report 05–08, Department of Geology, South Dakota School of Mines, 2008. In his interviews with John Neihardt, Black Elk called the site of his vision the "center of the earth," which today is usually identified with Black Elk Peak (formerly Harney Peak). By other accounts, however, the vision took place on what is now Mount Rushmore. According to a Lakota tradition, this mountain is called Tunkasila Sakpe because (prior to Borglum's carving) it resembled a group of wizened faces. According to Peter Gardella, Black Elk prayed to the Grandfathers under the name of Tunkasila at the dedication of Jefferson's head in 1935.

10. DeMallie, *Sixth Grandfather*, 51.

11. Theodore Roosevelt, "Report of the Honorable Theodore Roosevelt Made to the Civil Service Commission" (1892), ed. Richard E. Jenson, *Nebraska History* 62 (1981): 85–106, 89. Hereafter, "Report to the Civil Service Commission."

12. James Mooney, *The Ghost Dance Religion and the Sioux Outbreak of 1890* (Washington: U.S. Government Printing Office, 1896), 871.

13. Heather Cox Richardson, *Wounded Knee: Party Politics and the Road to an American Massacre* (New York: Basic Books, 2010), 175; John Koster, "Sioux Agent Daniel F. Royer Saw Dancing and Panicked," *Indian Life*, December, 2010, 24.

14. Theodore Roosevelt to Herbert Welsh, February 13, 1891, quoted in William T. Hagan, "Civil Service Commissioner Theodore Roosevelt and the Indian Rights Association," *Pacific Historical Review* 44, No. 2 (May, 1975): 191–92.

15. Roosevelt, "Report to the Civil Service Commission," 89.

16. DeMallie, *Sixth Grandfather*, 271–81.

17. Mooney, *Ghost Dance Religion*, 662–763; Joel W. Martin, "Before and Beyond the Sioux Ghost Dance: Native American Prophetic Movements and the Study of Religion," *Journal of the American Academy of Religion* 59, No. 4 (Winter, 1991): 677–701; Raymond DeMallie, "The Lakota Ghost Dance: An Ethnohistorical Account," *Pacific Historical Review* 51, No. 4 (November, 1982): 385–405; Lee Irwin, "Freedom, Law, and Prophecy: A Brief History of Native American Religious Resistance," *American Indian Quarterly* 21, No. 35 (1997): 35–55.

18. Mooney, *Ghost Dance Religion*, 764, 771.

19. "Indian Conference: The True Inwardness of the Fight at Wounded Knee," *McCook Tribune*, February 20, 1891.

20. Mooney, *Ghost Dance Religion*, 787–88.

21. Ibid., 766.

22. Ibid., 777.

23. DeMallie, *Sixth Grandfather*, 50.

24. Ibid., 290.

25. Dawes Severalty Act of 1887, 25 U.S.C. §§ 331–333. Repealed. Pub. L. 106–462, Title I, § 106(a)(1), Nov. 7, 2000, 114 Stat. 2007.

26. Roosevelt, "Report to the Civil Service Commission," 97.

27. Joseph Epes Brown, *The Sacred Pipe* (Norman: University of Oklahoma Press, 1953, 1972), xiv.

28. Indian Reorganization Act of 1934, 25 U.S.C. §§ 461–479. Both the allotment policy and the assimilation policy (prohibiting traditional practices) were legally ended with the Indian Reorganization Act.

29. DeMallie, *Sixth Grandfather*, 260–62; Mooney, *Ghost Dance Religion*, 789–90.

30. Roosevelt, *Hunting Trips*, 23–24; Roosevelt, *Winning of the West*, 1:90.

31. Roosevelt, *Winning of the West*, 4:53–54.

32. Roosevelt, "Report to the Civil Service Commission," 100–101.

33. Theodore Roosevelt, *An Autobiography* (New York: Macmillan, 1913), 159–60. *See also* Theodore Roosevelt, "Duty and Self-Control," Address at University of Wisconsin at Madison, April 15, 1911, Almanac of Theodore Roosevelt, http://www.theodore-roosevelt.com/images/research/speeches/trdutyandcontrol.pdf.

34. Roosevelt, "Report to the Civil Service Commission," 96–97, 101–2.

35. Reuben Quick Bear v. Leupp, 210 U.S. 50 (1908).

36. *Rules Governing the Court of Indian Offenses*, March 30, 1883, Department of the Interior, Office of Indian Affairs, Washington, DC.

37. Roosevelt, "Report to the Civil Service Commission," 90.

38. United States v. Sioux Nation, 448 U.S. 371 (1980) at 379; Doane Robinson, *A History of the Dakota or Sioux Indians* (Aberdeen, SD: News Printing Company, 1904), 419; DeMallie, *Sixth Grandfather*, 168–69.

39. Actual federal expenditures for 1875 were approximately $275 million. *Statistical Abstracts of the United States*, First Number (Washington, DC: U.S. Government Printing Office, 1878).

40. *Report of the Commission Appointed to Treat with the Sioux Indians for the Relinquishment of the Black Hills* (Washington, DC: U.S. Government Printing Office, 1875), 17–18.

41. Johnson's Lessee v. M'Intosh, 21 U.S. 543 (1823) at 588, 590. *See also* Stuart Banner, *How the Indians Lost Their Land: Law and Power on the Frontier* (Cambridge: Belknap, 2007).

42. Johnson's Lessee v. M'Intosh at 573. *See also* Robert Berkoffer, *Salvation and the Savage: An Analysis of Protestant Missionaries and American Indian Response, 1787–1862* (Conway, SC: Athenaeum, 1972); R. Pierce Beaver, *Church, State and the American Indians: Two and a Half Centuries of Partnership in Missions between Protestant Churches and Government* (St. Louis: Concordia, 1966); David Wallace Adams, *Education for Extinction: American Indians and the Boarding School Experience, 1875–1928* (Lawrence: University of Kansas Press, 1995).

43. The Indian Rights Association was the Protestant nativist group that supported the plaintiff in the case of Quick Bear v. Leupp (1908).

44. John R. Wunder, *"Retained by the People": A History of American Indians and the Bill of Rights* (New York: Oxford University Press, 1994).

45. Indian Removal Act of 1830, 25 U.S.C. §§ 171–173. Repealed May 21, 1934, c. 321, 48 Stat. 787.

46. State Legislature of Georgia, "An Act to Prevent the Exercise of Assumed and Arbitrary Power by All Persons under the Pretext of Authority of the Cherokee Indians," December 22, 1830, cited by U.S. Supreme Court in Worcester v. Georgia, 31 U.S. 515 (1832) at 516.

47. Worcester v. Georgia at 520.

48. Cherokee Nation v. Georgia, 30 U.S. 1 (1831); Indian Appropriations Act of 1871, 25 U.S.C. § 71.

49. United States v. Sioux Nation at 371.

50. Ibid. at 377–78. *See also* "The Black Hills Gold Fields," *New York Herald*, August 26, 1875.

51. DeMallie, *Sixth Grandfather*, 183, 194.

52. United States v. Sioux Nation at 371; An Act to Ratify an Agreement with Certain Bands of the Sioux Nation of Indians and Also with the Northern Arapaho and Cheyenne Indians, 44 Cong. Ch. 72, February 28, 1877, 19 Stat. 254, Art. IV.

53. Thomas Wentworth Higginson, "Saints and Their Bodies," *Atlantic Monthly* 1, No. 5 (March, 1858).

54. Roosevelt, *Autobiography*, 8–12. *See also* Joshua David Hawley, *Theodore Roosevelt: Preacher of Righteousness* (New Haven: Yale University Press, 2008), 4–15; Kathleen Dalton, *Theodore Roosevelt: A Strenuous Life* (New York: Random House, 2002), 18–19.

55. Roosevelt, *Autobiography*, 7.

56. Alphonso David Rockwell, *Rambling Recollections: An Autobiography* (New York: Paul B. Hoeber, 1920), 261.

57. Corinne Roosevelt Robinson, *My Brother Theodore Roosevelt* (New York: Scribner's, 1921), 50; Roosevelt, *Autobiography*, 29–30.

58. Roosevelt, *Autobiography*, 359–60.

59. Theodore Roosevelt, "Work and Religion," Theodore Roosevelt Digital Library at Dickinson State University, https://www.theodorerooseveltcenter.org/Research/Digital-Library/Record?libID=o286535.

60. Theodore Roosevelt, "True Americanism," *Forum Magazine*, April, 1894.

61. Theodore Roosevelt, "The Strenuous Life," Address to the Hamilton Club, Chicago, Illinois, April 10, 1899, in *The Strenuous Life: Essays and Addresses* (New York: Century, 1900), 1–18.

62. Theodore Roosevelt, "The Expansion of the White Races," Address at the Celebration of the African Diamond Jubilee of the Methodist Episcopal Church in Washington, DC, January 18, 1909, Almanac of Theodore Roosevelt, http://www.theodore-roosevelt.com/images/research/speeches/trwhiteraces.pdf.

63. Gail Bederman, *Manliness and Civilization: A Cultural History of Gender and Race in the United States, 1870–1917* (Chicago: University of Chicago Press, 1995), 170.

64. Morris, *Rise of Theodore Roosevelt*, 183.

65. Ibid., 182.

66. Carleton Putnam, *Theodore Roosevelt: The Formative Years* (New York: Scribner's, 1958), 151.

67. Morris, *Rise of Theodore Roosevelt*, 296–97.

68. Simon Moya-Smith, "Sacred Black Hills: An Ideological Battle Ground," *Indian Country Today*, June 25, 2013, https://newsmaven.io/indiancountrytoday/archive/sacred-black-hills-an-ideological-battle-ground-VFoRFEN4bkWpEHMZWJ7Zcg/.

69. DeMallie, *Sixth Grandfather*, 97; Alexandra Witkin-New Holy, "Black Elk and the Spiritual Significance of the Black Hills," in *The Black Elk Reader*, ed. Clyde Holler (Syracuse: Syracuse University Press, 2000), 188–206.

70. DeMallie, *Sixth Grandfather*, 229–38.

71. Ibid., 241.

72. Francis Paul Prucha, *American Indian Policy in Crisis: Christian Reformers and the Indian, 1865–1890* (Norman: University of Oklahoma Press, 1972).

73. DeMallie, *Sixth Grandfather*, 12.

74. Hiram Price, Commissioner of Indian Affairs, "Rules Governing the Court of Indian Offenses," March 30, 1883, U.S. Department of the Interior, Office of Indian Affairs.

75. DeMallie, *Sixth Grandfather*, 245.

76. Ibid., 9–10.

77. Ibid., 8–9.

78. Ibid., 294.

79. Ibid., 285.

80. § 6, Dawes Severalty Act of 1887, 25 U.S.C. §§ 331–333.

81. Theodore Roosevelt, "The Search for Truth in a Reverent Spirit," in *History as Literature and Other Essays* (New York: Scribner's, 1913), 247–74, 256.

82. Hawley, *Theodore Roosevelt*, 35–39.

83. Roosevelt, *Autobiography*, 411–12. Roosevelt did not believe that Japanese civilization was inferior to white civilization, but did think that "Asiatic races" were too different from whites to blend into American culture.

84. Theodore Roosevelt, "Review of *National Life and Character: A Forecast*, by Charles H. Pearson," *Sewanee Review*, August, 1894.

85. Theodore Roosevelt, "On American Motherhood," Speech to the National Congress of Mothers, March 13, 1905, Theodore Roosevelt Digital Library at Dickinson State University, https://www.theodorerooseveltcenter.org/Research/Digital-Library/Record?libID=o280100.

86. Roosevelt, *Winning of the West*, 1:1–28.

87. Ibid., 20.

88. Frederick Jackson Turner, "The Significance of the Frontier in American History," *Annual Report of the American Historical Association*, 1893, 197–227. See also Richard Slotkin, "Theodore Roosevelt's Myth of the Frontier," *American Quarterly* 30, No. 5 (Winter, 1981): 608–37.

89. Roosevelt, *Hunting Trips*, 32.

90. Roosevelt, *Winning of the West*, 1:132–71.

91. Ibid., 2:197.

92. Ibid., 3:56.

93. Roosevelt, *Ranch Life*, 105.

94. Hagedorn, *Roosevelt in the Badlands*, 355.

95. Roosevelt, *Winning of the West*, 2:194–95.

96. Theodore Roosevelt to William Arthur Jones, December 12, 1903, Theodore Roosevelt Digital Library at Dickinson State University, https://www.theodorerooseveltcenter.org/Research/Digital-Library/Record?libID=o186703.

97. Theodore Roosevelt to William F. Round, July 25, 1903, Theodore Roosevelt Digital Library at Dickinson State University, https://www.theodorerooseveltcenter.org/Research/Digital-Library/Record?libID=o185478.

98. Roosevelt, *Winning of the West*, 1:20.

99. Roosevelt, *Hunting Trips*, 18–19.

100. Remarks of President Roosevelt to the School Children at Salem, Oregon, May 21, 1903, Theodore Roosevelt Digital Library at Dickinson State University, https://www.theodorerooseveltcenter.org/Research/Digital-Library/Record?libID=o289895.

101. *See also* Gary Gerstle, "Theodore Roosevelt and the Divided Character of American Nationalism," *Journal of American History* 86, No. 3 (December, 1999): 1280–1307.

102. Roosevelt, "Report to the Civil Service Commission," 93–94, 97.

103. Curtis Act of 1898, 25 U.S.C. § 357.

104. Roosevelt, "Duty and Self Control."

105. Roosevelt, *Winning of the West*, 3:123.

106. Roosevelt, "True Americanism."

107. DeMallie, *Sixth Grandfather*, 14, 59, 90, 294.

108. Michael F. Steltenkamp, "A Retrospective on *Black Elk: Holy Man of the Oglala*," in Holler, *Black Elk Reader*, 104–26, 108.

109. DeMallie, *Sixth Grandfather*, 72.

110. Clyde Holler, *Black Elk's Religion: The Sun Dance and Lakota Catholicism* (Syracuse: Syracuse University Press, 1995).

111. Vine Deloria, foreword to the 1979 edition, in *Black Elk Speaks: The Complete Edition*, by John Neihardt, Philip Deloria, and Vine Deloria (Lincoln: University of Nebraska Press, 2014), xiv.

112. DeMallie, *Sixth Grandfather*, 32.

113. Holler, *Black Elk Reader*.

114. Neihardt, Deloria, and Deloria, *Black Elk Speaks: The Complete Edition* (2014), 153.

115. DeMallie, *Sixth Grandfather*, 52.

116. Ibid., 56.

117. John G. Neihardt, preface to the 1972 edition, in Neihardt, Deloria, and Deloria, *Black Elk Speaks: The Complete Edition* (2014), xxvii–xxviii.

118. DeMallie, *Sixth Grandfather*, 21.

119. Theodore Roosevelt, and Theodore Roosevelt Association Collection, *Hopi Indians Dance for TR at Walpi, Ariz. 1913*, video, Library of Congress, http://hdl.loc.gov/loc.mbrsmi/trmp.4121. *See also* Tisa Wenger, *"We Have a Religion": The 1920s Pueblo Snake Dance Controversy and American Religious Freedom* (Chapel Hill: University of North Carolina Press, 2009), 135–81.

120. DeMallie, *Sixth Grandfather*, 59–60.

121. Ibid., 290.

122. Ibid., 47.

123. Hagedorn, *Roosevelt in the Badlands*, 45.

124. Roosevelt, *Hunting Trips*, 260, 267.

125. Philip J. Deloria, *Playing Indian* (New Haven: Yale University Press, 1999); Rayna Green, "The Tribe Called Wannabee: Playing Indian in America and Europe," *Folklore* 99, No. 1 (1988): 30–55.

126. Robert Berkoffer, *The White Man's Indian: Images of the American Indian from Columbus to the Present* (New York: Knopf, 1978).

127. Alvin Schmidt, *Fraternal Organizations* (Westport, CT: Greenwood, 1980), 287.

128. Jesse Rhodes, "Indians on the Inaugural March," Smithsonian.com, January 14, 2009, http://www.smithsonianmag.com/history/indians-on-the-inaugural-march-46032118/.

129. Douglas Brinkley, *The Wilderness Warrior: Theodore Roosevelt's Crusade for America* (New York: Harper-Perennial, 2010).

130. Mark David Spence, *Dispossessing the Wilderness* (New York: Oxford University Press, 1999).

131. Ward v. Race Horse, 163 U.S. 504 (1896) at 509.

132. Theodore Roosevelt, "Addition to Pine Ridge Reservation, South Dakota," Executive Order, January 25, 1904.

133. DeMallie, *Sixth Grandfather*, 66; Gardella, *American Civil Religion*, 240.

134. DeMallie, *Sixth Grandfather*, 64.

135. John Taliaferro, *The Great White Fathers: The Story of the Obsessive Quest to Create Mount Rushmore* (New York: Public Affairs, 2002), 320–21.

136. Ibid., 51–54, 309–10.

137. John Fire Lame Deer and Richard Erodes, *Lame Deer, Seeker of Visions: The Life of a Sioux Medicine Man* (New York: Simon and Schuster, 1972), 80–95; Matthew Glass, "Producing Patriotic Inspiration at Mount Rushmore," *Journal of the American Academy of Religion* 62, No. 2 (Summer, 1994): 265–81; Albert Boime, "Patriarchy Fixed in Stone: Borglum's Mount Rushmore," *American Art* 5, Nos. 1–2 (Winter–Spring, 1991): 142–67.

138. Lincoln Borglum, *Mount Rushmore: The Story behind the Scenery* (Whittier, CA: KC Publications, 1996), 13–14.

139. Lincoln Borglum, *Mount Rushmore*, 16.

140. Brown, *Sacred Pipe*.

141. Black Elk, foreword to Brown, *Sacred Pipe*, xix–xx.

142. Bowen v. Roy, 476 U.S. 693 (1986) at 699–700.

143. Lyng v. Northwest Cemetery Protective Association, 485 U.S. 439 (1988) at 453.

144. Johnson's Lessee v. M'Intosh (1823); Cherokee Nation v. Georgia, 30 U.S. 1 (1831).

145. Lyng at 451, citing Sherbert v. Verner, 374 U.S. 398 at 412.

146. Omer C. Stewart, *The Peyote Religion* (Norman: University of Oklahoma Press, 1987), 131; George Wood and Franklin Bache, *Dispensatory of the United States*, 19th ed. (Philadelphia: Lippincott, 1907), 1386–87.

147. Traditional Indian Use of Religious Peyote, 42 U.S.C. § 1996a. Native American Graves and Repatriation Act of 1990, 25 U.S.C. §§ 3001–3013.

148. United States v. Sioux Nation (1980).

Chapter Five. Creationists and Evolutionists

Epigraph: "You Can't Make a Monkey Out of Me," words and music by Billy Rose and Clarence Gaskill (July, 1925).

1. Art Swift, "In U.S., Belief in Creationist View of Humans at New Low," Gallup, May 22, 2017, https://news.gallup.com/poll/210956/belief-creationist-view-humans-new-low.aspx; Cary Funk and Becka Alper, *Religion and Science* (Washington, DC: Pew Research Center, 2017).

2. Noah Feldman, *Divided by God: America's Church-State Problem—and What We Should Do about It* (New York: Farrar, Straus, and Giroux, 2005).

3. Everson v. Board of Education, 331 U.S. 1 (1947).

4. David Masci, "For Darwin Day, Six Facts about the Evolution Debate," Pew Research Center, 2017, http://www.pewresearch.org/fact-tank/2017/02/10/darwin-day/.

5. Cheryl I. Harris, "Whiteness as Property," 106 *Harvard Law Review* 8 (1993): 1707–91.

6. Andrew Dickson White, *A History of the Warfare of Science with Theology in Christendom* (New York: D. Appleton, 1896, 1898); John William Draper, *History of the Conflict between Religion and Science* (New York: D. Appleton, 1881).

7. Auguste Comte, *Cours de philosophie positive* (1830–1842), trans. Harriett Martineau as *The Positive Philosophy of August Comte* (New York: Calvin Blanchard, 1858).

8. James Orr, "Science and Christian Faith," and George F. Wright, "The Passing of Evolution," in *The Fundamentals: The Famous Sourcebook of Foundational Biblical Truths*, ed. R. A. Torrey (Grand Rapids, MI: Kregel, 1958, 1990), 125–36, 613–27; George M. Marsden, *Fundamentalism and American Culture*, 2nd ed. (New York: Oxford University Press, 2006); Ronald Numbers, *The Creationists: From Scientific Creationism to Intelligent Design*, expanded ed. (Cambridge: Harvard University Press, 2005), 19–25.

9. State of Tennessee v. John Thomas Scopes, Criminal Court of Tennessee (July 21, 1925); Epperson v. Arkansas, 393 U.S. 97 (1968); Edwards v. Aguillard, 482 U.S. 578 (1987); Kitzmiller v. Dover, 400 F. Supp. 2d 707 (M.D. Pa. 2005).

10. Tenn. Code Ann., Title 49, § 1922.

11. H. L. Mencken, *A Religious Orgy in Tennessee* (New York: Melville House, 2006), 11–17, 41, 61, 99, 129.

12. Clarence Darrow, *The Story of My Life* (New York: Scribner's, 1932), 254.

13. H. L. Mencken, *Men versus the Man: A Correspondence between Robert Rives LaMonte, Socialist, and H. L. Mencken, Individualist* (New York: Henry Holt, 1910), 116.

14. "What Would Their Verdict Be?," *Montreal Daily Star*, July 25, 1925; "Cranks and Freaks Flock to Dayton," *New York Times*, July 11, 1925, 1; "Professor Darwin," *Figaro's London Sketchbook*, February 18, 1874; "A Veritable Orang-Outang: A Contribution to Unnatural History" (cartoon), *Hornet*, March 22, 1871; "Bryan Flays Darwinians: Says in Address They Can't Make a Monkey Out of Him," *New York Times*, March 6, 1922, 10; William Jennings Bryan, *The Menace of Darwinism* (New York: Fleming H. Revell, 1921, 1922), 20; Edward Larson, *Summer for the Gods: The Scopes Trial and America's Continuing Debate over Science and Religion* (New York: Basic Books, 1997), 138.

15. L. Rogers, "Do You Believe Fiends Like That Are Descendants of Ours?" (cartoon), *Chicago Defender*, June 20, 1925.

16. Josiah Nott and George Glidden, *Types of Mankind* (Philadelphia: Lippincott, Grambo, 1854), 182.

17. Charles Carroll, *The Negro a Beast* (St. Louis: American Book and Bible House, 1900). *See also* George M. Frederickson, *The Black Image in the White Mind: The Debate on Afro-American Character and Destiny, 1817–1914* (New York: Harper and Row, 1971), 228–55, 232.

18. George William Hunter, *Civic Biology* (New York: American Book Company, 1914), 195–96.

19. Larson, *Summer for the Gods*, 88–89, 100.

20. Bryan, *Menace of Darwinism*, 4–5; Clarence Darrow, *Why I Am an Agnostic* (Girard, KS: Haldeman-Julius, 1929), 39.

21. Hunter, *Civic Biology*, 263.

22. *Fighting to the Death for the Bible: The Last Message of William Jennings Bryan* (Dayton, TN: Bryan College, 1975), 21.

23. Larson, *Summer for the Gods*, 27; Stefan Kuhl, *The Nazi Connection: Eugenics, American Racism, and German National Socialism* (New York: Oxford University Press, 1994), 39–43, 69.

24. William Jennings Bryan, "The White Man's Burden: An Address at the Independence Day Banquet of the American Society of London," July 4, 1906, Social Justice Speeches, http://www.edchange.org/multicultural/speeches/w_bryan_white.html; Bryan, "The Negro Question," in *The Commoner Condensed*, ed. William Jennings Bryan (New York: Abbey Press, 1908), 288–94; "North Would Act as South Did on Negro Question," *New York Times*, March 18, 1923.

25. Larson, *Summer for the Gods*, 44.

26. "Convention, by One Vote, Defeats Plank Naming Klan, Bryan, in Bitter Debate, Pleading for Party Unity," *New York Times*, January 29, 1924; Wyn Craig Wade, *The Fiery Cross: The Ku Klux Klan in America* (New York: Oxford University Press, 1987), 248–50; Angie Maxwell, *The Indicted South: Public Criticism, Southern Inferiority, and the Politics of Whiteness* (Durham: University of North Carolina Press, 2014), 37; Paxton Hibben, *The Peerless Leader: William Jennings Bryan* (New York: Farrar and Rinehart, 1929), 381–83; Randy Moore, *Evolution in the Courtroom: A Reference Guide* (Santa Barbara: ABC-CLIO, 2002), 189–90; "The Klan Walks in Washington," *Literary Digest*, August 22, 1925; Gerard Magliocca, *The Tragedy of William Jennings Bryan: Constitutional Law and the Politics of Backlash* (New Haven: Yale University Press, 2011).

27. Darrow, *Story of My Life*, 301–11; "Closing Argument in the Case of *People v. Ossian Sweet et al.*," Recorders Court, Detroit, MI (November 24–25, 1925); "Closing Argument in the Case of *People v. Henry Sweet*," Recorders Court, Detroit, MI (May 11, 1926); "The Eugenics Cult," in *Closing Arguments: Clarence Darrow on Religion, Law, and Society*, ed. S. T. Joshi (Athens: University of Ohio Press, 2005), 197–212.

28. Larson, *Summer for the Gods*, 113–14; Hunter, *Civic Biology*, 263–68; Kuhl, *Nazi Connection*, 39–43; Edward McNall Burns, *David Starr Jordan: Prophet of Freedom* (Redwood City, CA: Stanford University Press, 1953), 61–66; Maynard Metcalf, "Eugenics and Euthenics," *Popular Science Monthly* 84 (April, 1914): 383–89.

29. Jeffrey P. Moran, "Reading Race into the Scopes Trial: African American Elites, Science, and Fundamentalism," *Journal of American History* 90, No. 3 (December, 2003): 891–911; Moran, "The Scopes Trial and Southern Fundamentalism in Black and White: Race, Region, and Religion," *Journal of Southern History* 70, No. 1 (February, 2004): 95–120; Moran, *American Genesis: The Evolution Controversies from Scopes to Creation Science* (New York: Oxford University Press, 2012), 72–90.

30. Charles Satchell Morris, "Up from the Monkey or Down from God," *Norfolk Journal and Guide*, June 27, 1925, 12; John Norris, "Evolution Not a Fact—the Bible a Fact," *A.M.E. Church Review* 42 (October, 1925): 323–25.

31. John Jasper, *The Sun Do Move* (New York: Brentano's, 1882); Cleophus J. La Rue, *The Heart of Black Preaching* (Louisville: Westminster/John Knox, 2000), 34.

32. "If Monkeys Could Speak," *Chicago Defender*, May 23, 1925; "Evolution and Life," *Topeka (KS) Plaindealer*, July 24, 1925, 3; "A Typical Southern Jury," *Pittsburgh American*, July 17, 1925, 4, cited in Larson, *Summer for the Gods*, 154; W. E. B. Du Bois, "Scopes," *Crisis* 30 (September, 1925): 218.

33. "Attack 'The Sun Do Move' Preacher," *Buffalo American*, April 23, 1925, 1; Moran, "The Scopes Trial," 104–10.

34. W. N. Moses, "Rev. W. N. Moses, Attending Evolution Trial, States Reaction Will Favor Race," *Pittsburgh Courier*, July 25, 1925, 9.

35. *Transcript: The World's Most Famous Court Case* (Dayton, TN: Bryan College, 1990), 56, 78.

36. Ibid., 77.

37. Ibid., 66.

38. Ibid., 82.

39. In the Supreme Court of Tennessee, Brief and Argument in Behalf of Thomas John Scopes, September, 1925, 44; Bryan, *Menace of Darwinism*, 56.

40. *Transcript*, 89.

41. Ibid., 288, 304.

42. Darrow, *Story of My Life*, 257.

43. *Transcript*, 281, 282.

44. Darrow, *Story of My Life*, 94.

45. *Transcript*, 181.

46. Ibid., 287.

47. Ibid., 290, 298–99; Numbers, *Creationists*, 58.

48. *Transcript*, 292, 295.

49. Larson, *Summer for the Gods*, 190–91.

50. "Bryan and the American Press," *Pittsburgh Courier*, August 1, 1925, 16; "The Sudden Passing of William Jennings Bryan," *Chicago Broad Axe* 30 (August 1, 1925): 1; "Bryan, in His Last Days Was Admired by Many of Race," *Norfolk Journal and Guide*, August 1, 1925, 1.

51. Mencken, *Religious Orgy*, 103, 109, 119, 121.

52. Scopes v. State, 1 Smith (TN) 105 Supreme Court of Tennessee (Jan. 17, 1927) at 364.

53. Jerome Lawrence and Robert Edwin Lee, *Inherit the Wind* (New York: Dramatists Play Service, 1951, 1955); Stanley Kramer, *Inherit the Wind* (1960).

54. Mary L. Dudziak, *Cold War Civil Rights: Race and the Image of American Democracy* (Princeton: Princeton University Press, 2000), 145.

55. Glenn Smiley, "Report on Little Rock, September 23–29, 1957," Martin Luther King Jr. Papers Project, Stanford University, https://kinginstitute. stanford.edu/sites/default/files/smiley.pdf.

56. Reed Cartwright, "The Biology Teacher Next Door: Susan Epperson on Evolution," *Panda's Thumb*, July 3, 2004, https://pandasthumb.org/ archives/2004/07/the-biology-tea.html; Susan Epperson, "Reconciling Faith and Evolution in the Classroom: A Conversation with Susan Epperson, 42 Years Later," American Civil Liberties Union, December 9, 2010, https://www.aclu.org/other/reconciling-faith-and-evolution-classroom-conversation-susan-epperson-42-years-later.

57. Epperson, "Reconciling Faith."

58. Moore, *Evolution in the Courtroom*, 44.

59. Epperson v. Arkansas at fn. 16.

60. Ibid. at fn. 8.

61. Marsden, *Fundamentalism*, 236–39.

62. Jerry Tompkins, "Anti-Evolution Law Tested," *Science News Letter* 89, No. 1 (January 1, 1966): 7.

63. Edward J. Larson, *Trial and Error: The American Controversy over Creation and Evolution*, 3rd ed. (New York: Oxford University Press, 2003), 99; Bates et al. v. City of Little Rock, 361 U.S. 516 (1960).

64. George William Hunter, *New Civic Biology* (New York: American Book Company, 1926), 250, 400.

65. Vic Lockman, " 'Bill' Is a Product of Devilution" (cartoon), *Christian Beacon*, May 7, 1964.

66. Epperson v. Arkansas at 99.

67. McCollum v. Board of Education, 333 U.S. 203 (1948).

68. Engele v. Vitale, 370 U.S. 421 (1962); Abington v. Schempp, 374 U.S. 203 (1963).

69. Abington v. Schempp at 212, 226.

70. Zorach v. Clausen, 343 U.S. 306 (1952) at 313.

71. "The Most Hated Woman in America," *Life Magazine*, June 19, 1964; Douglas Martin, "Vashti McCollum" (obituary), *New York Times*, August

26, 2006, A13; Linda Wertheimer, "Fifty Years after Abington v. Schempp: A Dissenter Looks Back on School Prayer," *Atlantic*, June 17, 2013.

72. Ark. Stat. Ann. §§ 80–1627, 80–1628.

73. Steve Suitts, *Hugo Black of Alabama* (Montgomery, AL: NewSouth, 2005), 20; Epperson v. Arkansas at 109–14.

74. Laura Kalman, *Abe Fortas: A Biography* (New Haven: Yale University Press, 1992), 7–26; Epperson v. Arkansas at 98, 107–8.

75. Epperson v. Arkansas at 103, 106.

76. Everson v. Board of Education at 15; Zorach v. Clausen at 312, 314, 315.

77. Alana Semuels, "How Segregation Has Persisted in Little Rock," *Atlantic*, April 27, 2016.

78. Fred de Cordova, *Bedtime for Bonzo* (1951).

79. Ronald Reagan, Address to the Roundtable National Affairs Briefing, Dallas, August 22, 1980, Carnegie Mellon digital archive transcript as prepared for delivery, http://digitalcollections.library.cmu.edu/awweb/aw archive?type=file&item=684006.

80. James Guth, "The New Christian Right," in *The New Christian Right: Mobilization and Legitimation*, ed. Robert Liebman and Robert Wuthnow (New York: Aldine, 1983), 36.

81. John F. Kennedy, Speech to the Greater Houston Ministerial Association, September 12, 1960, John F. Kennedy Library, Pre-Presidential Papers, https://www.jfklibrary.org/Asset-Viewer/Archives/JFKSEN-0911-027.aspx.

82. James Madison, "Memorial and Remonstrance against Religious Assessments," July 28, 1785, Founders Online, https://founders.archives.gov/documents/Madison/01-08-02-0163.

83. "Reagan Tries to Cement His Ties with TV Evangelicals," *Los Angeles Times*, August 23, 1980, 1, 17; "Reagan Favors Creationism in Public Schools," *Creation-Evolution Journal* 1, No. 2 (Fall, 1980): 45.

84. Balanced Treatment for Creation-Science and Evolution-Science in Public School Instruction Act (Creationism Act), La. Rev. Stat. Ann. §§ 17:286.1–17:286.7.

85. Philip J. Hilts, "Creationism Back in Schools as Science," *Washington Post*, July 23, 1981.

86. *Science Framework for California Schools* (Sacramento: California Department of Education, 1970), 106.

87. Nell J. Segraves, *The Creation Report* (San Diego: Creation Science Research Center, 1977), 17, 30.

88. Numbers, *Creationists*, 339–49, 349, 352.

89. Henry Morris, "Evolution and Modern Racism," *Acts and Facts* 2, No. 7 (October 23, 1973).

90. Martin Luther King, "Letter from Birmingham Jail," April 16, 1963, Martin Luther King, Jr., Research and Education Institute, Stanford University, http://okra.stanford.edu/transcription/document_images/undecided/630416-019.pdf.

91. Randall Balmer, "The Real Origins of the Religious Right," *Politico*, May 27, 2014; Coit v. Green, 404 U.S. 997 (1971); Bob Jones, "Is Segregation Scriptural?," WMUU radio address, April 17, 1960 (Greenville, SC: Bob Jones University, 1960).

92. Reagan, Address to the Roundtable National Affairs Briefing, 4.

93. Henry Morris and John Whitcomb, *The Genesis Flood: The Biblical Record and Its Scientific Implications* (Phillipsburg, NJ: Presbyterian and Reformed Publishing, 1961).

94. Numbers, *Creationists*, 217–38.

95. Lemon v. Kurtzman, 403 U.S. 602 (1971).

96. Torcaso v. Watkins, 367 U.S. 488 (1961) at fn. 11.

97. "Note: Freedom of Religion and Science Instruction in Public Schools," 87 *Yale Law Journal* (January, 1978): 515–70.

98. "Ridicule Sparked Creationism Law," *St. Petersburg Times*, June 20, 1981; Balanced Treatment for Creation-Science and Evolution-Science in Public School Instruction Act (Creationism Act), La. Rev. Stat. Ann. §§ 17:286.1–17:286.7.

99. Edwards v. Aguillard at 592, 600, 604.

100. Cooper v. Aaron, 358 U.S. 1 (1958).

101. McLean v. Arkansas Board of Education, 529 F. Supp. 1255 (E.D. Ark. 1982) at 1264.

102. Edwards v. Aguillard at 610, 615, 617, 637.

103. Abington v. Schempp, Brennan, J., concurring, at 266–87, 273–74.

104. Roe v. Wade, 410 U.S. 113 (1973); Nina Totenberg, "A Tribute to Justice William J. Brennan, Jr.," 104 *Harvard Law Review* 33 (1990): 37.

105. Bowers v. Hardwick, 478 U.S. 186 (1986); Lawrence v. Texas, 539 U.S. 558 (2003).

106. Maureen Fiedler, "Antonin Scalia: A Very Traditional Catholic," *National Catholic Reporter*, February 15, 2016.

107. Oregon v. Smith, 94 U.S. 872 (1990), Scalia, J., dissenting, at 890.

108. Lee v. Weisman, 505 U.S. 577 (1991), Scalia, J., dissenting, at 646.

109. Edwards v. Aguillard at 633.

110. Kitzmiller v. Dover at 708–9; Edward Humes, *Monkey Girl: Education, Evolution, Religion, and the Battle for America's Soul* (New York: Harper Perennial, 2007), 41–42.

111. Kitzmiller v. Dover at 753.

112. Margaret Talbot, "Letter from Pennsylvania: Darwin in the Dock," *New Yorker* 81, No. 39 (December 5, 2005): 66–77.

113. Kitzmiller v. Dover at 748, 751.

114. Dover Area School Board of Directors, Intelligent Design Resolution, October 18, 2004, Kitzmiller v. Dover at 708; Percival David and Dean Kenyan, *Of Pandas and People: The Central Question of Biological Origins*, 2nd ed. (1989; Richardson TX: Foundation for Thought and Ethics, 1993).

115. Kitzmiller v. Dover at 752.

116. Humes, *Monkey Girl*, 183.

117. Steve Bensen, "Evolution v. 'Intelligent Design' " (cartoon), *York Daily Record*, December 21, 2004.

118. U.S. Census Bureau, Census 2000, "Profile of General Demographic Characteristics, Dover Borough, Pennsylvania," and "Educational Attainment and Employment Status by Language Spoken"; "Cranks and Freaks Flock to Dayton."

119. Phillip E. Johnson, *Darwin on Trial* (Downer's Grove, IL: Intervarsity Press, 1991).

120. Kitzmiller v. Dover at 745.

121. Testimony of Bryan Rehm, Kitzmiller v. Dover, Trial Transcript, Day 2 (September 27, 2005), 94; Kitzmiller v. Dover at 760, 762.

122. Robert Wuthnow, *The Restructuring of American Religion: Faith and Society since World War II* (Chicago: University of Chicago Press, 1988).

123. Humes, *Monkey Girl*, 38, 79.

124. Kitzmiller v. Dover at 752, 760.

125. Richard Dawkins, *The Blind Watchmaker: Why the Evidence of Evolution Reveals a Universe without Design* (London: Norton, 1986).

126. Richard Dawkins, *The God Delusion* (New York: Mariner, 2006); Daniel Dennett, *Darwin's Dangerous Idea: Evolution and the Meaning of Life* (New York: Touchstone, 1995); Dennett, *Breaking the Spell: Religion as a Natural Phenomenon* (New York: Penguin, 2006); Sam Harris, *The End of Faith: Religion, Terror, and the Future of Reason* (New York: Norton, 2004); Harris, *Letter to a Christian Nation* (New York: Knopf, 2006).

127. Lauri Lebo, *The Devil in Dover: An Insider's Story of Dogma v. Darwin in Small-Town America* (New York: New Press, 2008), 186–87.

128. Johnson, *Darwin on Trial*.

129. Dick Staub, "Interview: Phillip Johnson," *Christianity Today*, December 1, 2002, http://www.christianitytoday.com/ct/2002/decemberweb-only/12–2–22.0.html?start=3; Harris, *End of Faith*, 29–36, 108–52; Christopher Hitchens, *God Is Not Great: How Religion Poisons Everything* (New York: Hatchette, 2007), 123–48; Daniel Dennett, "Dangerous Memes," TED Talk, February, 2002, https://www.ted.com/talks/dan_dennett_on_dangerous_memes.

130. Kitzmiller v. Dover at 751, 752, 760.

131. Ibid. at 735, 765, 766.

132. Ibid. at 756.

133. Testimony of Barbara Forrest, Kitzmiller v. Dover, Trial Transcript, Day 6 (October 5, 2005); Susan Spath, "Cdesign Proponentsists," *Reports of National Center for Science Education* 23, No. 12 (September 25, 2008).

134. Lynch v. Donnelly, 465 U.S. 668 (1984) at 688. Jones also employed the *Lemon* test, although only secondarily.

135. Kitzmiller v. Dover at 722, 732–34.

136. Ibid. at 720, 736, 740–41.

137. Ibid. at 754.
138. Ibid. at 718.
139. Talbot, "Darwin in the Dock."
140. Joseph O. Baker, "Acceptance of Evolution and Support for Creationism in Public Schools," *Journal for the Scientific Study of Religion* 52, No. 1 (2013): 216–28.

Chapter Six. Religion, Race, and Science

Epigraphs: Bowers v. Hardwick, 478 U.S. 186, Burger, C.J., concurring, at 197–98; Stevens, J., dissenting, at 216.

1. I use the expressions "sexual difference" and "sexual nonconformity" to embrace sexual preference/practice as well as gender. Throughout the chapter, I use a range of more specific terminology that reflects the usage among the parties or in periods and events under consideration.
2. Obergefell v. Hodges, 576 U.S. ___ (2015). A brief in support of respondents was filed by major religious organizations and signed by many religious groups, including the ones mentioned. Briefs in support of respondents also were filed by Agudath Israel of America and the U.S. Conference of Catholic Bishops. Briefs in support of petitioners were filed by the Anti-Defamation League, the president of the Episcopal House of Deputies, and the Leadership Conference on Civil and Human Rights and joined by the religious groups mentioned. The American Humanist Association filed a separate brief in support of petitioners.
3. Bowers v. Hardwick, 478 U.S. 186 (1986); Romer v. Evans, 517 U.S. 620 (1996).
4. Steven Greenberg, "In the Name of Partnership," *Maariv*, March 5, 1999; Sandi Simcha DuBowski, *Trembling before G-d* (New Yorker Films, 2001); Steven Greenberg, *Wrestling with God and Men: Homosexuality in the Jewish Tradition* (Madison: University of Wisconsin Press, 2004).
5. Lawrence v. Texas, 539 U.S. 558 (2003); United States v. Windsor, 570 U.S. 744 (2013).
6. Emilie Townes, interview with author, Martha's Vineyard, MA, July 5, 2017. All quotations in this section are from this interview.
7. Shelby County, Alabama v. Holder, 133 U.S. 2612 (2013); United States v. Windsor (2013). The *Shelby* decision, striking down Section 5 of the 1965 Voting Rights Act, was issued on June 25; the *Windsor* case, striking down Section 3 of the 1996 Defense of Marriage Act, was decided the following day.
8. Steven Greenberg, interview with author, Boston, July 5, 2017. Unless otherwise noted, all quotations in this section are from this interview.
9. Greenberg, *Wrestling with God and Men*, 4.
10. Leviticus 18:22, "you shall not lie with a man as with a woman, it is an abomination"; Lev. 20:13, "If a man lies with another man as with a

woman, both of them have committed an abomination; they shall surely be put to death."

11. Greenberg, *Wrestling with God and Men*, 54, 65, 87, 90, 94.

12. Ibid., 203.

13. Ibid., 203, 207–9.

14. Greenberg, interview, July 5, 2017.

15. Townes, interview, July 5, 2017.

16. Greenberg, *Wrestling with God and Men*, 69–73.

17. "American Baptist Churches USA: Responses/Actions Pertaining to Homosexuality," June, 2012, http://www.abc-usa.org/wp-content/uploads/2012/06/homosexuality1.pdf; General Board of the American Baptist Church, USA, "Resolution Calling for Dialogue on Human Sexuality," June, 1993.

18. Townes, interview, July 5, 2017. Rev. E. Spencer Parson (1919–2013) was dean of the Rockefeller Chapel at the University of Chicago.

19. Mark Stern, "Gay Rights and Orthodox Response," *Tradition: A Journal of Orthodox Jewish Thought* 38, No. 1 (Spring, 2004): 123–40, 123, 128.

20. Bowers v. Hardwick at fn. 1.

21. Palko v. Connecticut, 302 U.S. 319 (1937) at 320, 324–25; Moore v. East Cleveland, 431 U.S. 494 (1977) at 503.

22. Bowers v. Hardwick at 218, citing Griswold v. Connecticut, 381 U.S. 479 (1965) at 485.

23. Bowers v. Hardwick at 194, Burger, J., concurring, at 197.

24. Jeremy Bentham, "Offenses against Oneself" (1785), *Journal of Homosexuality* 3, No. 4 (1978): 389–405; Michel Foucault, *Discipline and Punish: The Birth of the Prison*, trans. Alan Sheridan (New York: Vintage, 1977, 1995), 200.

25. Emilie M. Townes, *Breaking the Fine Rain of Death: African American Health Issues and a Womanist Ethic of Care* (Eugene, OR: Wipf and Stock, 1998), 121, 139, 140, 143.

26. Greenberg, interview, July 5, 2017.

27. Yaakov Levado, "Gayness and God: Wrestlings of an Orthodox Rabbi," *Tikkun* 8, No. 5 (September–October, 1993): 54–60.

28. Bowers v. Hardwick, Blackmun, J., dissenting, at 199, 204, 207.

29. Lawrence v. Texas at 562, 574, quoting Planned Parenthood of Southeastern Pennsylvania v. Casey, 505 U.S. 833 (1992) at 851.

30. Bowers v. Hardwick, Blackmun, J., dissenting, at 211.

31. Ibid. at 210–11.

32. Ibid. at 206.

33. Ibid. at 205.

34. Romer v. Evans (1996); United States v. Windsor (2013); Obergefell v. Hodges (2015).

35. Pope Paul VI, *Gaudium et Spes*, December 7, 1965, http://www.vatican.va/archive/hist_councils/ii_vatican_council/documents/vat-ii_const_19651207_gaudium-et-spes_en.html.

36. Lawrence v. Texas at 567.
37. Everson v. Board of Education, 330 U.S. 1 (1947).
38. Bowers v. Hardwick at 196.
39. Lawrence v. Texas, Scalia, J., dissenting, at 591.
40. Bowers v. Hardwick, Stevens, J., dissenting, at 216.
41. Loving v. Virginia, 388 U.S. 1 (1967).
42. Bowers v. Hardwick, Blackmun, J., dissenting, at fn. 3/5.
43. Orthodox Union Advocacy Center, "Orthodox Union Statement on Supreme Court's Ruling in *Obergefell v. Hodges*," June 26, 2015, https://advocacy.ou.org/orthodox-union-statement-supreme-courts-ruling-obergefell-v-hodges/.
44. Townes, interview, July 5, 2017.
45. Coretta Scott King, press conference on the introduction of ENDA, Washington, DC, June 23, 1994, Iowa State University Archives of Women's Political Communication, https://awpc.cattcenter.iastate.edu/2017/03/09/remarks-on-the-introduction-of-the-employment-non-discrimination-act-of-1994-june–23–1994/. The NAACP filed an amicus brief in support of gay civil rights in Romer v. Evans (1996).
46. Romer v. Evans at 624.
47. Plessy v. Ferguson, 163 U.S. 537 (1896).
48. Ibid. at 623.
49. Ibid. at 635.
50. Carlos Ball, *From the Closet to the Courtroom: Five LGBT Rights Cases That Have Changed Our Nation* (Boston: Beacon, 2011), 136.
51. United States v. Carolene Products Company, 308 U.S. 144 (1938) at fn. 4; Department of Agriculture v. Moreno, 413 U.S. 528 (1973) at 533; City of Cleburne, Texas v. Cleburne Living Center, Inc., 473 U.S. 432 (1985).
52. Emilie M. Townes, *Womanist Ethics and the Cultural Production of Evil* (New York: Palgrave Macmillan, 2006), 67. *See also* Michael Omi and Howard Winant, *Racial Formation in the United States* (New York: Routledge, 1986, 1994, 2015).
53. Michel Foucault, *The History of Sexuality*, vol. 1, *An Introduction*, trans. Robert Hurley (New York: Vintage, 1980).
54. Varnum v. Brien, 763 N.W. 2d 862 (Iowa 2009). In this case the Iowa Supreme Court characterized sexuality as a quasi-suspect classification.
55. Romer v. Evans at 621, 635. *See also* Janet E. Halley, "Sexual Orientation and the Politics of Biology," 46 *Stanford Law Review* (1993): 503–67.
56. Romer v. Evans at 624.
57. Ibid. at 634, citing Davis v. Beason, 133 U.S. 333 (1890).
58. Romer v. Evans, Scalia, J., dissenting, at 636–37.
59. Romer v. Evans at 632.
60. Ibid. at 630, 632, 635.
61. Ibid. at 634, citing Department of Agriculture v. Moreno, 413 U.S. 528 (1973) at 534.

62. Romer v. Evans, Scalia, J., dissenting, at 636, 644, 652.
63. Greenberg, interview, July 5, 2017.
64. W. E. B. Du Bois, *The Souls of Black Folk: Essays and Sketches* (Chicago: A. C. McClurg, 1903), 3.
65. Obergefell v. Hodges, Roberts, C.J., dissenting, at 2611–14.
66. Ibid. at 2613.
67. Affidavit of Rabbi Steven Greenberg on behalf of applicants, Halpern et al. v. Canada and Metropolitan Community Church of Toronto v. A.G. Canada, Ontario Superior Court of Justice (June, 2001), ¶¶ 11, 12, 16.
68. Obergefell v. Hodges, Roberts, C.J., dissenting, at 2616.
69. Greenberg, affidavit, June, 2001, ¶¶ 3, 4.
70. Clare Virginia Eby, *Until Choice Do Us Part: Marriage Reform in the Progressive Era* (Chicago: University of Chicago Press, 2014); Nancy F. Cott, *Public Vows: A History of Marriage and the Nation* (Cambridge: Harvard University Press, 2002); Stephanie Coontz, *The Way We Never Were: American Families and the Nostalgia Trap* (New York: Basic Books, 1992, 2000).
71. Steven Greenberg, email message to author, August 4, 2017.
72. Greenberg, affidavit, June, 2001, ¶ 6.
73. Ibid., ¶ 7.
74. Greenberg, *Wrestling with God and Men*, 14.
75. Baehr v. Lewin, 74 Hawai'i 530 (1993).
76. United States v. Virginia, 518 U.S. 515 (1996); Mississippi University for Women v. Hogan, 548 U.S. 718 (1982); Frontiero v. Richardson, 411 U.S. 677 (1973).
77. Obergefell v. Hodges, Roberts, C.J., dissenting, at 2623.
78. Loving v. Virginia at 12.
79. United States v. Windsor, Scalia, J., dissenting, at 2708.
80. Obergefell v. Hodges, Alito, J., dissenting, at 2642–43.
81. Obergefell v. Hodges, Roberts, C.J., dissenting, at 2614.
82. Ibid.
83. Townes, *Womanist Ethics*, 29–36.
84. Martha Hodes, *White Women, Black Men: Illicit Sex in the Nineteenth Century* (New Haven: Yale University Press, 1997).
85. Michelle Alexander, *The New Jim Crow: Mass Incarceration in an Age of Colorblindness* (New York: New Press, 2010, 2012); Robert Perkinson, *Texas Tough: The Rise of America's Prison Empire* (New York: Metropolitan Books, 2010).
86. Townes, *Womanist Ethics*, 115–20; Daniel Patrick Moynihan, *The Negro Family: The Case for National Action* (Washington, DC: U.S. Government Printing Office, 1965).
87. Emilie Townes, "Roundtable Response: Same Sex Marriage and Relational Justice," *Journal of Feminist Studies in Religion* 20, No. 2 (Fall, 2004): 100–104.
88. Obergefell v. Hodges at 2602.

89. Ibid. at 2598–2601.
90. Ibid. at 2601.
91. Ibid. at 2602.
92. Ibid. at 2607.
93. Ibid. at 2596.
94. Greenberg, email message to author, August 4, 2017.
95. Brown v. Board of Education of Topeka, Kansas, 347 U.S. 483 (1954) at 495.
96. Obergefell v. Hodges at 2591.
97. West Virginia State Board of Education v. Barnette, 319 U.S. 624 (1943) at 642.
98. Emilie Townes, "Gay Marriage and Religion: What Marriage Means to Me," *Huffington Post*, June 22, updated August 21, 2012.
99. Steven Greenberg, email message to author, September 26, 2017.
100. Greenberg, email message to author, August 4, 2017.

Conclusion

1. West Virginia State Board of Education v. Barnette, 319 U.S. 624 (1943) at 642.
2. Ulysses S. Grant, Speech at the Reunion of the Army of the Tennessee, October 6, 1875, Ulysses S. Grant Papers, Series 10, Addition III, 1819 to 1969, http://hdl.loc.gov/loc.mss/ms008146.mss23333.0375.
3. "Eisenhower Tells of Zhukov Ouster," *New York Times*, December 23, 1952, 16; Ronald Reagan, Address to the Roundtable National Affairs Briefing, Dallas, August 22, 1980.
4. Lynch v. Donnelly, 465 U.S. 668 (1984); Town of Greece v. Galloway, 572 U.S. 565 (2014); Zelman v. Simmons-Harris, 536 U.S. 639 (2002).
5. Kitzmiller v. Dover, 400 F. Supp. 2d 707 (M.D. Pa. 2005).
6. Reynolds v. United States, 98 U.S. 145 (1879) at 164, 167.
7. Cantwell v. Connecticut, 310 U.S. 296 (1940); United States v. Ballard, 322 U.S. 78 (1944); Sherbert v. Verner, 374 U.S. 398 (1963); Wisconsin v. Yoder, 406 U.S. 205 (1972).
8. *Cf.* Braunfield v. Brown, 366 U.S. 599 (1961).
9. Lyng v. Northwest Cemetery Protective Association, 485 U.S. 439 (1988) at 456; Oregon v. Smith, 494 U.S. 872 (1990).
10. Oregon v. Smith at 885, 888.
11. Ibid. at 890.
12. 42 U.S. Code, Ch. 21B, Religious Freedom Restoration Act of 1993; City of Boerne v. Flores, 521 U.S. 507 (1997).
13. Burwell v. Hobby Lobby Stores, Inc., 573 U.S. ___ (2014); Masterpiece Cakeshop, Ltd. v. Colorado Civil Rights Commission, 584 U.S. ___ (2018).

Index

Page numbers in *italics* refer to illustrations.

7/20